TESTIMONIALS

From the moment I met Stacy, her energy and love for the sport of cheer and dance were unmistakable. She is an incredible mentor to so many athletes, coaches, coworkers and friends. She tells this history through the most genuine and honest perspective. She has gone through every step and every emotion each one of us has experienced as a coach, manager, director, or owner. She knows the love you must have for this sport and its athletes, and she knows the drive that's required to keep pushing to the next level. She is a pioneer herself.

– Rosalind Schmidt, *Premier Athletics NKY*

When I think of people who have influenced me more than anyone else in my career and life, Stacy tops that list. I continue to strive to motivate the people around me the way Stacy has motivated me and so many others. Stacy's steadfast determination to remind us that we do this for the kids is one of her most admirable traits. This book is a wonderful opportunity for all of us to look back at where All Star began, and I can't imagine a better person than Stacy to bring those memories to life and show the world how wonderful the people are who helped guide the way.

– Susan Traylor, *Premier Athletics*

People slip in and out of your life, typically in seasons. Some people make a lasting impression with their character, passion, authenticity, drive, loyalty, and like-mindedness, or because they're just plain fun. That's Stacy.

I treasure the honor of working closely with Stacy, the gym franchise owner; Stacy, the dance director and coach; and Stacy, the former committee member as USASF regional director. She's not only brilliant, she's a person of integrity. She not only poured her heart and soul into the athletes she coached and the successful gym franchise she managed, she accomplished the same in her research to collect the history of our sport that needs to be shared with hundreds of thousands of athletes, coaches, and parents. This historical account is long overdue, and I couldn't think of anyone who would be more qualified to present this rich history than Stacy Rowe.

– Glenda Broderick, *USASF*

Stacy is an award-winning author who has dedicated her professional life to the cheer and dance industry. It is an honor to be a part of this book, and I couldn't think of a better person to pour her blood, sweat, and tears into its creation than Stacy Rowe.

– Sean Timmons, *Nfinity Athletic*

I met Stacy when she was a freshman and I was her cheerleading coach at Methodist College, now Methodist University, in Fayetteville, North Carolina. She was a young, enthusiastic, and ambitious athlete, always ready to go above and beyond to succeed. Our friendship extended beyond her college years when I realized that her passion was to stay in the cheerleading industry. Throughout our time at Premier Athletics, Stacy's critical thinking skills and optimistic view of the industry helped shape the company. Stacy filled all my gaps and weaknesses as a leader and, ultimately, improved my role. She continues to be a well-respected guest lecturer, visionary, and pillar in the cheerleading industry. I can't wait to see what she does next.

– Abel Rosa, *Deep South Spirit, The Cheer Tour*

When I met Stacy she tried to talk me into opening a cheer gym with her in a small town in North Carolina. Although I was skeptical, I admired her confidence and persistence. Against my better judgment I agreed to join her, and we opened the gym with her in charge. It was tremendously successful. It's been incredible to watch Stacy develop into one of the leaders in the All Star industry. In addition to her knowledge, her concern for the overall well-being of her students—children or adults—has made her a great teacher.

– Boog Potter, *Premier Athletics*

It's rare to encounter someone who not only challenges you to be better but also supports you in that journey. I've known Stacy for over fifteen years, and our paths have crossed in ways that have only deepened my respect for her as both a person and as a professional.

Stacy has always exemplified qualities that I admire: unparalleled business acumen, a fierce commitment to excellence, and unwavering patience that helps guide those around her toward their own success. Her expertise in the All Star cheer industry is matched only by her generosity in sharing that knowledge. She has lifted others up, not just on the mat and in the gym but also in everyday life. I am grateful to have learned from her at every step of my own journey.

– Chad Wright, *Cheer Athletics*

I can't wait to read *The Pioneers of All Star Cheer* because Stacy has put her heart into making our industry better and continues to help it grow every day. She inspires small business owners to be just as successful as the big names.

– Jessica Moltisanti, *Zone Cheer All Stars*

Stacy's extensive experience, leadership, and deep understanding of both the cheer industry and business make her uniquely qualified to write *The Pioneers of All Star*. She has lived through successes, learned from challenges, and continuously inspired those around her with her wisdom and passion.

– Michelle Ford, *Showtime Elite*

Stacy transformed several of my unrelated side projects into a cohesive career. Without her, I wouldn't be where I am today. She is fierce, encouraging, and direct. She'll let you know if you have broccoli in your teeth. If she cares about you, she'll move mountains for you. She's qualified to write this book because she's one of the pioneers of All Star who's been around since the beginning.

– Carly Byman, *Varsity All Star Dance*

Stacy gave us some of the best times of our lives. I am so thankful that she helped make my daughter the person she is. Coaching an

All Star team is more than winning a trophy or a title. It's an experience that will last a lifetime. Thank you isn't enough to say to Stacy and her All Star program.

– Susan George, *All Star Cheer Parent*

I met Stacy Rowe when she opened Premier Athletics Clayton in 2001. I had never cheered or danced in that capacity before she became my coach. She not only taught me skills and techniques but also how to be a better teammate and leader. She always encouraged us to work as a team, even when it was challenging. She knows the technical ins and outs of the business, but she also has shown a drive to succeed that gives her the credibility to write this book. I will forever remember my time as her athlete, and now, as her friend. I am a better person, teacher, and leader because of my time as her athlete.

– Megan Parker, *Former All Star Cheerleader and Dancer*

I am privileged to say that Stacy is my aunt, but I also spent nearly ten years with her as my All Star cheer and dance coach. She pioneered All Star cheer and dance in our quaint little corner of North Carolina. Through her passion for the sport and dedication to her role as a model for young athletes in the community, she created something that almost every young person wanted to be a part of. Stacy not only brought the world of All Star sports to our area for the first time, but she also created an atmosphere that encouraged young people to dream and to work together for a common goal. In addition, she provided a safe space for those who needed one.

Her unwavering character, outspoken nature, intelligence, and huge heart have contributed to her success. I am so proud to have both an aunt and a coach who has been an inspiration to me and many others.

– Lauren Vaudry, *Former All Star Cheerleader and Dancer*

Stacy has been an integral part of my career and my life in general, from our industry pep talks to listening to me vent. Seeing her success has changed my life. I realized I can do other things beyond my career. Stacy writes books. I plant flowers.

Stacy's experience in our remarkable industry prepared her to assist others. She has been both a winner and a loser, but she has remained the same person. That is a testament to who she is.

– Tracey Pauley, *TCLM Events*

Stacy always has been generous with her time and willing to do anything she could to help colleagues excel. She continually shares her expertise in coaching, event management, and entrepreneurship. Stacy has done it all and has a wealth of knowledge in all facets of our industry. That background allows her to structure both large-scale building blocks and minute details that ensure anything she touches—a business, team, event planning, culture creation, staffing perspective—will lead to success.

– Brown Walters, *Senior Event Coordinator Varsity*

THE PIONEERS OF ALL STAR CHEER

ALSO BY S.R. FABRICO

NONFICTION

- *The Pioneers of All Star DANCE* [Coming Soon!]
- *My Firefly Journal*

MY JOURNAL SERIES: 52 weeks of goals, growth, and gratitude for athletes

- My Cheer Journal
- My Dance Journal
- My Gymnastics Journal
- My Swim Journal
- My Soccer Journal
- My Basketball Journal
- My Volleyball Journal
- My Crew Journal

FICTION

- *The Secrets We Conceal*
- *Call Her Janie*
- *Keeping Janie*
- *Janie's Hope*
- *Ten Thousand Steps* [Coming Soon!]

THE PIONEERS OF ALL STAR CHEER

THE HISTORY AND EVOLUTION OF THE SPORT WITH TIPS FROM GYM OWNERS AND ENTREPRENEURS

S.R. FABRICO

Copyright © 2025 by S.R. Fabrico. All rights reserved.No part of this publication may be reproduced, stored in a retrieval system, or transmitted in any form or by any means, electronic, mechanical, photocopying, recording, scanning, or otherwise, without the prior written permission of the author.

Limit of Liability/Disclaimer of Warranty: This publication is designed to provide accurate and authoritative information in regard to the subject matter covered. While the publisher and author have used their best efforts in preparing this book, they make no representations or warranties with respect to the accuracy or completeness of the contents of this book and specifically disclaim any implied warranties of merchantability or fitness for a particular purpose. No warranty may be created or extended by sales representatives or written sales materials. The advice and strategies contained herein may not be suitable for your situation. You should consult with a professional when appropriate. Neither the publisher nor the author shall be liable for any loss of profit or any other commercial damages, including but not limited to special, incidental, consequential, personal, or other damages.

The Pioneers of All Star Cheer:The History and Evolution of the Sport with Tips from Gym Owners and Entrepreneurs
By S.R. Fabrico

Paperback ISBN: 978-1-962546-11-9
Hard Cover ISBN: 978-1-962546-10-2
Ebook ISBN: 978-1-962546-12-6

Cover design by The Paperhouse Books
Printed in the United States of America
SRF Creations

To my friends and colleagues at Premier Athletics, you have been an influential part of my entire adult life. Our culture and history are woven into the fabric of my being. You helped shape me into the person I am, so I'm eternally grateful for every one of you. You are like family and, together, we have built something special.

Cole Stott, you have pushed me throughout my career and helped me evolve into the person you always knew I could become. You challenged me from the moment we met and continue to challenge me in positive ways every day. You are my business ride or die and, occasionally, you're fun to tease. I appreciate your vision and your courage as you steer the ship. I'll be your first officer any day of the week and twice on Sundays.

Boog Potter and Mike Martinez, thank you for believing in a Yankee girl from New Jersey who wanted to open a gym in the small town of Clayton, North Carolina, where there was only one stoplight and no Walmart.

TABLE OF CONTENTS

Foreword xvii

Preface xix

Introduction 1

Section I: The History 6

   Part I: Early Development Era 6
   Part II: Creation Of All Star 19
   Part III: Growth Era 25

Section II: Modern-Day-All Star 42

   Part I: Modernization & Expansion Era 42
   Part II: The Contemporary Era 59

Section III: Looking To The Future 77

   Part I: Building The Future 77

Section IV: The Pioneers 80

      Jeff Webb 84
      Lance Wagers 103
      Cathy Buckey 112
      Debbie Love 121
      Kevin Jones 129
      Hilda Mcdaniel 138
      Bill Seely 151
      Kathy Gaffney 166
      Regina Symons 173
      Steve Wedge 182
      Gwen Holtsclaw 190
      Dawn Duncan Walters 197
      Eric Little 204

Ray Jasper	212
Danny Kahn	219
Amy Tyler	226
John Newby	232
Jim Chadwick	242
Kevin Brubaker	255
Brad Page & Ladd Lebus	269
Tammy Skinner	278
Jamie Parrish	285
James Speed	293
Courtney Pope	308
Elaine Pascale & Joelle Antico	312
Victor & Kristen Rosario	322
The Three Amigos	335
Brett Hansen	346
Don Collins	353
Robin Coe	364
Aaron Flaker	376
Morton Bergue	388
Justin Carrier	396
Orson Sykes	404
Tate Chalk	412
Randy Dickey	425
George "Boog" Potter	433
Mike Martinez	444
Cole Stott	456
Casey Jones	465
Roger Schonder	480
Brian Elza	490
Happy Hooper	500
Sean Timmons	509
Dennis Worley	521
Damianne Albee Steward	532

Tres Letard 539
Becky Herrera 548
Leon Reynolds 558
NACCC 568
USASF 578
Steve Peterson 598
Amy Clark 600
Meredith Walker 602
Heidi Weber 604
Cathryn "Cat" Weeden 615
Brooke Plack 629
Kali Seitzer & Sean Guzman 639

Suggested Reading From The Pioneers **651**

About The Author **656**

Acknowledgments **660**

Join The Movement **663**

Podcast **664**

Index **665**

Also By S.R. Fabrico **680**

Sources **681**

FOREWORD

Cheerleading has been a part of my life for more than thirty years. From my start as a college cheerleader I moved to working in some of the first up-and-coming cheerleading training gyms and then to owning several cheer-related businesses. At every stop I have been blessed to find a sport that fulfills both my competitive and professional aspirations. I have worked with thousands of athletes, families, and colleagues and am honored to be part of a community that has made such a profound and positive impact on both my family and me.

It was through this community that I crossed paths with Stacy Rowe. Although we had been acquainted for a long time, it was only four or five years ago that I came to know Stacy well. As opportunity—in the form of COVID—would have it, we became business partners, but more important, we became close friends.

I was immediately drawn to Stacy's no-nonsense, get-it-done approach to business. It didn't take long to see beyond her directness and recognize the person underneath, a woman of deep character who cares fiercely about everything she takes on and everyone she works with. Stacy doesn't do anything halfway. Her tireless work ethic, combined with a rare ability to blend structure and creativity, makes her a formidable businesswoman. Where creative minds struggle with structure, Stacy thrives. She is systematic yet innovative in everything she pursues. She is both the artist and the architect.

When Stacy shared her vision for writing a positive and accurate book about All Star cheerleading, I had no doubt she would make it happen. We often talk about our gratitude for this sport and the incredible people who have helped shape it. Now Stacy has put that gratitude into print with *The Pioneers of All Star Cheer*.

In this book Stacy explains the history of All Star cheer and honors the athletes, coaches, entrepreneurs, and trailblazers who helped build the sport and who continue to lead it today.

Cheerleading has always been a powerful expression of athleticism, creativity, and community spirit, yet few know the story of how All Star cheer was created. Through Stacy's work, readers are invited to glimpse the perseverance, vision, and culture that pushed the boundaries of traditional cheerleading and redefined what it could be.

As you read these pages, please take a moment to appreciate the athletes who competed, the coaches who dared to dream bigger, and the entrepreneurs who built the foundation of this sport we love so deeply. Stacy has done a fantastic job of honoring their contributions, and I hope you are as inspired by their stories as I am.

Dream big and keep pushing the boundaries of All Star cheer.

– Casey Jones, The Stingray Allstars

PREFACE

Cheerleading has been part of my life since I was ten years old and I cheered for St. Mary's Elementary School. I still remember the white sweatshirt that featured a blue megaphone with the letters *SMS* in the center. Our blue skirts fell to our knees, and we wore white and black saddle shoes. I vividly recall the cheer we performed at each basketball game to welcome the visiting squad. My favorite part was jumping to face the crowd, hands on hips, and shouting my name. Instantly, I caught the cheerleading bug.

Wanting to get more serious about cheerleading, I begged my parents to let me join the Monroe Township Cheerleading Organization where I would cheer on the sidelines for local soccer teams and learn a routine for competition. Those competitions fueled my growth, and my passion deepened.

In high school I cheered all four years for the football team, the men's and women's basketball teams and, occasionally, competed. But I wanted more. About thirty minutes from my hometown, a new team called Rainbow All Stars had recently formed. My tumbling coach, Tara Charleton, convinced me to join her senior team at Rainbow. We practiced inside a gymnastics facility and trained solely for competition. I thought it was the coolest thing ever.

I was especially passionate. I trained several days a week by working out and running in preparation for cheering in college. Little did I know those early cheerleading decisions would mold the rest of my life.

After cheering for three years in college, I graduated early and went on to teach high school math and serve as the assistant coach for both the junior varsity and varsity cheer teams. Once again, my passion soared. I dreamed of one day opening my own gym and coaching full time. Lo and behold, I found an organization, Premier Athletics, that helped me realize my dream—to open a cheerleading gym and do what I loved as a career. Eventually, I became part owner of Premier Athletics—what a gift.

Throughout my career in cheerleading and dance I coached thousands of athletes. I retired from coaching in 2018 and began writing to scratch my creative itch. Since then I have written four novels and nine goals, gratitude, and reflection journals. As All Star cheer celebrates approximately forty years of existence, I felt compelled to write about its history and evolution and to celebrate the stories of gym owners and cheer business professionals who helped shape the industry.

When I look back, my career seems like a blink of an eye. Many of us were young adults who didn't want to grow up and find a real job. Even today we're sometimes asked when we'll stop the silliness and do something for real. But All Star cheer is real, and countless people helped forge the path to create an entertaining, innovative sport that helps so many diverse individuals thrive.

I began writing novels in 2018 after retiring from coaching, believing that writing would fill my need to be creative. After years of writing and publishing, my business partners suggested I write a book about the cheerleading industry. Little did they know I already had that exact book idea on my wish list. Their suggestion was the push I needed to start the process.

My intention with this book is to remind everyone of the nostalgia we feel when we think about the cheerleading of the past. I want to create a true understanding of how All Star cheerleading came to be. The pioneers of our sport literally created an industry out of thin air, an industry that allowed many people to build thriving businesses centered around their passion, one that created wonderful life lessons and memories for young athletes. Being able to provide for your family while doing something you love is the greatest gift. All Star cheer has done that for so many, and it's still doing it.

The cheerleading industry has grown so much within my lifetime that I had forgotten what a small community All Star really is. As I began my interviews, I realized how interconnected everyone is. The All Star community is remarkable, a large family of people who have your back, even when you don't know them personally. I couldn't imagine my life without All Star cheer and dance, and I hope this book shines a light on the wonder and magnificence of the sport.

"We rise by lifting others." – Robert Ingersoll

This quote is my personal favorite. It reminds us that our own growth is connected to the growth of those around us. As a society, we rise by uplifting the people in our lives.

At my core, I am a teacher. My degree is in mathematics, and I've been a business owner for over twenty-five years. I'm an award-winning author, a sister, an aunt, a friend, a mother, and a wife of twenty-five years, but intertwined with all that, I am a teacher.

I crave knowledge and understanding, and I strive to be the best at my craft. I love pouring myself into those around me because I genuinely enjoy helping others succeed. Teaching fulfills me. It doesn't matter if I'm teaching math, business, cheerleading, dance, gymnastics, or writing, I love helping others grow. I enjoy providing helpful tools and celebrating others' successes. Celebrating each other is an integral part of life, and I am excited to write this book as a celebration of All Star cheer.

All Star isn't perfect, and I've personally had my ups and downs with the sport. But after interviewing over one hundred people to create this book, I can honestly say I am genuinely proud to be part of All Star. I'm proud of what we've built, and I'm proud of the people who have poured their lives into creating this amazing community where athletes can thrive. I can't wait to see how we come together again—especially in this time of division—to build something even bigger, better, and stronger so it will last for centuries.

Writing *The Pioneers of All Star Cheer* has been a labor of love. I'm grateful for my business partners Cole Stott, Casey Jones, and Kevin Brubaker who helped connect me to so many incredible cheer professionals who contributed to this book. The project took on a life of its own and, at times, it became daunting. Sifting through the information was a monumental task, and I must give special thanks to my husband who immediately jumped on board as my research assistant.

After countless hours of interviews with some of the greatest minds in our sport, I was filled with gratitude. Each person was genuine, gifted, kind, and innovative. As I listened to story after story, I was honored to be part of a sport that so many brilliant people had the courage and boldness to create.

Initially, I began with an interview list of twenty-five people in the All Star cheer. During the interview process I asked each person if there was anyone they would recommend I interview for the book. The list grew massively. Some people could not be reached; some people declined, but over one hundred interviews were conducted to collect as much knowledge as possible with the goal of telling the story of how All Star cheer came to be and how it has evolved into what it is today. The intention for *The Pioneers of All Star Cheer* is to share the positive impact All Star cheer has had on so many, including me, and to record the sport's history for future generations to appreciate and understand.

I've done my best to capture the spirit of the sport. Certain aspects reflect my perspective, drawn from being part of All Star for several decades. Where appropriate, I have sprinkled in my personal opinions. Each interview played a part in creating the history and evolution of the sport.

The first edition has been written with the intention of updating it as I learn more and continue to add the stories of impactful gym owners, coaches, and businesses. If you have information you'd like to contribute, please email srfabricoauthor@gmail.com.

INTRODUCTION

FOR THOSE WHO MAY NOT KNOW:

THIS IS ALL STAR CHEERLEADING

Here's Merriam-Webster's definition of cheerleader: "one that calls for and directs organized cheering (as at a football game.)" Merriam-Webster, America's most trusted dictionary, boasts that you can "find definitions for over 300,000 words from the most authoritative English dictionary, continuously updated with new words and meanings," yet "All Star cheerleading" cannot be found anywhere in its listings.

As defined by the US All Star Federation (USASF), All Star cheerleading is "a high-energy, team-based performance sport combining athleticism, artistry, and acrobatics."

But the meaning of All Star for those who participate is difficult to quantify. The sport transcends the eight counts performed in a routine. All Star cheer is a community of individuals who form teams that stand alone for the sake of competition and the pursuit of excellence. Those competitors are All Star cheerleaders.

All Star cheerleaders strive to entertain. Their purpose is to celebrate others and uplift those around them by executing a routine that will evoke emotion. All Star cheerleaders crave the feeling of bringing joy to a crowd. There is no better feeling for cheerleaders than to hear the audience scream in excitement for the performance they have delivered. It's exhilarating to sense the energy a routine evokes from the audience. It's what every team strives for. When performed flawlessly, a cheerleading routine resembles a symphony with various elements coming together to create a harmonious performance. Cheerleaders are unwavering in their commitment to spreading cheer and are instructed to suppress their emotions so they can fully perform their job and uplift those around them. That is the task. That is what "cheer" leaders are called to do.

All Star includes a competitive element, prompting teams to take everything I mentioned earlier, apply a scoring rubric, and enhance it with lights, music, and staging. It's a battle to determine who can deliver the most difficult and flawless performance while exciting the crowd. All Star cheerleaders are highly competitive, and they work tirelessly to excel. While the competition is fierce, All Star cheer is an incredible community where members inevitably reach out to help one another.

To provide a clearer explanation, here's the definition of All Star from the USA Cheer website: "All Star cheer is a form of cheerleading in which athletes perform a two-and-a-half-minute routine that includes tumbling, stunting, pyramids, dance, and cheer segments."

All Star cheer differs from traditional school cheerleading in that its main focus is on competition, whereas school cheerleading features crowd leading and other school-related roles, although there is the possibility of competition. All Star cheer teams are typically organized by a club and welcome athletes from the entire area to join their teams.

Teams are organized into tiers for every skill level, beginner to elite. All Star rules are tailored to skill progressions commonly performed in cheerleading, ensuring they match the competitor's developmental stage. Teams range from Tiny Novice Level 1 to adults at Level 7.

In the United States, most All Star clubs, teams, and competitions fall under the USASF, which also encompasses All Star dance. Often, a single club offers both All Star cheer and All Star dance. USASF delivers rules, resources, credentials, and essential information for athletes, coaches, parents, and clubs.

But All Star transcends its literal definitions by instilling crucial life lessons that empower athletes to confidently attack life. Key lessons include teaching athletes self-respect, respect for others, and the power of teamwork to achieve a common goal. Empowering athletes, especially young women, to assert themselves is another major focus. And our athletes learn that we rise together by lifting others.

HOW TO READ THIS BOOK

Dive into the history of All Star. Discover the origins of cheerleading and its evolution into All Star. Explore the most impactful moments in All Star history and learn about the vision and courage of those who paved the way by taking bold leaps as pioneers.

Many of those pioneers are featured in chapters that focus on their personal All Star journeys. Explore these incredible individuals to learn more about who they are and how they made their contributions to All Star. *The Pioneers of All Star Cheer* provides a retrospective on the history of our sport that details its origins and evolution to the present day.

THIS BOOK IS A SMORGASBORD. BE SURE TO TASTE IT ALL.

The Pioneers of All Star Cheer is designed for you to explore freely, but please do so thoughtfully. It's organized chronologically, but it can be understood in any order you choose.

Section I provides a general overview of the origins of All Star cheer, tracing the series of events from the first cheerleader in 1898 to the inaugural All Star team, the first All Star competition, and numerous other milestones.

Section II examines the mergers and acquisitions in the sport's history, the inception of the NACCC and USASF, and the evolution of All Star up to 2025.

Section III briefly explores what the future holds: Where is All Star headed, and how do we get there?

Section IV offers an in-depth look at the individual pioneers of the sport. Read a more detailed account of how the pioneering programs, gyms, and businesses were developed. Gain insight into their challenges as well as their most cherished memories and advice.

Learn about the pioneers as individuals and what they specifically contributed to All Star.

At the top of each pioneer's dedicated chapter you'll find powerful quotes selected by each individual. I believe those quotes offer a glimpse into the wisdom and knowledge each pioneer has gained throughout their All Star journey. You'll be inspired by their stories of how they started and developed their businesses. You'll also discover entertaining facts and tips for gym owners and coaches.

I've also included messages from the All Star pioneers to others in the industry, along with books that each pioneer has found impactful.

THE AUTHOR'S WISH

I hope readers will gain a deeper insight into All Star cheer and learn from the pioneers who shaped it. I hope you will enjoy this book as you journey down memory lane, discover a bygone era, or dive into All Star cheer for the first time.

All Star cheerleaders are fueled by a fierce passion that drives them to work tirelessly for their team, friends, and families. And they do it all with a smile. All Star cheerleaders are among the toughest people I know. People stay in the world of All Star because they love it.

SECTION I: THE HISTORY

"The beginning is the most important part of the work."
– Plato

PART I: EARLY DEVELOPMENT ERA
1898-1981

THE POWER OF ENCOURAGEMENT

A group of cheer gym owners gathered for a business leadership meeting, and I split the group into three equal lines. Ten feet from the end of each line I placed a bucket. Each person in line received three pennies. Each line had its own leader positioned in front of their respective bucket. I gave the three leaders separate instructions to follow while the members of their lines attempted to toss their pennies into the bucket.

The leader of the first line crossed his arms and remained silent. His instructions were clear: He was to ignore his line completely.

The second leader smiled brightly while he clapped and cheered, "Come on! You've got this! You can do it! Let's go!"

The third leader, by contrast, shouted insults at his group: "You suck! Losers! You couldn't drop your penny in the bucket if it was right in front of you. Just quit. You're awful!"

The second line, led by the individual shouting encouragement, won the game by tossing the most pennies into the bucket.

People thrive on positive reinforcement. It fuels our desire to succeed. Encouragement builds confidence and reinforces our sense of self-worth. It motivates us to persevere by affirming our abilities and helping us feel seen. Given the powerful role encouragement plays in human achievement, it's no surprise that cheerleading came into existence.

Johnny Campbell is regarded as the first US cheerleader after he organized a group of students to lead the crowd from the sidelines at a University of Minnesota football game in 1898.

FROM SIS BOOM RAH TO SKI-U-MAH: CHEERLEADING'S ORIGINS

It was a typical twenty-eight degrees in Minneapolis on Nov. 5, 1898. The University of Minnesota Gophers had lost three consecutive games, and medical student Johnny Campbell was determined to help his school avoid making it four. So he marched passionately onto the field with a group of students and led the crowd in a cheer:

Rah! Rah! Rah!

PIONEERS OF ALL STAR

Ski-u-mah!
Hoo-Rah! Hoo-Rah!
Varsity. Varsity. Varsity,
Minn-e-So-Tah!

Captivated by such school spirit, the crowd joined in, repeating the chant in unison. Many believed the overwhelming encouragement helped lead Minnesota to a 15-0 victory over North Dakota. Competing universities soon adopted Campbell's model, and the tradition of cheerleading was born.

Long before that frigid day in Minneapolis, in the 1860s students in Great Britain shouted chants for their favorite soccer players. When the tradition made its way across the Atlantic, it found fertile ground in the United States. When Princeton and Rutgers hosted the first intercollegiate football game in 1869, student fans rallied with cries of "Sis Boom Rah!"

Shortly after Campbell's impromptu moment, the University of Minnesota created the first official "yell leader" squad, composed of six male students. To this day, Minnesota continues to use Campbell's cheer.

Throughout the early 1900s cheerleading squads—entirely male—were formed across the country at universities from Princeton to the University of Oregon. In the 1920s the Oregon squad introduced the use of flash cards to engage the crowd and encourage coordinated chants. Meanwhile, Minnesota's cheer squad established a fraternity called Gamma Sigma, dedicated to the art and leadership of cheering.

The 1920s, known as the Golden Age of Sport, burst with emerging talent across all disciplines. Sports competition became the centerpiece of people's lives. Women were urged to compete, but only in swimming, golf, and tennis. Despite the increasing number of women attending college during that time, their sports opportunities remained limited.

In 1923 the University of Minnesota became the first college to include women in cheerleading by creating coed teams. Across the country in the late 1920s and early 1930s women cheered as colleges lifted gender restrictive policies. In 1930 Concordia College in Moorhead, Minnesota, launched a pep squad of nine freshman girls. Still, many collegiate newspapers and school manuals referred to cheerleaders as "chap," "fellow," and "man."

In September 1939 World War II erupted, calling countless men to arms. As a result, women took on cheerleading roles at universities nationwide to boost morale for the men who were lucky enough to avoid the war and continued playing sports. By 1945, when the war ended, cheerleading was predominantly female.

FROM CAMP TO POM-PONS:

BUILDING THE BUSINESS OF CHEER

Lawrence "Herkie" Herkimer competed as a gymnast at Southern Methodist University and became the AAU national champion on the rings. Herkie overcame a stutter and discovered his voice in cheerleading. He kicked off his cheerleading journey by offering private lessons to aspiring high school cheerleaders. As time progressed, private lessons evolved into group sessions, which eventually transformed into camps.

In 1945 Herkie launched the inaugural cheerleading camp at Sam Houston State University in Huntsville, Texas, attracting fifty-three participants and backed by $600 borrowed from his father-in-law. Herkie aimed to provide a platform for cheerleaders to hone their skills, expand their talent beyond the sidelines, and compete against other schools. One year later the camp surged to 350 participants. Eventually, Herkimer earned more from his cheerleading camps than from his Southern Methodist teacher's salary, prompting him to go all in on his cheerleading business when he started the National Cheerleaders Association (NCA). Herkie was the first to transform cheerleading into a thriving business. This single moment would be the catalyst for the growth of an entire sport.

Cheerleading soon spread nationwide. Cheerleading squads filled nearly every American school, from elementary to college. The expansion created a fantastic opportunity for women to engage in a school activity. This likely explains why cheerleading wasn't deemed a sport back then. If it had been, girls might not have been encouraged to participate.

In the 1950s the Universal Spirit Association (USA) was founded as a groundbreaking camp company. Originally named California Specialty Camps, USA was launched under the leadership of Robert Olmstead, who had served as the drum major for the US Army Band in

World War II. Olmstead's parents were vaudeville actors, and Robert walked the high wire himself. Marching bands nationwide owe their creative transitions, formations, and thrilling entertainment elements to Robert Olmstead.

The Olmstead family also taught music lessons in their garage studio. Robert and his wife, Edith, pioneered the concept of drill teams and song leaders, which evolved into pom teams and, ultimately, into "dance teams," a term that Jeff Webb coined to capture every form of dance.

With USA, Robert started camps for majorettes. He envisioned a grand production on the field and created a group he called flag girls. Robert personally instructed every camp until he added cheer. He eventually hired Herkimer to lead cheer camps for USA on the West Coast. Mike Olmstead, Robert's youngest son, eventually took the reins of the company. In 2012 Varsity acquired USA, and Mike now leads Y2K Event Production.

In the 1960s, while most schools technically didn't forbid girls from participating in sports, they didn't offer many options for them either. Excitement for girls to join cheerleading surged as college cheerleaders nationwide began working with NCA camps, training tens of thousands of high school cheerleaders across the country. Camp training emphasized sideline cheers, chants, and basic stunts—like shoulder sits—far different from today's camp experience.

As cheer evolved into a more structured activity with teams attending camps, Herkie realized his customers needed a solution for their attire. He launched the first cheerleading uniform company, Cheerleader Supply. The company began when Dorothy Herkimer, Herkie's wife, began sewing uniforms for the teams her husband coached. Building on the success of NCA cheer camps, Dorothy transformed the uniform business into a thriving manufacturing enterprise with a dedicated sales team.

By the late 1960s and early 1970s, peewee and youth football organizations started adding cheerleading teams to their games. By then about 95 percent of television broadcasts were in color, replacing the outdated black and white. This pivotal moment fueled a marketing boom. Herkie aimed to create a new crowd-leading tool that people would remember for a lifetime.

Herkie imagined a vibrant apparatus for cheerleaders to use on the sidelines. He thought such an innovation would be more visually appealing to TV audiences with color televisions in almost every home. In 1971 Herkie patented the pom-pon, featuring a concealed handle. While most people call it a pom-*pom*, Herkie deliberately named the device a pom-*pon* after discovering that pom-pom had vulgar connotations in some countries. Every cheerleader worldwide knows the pom-pon remains a staple today. You'll still spot the pom-pon on the sidelines of most football and basketball games as well as in cheerleading competitions. Additionally, pom has emerged as its own distinct school and All Star dance division.

THE SPORT THAT WASN'T: THE TITLE IX PARADOX

On June 23, 1972, President Richard M. Nixon signed Title IX into law, ensuring equal education for all, regardless of gender. The law governs every aspect of education including admissions, sports, academic programs, financial aid, and student services. Any college, university, or K-12 school seeking federal funding must adhere to Title IX. Originally aimed at academic opportunities, this law is now recognized for finally giving women the chance to play sports.

Cheerleading met almost every definition of a sport. According to Merriam-Webster, a sport is "a specific activity—such as an athletic game engaged in for pleasure—an athletic activity requiring skill or physical prowess, or an activity that is often competitive." Although cheerleading met those criteria, except for being competitive, it was not included under Title IX.

Title IX determined that any sport it covered must be for the sole purpose of competition, and cheerleading in schools, of course, was not solely for that purpose. But Title IX also increased funding for women's sports. The revenue generated by successful men's sports, such as football, would fund the addition of new sports for women. If every school had included cheerleading as a sport, they might have had to include the marching band, majorettes, and dance teams. Where should they draw the line?

I believe the decision was largely influenced by money, but also by the fact that male lawmakers from previous decades permitted women to participate in cheerleading at a time when women were generally excluded from sports. After all, girls nationwide were participating in cheerleading long before the Title IX law was enacted.

In my opinion, the passage of Title IX paved the way for All Star cheer to explode. Although not considered a sport at first, female participants inadvertently set out to prove they deserved to be recognized as athletes and that cheerleading deserved to be recognized as a sport. Thus, cheerleaders pushed themselves further and further, challenging their ability to create more difficult and daring performances with the intention of being recognized as athletes in a unique sport.

HOW JEFF WEBB CHANGED CHEER FOREVER

Among the top instructors at NCA Camp was Jeff Webb. In addition to teaching NCA camps, Herkie asked Jeff to teach college camp for USA who partnered with Herkie to teach cheer camps on the West Coast. In 1975 Webb resigned from his role at the National Cheerleaders Association to return to law school. Herkimer requested that Webb stay over the summer to teach at his camps. Webb agreed.

Jeff Webb envisioned making the elements of cheer more dynamic and entertaining, so he developed new techniques for transitioning from one skill to another. Many of those techniques are still in use today. According to Jeff, word leaked that he would be leaving NCA at the end of the summer, prompting a few camp staffers to suggest he start his own company. They were enthusiastic about the new athletic cheer concept Jeff had created and wanted to continue his exciting approach to cheerleading.

Jeff said he never seriously considered starting his own company until someone suggested it to him. He completed his camps and, at summer's end, he cleaned out his desk and went home. He discussed possible next steps with his parents, who encouraged him to start his own company and forgo law school.

Kline Boyd, a friend of both Jeff and Jeff's dad, rallied friends and family to raise enough money to launch Jeff's new company. But it needed a name. The terms "US" and "national" were already in use, and he wanted something more expansive than national anyway, so he landed on Universal Cheerleaders Association, and UCA was born. After Jeff launched UCA, it became the official cheer summer camp partner for USA Cheer which, in turn, supported UCA in staffing its dance camps.

Jeff was committed to making cheerleading more exciting, so he continued to develop innovative elements, including new transitions between stunts and within pyramids. He conducted stunt clinics to promote UCA and attract teams to enroll in summer camp.

Jeff Webb relocated to Memphis, Tennessee, where he established his corporate headquarters in his apartment with his first and only employee at the time, Robert Tisdale. Robert went on to work for Jeff for forty-five years before retiring in 2019. Robert also had worked for NCA and had just finished graduate school when Jeff started UCA. Robert assisted with all back-of-house tasks, from accounting to staff shirts.

Jeff and his small staff, which later included his brother Greg, started conducting clinics across the South and parts of the Midwest. They referred to them as "gymnastics clinics for cheerleaders" that included tumbling, partner stunts, pyramids, and mini tramp—yes, mini tramp was a thing. No one had been doing camps like that.

Jeff and his team at UCA began teaching his straight leg building techniques that had never been used before. The new techniques enabled teams to learn stunts and pyramids more quickly. The squads were astonished by what they could learn from the UCA staff in just one day. Jeff aimed to teach cheerleaders skills that would capture the crowd's attention and enhance the excitement of partner stunts and pyramids. In the early years Jeff provided the clinics for free as a marketing strategy to promote his summer camps. There was no internet to promote a business back then, so appearing in person to give the squads a glimpse of the UCA magic was the best way to sell summer camps. After each clinic, Jeff would collect the coaches' names and addresses and send each one a summer camp brochure with registration information. Essentially, it was the 1970s version of a marketing funnel. To register for a UCA summer camp you simply filled out the bottom of the flyer and mailed it in along with your check.

After a successful first summer with more than a thousand campers, Webb focused on further growth in the cheer camp and clinic model. The number of new stunts and pyramids continued to increase. These new building elements were more challenging and required greater agility, leading to a need for uniforms made from more flexible fabric. Heavy sweaters and skirts were no longer appropriate. This demand for new outfits was addressed by the emerging uniform company, Varsity Spirit Fashions, a UCA affiliate.

Jeff Webb and UCA were laser focused on figuring out how to continue funding their new uniform endeavor, oblivious to what anyone else was doing. The UCA team determined that, to achieve greater national exposure for cheerleading, they needed to appear on television.

In 1980 a sports syndicator in New York City covered soccer, basketball, football, and various other sports. Jeff journeyed to New York City to pitch his televised cheerleading competition idea. He invited George Gallup, the head of the television network, to a UCA cheerleading summer camp to explore the potential for a cheerleading show.

That summer the Television Sports Network (TVS) visited a UCA camp where Jeff showcased a college demo choreographed to the *Rocky* theme, a routine that teams could perform in competition. As a result, TVS signed a three-year deal with UCA to cover its events.

That was great news, but UCA needed to host an event in a prime location for television. Walt Disney World declined the opportunity, so the first televised national cheerleading competition was held at Sea World in Orlando, Florida, between ski shows on a specially constructed stage in the water. Twenty teams were invited to compete in the first televised cheerleading competition known as the National High School

Cheerleading Championships. The event achieved excellent TV ratings throughout its three-year contract.

At the end of the third year, George reached out to Jeff and said, "I'm leaving my position as president of TVS and going to work for an upstart cable company." Given that cable was in its infancy, it seemed insane to leave a great job as president of an established organization for a new cable company. But Jeff was curious, so he asked, "What's the name of this cable company?"

George replied, "Entertainment and Sports Programming Network, ESPN."

Jeff decided to stick with George and move his show to the fledgling network. As ESPN grew, so did the national exposure for cheerleading. Such exposure led to a demand for more shows, additional divisions, and worldwide cheerleading visibility. UCA, now known as Varsity Spirit, is ESPN's longest-standing television partner.

At the same time, Herkimer and his team at NCA required a unique and exciting approach to attract new customers. As a result, NCA established the High School National Cheerleading Championship in Dallas, Texas, during the 1981-1982 school year. Teams would be evaluated on their sideline cheers, acrobatic elements, and song routines that included dance with pom-pons.

"Creativity is intelligence having fun." – Albert Einstein

PART II: CREATION OF ALL STAR
1982-1991

FROM RADIO STATION TO ALL STAR CHEER

Take a moment to immerse yourself in the 1980s. The economy was thriving. Materialism and consumerism were on the rise. Blockbuster movies were common, cable television was rapidly spreading across the country, but children still went outside to play. Cheerleaders practiced on grass, but if they were fortunate, they might have a few minutes to practice on the wrestling mats in the school cafeteria. The eighties also were a remarkable era of technological innovation and optimism.

But the eighties didn't have the internet, cell phones, email, or social media. Snail mail, fax, or phone were the only means of communicating with other businesses, and unless you saw something on television or in newspapers or magazines, you were unaware of what was happening around the country.

In that context, Hilda McDaniel coached a recreational cheerleading squad called the Tuckahoe Tomahawks in Virginia because her daughter, Kendall, was a cheerleader. Hilda was creative and determined to make her team successful. She didn't like the typical cheers and chants, and she was talented at rhyming and making up words, so she created a unique rap style for her teams to perform.

Hilda didn't want anyone on her team to be left out, so she created long pyramids that extended twenty or even thirty feet in length to ensure every girl had a spot. Some of her teams boasted fifty participants. In addition, she infused a theatrical element into her routines from years spent in the auditorium watching Kendall perform.

Hilda brought her team to the Eastern Cheerleading Association (ECA) camp where they became the center of attention because she insisted that all the girls wear matching outfits, including hair bows, which was not common like it is today. Hilda ultimately became the director of the entire Tuckahoe organization. While at camp she met Don Collins, who would later become the cheerleading coach at the University of North Carolina at Chapel Hill and the owner of Spirit Xpress summer camps and All Star Challenge competitions.

As Kendall grew older and prepared to age out of Tuckahoe, Hilda was not ready to stop coaching. In 1982, a friend of hers was working in marketing at radio station WRXL in Richmond, Virginia. The station organized a basketball team of disk jockeys to compete against local schoolteachers in a fundraiser and sought a group of cheerleaders to attend their games. WRXL asked Hilda if she would organize a cheerleading team to support the disk jockey basketball team.

Hilda asked, "Can I compete with my team?"

"We don't care what you do," the station said, "as long as you show up and cheer at our basketball games."

Hilda was thrilled. Her opportunity to keep coaching her daughter had landed in her lap, and since her team would be cheering for a basketball team, her cheer squad would be allowed to compete. After a year, her marketing friend moved to Richmond's Q94, and Hilda and her team followed, breathing life into the Q94 Rockers, an independent cheerleading team made up of local athletes from various schools that was formed to cheer for the Q94 disk jockeys basketball team and to compete in cheerleading competitions. Hilda maintained her tradition of cheer raps, large pyramids, matching outfits, and hair bows, and in 1983 she rented a charter bus for her team to travel to Dallas, Texas for the NCA High School National Championship. Unfortunately, a severe ice storm struck, preventing the team from reaching the competition. A year's worth of effort had been wasted. As a result, Hilda' team chartered a plane the following year to guarantee they would compete in the JV High School division at the 1984NCA High School Nationals.

In 1985 the Clayton Valley All Stars from California competed at the NCA High School Nationals alongside several other teams, including Rebel Cheer Company from Texas. I found myself entangled in a spirited debate while gathering research to determine who was the first All Star team. The debate was ultimately settled, the Q94 Rockers were the first All Star "type" of team, but the Clayton Valley All Stars was the first team to use the term All Star in its name, which led to the division eventually being named All Star. These teams had something in common: Although the participants on each of those teams were of the appropriate age for their division, they didn't cheer for the same schools as traditional school cheer teams. Instead, they were a group of athletes from the local area who put together a routine solely for the purpose of competing.

The sport of cheer was growing in popularity across the country, and the athletes who participated wanted to continue pushing the envelope, challenging themselves each year to invent something new, something more creative, something more difficult, something more entertaining. Meanwhile, the narrative that "cheerleading is not a sport" continued, which only motivated the participants to push themselves even further.

AN INDEPENDENT SPIRIT: THE RISE OF ALL STAR

NCA leadership coined the term "All Star" in 1985 when it introduced an All Star division at the High School National Championship event in Dallas. All Star teams were made up of athletes from neighboring schools who united to form a team solely for the purpose of competition. These teams did not cheer for any sport. Teams such as the Q94 Rockers and Clayton Valley All Stars were barred from competing in the traditional school divisions because they selectively chose athletes from across their community, which was considered unfair.

The All Star division was initially established because Lance and Carol Wagers, who were running NCA, recognized that permitting All Star teams to keep competing would upset their school team customers. At the same time, they didn't want to turn away these new teams. In the beginning, All Star was a single division, and routines consisted of traditional cheer routines with no music.

Essentially, anyone who wasn't part of a school team competed in the single All Star division. All-girl teams complained that they were at a disadvantage when competing against coed teams. Eventually, the division split into an all-girl division and a coed division. In 1987, at the direction of Kevin Jones, NCA hosted the first strictly All Star cheer competition with seventy-seven teams in the junior and senior divisions from around the United States, thanks to Carol and Lance Wagers. They understood the potential for All Star competition, but had they turned away teams like the Q94 Rockers, Rebel Cheer Company, and Clayton Valley All Stars, All Star may never have come to fruition.

Girls across the country continued to be drawn to cheerleading where they could work together to perfect a routine to perform on stage in front of a crowd and compete against other teams of girls doing the same thing, all while wearing skirts, hair bows, and makeup. Athleticism, toughness, intelligence, camaraderie, and teamwork motivated more girls to participate every day.

As the sport grew, it provided Lawrence Herkimer with the opportunity to sell his NCA business to BSN Corporation for twenty million dollars in 1986. Two years later, BSN sold NCA to Prospect Group with

Herkie remaining at the helm. The cheerleading industry was taking off, and Herkie anticipated that NCA would generate $50 million in revenue by 1990.

The Midwest added to the cheerleading boom in 1988 with the formation of Steve Wedge's Cheerleaders of America (COA). A young accountant with a cheerleading background, Wedge worked part time on the board of Song Leaders and Cheerleaders of America. The organization struggled briefly after the president abruptly resigned, but young and full of passion, Wedge helped pick up the pieces and, as you know, rebranded the company in 1988. COA has impacted many cheerleaders and dancers over the years, but most notable is the $400,000 in college scholarships provided through its nonprofit organization that retained the original Song Leaders and Cheerleaders of America name.

Also in 1988, down south in Fayetteville, North Carolina, Gwen Holtsclaw became the first female owner of a cheer company. It was called Cheer Ltd. Gwen also was the cheerleading coach at Methodist College, now Methodist University. Cheer Ltd. started with private summer camps for school teams that evolved into private cheerleading camps for All Star teams. All Star offered no camp options, aside from attending one of the school camps held at various college campuses across the country. Cheer Limited customized its camps to meet its customers' needs. Soon several All Star programs asked Cheer Ltd. to provide summer camps for their teams.

"Growth is never by mere chance; it is the result of forces working together." – James Cash Penney

PART III:
GROWTH ERA
1992-2002

INTO THE WAREHOUSE: THE BIRTH OF ALL STAR FACILITIES

In the late 1980s and early 1990s, many new All Star teams began to pop up across the country. The introduction of new divisions that included Senior,

Senior Prep, Junior, and Junior Prep, enabled the formation of more teams, resulting in fully developed All Star programs.

Many program owners were renting space in gymnastics facilities. In several instances, gymnastics facilities sought to incorporate All Star programs as a supplemental revenue source, but they were not interested in understanding the sport or coaching the cheer teams. Gymnastics facilities were essentially a springboard for many of the initial All Star programs. When gymnasts burned out from practicing twenty hours a week, they could transition to All Star cheer where the competition intensity remained high, but the number of practice hours was significantly reduced.

Initially, it was a win-win for both gymnastics' facilities and cheer program owners, but as cheer outgrew them, dedicated All Star cheer locations began to emerge.

In the 1990s a typical cheer gym was packed with wall-to-wall carpeted foam rolls, a few cheese wedges, panel mats, a tumble track, and a trampoline. Many lacked a viewing area for parents and often had no room for a proper office. During my interview with Kristen and Victor Rosario about their first facility, Kristen revealed that kids would stand on her desk and use it as a runway to kick off their tumbling pass on the tumble track.

Initially, there were no spring floors, rod floors, or in-ground pits. Some gym owners operated their facilities without heating or air conditioning. During his interview, Randy Dickey mentioned sharing warehouse space with storage shelves, day workers, and forklifts. He paid monthly rent to install a carpet-bonded foam floor in the center of the warehouse and practiced with his teams at night after daytime operations had ceased.

The establishment of All Star cheer facilities created more opportunities for athletes to receive standardized training in spaces tailored specifically for their sport. Opportunity also increased for owners and coaches to manage more teams, classes, school teams, and additional programs, laying the groundwork for All Star to become both a business and a career.

NO RULES, NO LIMITS: THE GOLDEN AGE OF INNOVATION

By the mid-1990s the two major All Star entities had begun to take shape. Almost every All Star team in the country trained year-round in pursuit of the bragging rights that belonged to the winner of NCA or UCA All Star Nationals. All Star teams would attend local competitions or host their own competitions in preparation for the big national events. Programs didn't compete at both NCA and UCA All Star nationals. Instead, they formed an allegiance to one brand, usually based on routine style.

NCA expanded its divisions to include Junior Prep (grades 5 and below), Junior (grades 6-8), Senior Prep (grades 10 and below), and Senior (grade 12 and below), offering all-girl and coed options in each. Prep did not have the different rules or skill levels it does today. It was simply preparation for the junior and senior divisions. NCA also provided teams with the option to create routines using music exclusively or to compete with a mix of music and cheer instead of the previously mandatory all cheer routines. The new option to compete with all music routines introduced an additional dance component to All Star that had not existed before.

Choreographers from New York and Los Angeles entered the All Star space as coaches and gym owners sought their expertise to create eye-catching, energetic dances to elevate their routines. It wasn't long before most teams across the country employed some form of dance choreography. This change eventually led to stunt choreographers, pyramid choreographers and, ultimately, to full routine choreographers, creating additional opportunities in cheer.

Varsity was established as the corporate identity of UCA and Varsity Spirit Fashion Uniforms. UCA remained the name of the summer camp and competition companies. To promote growth and keep up with demand, UCA also expanded its All Star division offerings to include Youth (grade 5 and below), Junior (grade 9 and below), and Senior (grade 12 and below). UCA routines focused more on stunt elements and tumbling and less on dance, but a cheer was still required. There was no limit on team size, but it was beneficial for the team to be larger. Additional stunts in the air were more impressive and typically garnered higher scores.

I once had a senior cheer team with forty-four athletes, and I spoke with several other coaches who had close to fifty athletes. Even with the ability to add that many athletes to a team, there still wasn't enough room for everyone who wanted to participate at the All Star level. All Star attracted athletes of all shapes, sizes, and ability levels. Gyms were literally turning athletes away. The addition of new divisions allowed programs to add more teams and train more athletes, which created better, safer, and more appropriate training opportunities for all participants, but there was still not enough team space.

TO CATEGORY SCORING AND BEYOND

To bring more credibility to the scoresheet, in 1992 Steve Wedge of COA developed a method of scoring competitions known as "category scoring," which he began to use at his events. He adapted this concept from his experience with high school marching band. Prior to Steve's concept, each judge on the panel was responsible for judging all elements in a routine, which was difficult and left tremendous room for subjectivity. Steve's new category scoring method was the first step in a more effective way to score routines, which resulted in more precise and fair placements.

Steve's scoring method initially assigned one person to judge each element of a routine—tumbling skills, building elements, jumps, and dance. Each judge also would provide a score for overall effect and impression of the routine.

In addition, at Steve's direction, COA implemented a safety judging system. With this new system teams had the opportunity to sign up for practice time the night before a competition. At that practice a safety judge would review their routine to ensure it complied with the rules. On the day of competition, safety judges would monitor whether participants' skills were legal under the specific competition's rules. Teams were notified immediately after their performance if they had any infractions.

As gyms continued to search for their identity, coaches tried to create innovative skills, pushing the envelope every year. The Top Gun All Stars from Miami, Florida, for instance, unveiled the pike open split basket toss to the world in 1995. Later Top Gun created the kick full basket toss. A basket toss is a required element in a cheer routine in which three or four bases throw a girl into the air as high as they can. The flyer performs a skill in the air before being caught by the base(s) on the ground in what cheerleaders call a cradle.

WHEN THE MUSIC NEVER STOPPED

Prior to the 1995-96 season, All Star routines still mirrored their school counterparts, complete with a traditional cheer. But when the rules changed to allow teams to perform their routine entirely to music or a mix of music and cheer, teams chose the style that worked best for them. During that crucial time some teams maintained traditional cheer sections while others fully transitioned to music-driven routines. The competitive results soon made the choice clear. During my interview with Justin Carrier, he remembered the legendary coed team from Top Gun performing a cheer that spelled out "T-O-P-G-U-N" with full twisting layouts, but it lost to teams that kept the music going throughout their routines.

"The big question was do we need to go *all* music in order to remain competitive?" Justin said. The answer quickly became apparent: Yes.

What followed was a series of evolutionary steps that moved All Star further away from its school-based roots, including the following:

- Teams began incorporating two eight-count cheer sections layered over music.

- Programs like Cheer Athletics introduced signature "program" cheers that engaged the crowds.

- Cheer sections continued over the music, but with fewer traditional motions.

- Eventually, cheers disappeared entirely.

This evolution marked a deliberate shift. All Star cheer was no longer a derivative of school cheerleading. It was forming its own distinct identity.

The first magazine dedicated specifically to cheer hit the market in 1995. *American Cheerleader Magazine* gave a written voice to the sport of cheer around the country. Companies like ECA, COA, and Cheer Ltd. clamored for ad space to show their business to the world. *American Cheerleader Magazine* focused primarily on high school and collegiate cheer teams. The magazine grew in popularity by featuring one lucky cheerleader on its cover each month. As young cheerleaders, my friends and I eagerly ripped the little postcard out of the fold of the magazine to apply for that coveted spot on the cover.

In 1997 the first multilocation gym business model emerged, demonstrating that All Star cheer could be a viable business for entrepreneurs. Premier Athletics opened three locations in one year and added five more locations over the next three years, thus setting the stage for multilocation franchises.

Toward the mid to late 1990s more event producers joined the scene with their own sets of rules, divisions, and scoresheets. The unique set of rules and divisions became a selling point, enticing customers to attend their events instead of other brands. For example, some events allowed flipping basket tosses and round-off back handspring double backs even though both skills were extremely dangerous if not taught and performed correctly. Many still say that was the beginning of the wild, wild west in cheer competition. Imagine a basketball tournament where a three-point shot is worth five points and a half-court shot is worth ten points. The following weekend, at another tournament, every basket is only worth one point. That was the wild, wild west of All Star cheer.

While many event producers followed the rules and divisions set by NCA or UCA, there was a no-holds-barred component that allowed virtually any skill, team size, or level. Many events were regional and catered to a specific style. Programs became accustomed to their local way of doing things and to their regional event producers' scoresheet. It was difficult for event producers to break into a new region because, in most cases, it was a dramatically different market.

In some ways I think the wild, wild west added to the fun and excitement. As I mentioned earlier, cheerleaders have an inherent desire to push boundaries, explore their creativity, demonstrate their value, and gain recognition as athletes competing in a sport. All Star thrived during this unrestrained period, attracting both more participants and more fans.

This period also allowed the gyms to find their identities and compete where their style fit best. Some event producers preferred a more entertaining routine with creative elements that impressed the crowd while others favored a clean, well-executed routine. There were no specified point deductions for mistakes in a routine, so almost everyone challenged themselves as much as they could.

As more teams and events emerged, the competitions grew more challenging. A major focus on skill development, progression, and technique began to take shape. Coaches sought an advantage, leading them to enlist technicians who could train their athletes and provide targeted drills and strength training to improve their teams' skills on stage.

By the end of the 1990s almost all routines were performed entirely with music. As a result, music producers crafted custom mixes designed to enhance routines and provide teams with a competitive edge.

Programs such as World Cup from Freehold, New Jersey, and Cheer Extreme from Kernersville, North Carolina, exemplify custom mixes that significantly influenced the overall feel and energy of a team's performance during this period. I still remember Cheer Extreme's Senior Elite executing its pyramid like a transformer, shifting in and out of poses and hitting picture after picture in perfect harmony as Celine Dion belted out her latest ballad.

Without social media at their fingertips, fans couldn't view their favorite routines with a single click. Instead, they had to gather like a herd of cattle, filling a competition hall to see Top Gun's newest invention, the incredible tumbling from Cheer Athletics, or the precision of The Stingray Allstars. The excitement was palpable as the crowds clambered to watch team after team take the stage and perform. Routine after routine, the music pulsated through the audience, building excitement with each performance and breathing life into every routine. Back then, events were an exciting celebration of athleticism, innovation, and sportsmanship.

THE GREAT COMPETITION BOOM

The growth of major national competitions exploded as the twenty-first century arrived. Typically, cheer competitions were held in high school or college gymnasiums, but as more event producers emerged, they tried to outdo each other. UCA was held at Walt Disney World in Orlando, Florida, for example, so the bar was set high. New national competitions were held in a convention center where the competition floor was elevated on a stage with a large backdrop in a rock concert style production.

The trend for gyms to attend four or five two-day national competitions per season became more common. In most sports, to compete in a national event a team must win at the state level, move on to and win at the regional level, and ultimately secure a spot in the national competition. But it was the wild, wild west, so a gazillion "national championship" events were held. Almost everyone was a "national champion."

In 1995 the Pepsi Cheerleading Championship took place at Kentucky Kingdom in Louisville. The event was the brainchild of college friends Aaron Flaker and Emmitt Tyler. It later became JAMfest, and their team infused the industry with family fun by creating their mascot, Jammy.

Aaron had been the University of Louisville Cardinal Bird mascot, so it was only fitting that he became the mascot for his own event brand. This new element, along with the fun and celebration at JAMfest events, injected fresh excitement into All Star cheer competitions. JAMfest emphasized family by offering game areas, dedicated spots for cheer dads to gather and enjoy themselves and, of course, the Jammy mascot.

Another emerging event was Kevin Brubaker's CHEERSPORT, which revolutionized All Star. The CHEERSPORT team developed the concept of level play. When he hosted his first event in 1997, Brubaker and his team created levels that allowed teams to compete in a division suited to their ability. Intermediate teams, for example, were limited to performing tumbling skills no more difficult than a back tuck and were prohibited from using twisting cradles.

At that time only straight and twisting cradles existed. Advanced teams could execute any skill as long as it adhered to the safety guidelines and rules. Level play not only created a fairer playing field but also propelled the sport to new heights. Gyms skyrocketed from hosting four or five teams to hosting ten, twenty, or more.

In addition to creating level play, CHEERSPORT was the first event producer to add spring floors to its competitions. A year or two after its first event it added a Novice division and, later, Excel and Basix.

Julie O'Brien, Kevin's dear friend and partner at Charlotte Allstars, worked with Kevin for years to develop the rules and regulations for the six levels, standards that were subsequently adopted by the United States All Star Federation (USASF) in conjunction with the updated NACCC rules, forming the basis for the current All Star cheer rules.

It's fortunate that CHEERSPORT didn't give up after its first moderately attended event, because it rapidly grew to become the largest cheerleading competition in the world with over 1,200 teams at its peak, a brilliant example of what was achievable in All Star. No one then could comprehend managing an event of such magnitude. Today, there are at least six cheerleading competitions of equal or greater size.

Every All Star knows that nothing compares to the CHEERSPORT warm-up room, the first wonder of the cheer world. Most athletes are in awe when they see that warm-up room for the first time. Every year, twelve 53-foot trailers loaded with 500 rolls of carpet-bonded foam travel down the highway to CHEERSPORT.

The turn of the twenty-first century introduced a new wave of gyms to the sport along with event producers, apparel, camps, shoes, and more. Athletic Championships emerged in Chattanooga, Tennessee, in 2000. Owner Mike Martinez added a personal touch to his events by fostering meaningful relationships with his customers. The coaches' celebrations at the Athletic Championship were legendary as well. Those gatherings allowed owners, coaches, and cheer industry vendors to connect and collaborate.

Martinez was part owner of Premier Athletics, which had expanded to include over twenty franchise locations. Additionally, it launched the Premier Network to offer discounts to programs that attended specific events and purchased uniforms from the Cheerleader Dance Team, NCA's uniform brand, which evolved into what became known as the Varsity Family Plan.

Also in 2000, Kevin Jones founded a new competition brand, America's Best. By 2001 he had expanded to eight events nationwide. NCA and UCA maintained their focus on one major event and a few smaller, one-day competitions while All Star–focused companies hosted multiple two-day national competitions in convention centers across the country.

Spirit Sports, owned by James Speed and Shannon Smith, also became part of the scene. It hosted its first competition in Myrtle Beach, South Carolina, a destination event for families to enjoy the beach as well as to compete. The first-year event was scheduled for the baseball stadium, but the weather had different ideas. James and Shannon had to find another solution in a hurry. Fortunately, the Myrtle Beach Convention Center had an exhibition hall available, allowing them to move the event indoors. Spirit Sports in Myrtle Beach is still taking place at the Myrtle Beach Convention Center today.

James and Shannon invented cheer's initial video replay system and a simple rubric to help score teams appropriately within their respective levels. Before Spirit Sports, if you had a question about your scoresheet, you had to wait until the event producer unpacked the truck and dug out the box of paper scoresheets back at the office to get an answer. James and Shannon wanted coaches to be able to question scores immediately, leading to the invention of the sport's first form of video replay and Accuscore.

Don Collins launched the All Star Challenge in 2001, adding theatrics to the competitions with themed events and dynamic, Hollywood-quality scenery. Spectators dressed up to fit the theme, which added to the fun and excitement.

My own program attended Clash of the Titans dressed like Greek gods with white togas draped over their clothes and gold leaf crowns on their heads. The All Star Challenge events placed an emphasis on its unique awards that coincided with each event's theme. The All Star Challenge also originated the Thalia Awards, named after the Greek goddess of festivity.

On the heels of Athletics Championships, Spirit Sports, and All Star Challenge came the World Spirit Federation (WSF), known for inventing the first digital scoring system. Judges no longer had to score with a pencil and tabulate their scores. Instead, they could easily type them into a computer, which then tallied the scores accurately for coaches to review.

The wild, wild west gave way to the innovation and development of All Star. Coaches and owners pushed each other to invent new skills. Event producers challenged the status quo by introducing new levels, new technology, new ideas, and enhancements that created more fun and better experiences for everyone.

Many brilliant ideas emerged from that period of chaos. But as a coach you needed to adjust your routine from event to event to align with the specific safety guidelines, rules, and scoresheets of each event producer. It was difficult to train your team and polish routines when the rules changed so often.

To be clear, these were not changes to try and hit a scoresheet that provided a how-to guide to maximize your score. These changes were necessary to ensure that your team wouldn't be penalized for performing a skill that was illegal or out of level at a particular event. For instance, what was legal in the Intermediate division at one competition could be illegal the next weekend at a different competition.

Victor Rosario of Top Gun All Stars was the master of navigating the gray areas of the rules. He taught the rest of the industry to think outside the box. But as the sport grew in popularity and participation, the chaos persisted.

Divisions were plentiful, yet teams were often left without competition. Rules and age requirements were often violated, and enforcement was left to the event producers, some of whom enforced the rules while some did not. The constant changes and inconsistencies frustrated coaches and athletes alike, leaving parents equally bewildered and annoyed. The chaos hindered All Star's growth. Direction was necessary.

THE NATIONAL ALL STAR CHEERLEADING COACHES CONGRESS, NACCC

In 2003 the National All Star Cheerleading Coaches Congress (NACCC) was formed in response to the inconsistent rules among competition companies. As the level of difficulty increased for performers, ensuring safety, technique, and proper progressions became more difficult due to the varying rules. The NACCC was founded by Kristen and Victor Rosario, Elaine Pascale, Joelle Antico, Jamie Parrish, and John Metz under the legal guidance of Dennis Worley. Coaches and owners were frustrated, so the NACCC brought their voices together.

The NACCC organized its first major meeting in 2004 at the Georgian Terrace Hotel in Atlanta. Coaches gathered to discuss a unified set of rules and to determine the best approach to advance the sport. The internet was hardly a thing, so the conference employed a paddle system for coaches to vote on specific rules.

Once the rules were established, the NACCC presented its proposals to the event producers. The fee for an event producer to join the NACCC was $500, which included an agreement to adhere to the rules established by the NACCC coaches and owners. Approximately thirty event producers participated, leading to a gradual unification of the All Star industry.

Rules voting still exists today within the USASF, but fewer than ten percent of the industry participates.

You can learn more about the NACCC in its dedicated chapter on page 568.

SECTION II: MODERN-DAY-ALL STAR

"In union there is strength." – Aesop

PART I:
MODERNIZATION & EXPANSION ERA
2003-2012

VARSITY AND NCA: WHEN TWO GIANTS UNITED

In 2003 Leonard Green & Partners, a boutique private equity firm founded in 1989, acquired Varsity Spirit, then known as Varsity Brands, for $130 million, over six times what Lawrence Herkimer had sold NCA for in 1986.

At that time Leonard Green & Partners relied on the Varsity leadership to make growth decisions for both school and All Star cheer and to guide the business. There were growth targets and financial goals but, ultimately, Green trusted the cheerleaders to determine the best path forward.

With Leonard Green & Partners came the essential capital to make strategic moves that would advance All Star. After much consideration, Varsity Brands purchased the National Cheerleaders Association (NCA) in 2003. In the initial meeting with Jeff Webb and several other Varsity leaders, the newly acquired NCA employees and the NCA staff were, according to their own account, terrified that NCA would be shut down. But Jeff stood in front of the room and asked, "Okay, gang, where do we want this to go? Where do we want to be in five years?"

Just like that, the two biggest names in cheerleading joined forces.

The employees believed the major difference between Varsity and every other player in the game was that Varsity took responsibility for how the sport appeared to both its participants and the public. Jeff spent lots of time listening to his team to determine how to make the best decision for the sport and, primarily, for the athletes.

Then, as now, Jeff had two core objectives: to grow the sport of cheerleading globally and to provide quality experiences for the athletes who participate in it. His motivation was, and is, that simple.

THE GREAT UNIFICATION: HOW THE USASF CHANGED ALL STAR FOREVER

Varsity decided to become more involved in All Star. Jeff Webb believed that if Varsity was going to be more invested in All Star, then All Star needed unified skills and standard rules to help make the sport safer for the athletes. The USASF emerged from a brainstorming session that included Jim Chadwick, Jeff Webb, Chris

Shepherd, Bill Seely, Greg Webb, and a few other Varsity employees.

Jim also believed that Varsity should be involved in All Star, and that the world of All Star needed a standardized set of divisions, guidelines, and rules. He believed the organization should be compromised of one-third event producers, one-third coaches and owners, and one-third the governing authority, but that required funding.

Jim figured it would take about $500,000 to set up the organization properly. He arranged a meeting with the top twenty event producers and explained his vision. He pitched his idea and asked each participant to contribute $25,000 to help get the organization started. Every single event producer declined. Jim even asked his uncle, Herkie Herkimer himself, but he, too, declined.

Jeff agreed with Jim that a structure for All Star was necessary and begrudgingly agreed to fund the organization. Varsity was owned by a venture capitalist, and Jeff was not looking forward to explaining this new expense to him.

Nonetheless, on January 29, 2004, the US All Star Federation, Inc. official charter was signed. CHEERSPORT was the first event company to join, followed by Athletic Championships. This is the USASF Mission Statement: "To support and enrich the lives of our All Star athletes and members. We provide consistent rules, strive for a safe environment for our athletes, drive competitive excellence, and promote a positive image of the sport."

To this day, USASF's core principles aim to make All Star a safer sport by establishing fair and consistent rules and competition standards. The organization credentials coaches, certifies legality officials, sanctions events, and maintains and updates safety guidelines, all to promote the safest possible environment for All Star cheer and dance athletes to train and compete.

So the USASF was established with the mission to unify the sport, but how would it convince event producers to join? An invitation only, prestigious event would set the standard for others to follow. Thus, the inaugural USASF World Cheerleading Championships were held at Disney World in Orlando, Florida, in April of 2004, featuring fourteen teams. Teams were hand selected to attend the first year.

The event was established to celebrate the end of the season and to create a prestigious occasion that all event producers, gyms, and athletes would aspire to participate in, aiming to unify the sport and establish standards. In its second year the first invitations to The Cheerleading Worlds, known as Worlds bids, were awarded at events nationwide. In addition, international teams attended The Cheerleading Worlds, proof that All Star cheer had spread around the globe.

"The annual Cheerleading Worlds event is a dedicated tribute to the expertise, athleticism, determination, and shared passion that characterize All Star cheer," the USASF website declared. It went on to note that over

10,500 All Star athletes from twenty-five nations gathered each year for The Cheerleading Worlds, the ultimate reward after a season of hard work.

Producing the World Championships provided the USASF with the ability to establish the standards the sport so desperately needed, and so a standard set of rules and divisions was created. Event producers also established a standard for their competitions, leading to sanctioned events.

To be recognized as a sanctioned event it was necessary to adhere to the guidelines set by the group. For instance, nine-panel mats, which later evolved into a nine-panel spring floor, were the standard. Interestingly, before these standards were established, event producers could utilize any type and size of mats they preferred. The USASF regulations focused on the well-being of athletes and the development of the sport.

This unification created explosive growth for everyone involved. Cheer gym programs grew in number and size. Event producers who were previously limited to their region due to varying rules, guidelines, and terminology were now able to expand and offer events throughout the country. Athletes were receiving better quality training and additional opportunities. Unifying the sport did exactly what everyone had hoped it would: It led to the massive growth of All Star and promoted athlete safety and consistent standards.

(For a more in-depth understanding of the USASF's impact on All Star and its specific contributions to the sport, please refer to the USASF chapter in Section IV on page 578.)

Coincidentally, in perfect timing with the formation of the USASF and the Cheerleading Worlds, *Inside Cheerleading* magazine entered the scene, and Chris Korotky turned the focus to All Star. *Inside Cheerleading* was the first publication to put an emphasis on celebrating All Star cheer. Its inaugural edition covered the first Cheerleading Worlds in 2004. Inside Publications now offers six magazines: *Inside Cheerleading, Inside Dance, Inside Gymnastics, Inside Action Sports, Coaches Handbook for Cheerleading* (annual), and *Coach's Resource Guide for Gymnastics* (annual).

GOING GLOBAL: FORMATION OF THE INTERNATIONAL CHEER UNION (ICU)

On April 26, 2004, the International Cheer Union (ICU) was recognized as the world governing body of Cheer. To be clear, this was for all types of cheer including school, recreational, and All Star. The ICU boasts 120 National Cheer Federation members and ten million athletes spread across all continents except Antarctica. The ICU hosts World Championships that welcome over seventy nations in addition to many continental and regional championships. The ICU continues to grow as a unified voice for all those dedicated to the advancement of cheerleading throughout the world.

According to the ICU's website, it is legally registered as an international nonprofit governing entity. Its mission and purpose are strictly to advance the sport of cheer.

No corporations or individuals will financially benefit from it. ICU's statutes are approved by SportAccord and have been adopted by the ICU General Assembly. The ICU is a fully democratic international sports federation.

The ICU aims to promote, organize, and assist all cheer-related activities and disciplines worldwide while working to perpetuate and improve the sport on a global scale. It focuses on encouraging the growth and development of cheer programs and opportunities for youth worldwide while communicating with and supporting formation of new national cheer federations and assisting countries interested in starting cheer programs, activities, and events. Jeff Webb, Karl Olson, and the ICU team gained official recognition from the International Olympic Committee (IOC) in 2021, a monumental achievement for cheer and its future.

The ICU also encourages countries to form national teams for international events, exchanges, and competitions while coordinating with other organizations that promote cheer. The ICU collaborates with companies, manufacturers, agencies, and other entities that can support Cheer's growth, development, and promotion while acknowledging exceptional contributions from groups, individuals, and organizations.

The ICU provides its 120 National Cheer Federations, coaches, teachers, and educators with tools for researching trends, technology, ideas, and solutions to cheer-related challenges while creating opportunities to discuss, enhance, and evaluate changes in the sport. It promotes moral standards enhanced through sports experiences and education in accordance with the laws of the IOC and the World Anti-Doping Agency.

The ICU establishes rules and regulations for international competitive events and programs, setting eligibility criteria that align with IOC standards while collaborating with National Cheer Federations to maximize international athlete participation. The ICU creates, promotes, disseminates, and maintains jurisdiction over rules of conduct for international competitions, including the World Championships, Pan American Games, and potential Olympic Games participation. The organization establishes and sanctions eligibility standards for these major competitions, conducts international athletic competitions in cheer, represents the sport to the IOC, and undertakes all necessary actions to accomplish its organizational purposes and goals.

BUILDING THE NETWORK

With the acquisition of NCA came a larger presence in the All Star space for Varsity, but competing companies were emerging and excelling rapidly in All Star. Many of Varsity's employees felt strongly that the company needed to expand its All Star footprint by placing a stronger emphasis on All Star. Varsity had two options: (1) organically develop and perfect the All Star events it already operated, or (2) purchase an established All Star company and learn from it.

Varsity needed a better understanding of what All Star gym owners and athletes wanted, so it chose the second option and purchased Athletic Championships in 2005. That purchase gave Varsity a boots-on-the-ground insight into the sport of All Star. Owners Boog Potter, Mike Martinez, and Cole Stott also owned Premier Athletics, so they brought their own level of brilliance along with their businesses. As a result, Varsity acquired tremendous talent.

Athletic Championships and Premier were filled with creative minds who helped navigate the All Star space and assisted Varsity in gaining a better understanding of the difference between school cheer and All Star cheer.

Boog, Mike, and Cole understood the day-to-day struggles of gym owners and told Varsity's Jeff Webb that gyms often faced difficulties during the summer when there were no competitions. In the early 2000s tryout time was a challenging month for gym owners, and they almost always needed cash flow.

Varsity took the Premier Network concept and turned it into the Varsity Family Plan, a rebate program that allowed gyms to earn money for their Varsity spending. The checks would be sent out at the end of the season with the intent of helping gym owners survive the slow summer.

As Varsity grew, a new major player emerged. JAMfest rapidly expanded the number of events it hosted across the country. Varsity took notice and approached the JAMfest team about purchasing the company. Although a letter of intent had been signed, the JAMfest team ultimately decided not to sell.

In 2006 Varsity added the World Spirit Federation (WSF), Spirit Sports, and American Championships to its team, expanding its footprint and increasing the number of gyms participating in Varsity Brands events.

INTERNATIONAL ALL STAR FOUNDATION (IASF)

The IASF was created in 2006 to bring structure, consistency, safety, and growth to the global community of All Star cheer and dance. The IASF works to establish common ground among all countries involved in All Star, not just the United States. IASF conducts the World Championship for international divisions at The Cheerleading and Dance Worlds. Essentially, it is the USASF's counterpart to the international cheer community.

USA FEDERATION FOR SPORT CHEERING, USA CHEER

In 2007 USA Cheer was formed to serve as the official national governing body for all types of cheerleading in the United States. It is recognized as such by the International Cheer Union and the US Olympic and Paralympic Committee. USA Cheer exists to serve the cheer community, including All Star, youth recreational cheer, traditional school-based programs, and the sport of STUNT.

USA Cheer pursues the following three primary objectives:

1. To promote safety and provide safety education for cheer in the United States

2. To grow and develop interest and participation in cheer across the country

3. To represent the United States in international cheer competitions

The affairs of USA Cheer are managed by a board of directors that has the primary responsibility for all USA Cheer programs, including decisions regarding strategy and policy. The board approves the actions of any committees that administer or implement programs on behalf of USA Cheer, an organization that played a crucial role in the push to include cheerleading in the Olympics.

THE DANCE WORLDS

As All Star cheer continued to grow, All Star dance emerged. Many gyms throughout the country added All Star dance teams to their facilities to expand participation. With the increase in All Star cheer divisions, technical difficulty also increased, and some athletes chose not to continue. Initially, All Star dance was a way to encourage athletes to remain committed to All Star. In 2007 USASF Dance was formed as a division dedicated to the education and growth of All Star dance, and the first Dance Worlds was held at EPCOT at the American Showplace Arena in Orlando, Florida.

All Star dance has grown significantly in the last twenty years and is no longer just a place for cheerleaders to continue All Star. It has become a welcoming environment for dancers of all ages, styles, and abilities, including any cheerleaders who may want to stick with All Star but no longer wish to cheer.

PREMIUM VS. PRACTICAL: ALL STAR GROWS IN TWO DIRECTIONS

Participation in the sport of cheer continued to grow, and more All Star facilities opened, but toward the end of 2008, growth began to stall during the financial crisis in the United States. All Star slowly began to increase its price tag at the same time, creating a barrier to entry, especially when so many families were struggling.

During this time Varsity acquired All Star Challenge, American Cheer Power, Xpress Brands, and Spirit Cheer. Varsity also established an official All Star division. The sport continued to evolve from an informal recreational activity to a standardized competitive program with consistent rules, divisions, and organizational structure.

All Star began with a group of young college students who wanted to continue participating in cheer and continued to evolve until a level of professionalism took hold. Gym owners started running businesses rather than just coaching cheer. Event producers elevated the standards at competitions and began to run more efficient events with enhanced production values, quality staff, and additional checks and balances on scoresheets for coaches.

Due to Varsity's growth, non-Varsity event producers united to form the Independent Event Producers (IEPs) and establish its own niche, separate from Varsity.

Essentially, anyone who didn't wish to compete with Varsity was welcome to compete with an IEP. At that point it was standard that to compete in a USASF sanctioned event or to send teams to The Cheerleading Worlds you had to be a member of the USASF.

Most industry professionals had come from a world where the USASF didn't exist, but they fully supported USASF standards. Yet many event producers and gyms didn't want to support Varsity. It was like a "shop local" campaign: Support the Independent Event Producers.

As the fame and excitement for Worlds grew, so did the number of rhinestones, the size of the hair bows, and the expense of the sport. The All Star community unintentionally created an elite environment. The Independent Event Producers fully supported the USASF's mission and The World Championships, but the focus turned to bringing fair, fun, and affordable events to the industry.

Varsity had venture capitalists to answer to, so it was driving up the cost of the sport. But Varsity also elevated its standards. In fairness, many gym owners, parents, and athletes wanted what Varsity was selling so, to them, the cost didn't matter.

To provide new experiences to All Star athletes, Cole Stott, president of the Varsity Knoxville office, launched the first All Star Dance-only brand. In 2009 there were several All Star cheer events that included dance competitions, but dance was secondary to All Star cheer, serving primarily to generate additional revenue for an already existing cheer event. Because Stott had been part of Premier Athletics, which had many All Star dance teams, he understood the importance of creating events that catered to All Star dancers.

The Groove Experience was initiated in the Varsity Knoxville office by Sabrina Tull and Cheryl Passalacqua. They introduced a new experience to the All Star dance world, further expanding Varsity's presence in All Star dance. The Groove Experience was an All Star dance-specific event brand that provided dance competitions for All Star dancers across the country.

In 2011 Varsity acquired Spirit Festival and merged with Herff Jones, a company founded in 1920 that manufactures class rings, medal pins, and other emblematic jewelry. Herff Jones later expanded to include graduation announcements, diplomas, caps and gowns, and diploma frames.

The merger of Herff Jones and Varsity was sensible and mutually beneficial. Herff Jones believed in the magic of a healthy school environment while Varsity focused on enhancing the student experience and creating memorable moments for young people. And Herff Jones was one of the few companies that provided an employee stock ownership plan (ESOP) for its employees.

Herff Jones partnered with Varsity to align their values, creating incredible opportunities that elevated the student experience. Herff Jones was a welcome addition for Varsity employees, enhancing the culture and reinforcing the commitment to creating unforgettable moments for America's youth. During the initial merger,

Jeff Webb became vice chairman and, within a year, ascended to chairman and CEO. Following the merger, Jeff Webb envisioned the new company as America's go-to partner for extracurriculars in schools.

JAMfest launched The MAJORS in 2011, a prestigious, invitation-only event designed to celebrate and showcase the top All Star cheer teams. The MAJORS created a new growth opportunity in the Midwest. Teams from across the country converged in Kentucky for JAMfest Super Nationals to catch a glimpse of The MAJORS.

JAMfest's creativity kept it at the forefront, fueling innovation and excitement in the sport. Previously, the major competitions that attracted significant attention took place in Dallas, Texas, and Orlando, Florida. The MAJORS demonstrated to event producers that prestigious events could take place outside those locations.

EXTRA! EXTRA! CHEER ALL ABOUT IT!

The first online cheer media spread rapidly throughout All Star. DJ Yeager, somewhat accidentally, created cheerUPDATES in February 2012. He was invited to The MAJORS cheerleading competition and chose to use Twitter to share updates with those unable to attend. At that time fans had no centralized method to keep up with cheerleading competitions.

In DJ's own words, "I had no interest in being in a group text with fifty people. That sounded exhausting."

He took the next best step and created a Twitter account. He initially believed Twitter was solely for "posting really stupid updates about having Chipotle for lunch," but he began tweeting competition results from The MAJORS event. To his surprise, about 500 followers joined on the first night, and that number increased to about 1,100 by the end of the event.

The cheerUPDATES continued to expand rapidly. By the time the World Championship came around a few months later, cheerUPDATES had increased its following to about 11,000. For the first year, DJ maintained anonymity as the person behind cheerUPDATES, generating intrigue within the cheerleading community.

DJ describes cheerUPDATES as "a truth teller" and "a reality seeker" that treats cheerleading as a legitimate sport. He believes the sport should be covered honestly, which includes reporting on teams' mistakes and failures, just as in any other sport. DJ said his motivation was to enhance transparency and elevate cheerleading coverage to the level of other mainstream sports. As a result, cheerUPDATES was the first coverage of its kind in the All Star world and took it by storm.

Another source of information was created in 2012 when the private Facebook group, All Star Gym Owners Association, was established by Randy Dickey and Courtney Pope. The initial purpose of the page was to provide All Star Gym Owners with a space where they could work together, ask questions, and share information. In addition, there would be a national conference for owners to gather, discuss industry topics, and share ideas.

Not long after the Facebook group was created, many additional industry professionals were added to the page including coaches, vendors, and other industry professionals. Today, the page has 15,200 members and serves as a source for people to ask questions about scoring, events, business, and coaching tips, and it even includes some cheer gossip.

"The price of greatness is responsibility." – Winston Churchill

PART II:
THE CONTEMPORARY ERA
2013-2024

A NEW PEAK TO CLIMB

In 2013 All Star launched The Summit by Varsity Brands, a season-ending event for all teams, Youth to Senior, that were ineligible to attend The Cheerleading Worlds. Gym owners struggled to retain athletes in their programs if they lacked sufficient Level 6 participants to form a Cheerleading Worlds team, so they appealed for a championship that would grant prestige and recognition to teams across different ages and levels.

Before The Summit a few end-of-season events had already begun to take shape including Final Destination, US Finals, The One, and the All-Levels Championships. Those events were regional, giving teams around the country the opportunity to compete close to home.

In some cases, the winners of each region would be judged virtually to select a grand national champion. While the events were fun and well run, they lacked prestige, but they did provide a meaningful way to wrap up the season. Even so, gym owners and athletes alike longed for one definitive season finale, a true national stage where the best teams from across the country could compete head-to-head to determine the best of the best in each age group and level.

Varsity initially resisted the craze surrounding end-of-season events. It genuinely believed that all athletes should strive to attend The Cheerleading Worlds, but the All Star gyms continued to request an event to celebrate their non-Worlds teams. And as the industry grew and new gyms and teams formed, many didn't have a team ready to take on the World Championship, but they did have great teams who wanted to compete against the best in their respective division.

Varsity couldn't continue to ignore its customers. Gyms all over the country were devasted by a troublesome pattern: Athletes were gym hopping in pursuit of more decorated programs, and that process didn't foster good sportsmanship or sustainable growth. All Star had grown tremendously, and there were many great teams that needed the opportunity to compete at a national event.

Recognizing reality, Varsity took a bold and significant gamble with John Newby, Dennis Worley, and Damianne Albee Steward working together to create a prestigious national event. The Varsity group developed a bidding system whereby teams could earn invitations to attend The Summit by participating in Varsity Brand events. The first year, 457 bids were distributed across hundreds of events. All but one of those bids was accepted. A bid was an earned invitation to attend the event. If you did receive a bid from a qualifying in-season event, you weren't allowed to attend the end-of-season event, in this case, The Summit. The national event took place in May 2013 at Disney World in Orlando, Florida. The Summit quickly became popular as more and more teams worked to attend, thereby increasing participation in Varsity Brand events throughout the year.

Steward recalled that the first event ran smoothly, largely because Varsity was an experienced host of major events. "When I walked into the Milkhouse and saw The Summit mountains on the background of the stage," she said, "I cried."

She poured hours into bringing The Summit to life and accepted personal responsibility for ensuring that every athlete who took the stage felt celebrated.

LEVELING THE FIELD: EXPANDING ALL STAR'S REACH

All Star continued to grow as new generations entered the fray. As new gyms opened, they were usually smaller, and their athletes were less experienced in the sport. Many felt defeated before they even started. They entered an established All Star world with programs that had been in the game for decades, and they needed a fair playing field to grow and time to catch up. In addition, new event producers entered the All Star space with fresh perspectives and ideas. They catered to the newcomers as they figured out how to navigate the world of All Star together.

After extensive discussion of member feedback, the USASF introduced the first prep divisions for teams that were not yet ready to compete in the six existing elite divisions. This move provided athletes who were inexperienced in cheer a place to compete. Today, many gyms use the prep divisions as a stepping stone toward the commitment and experience needed for their elite teams.

Establishing prep divisions leveled the playing field and provided more athletes with the opportunity to participate while creating additional growth for gym owners and event producers. In addition, the prep divisions helped provide a more affordable option, creating the possibility for even greater participation and overcoming the financial barrier to entry.

During this same time Herff Jones acquired BSN Sports, the leading marketer, manufacturer, and distributor of sporting goods and team uniforms in the United States. BSN Sports, formerly known as Sports Supply Group, Inc. purchased NCA in 1986. The acquisition rounded out Jeff Webb's vision of being an extracurricular partner in America's schools. In addition, Herff Jones eventually rebranded as a subsidiary of Varsity Brands.

Another newcomer to the scene, Karen Noseff Aldridge, founded Rebel Athletic with a simple goal: She wanted to provide high-end couture cheer uniforms at the best value. She aimed to provide the best service, selection, and designs to cheer athletes everywhere. Rebel Athletic took the All Star market by storm, creating sparkling masterpieces to be debuted by magnificent teams at The

Cheerleading Worlds. Rebel designed uniforms like a fashion house, creating looks that made the difference between winning and merely placing. Rebel Athletic brought the bling to cheerleading uniforms.

As The Groove Experience gained popularity and many other event producers began to grow and create dedicated dance events, the All Star dance community wanted a Dance Summit, a prestigious event for dancers, similar to their cheer counterparts. As a result, in 2014 Varsity hosted the first Dance Summit at EPCOT in Disney World, Orlando, Florida. Run by Cheryl Passalacqua, the event attracted about sixty teams in its first year and almost doubled that number in its second year. Today, the event boasts over 300 teams from sixteen countries. Varsity, along with the independent event producers, uniform companies, and shoe companies flourished while All Star thrived.

CHEERSPORT had grown to over 1,200 teams before it was sold to Varsity in 2014, creating a ripple effect. The older, more established independent companies that had been around from the start were tired of walking the path alone. (By independent I mean those organizations that were not Varsity event producers.) Between the Varsity Family Plan and the Cheer and Dance Summit, the incentives to compete and remain loyal to Varsity were difficult for smaller, independent companies to overcome.

Many suggested that Varsity was a monopoly, but I believe it simply had great leadership with Jeff Webb and many other talented, smart people who made intelligent decisions that not only grew Varsity but also advanced the sport of All Star and every other business within the industry.

Back on the competition floor, new divisions emerged to accommodate growth and new opportunities. The recently created Prep division, originally intended as a path into All Star, had evolved into a division of professional cheerleaders who had perfected the basic skills needed for prep. I'm kidding, but Prep had improved to the point that it had become an arduous starting place for new participants in All Star, so in response to its members' demands, the USASF added the All Star Novice division.

Novice was created as a nonranking performance team option for athletes with little to no experience. This new division provided a space for athletes to experience the competitive atmosphere without the pressure of competing against other teams. As prep had done previously, adding the Novice level offered a lower price point and commitment option for new participants.

SUMMIT FEVER

The previous few years had every gym in the country scrambling to claim its spot atop the Summit mountain. Almost every gym owner everywhere was convinced that if their program won Worlds or could win one of the summits, they would grow beyond their wildest dreams. Everyone was lining up at the grand Varsity gates to earn their rite of passage to these prestigious events, making Varsity a prime target to be acquired once again.

Enter Charlesbank Capital Partners, which acquired Varsity Brands for approximately 1.5 billion dollars, providing liquidity to the employee owners. Because the previous owner, Herff Jones, had an ESOP, the Varsity employees were given a share of the company's sale to roll into a long-term retirement account or to cash out. Charlesbank was more aggressively involved in the day-to-day operations than previous ownership, but it still relied on the leadership team for guidance.

Although I was a Varsity employee then, I believe it was during this period that a notable shift in focus began, a shift from the athlete experience to the bottom line.

As the new crop of gym owners gained a few years of experience, their teams became better and stronger, but they still found it difficult to compete against programs with double or triple the number of athletes. The industry responded with a Division II (DII) option. Smaller programs could compete against each other in DII, which they believed would level the playing field again.

Varsity responded in kind. In May 2015 it hosted the first DII only competition, the DII Summit, held in Tampa, Florida. DII was for teams with no more than 125 All Star Elite participants.

The following year the event moved to the Wide World of Sports at Disney World in Orlando, Florida. Today, Varsity hosts four separate Summit events along with a series of regional summits, US Finals, and the Youth Celebration. These events bring together about 3,500 teams to commemorate and celebrate their seasons at a final event.

With a surge of new capital from Charlesbank and the addition of three summits, JAM Brands, formerly JAMfest, the single largest competitor in the market, finally decided to sell in 2015 after rejecting three previous offers. JAM Brands, like Varsity, had purchased several event producers over the previous decade and had created its own dynasty.

Among those acquisitions were the Golden State Spirit Association owned by Tammy VanVleet, the Aloha Cheer and Dance Championships in Hawaii, Coastal with Serena Andrews, the Great Lakes Cheerleading Championships, COA with Steve Wedge, and America's Best and Spirit Innovations with Kevin Jones. When Varsity purchased JAM Brands, it acquired all those brands at once. With that purchase, Varsity acquired almost all the original companies in All Star.

THE $2.5 BILLION TURN

DII gyms were on the rise and realized that if they came together as a group, they could have a stronger voice on important topics like rules, divisions, and scoring. Previously, they thought they had no voice because they were "just the little guy"—their words, not mine.

In 2018, organized by Tabbi McCallister, Cat Weeden, and Angela Harvard, the DII gyms formed the Small Cheer Gym Association to vote as a group and have their voices heard. Through the unity of shared interests, they created a voice for small gyms in All Star.

Small gyms believed the larger, more established All Star gyms controlled the rules and had a louder voice because of their size.

The Xtra Small division was created at The Cheerleading Worlds, allowing a maximum of fourteen members per team. The division was reserved for programs that fielded only one team, which excluded the big gyms. Eventually, the division would be open to any USASF member gyms, and a series of limited divisions were added in 2022, specifically for programs that fielded only one team.

In 2018 Bain Capital acquired Varsity Spirit for $2.5 billion. Yes, that's billion with a B. As a global private investment firm, Bain was known for making sizable investments with the expectation of significant returns.

The acquisition marked a notable shift in management style. Jeff Webb, long seen as the visionary behind Varsity's growth, stepped away to focus on his work with the ICU. In his absence, the company's leadership style began to reflect a more traditional corporate structure. Across the industry—both within and outside of Varsity—many noticed a stronger emphasis on financial metrics.

Under Webb's leadership Varsity had felt like a speedboat—quick to innovate and eager to elevate the entire cheer community with a focus on the athlete experience. In contrast, the Bain-owned Varsity resembled a barge. It was still powerful but slower to pivot and with a major focus on the bottom line. It was a different vessel for a new era in the sport.

Everyone in the industry felt the shift. Prices increased, and quality was diluted. Where events once offered unique individual experiences and a personal touch, they became streamlined and cookie cutter.

A narrow focus was placed on profit, and decisions were made based on financial outcomes instead of the continued enhancement of the athlete's experience. The employees who loved All Star did their best to continue creating lasting memories for each athlete, but despite their efforts, the focus was on maximizing every cent of profit. Long gone were the days of looking toward the future and planning where All Star would be ten years down the road. It had become more about Bain Capital squeezing every cent out of its investment. Business is business, but for those who loved All Star and were passionate about helping athletes find their confidence, the change stung like a murder hornet.

The lack of leadership also left a void in the industry, and the Cheer and Dance Industry Professionals (CDIP) saw an opportunity to fill that gap. The CDIP, led by Vice Chair Heidi Weber, rekindled the mission of the Independent Event Producers to create an affordable experience for All Star. Countless gyms told the CDIP they couldn't continue the path they were on, and they couldn't charge their customers one more penny. As a result, the CDIP and its members tried to create a more cost-effective product without sacrificing the quality of All Star cheer.

The two biggest complaints Heidi Weber heard were cost and predictability. Gym owners were growing frustrated with The Summit bid system because they couldn't plan their season without knowing whether their team would receive a bid. If a team didn't receive a bid, it wouldn't have an end-of-season celebratory event. In addition, the CDIP event producers were frustrated. They, too, were struggling to provide new products for their customers that would allow their events to grow.

Listening to the complaints of both gym owners and competition companies and taking advantage of the All Star climate, Heidi Weber and three other event producers—David Owens, David Hanbery, and Jeb Harris—came together to create The Open Championship Series. The event was held at Universal Studios in Orlando, Florida. They called it The Open Championship Series because it was open to anyone. You didn't need a bid to attend. The Open Championship Series was a new opportunity for independent event producers and a reliable event for gym owners.

The first competition included fewer than one hundred teams and was not the prestigious end-of-season event that Heidi Weber and her partners had expected. But they forged ahead and planned The Open Championship Series again for 2020. This time, they would offer event options in different cities. They had a good marketing strategy and pounded the pavement, but the customers said they wanted invitational bids, even though they had previously said they didn't. As a result, The Open Championship Series fell short of expectations.

THE PANDEMIC PIVOT

I remember first hearing about the coronavirus on TV. I was overseeing nine All Star facilities that were about to go on spring break. I proposed that all facility managers close a week early to allow for two full weeks of cleaning and disinfection. And then the whole country shut down. We aren't going to revisit the details. Insert your own dumpster fire here. Most of us have one.

The saying at the time was that we were all in the same storm, just in different boats. I felt like Rose DeWitt Bukater from *Titanic*, clinging to dear life with a broken paddle and a whistle tied to my life jacket, a whistle I didn't have the lung power to blow.

And because Bain Capital's Varsity was like a huge barge, it was unable to make swift turns or quick decisions. Instead, it was forced to navigate the bureaucratic seas before any decisions could be made.

During COVID, the company was able to evacuate 90 percent of its workforce from that metaphorical barge just two weeks after being stranded in the metaphorical sea. It was an interesting time in All Star after the entire industry was deemed nonessential. Gyms were closed, events were canceled, and All Star cheer and dance athletes everywhere were devastated that they couldn't end their season in the typical fashion.

Acting swiftly, Heidi Weber and her team announced a new and exciting event called the Allstar World Championship (ASWC) in Orlando, Florida, in conjunction with Universal Studios Orlando. Before this brazen move, The Cheerleading Worlds, hosted by the USASF, stood as the sole World Championship event, intentionally reserved for Level 6 and Level 7 Senior and Open teams.

With the introduction of ASWC, teams could compete at qualifying events held by select event producers to earn bids to the Allstar World Championship. This event expanded the opportunity for recognition by allowing teams across all ages and levels to end their season by being crowned world champions.

ASWC also introduced its own scoresheet and competition structure, which featured a distinct set of divisions and rules. This move created new opportunities for gym owners and athletes, but it also introduced a level of divergence in the industry that hadn't existed for over two decades. For many, it meant evaluating which competitive path aligned best with their values and goals.

ASWC chose to part ways with the USASF, opting instead to move forward with its version of a world championship and electing to follow a model of self-governance for their event producer partners and gym owners who attended their events. Choosing to use the name "Worlds" in the event title created conflict with the USASF event producer agreement and the original Cheerleading Worlds. This single decision divided the industry.

Without Jeff Webb's continued leadership in All Star and the onset of the pandemic, the resulting chasm provided the perfect opportunity to reinvent the wheel, and so they did. During the 2020-2021 All Star season, Bain Capital's Varsity, being the behemoth it was, experienced a slow recovery. Many of its events had been held in large downtown convention centers that were still closed, which caused many in-person Varsity competitions to be canceled. The CDIP event producers hosted in-person events in smaller, suburban areas. The gym owners, coaches, and parents were desperate to meet in person. Heck, we all were.

This opportunity allowed the CDIP event producers to capture the attention of new programs and build relationships with people who otherwise wouldn't have attended their events. Fast forward to April 2021 after a full year of planning when Heidi Weber, David Owens, David Hanbery, and Jeb Harris finally executed the first non-USASF world championship, the Allstar World Championship.

The event took place at the Orange County Convention Center in Orlando, Florida. The only date available was the same weekend as The Cheerleading Worlds. Once again, Heidi and her crew took advantage of the opportunity by hosting a USASF Worlds team showcase that allowed teams to perform on stage before competing the next day at the USASF Cheerleading Worlds. Of course, that was a great marketing opportunity to showcase their brand and continue building relationships.

The first year the ASWC hosted 425 teams. In year two the event tripled to 1,240 teams. ASWC turned the industry upside down, taking it back to the wild, wild west. After decades of moving toward consistency in the sport, All Star once again included a divided set of rules and a variety of divisions, forcing gyms to choose one path or the other.

Ironically, what had begun as a way to provide a cheaper, non-bid alternative for cheer athletes evolved into a new microcosm of cheer and, today, ASWC awards bids to attend its event, one of the most expensive in the cheer season.

BUILDING BRIDGES

Heidi and CDIP weren't the only opportunists to emerge from the pandemic pivot. Cheryl Passalacqua, with the support of Cole Stott, started Stage 8 Dance Brands, only the second brand to focus solely on All Star dance. It is ironic that a non-dancing male cheerleader from Knoxville, Tennessee, has done so much to provide tremendous experiences for All Star dancers around the country.

In 2021 Cheryl, managing partner of Stage 8 Dance Brands, and her partner, Janna Thomas, revolutionized the All Star Dance industry. They created five distinct All Star Dance experiences that had been unavailable to All Star dancers. The most notable are The Dance Connection and the Stage 8 Dance Battle.

The Dance Connection combines competition with convention and brings incredibly talented instructors, handpicked by the Stage 8 staff, to inspire and train the dancers. This unique experience is the first of its kind in the All Star dance space and is an incredible opportunity for athletes to learn and grow.

The Stage 8 Dance Battle is the first invitation-only All Star Dance event. All Star dance teams unite in a thrilling celebration, showcasing diverse styles as they battle head-to-head. The event ignites passion, celebrates teamwork, and elevates dance. I had the pleasure of assisting in the creation of this incredible event. After launching the Stage 8 Dance Battle, Varsity Spirit introduced The Dance MAJORS, a counterpart to The MAJORS for All Star cheer, creating even more opportunities for All Star dance.

Stage 8 Dance Brands also changed the game by providing judges with video reviews and audio critiques that made significant improvements for participating teams. When Cheryl founded Stage 8 Dance Brands she had two clear goals: to provide unique opportunities designed specifically for dancers, and to assist in making sure that teams left her events better than when they arrived. She works tirelessly to achieve those goals every day.

Stage 8 Dance Nationals at the Hilton Orlando was created as a new end-of-season celebration for All Star dancers. In addition to traditional competition, the event provides soloists with a title competition, allows selected dancers to participate in the opening number, and chooses dance ambassadors to celebrate Stage 8 Dance Brands by performing throughout the year. No such opportunities existed for All Star dancers prior to Stage 8 Dance Brands. Cole was ecstatic to watch Cheryl and her team grow Stage 8 Dance Brands, but he had some plans of his own.

Founding partners and friends Cole Stott, Casey Jones, Kevin Brubaker, and I (Stacy Rowe) began MotUS in 2022. Derived from the Latin word for movement, MotUS was created to bring unity and focus to All Star through a gym-led community of like-minded owners. The mission: to serve gym owners and coaches; to lead with courage, patience, and conviction; and to empower everyone to keep athletes at the heart of every decision.

MotUS is growing every day with over 200 gyms and two dozen affiliate members. Together, they strive to keep the athletes at the center of All Star and work collaboratively as a community to support one another. MotUS also formed the Prime Alliance, a group of event producers who believe in the MotUS mission. The first event producer members to join were CX Brands, All Out Brands, Choice Events, All Day Cheerleading, American Spirit Championships, and World Cheer Co. The Prime Alliance is proud to be a group of independent event producers who believe in and support the USASF's mission.

As new companies and events emerged through the industry in 2024, Varsity Spirit was sold once again, this time to Kohlberg Kravis Roberts (KKR) for approximately $4.75 billion. KKR's co-CEOs plan to accumulate thirty trillion dollars in assets by 2030. For those in All Star, there appears to be a shift from focusing on profits to prioritizing athletes and quality experiences. Only time will reveal KKR's motives and its future in All Star.

ALL STAR LEVELS UP WITH PRO CHEER LEAGUE

The Pro Cheer League started by Varsity, is launching in 2025 as a groundbreaking professional cheerleading competition featuring four inaugural teams located in Miami, Atlanta, Dallas, and San Diego. Open to athletes over eighteen who have graduated high school, the league represents a new frontier in competitive cheerleading that elevates the sport to a professional level. These founding cities were strategically selected based on four key criteria: strong media and sports markets, partnerships with organizations that have proven track records of assembling elite teams, access to high-quality practice facilities, and established followings within the cheerleading community.

The league's vision extends far beyond its initial four-team launch, with plans for rapid expansion and a potential global reach. Tryouts for the inaugural season will take place in early September 2025 across all four cities. In an innovative twist, these tryouts were live-streamed, allowing teams to scout and potentially recruit talented athletes who may not make their local team due to positional abundance or specific skill needs. The first season will run from November practice sessions through a five-match tour starting in January 2026, with competitions in Indianapolis, Atlanta, Houston, and Anaheim before culminating in a championship finale in Nashville at the end of March. With media deals currently in development and exciting announcements planned for the future, the Pro Cheer League aims to transform cheerleading into a globally recognized professional sport.

SECTION III: LOOKING TO THE FUTURE

"The best way to predict the future is to create it together." – Joe Echevarria

PART I: BUILDING THE FUTURE
My Take – 2025

MOMENTS THAT MATTER

All Star is rare and special and beloved by those who are part of the sport. Hundreds of thousands of All Star athletes across the world find peace and comfort in the gyms they call home. Tens of thousands of gym owners and coaches pour their hearts and souls into the sport every single day to provide a positive environment for kids to train not only in the skills necessary for the competition stage but also in the skills necessary for a good life.

All the grit, tenacity, hard work, and dedication that every athlete, coach, gym owner, event producer, and parent put in day-to-day to make it all happen is commendable and remarkable. Literal blood, sweat, and tears culminate in the perfect moments on stage when an athlete takes the floor with their closest friends, when the house lights go down, when the stage lights fire up, when friends, family, and fans stand proudly and wait for the performance to begin.

As the athletes stand onstage their chest tightens for just a moment. They inhale deeply, exhale, and smile—maybe even give a little shimmy. The coach gives them a thumbs-up, the silent signal that the music is about to begin and their team is ready. Then the coach inhales deeply while hoping and praying their team will execute the routine as flawlessly as they know they can.

The athletes have prepared for this moment, and now they're going to give it everything they have. The music booms through the speakers. The bass pulses through everyone's veins, and muscle memory takes over as the crowd erupts in praise and excitement for the hard work they know has been done. The team hits every stunt, motion, jump, and flip exactly as they've been trained to do. The athletes try to stay in the moment, but they can barely keep up with the whirlwind of emotions flooding through their body.

Finally, the team reaches the dance, the last four eight counts of the routine. Their senses return to the mat. They feel every emotion simultaneously as they strike their final pose. And in that instant both the coach and the team know—with every fiber of their being—whether the team delivered the performance of a lifetime, or if there's still work to be done. Either way, everyone returns to the gym together to keep striving for excellence in every performance.

Never giving up—the relentless pursuit to be the most creative, the most daring, the most competitive—that is the grind. That is All Star.

Cheer is constantly growing and evolving, but one thing remains unchanged: No matter the challenges or mistakes along the way, it always comes back to the athletes—their growth, their resilience, their confidence, and the lifelong friendships they gain along the way.

BE BOLD TOGETHER

Varsity, without a doubt, was and still is the largest player in All Star cheer. Lawerence Herkimer started the business of cheer, and Jeff Webb was the bold leader whose clear vision paved the way. It's easy to criticize what's been done, but few have had the courage to take the first step and lead selflessly.

During my interview with Nicole Leago Devall, board chair of the USASF, she said, "We are who we are because of those that came before us." I agree. We are indebted to those who built the sport we all love, but it's in our hands now, all of us who are still part of All Star. The athletes deserve the best from us. We have a responsibility to put our differences and personal interests aside and work together to continue building our precious and wonderful All Star community so we can continue to create incredible experiences for the young people who participate in our sport.

SECTION IV: THE PIONEERS

As you read through this section, you'll see many paths intertwined in the fabric of All Star. Some have called it the "good ole boys club." And as a woman trying to find my footing in the industry, I used to feel that way too. But now I see it for what it is: It's just All Star. Lifelong friendships formed through cheerleading have led to relationships and connections that have lasted for decades and that will last for decades more. You know you've been part of something special when, in your thirties, you walk into a bank for an interview and the person across the desk lights up because they recognize you were an All Star. Instantly, there's a connection.

At the top of each chapter you'll find the pioneer's favorite quote. In addition, each pioneer chose an animal whose traits reflect their personality. This animal is featured at the top of the chapter and is described in the "Did You Know?" section. Enjoy reading about the All Star journeys as these pioneers share stories from their own experiences and offer insights into the evolution of the sport. Each chapter also includes an "Earned Wisdom" section. Please don't miss it. This is where pioneers share advice, lessons learned, common missteps, and heartfelt gratitude for the people and moments that shaped them.

One of my favorite parts is the personal section filled with fun facts and little-known tidbits that let you meet each pioneer on a more intimate level.

Last, each pioneer was asked to share a single message with the industry. If they could light up one message in neon on a backdrop for everyone in All Star to see, what would it be? You'll appreciate their answers.

There are many incredible people who pioneered our sport. I interviewed over one hundred of them to gather the facts for this book. Some pioneers declined to participate, some couldn't be reached, and some may not have made it onto my radar. If you know someone you think is a pioneer and needs to be celebrated in *The Pioneers of All Star Cheer,* please reach out to srfabricoauthor@gmail.com. They can be added in future editions.

WHAT MAKES PIONEERS DIFFERENT?

As I completed interview after interview I was overwhelmed by each person's genuine desire to make a positive impact on the young people in their community and, sometimes, beyond. Their genuine passion for helping others is tremendous.

They were mavericks, effectively creating an entire industry from scratch. Each contributed to the sport in their own ways, but these pioneers all shared one thing in common—an unrelenting pursuit of ingenuity, creativity, uniqueness, and vision.

The pioneers challenged each other to drive the sport forward. They were young and eager, fresh out of college, and they didn't want to stop cheering, so they invented an industry where they could make a living doing what they loved.

They were courageous, brilliant minds who paved the way for a future in All Star cheerleading. Today, the International Cheer Union (ICU) estimates there are 150,000 All Star cheerleaders in the United States and 7.5 million cheerleaders across 116 nations.

I'm humbled by the brilliance of every person I interviewed and it has been a great honor to share their stories. Their genuine care, joy, and courage are inspiring. They aren't just great people, they're individuals who have achieved greatness and who continue to instill that pursuit of greatness in All Star cheer athletes today. Personally, writing this book and interviewing each person made me immensely proud to be part of All Star and reminded me of what a great activity All Star cheer is for young people. It has truly been an honor to share their stories. Though our sport is indebted to hundreds of incredible people, I especially wish to thank the many industry professionals I interviewed and who grace the pages of this book. Here they are in alphabetical order (by first name):

Aaron Flaker
Amy Clark
Amy Tyler
Anastasia Miller Burns
Anna Love Logan

Jeff Webb
Jim Chadwick
Jody Melton
Joelle Antico
John Newby

Angela Rogers
Becky Herrera
Bill Seely
George "Boog" Potter
Brad Habermel
Brad Page
Brett Hansen
Brian Elza
Brooke Plack
Casey Jones
Cathryn Weeden
Cathy Buckey
Cole Stott
Courtney Pope
Damianne Albee Steward
Danny Kahn
Dawn Duncan Walters
Debbie Love
Dennis Worley
Don Collins
Douglas "DJ" Yeager
Elaine Pascale
Eric Little
Gwen Holtsclaw
Happy Hooper
Heidi Weber
James Speed
Jamie Parrish

Justin Carrier
Kali Seitzer
Kathy Gaffney
Kendall Tyler Battleson
Kevin Brubaker
Kevin Jones
Kristen Rosario
Ladd LeBus
Lance Wagers
Leon Reynolds
Lynn Singer
Meredith Walker
Mike Martinez
Morton Bergue
Orson Sykes
Randy Dickey
Rey Lozano
Regina Symons
Robin Coe
Roger Schonder
Sean Timmons
Steve Peterson
Steve Wedge
Tammy Skinner
Tate Chalk
Tegan Jemma Reeves, PhD
Tres LeTard
Victor Rosario

"There are a million great ideas, but it almost always comes down to execution." – Anonymous

JEFF WEBB
Varsity Spirit – 1975
ICU, USASF, & IASF

In the summer of 1975, twenty-four-year-old Jeff Webb cleaned out his desk at the National Cheerleaders Association (NCA) and stepped into the unknown. Armed with little more than ambition and a vision for a more athletic, dynamic approach to cheerleading, Webb founded the Universal Cheerleaders Association (UCA) from his Memphis apartment.

What began as a rebellion against the status quo transformed an American tradition into a global competitive sport and created an industry that eventually employed thousands and engaged millions. This is the story of how Webb's entrepreneurial spirit and willingness to innovate—adding acrobatics, creating national competitions, and bringing cheerleading to television—laid the foundation for modern cheerleading as we know it today.

THE EARLY DAYS

Jeff Webb began his cheerleading journey as a high school cheerleader at Hillcrest High School in Dallas, Texas. In the late 1960s high school teams were typically coed with an equal number of boys and girls, and squad members were elected by the student body. At least that's how it was at Hillcrest High School.

The school would host a preliminary tryout to determine if candidates had the skills required to make the team. After the preliminary tryout, the selected athletes would then try out in front of the entire student body to be elected for the team. Earning a spot on the cheerleading squad was an honor that was only offered to seniors.

Jeff made the team and attended the 1966 NCA summer camp at Southern Methodist University in University Park, Texas. It was there that Lawrence "Herkie" Herkimer gave Jeff an application to be an NCA instructor the following summer, a huge honor.

Jeff filled out the application and was offered a position as a camp instructor. He was bound for the University of Oklahoma in Norman and decided that running summer cheer camps beat mowing lawns or working on roofs, so he took the job. He spent most of the summer on the road, a stark change from his usual routine. Jeff said that when he went to college he figured everyone else would be trying to adjust, but he'd be happy to be in the same place for more than a week.

He continued teaching camps for NCA while attending college. Eventually, Herkie offered Jeff a position as head instructor. The NCA head instructors were in charge of the camp staff and responsible for administering the program to all the athletes. Herkie chose Jeff to lead NCA's largest camps across the country. Jeff has fond memories of working at NCA summer camps alongside Herkie.

FROM PROTÉGÉ TO GENERAL MANAGER

In 1971, while finishing his degree at Oklahoma, Jeff received a call from Herkie asking him to meet for lunch. Herkie knew Jeff planned to attend law school, so he asked, "What do you think about taking a year off before you head to law school? You can come work for NCA in the Dallas office and learn the ropes. I'll take you with me to run my big one-day clinics, and you can help me select staff for the summers." Herkie offered to pay him $10,000, equivalent to about $97,000 today.

That was a lot of money, and Jeff had been working three jobs to pay for his college tuition. He didn't have access to student loans because they either didn't exist, or he didn't know how to obtain one. Jeff thought about the offer and felt incredibly grateful for the opportunity. He could continue with school, work three jobs, and be dead broke, or he could take a little time off, work, and save money for law school. He chose to move back to Dallas and work for NCA.

The company was small, only about five or six employees, and Jeff was the underling. During the winter he would travel with Herkie and teach one-day clinics in various school districts.

Teams from several schools would come together, and Herkie would teach the kids about motion techniques, crowd control, and how to cheer at a game. He would then teach a few cheers, watch the teams, and give them advice. For twenty years Herkie was the only one to teach the clinics until he passed the torch to Jeff, because he trusted Jeff to do the job just as well as he had.

Jeff continued to receive promotions until Herkie asked him to be the general manager of NCA. Jeff was only twenty-three and had no significant management experience. Although Jeff was thrilled about the opportunity, many senior colleagues were less than pleased at the prospect of such a young, inexperienced person being their boss.

Jeff had big ideas that he wanted to implement in his new role, but he was thwarted by those who favored the status quo. The long-time employees didn't want to listen to the new guy. After all, they had been successful for many years without Jeff.

"The problem was that, being the newer person, I wanted to do some things differently than they'd been doing for twenty-something years," Jeff said. "They felt what they were doing was working, and I don't blame them. Looking back, it was the whole 'If it ain't broke, don't fix it.' But to an entrepreneur? If it ain't broke, keep looking."

Jeff grew more and more frustrated, so after about a year he decided to go to law school. Just before the summer of 1974, Jeff met with Herkie to thank him for the opportunity and to let him know that he planned to resign. Herkie was gracious but wanted Jeff to stay through the summer to work the large camps.

Jeff agreed. During his last summer with NCA, Jeff experimented with the other camp staff on creating more acrobatic elements with pyramids and partner stunts, moves that had never been done in cheerleading.

A DOLLAR FIFTY PROFIT: THE HUMBLE BEGINNINGS

> "We were flat broke!" – Jeff Webb

Jeff Webb credits his parents with having a significant impact on his life. His father grew up on a dairy farm during the Great Depression and worked as a cowboy. His mother was a tremendous tennis player and a great athlete. She could outrun Jeff until he was about fifteen. He didn't like that. He grew up in a middle-class household. His mother taught kindergarten. She was competitive and taught all three Webb children they could do anything they wanted.

"My mom would tell us even if we failed, go do it," Jeff said.

Jeff's father was known for his kindness and empathy. It was important to him that those qualities be extended not only to his colleagues but to everyone he encountered. As a former employee of Jeff's, I believe those values were clearly reflected in the culture of the company he built.

Just before the first UCA summer camps were to start that first summer, Jeff ran out of the original investment money. "We were flat broke!" he said. "I wasn't sure how we were going to survive."

Registrations had been slow, and the uncertainty made him sick to his stomach. "What was I going to tell my instructors who were also my best friends: 'Thanks a lot, but I don't have any work for you'?"

Then, on registration deadline day, the forms poured in. That summer over 2,000 athletes attended the first UCA summer camp held at the University of Mississippi in Oxford. Jeff was relieved and encouraged. The excitement boosted his confidence and drove him forward. Jeff recalls that they even made a little money that first summer.

"I think it was about $1.50 for the entire year," he said, and then he laughed. "We were a bunch of kids. I mean, I was the oldest person in the company at twenty-four. We were all about the same age, we were all good friends, we helped each other out, and we expected a lot from each other."

BEYOND THE SUMMER CAMPS: THE BIRTH OF VARSITY SPIRIT

Over the next four to five years, Jeff focused on clinics and summer camps. The business continued to grow, and Jeff and his team learned on the fly as they shaped the corporate culture that built Varsity.

The company was egalitarian, meaning that he and his early staff believed in the principle that all employees are important and deserve to have their opinions taken seriously. The expectation was that everyone would carry their weight and bring their best to work every day.

Instilling a positive, people-first culture was important to Jeff from the beginning. He ingrained those values into the foundation of the company, an approach he considered a key factor in both his personal success and that of Varsity.

Finally, after years of perfecting camps and clinics, Jeff decided to start a uniform company. "We didn't start the uniform company because we wanted to expand or create another division," he said. "We started it because the current uniform providers weren't creating uniforms that kept up with the athletic skills we were developing."

Cheerleading uniforms back then featured heavy sweaters, wool skirts, and saddle shoes. Stretch fabric was still a dream. Customers at UCA camps voiced their complaints, prompting Jeff and his team to find someone to make more appropriate uniforms. They discovered a Tennessee company that was already producing athletic uniforms. His team compiled a catalog and developed fresh designs and patterns.

"We sent out the catalog," Jeff said matter-of-factly, "and people started ordering. We put our reputation from camp on the line."

Then came a major setback: The manufacturer went out of business, but it already had all the uniform orders.

"Oh boy," Jeff recalled. "What are we going to do? We sent in the orders and the money. We don't have any money, and we don't have any uniforms."

Luckily, Jeff found another manufacturer. The uniforms were delayed, but they were delivered—with excellent quality—to every customer. And Varsity Spirit Fashion was born.

Over time, the larger company became known as Varsity Spirit with UCA representing the camp and competition brand and Varsity Fashions evolving into its dedicated apparel division.

TELEVISION DREAMS: CHEER IN THE NATIONAL SPOTLIGHT

To this day, Varsity Spirit is ESPN's oldest continuous television partner.

In 1980 Jeff had a vision to expand cheerleading nationally, but there was one problem: UCA didn't have enough money.

Every year, the company ran out of funds just before summer camps began. While UCA had excellent camper retention season after season, it had recently launched the uniform division, and the capital demands of the growing business had outpaced its revenue. Jeff asked himself, "How can we get people to see us, to see what we do, and pay us to come to them?"

Then it hit him: television.

No one in cheerleading had done TV. Jeff wanted to put his brand of cheerleading on the air, but who would tune in to watch a cheerleading camp?

As he brainstormed with his team, they tossed around the idea of having the squads compete. At the time, though, cheerleading was still focused on cheers and sideline dances.

"Eh," someone said, "that might be boring."

But then they thought about the high-energy camp demos the staff performed at the start of each session—fun, upbeat routines set to music and filled with exciting partner stunts, pyramids, and mini tramp action. That was what people would want to see. As a result, the group decided to let the squads compete in those routines, and the group would choose the winner.

Through Jeff's contacts he found a sports syndicator from New York City who worked with soccer, basketball, football, and a variety of other sports. Jeff took his first trip to New York City to pitch George Gallup of TVS the idea of a cheerleading competition on television.

"George looked at me like I was crazy," Jeff said. "He didn't quite grasp the idea."

Jeff, being the entrepreneur that he was, wouldn't take no for an answer and invited Mr. Gallup to a summer camp to see what cheerleading was all about. Not long after, George attended a UCA camp at Middle Tennessee State University in Murfreesboro and watched the different classes. Jeff turned to George and said, "Now imagine if we put all of this together into a routine with judges."

George said he'd been looking for something different, so he decided to give Jeff's idea a try. Jeff accomplished what he had set out to do—gain national television exposure for cheerleading. But he had never run a competition, and he didn't have a venue. As was his nature, Jeff didn't do anything small, so he went straight to Disney World and asked if it would host his competition. But Disney said no.

That's how the first competition came to be held at SeaWorld in Orlando, Florida. Sea World built a stage in the water for the ski show and placed a floor exercise mat on it that consisted of mats on top of foam. Jeff invited twenty high school teams.

Jeff called the first modern cheerleading event the National High School Cheerleading Championship, which is still in existence today. Technically, this was also the first invitation-only cheerleading event. In fact, without this concept of a competitive routine set to music, All Star may never have existed. In All Star today, this concept is used thousands of times each year.

The first televised cheerleading competition took place between ski shows and received tremendous ratings. As a result, UCA signed a three-year contract with TVS.

Right before the competition in year three, George met with Jeff and told him he would be leaving his position as president of TVS to work for an upstart cable company. Back then, hardly anyone had cable TV. Most people didn't even know what it was. Jeff thought George was making a mistake, but he asked him where the company was and what it was called.

George told him the company was based in Connecticut and was called the Entertainment and Sports Programming Network—ESPN. Jeff decided to move his show to ESPN with George, and the rest is history.

No one had heard of ESPN then, but as the network's footprint grew, so did cheerleading's national exposure. Soon, cheerleading spread across the country. Middle school and high school teams wanted to train, improve, and compete, so they started traveling to UCA camps.

As ESPN continued to grow, Varsity added additional divisions, including a collegiate showcase. Disney eventually jumped on board, and the competitions moved to Disney World in Orlando, Florida.

ESPN later launched ESPN II, which required twenty-four-hour programming, opening the opportunity for even more cheer events. Varsity added dance shows to the lineup. To this day, Varsity Spirit is ESPN's longest standing television partner. That's how Jeff built the Varsity franchise.

ESPN broadcast the competitions while Varsity promoted its own uniforms and camps. That was the magic ingredient. Right from the start, Varsity zeroed in on marketing, fueled by Jeff's big ideas and his unwavering determination to make them happen.

THE ALL STAR TRANSFORMATION: CREATING ORDER FROM CHAOS

All Star began taking shape in the early 1980s, and Varsity was worried that without structure and safety standards, this new form of cheerleading would affect their relationships with high school federations and, indeed, the reputation of the entire sport.

"We missed All Star strategically in the beginning," Jeff said.

One good thing about being larger is that you don't have to be first. Jeff credits many of his employees, including Jim Chadwick and Eddie Zagara, with pushing Varsity to enter the All Star space. They insisted that All Star was an important new space Varsity needed to be in. Jim wanted to lead the effort, so he put together a presentation for Jeff and the rest of the Varsity team, and they began to host All Star competitions.

As All Star cheerleading surged in popularity, so did emergency room visits for cheerleaders nationwide. With injuries on the rise, it was affecting all aspects of cheer. Routines had to change for every event, which put a lot of pressure and stress on the athletes and coaches.

Jeff genuinely felt that Varsity had a responsibility to implement additional safety measures for the sport. He knew that something needed to be done to unify the rules.

Jim Chadwick, vice president of Varsity at the time, worked with Jeff to develop the concept of an All Star cheerleading entity that would create standard rules for the sport. From this idea, the United States All Star Federation (USASF) was born.

Jeff and Jim agreed that, for the good of the sport, they should invite all event producers to participate in standardizing the rules. They approached twenty event producers and asked each to contribute $25,000 to help get the organization started. Every single event producer declined.

As a result, Varsity had to fund the entire project almost all on its own. It was an investment that grew to over $3 million, but it was eventually paid back.

Jim and Jeff understood and believed in the value of organizing the sport by establishing standard rules, divisions, and guidelines, not only for teams but also for events. This single decision shaped the future of All Star.

Many people today see this decision as a power play by Varsity to control the sport, but the rules entity was created to help ensure the longevity of the sport, and everyone who was part of All Star was offered an opportunity to participate.

Thus, the USASF was created in 2004, and Jim Chadwick was appointed president and chairman of the board of directors.

CHEERSPORT and Athletic Championships were the first non-Varsity members. At the time, CHEERSPORT specifically told Varsity it wasn't for sale, but it believed in what the USASF was doing and wanted a seat at the table.

UCA was a member, of course, and after Varsity purchased NCA, it became a member as well.

Remember that the goal was to unify the industry and establish a standard set of rules, divisions, and guidelines for everyone. To gain more traction and members, the USASF started the Cheerleading World Championships for All Star to be held in Orlando, Florida, at the end of April, creating a definitive end to the season. Previously, there had been no such thing. Varsity also convinced ESPN to cover the competition, which added exposure and legitimacy to the event and, therefore, to USASF.

Varsity purchased NCA shortly after establishing the USASF. Upon acquiring NCA, the staff and instructors who worked for NCA were concerned about losing their jobs if NCA would be merged into UCA. But that didn't happen. NCA employees kept their jobs, and NCA remains strong today because Jeff kept both brands.

The company would operate efficiently behind the scenes by collaborating with accounting, technology, and daily operations while Jeff maintained the camps, competitions, and staff as separate brands. The Cheerleader Dance Team Uniform Company was merged into Varsity Spirit Fashion, but that was the only consolidation.

"We could do this All Star thing a lot faster through acquisition rather than just organic growth," Jeff said.

Not long after, Jeff met Boog Potter and Mike Martinez from Athletic Championships through Cole Stott, one of the first USASF board members. Jeff liked the group of gentlemen and believed they had much in common.

With the acquisition of the Athletic Championships came Premier Athletics, marking Varsity's entry into the All Star space. Jeff began discussing how to leverage Varsity's resources and influence to scale the All Star business and promote the growth of the sport.

What occurred then were two major acquisitions involving a phenomenal talent pool. Jeff was excellent at utilizing his team, listening to ideas, and executing them. The masterful think tank of people Varsity had acquired shared ideas on how to grow All Star.

Many other event producers noticed the acquisitions and approached Varsity to express interest in their companies. Now that Jeff had assembled his All Star team, he collaborated with them to strategically evaluate which companies would be a good fit. Among these early event producers were World Spirit Federation, Spirit Sports, and American Championships. The All Star Challenge, Spirit Festival, and CHEERSPORT were acquired next, followed by JAM Brands in 2015, leading to further growth.

As Varsity and All Star grew, so did everything associated with All Star. "We should focus on our commonalities rather than our differences," Jeff said. "We should discuss how to do this together."

JEFF WEBB'S ENDURING VISION

Jeff is a visionary whose imagination transcends what most people can grasp. Every single person who participates in modern cheerleading has Jeff Webb to thank for those opportunities. His vision, drive, and determination have enabled tens of thousands of passionate All Star fans to earn a living doing what they love. Jeff is likely the most passionate person in cheerleading today. He has devoted his life to advancing the sport. He believes in cheer and what it has done for young people over the years.

Jeff shared a story about a time when he was walking the corridors at The Cheerleading Worlds. A woman approached him and began to cry. She continued to speak through her tears and expressed how much All Star had done for her daughters. She thanked Jeff for making it all happen.

"That remarkable moment hit me straight in the heart," Jeff said.

Today, Jeff remains deeply committed to the sport of cheer as president of the International Cheer Union (ICU) governing council. He believes a rising tide lifts all boats and frequently asks the following questions: What is good for the sport? What will make the sport better for the kids?

Anywhere there's cheer, there's Jeff Webb.

> "Success is doing something that makes a difference. It's also doing something that makes you happy." – Jeff Webb

EARNED WISDOM

★ **Success:** Success is respecting and appreciating everybody and what they do. Money doesn't define success, but if you have money and choose to do something with it that makes a difference, then that is success. Success is also doing something that makes you happy. Humans have ups and downs, but you're fortunate if you do something that makes you happy.

★ **Gratitude:** Jeff is grateful for his parents. He regrets that his father passed away so early. He wishes he were around to help guide his decisions and witness the sport's growth.

★ **Jeff's Wish:** Jeff wished he introduced cheerleading on a global scale sooner. He believes in the positive and uplifting nature of the sport and finds it frustrating that many young people in other countries can't afford to participate in cheer or don't have access to it.

★ **Mistakes:** "I've had many of them," Jeff said. His company almost went bankrupt. Several times the uniforms barely arrived in time. And he almost lost the television contract.

★ **To My Younger Self:** Jeff would sell Varsity to the employees if he could go back and do anything again, because he believed so deeply in the employees who loved and cared about the sport. An employee stock option would have been the better choice for his team rather than selling to another company.

★ **For Gym Owners:** Strive for continuous improvement. Make sure you spend your time trying to better yourself and the people around you. Be kind to your students and always put safety first.

★ **For Coaches:** Set clear expectations and do your best every day, regardless of how you feel, because the kids deserve the best you have to offer. Be a great teammate and support the people you work with. Show grace. Understand that everyone is human.

★ **Lessons Learned:** If you aren't constantly evolving, the end is near.

DID YOU KNOW?

★ Jeff enjoys duck hunting.

★ He loves dogs and owns champion Labrador retrievers that he takes on his duck-hunting adventures.

★ Jeff has his own plane and loves to fly.

★ His favorite All Star memory is standing in the small arena at Disney and watching the first World Championship for All Star cheerleading.

★ Jeff chose the bald eagle as his animal. The bald eagle symbolizes the divine spirit, sacrifice, connection to the creator, intelligence, renewal, courage, illumination of the spirit, healing, creation, freedom, and being a risk-taker.

> PUT THE ATHLETES FIRST, EVEN BEFORE YOUR BUSINESS.

"If you wake up tomorrow and only have what you thanked God for yesterday, what would that be? We should remember to be truly thankful for the good in our lives." – Max Lucado

LANCE WAGERS

National Cheerleaders Association (NCA) – 1977

THE BEGINNING OF A LIFELONG PASSION

Lance Wagers began cheering in his sophomore year at the University of Colorado. He continued to cheer for three years and was selected head cheerleader, or yell leader as it was called in 1969. He wore cowboy boots on the sidelines as he tumbled in the grass. He attended the NCA college camp in Colorado and received an application from Bob Shields to apply for the NCA camp staff. Lance then spent his summers working at NCA college camps. Carol Pojezny was the first head instructor.

Lance drove his white 1964 Chevy Corvair across the country to Lincoln, Nebraska, to teach his first camp, sporting his "hippie hair," as he described it. Being from Colorado, most people didn't know if Lance was talented or not. But he wanted to make sure they knew, and maybe he wanted to show off a little in front of Carol. When she introduced him for the staff demos, he did flip-flops (back handsprings) the length of the gym floor.

Carol's jaw hit the floor, and she said, "I didn't know you could do that."

Lance smiled and replied, "You didn't ask."

In his second year Lance became a head instructor and moved to Dallas, Texas, in 1977 to work at NCA headquarters.

Carol Pojezny, who later became Lance's wife, persuaded Herkie to hire him to oversee the advisor/sponsor program that NCA was starting. Lance packed his bags, left Colorado, and never looked back. Carol and Lance married in 1981 and worked together throughout their marriage.

Camp was often staffed with people from all over the country who didn't know each other, so Carol and Lance organized bonding games because a cohesive team led to a better camp experience. Lance was known as the kumbaya guy on staff because he shared positive stories with everyone.

"I think it's amazing," Lance said, "that seven strangers could turn into best friends after five days at camp."

A PIVOTAL DECISION

Around the early 1980s Carol approached Herkie with the idea of hosting a middle school and high school cheerleading competition. Prior to that, NCA had only hosted camps. The idea was that teams would compete with a sideline cheer and a pom-pon routine set to music. But the concept was new, and there weren't many rules.

It wasn't long after the event was created that teams composed of athletes from the local area began to compete. Those teams didn't have a school they cheered for. They cheered for the sake of cheering. Eventually, some of those teams started to place third, and then a team took second, which made Lance and Carol fear that the true school teams would become angry.

NCA held a meeting to discuss the predicament. The meeting lasted about ninety minutes, and when participants walked out of the room they had decided that those non-school teams could continue to compete with NCA in the newly created All Star division. That single 1984 decision to keep those non-school teams essentially created the opportunity for the All Star cheer world to flourish. A few short years later, NCA hosted the first ever All Star only competition.

5,6,7,8 – CHEEROBICS

Lance and Carol also started Cheerobics in 1984. They opened locations in North Dallas and Central Dallas. Cheerobics was a term used by NCA to refer to its camp warm-up. Lance purchased rights to the name from Herkie for $10.

"It was a personal thing," Lance said. "The name was trademarked, and I wanted to use it legally." Herkie insisted on approving Lance's request, and only asked for that token amount of money in return.

The gym was built for school cheer, classes, and to help kids who didn't make their middle school and high school teams prepare for tryouts the following year.

Eventually, they started the Cheerobics Chili Peppers All Star team. Lance and Carol hired Morton Bergue, a former NCA instructor, to run Cheerobics. Cheer Athletics, a well-known All Star program based in Plano, Texas, rented space from Cheerobics before opening its first facility.

Lance was an NCA camp instructor for twenty-three years and physically ran camps until he became president of the company. As president, he was needed more in the office to monitor staff and budgets. Lance worked for NCA for twenty-five years, and his wife Carol worked for NCA for twenty-nine years. In 1995 they decided their time at NCA and Cheerobics had come to an end, so they retired.

Following retirement, Lance and Carol traveled to Brazil on a mission trip. There, they met a woman with two beautiful daughters. She asked if they would consider adopting her children. The process took over a year and a half, but eventually they did adopt the girls, who were ten and eleven at the time. Today, their daughters are thirty-nine and forty.

Lance looked at Carol and said, "Well, maybe I should be thinking about their college educations." Not long after, he accepted a new position with the American

Cheerleaders Association (ACA), which had been acquired by Varsity.

THE ACA YEARS

For twenty years Lance managed the ACA high school competitions, camps, and All Star competitions. The All Star events grew rapidly, becoming their largest competitions. The ACA offered a leadership program focused on life skills that incorporated leadership into cheerleading.

When Lance began at ACA he gathered twelve of his closest friends from the cheer industry to spend an entire week at his house developing an incredible leadership program that could influence athletes nationwide. The ACA leadership program began with 1,100 kids in its first summer, but it expanded over the years.

The ACA evolved a powerful mantra: Attitude. Choices. Always. That legacy persisted throughout the company until Lance retired again in 2018.

Lance's extraordinary cheerleading journey reveals how one person's passion can ripple through and transform an entire industry. From his first back handsprings on the gym floor to the creation of the groundbreaking All Star division, Lance's contributions have transformed countless lives through cheerleading.

His story shows that leadership means spotting possibilities where others see obstacles, bridging divides instead of deepening them, and nurturing talent with skill and compassion. The cheerleading world today stands on the shoulders of pioneers like Lance and Carol whose vision and passion forged a path for generations of athletes.

Although Lance has officially retired, his legacy continues to tumble, fly, and soar through every competition, team, and athlete who revels in the joy of cheerleading. In the end, Lance's greatest achievement isn't counted in years served or programs built but in the countless lives he's inspired to reach higher, work harder, and cheer louder, both on and off the mat.

Lance still spends some weekends judging international competitions, and he often can be seen at The Cheerleading Worlds presenting awards. He enjoys seeing the joy on the athletes' faces, and he loves to dress up and present. He has five grandchildren ranging in age from three to twenty-one. He enjoys traveling and spending time with friends and family. He enjoyed his forty-plus years in the industry where he had a positive impact on the lives of those he encountered.

A TRIBUTE TO CAROL

Herkie trusted Carol implicitly. He gave her full reign over the NCA, and she saw the company through several mergers and buyouts. Back then there were no computers, so Carol acted as a human computer. She had all the knowledge stored in her brain. She hand-selected the staff for all 700 NCA summer camps. It was her idea to start the first competition. Carol did tremendous and tedious work for the NCA, and she was loved and revered by many.

Carol had a significant influence on Lance as they worked closely together throughout their entire marriage. "We loved being married," Lance said. "We loved working together." They literally spent 24/7 together and, according to Lance, they never seemed to have any conflicts. Lance believes their marriage was a blessed one. They almost never got on each other's nerves. "Well, maybe sometimes we got on each other's nerves," Lance said, "but not all the time."

"Success is putting in the work and effort." – Lance Wagers

EARNED WISDOM

★ **Success:** Success is pouring your heart and soul into what you're doing. Come up with an idea and work hard to bring it to fruition.

★ **Gratitude:** Lance credits Lawrence Herkimer for his career. He said Herkie was kind, gracious, and an incredible mentor. Lance also gave a heartfelt thank you to his late wife, Carol. He had genuine gratitude for her leadership, guidance, and friendship.

★ **Mistakes:** Mistakes are fixable. You just have to be willing to put in the work.

★ **For Gym Owners:** Enroll in a business course to learn how to effectively run your business and examine every aspect of it. Understanding how to run your business is extremely important. Many owners start off with a bang and then fizzle out because they don't know how to run a business. Second, make sure you hire quality individuals. Hire genuinely good people.

★ **For Coaches:** Put your ego aside and teach from the heart. Be sure you're doing work you can be proud of.

★ **Lessons Learned:** There's no job that's too big for you to handle.

DID YOU KNOW?

★ Lance's favorite part of cheer is watching all the pieces come together.

★ Carol and Lance hosted a Christmas party for forty-three years, and Lance did all the cooking, using recipes from his own cookbook. He prepared thirty-five hors d'oeuvres every single year. Lance is writing a hospitality book to honor their years as the hostesses with the mostess.

★ Lance loves to cook. The harder the recipe, the more relaxed he is.

★ Carol and Lance loved to jitterbug, and they were known to cut loose on the dance floor.

★ Lance and Carol are members of the Spirit Industry Hall of Fame and have received the Cornerstone Award, the Pioneer Award, and Varsity Legends Awards. Lance also has a choreography award named after him.

★ Lance has a lasagna ministry. He makes small pans of lasagna that feed a family of four, but he'll prepare ten or twelve of them at a time and freeze them. When someone needs food, he just goes to one of the four refrigerators and freezers in his shed.

★ For his animal Lance chose the horse because it symbolizes freedom, stamina, mobility, the land, travel, power, grace, and nobility.

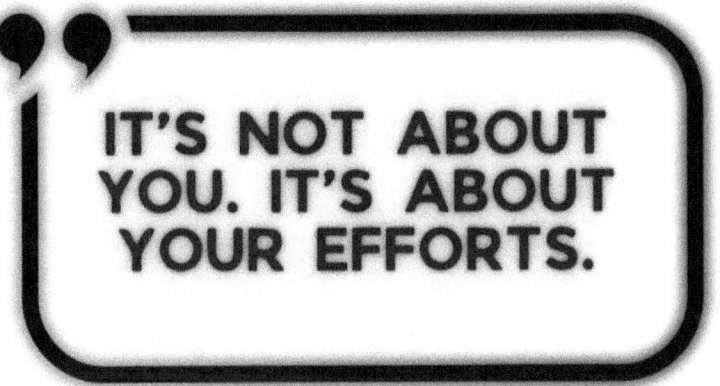

IT'S NOT ABOUT YOU. IT'S ABOUT YOUR EFFORTS.

"A coach is someone who tells you what you don't want to hear, who has you see what you don't want to see so you can be who you always knew you could be."
– Tom Landry

CATHY BUCKEY

NC State Cheerleading – 1979
Champion Cheerleading – 1980

THE FOUR-YEAR-OLD MASCOT

Cathy Buckey didn't just coach cheerleading, she revolutionized it. From her humble beginnings as a four-year-old mascot for her father's football team to becoming one of the most influential figures in cheerleading history, Cathy's journey embodies passion, innovation, and dedication.

When North Carolina State University in Raleigh hired her in 1979, the school couldn't have foreseen how this spirited coach from Ohio would transform not only its cheerleading program but also the entire landscape of competitive cheer throughout the Southeast and beyond.

Cathy's vision extended beyond sideline support. Her vision created a comprehensive cheerleading ecosystem that developed athletes from childhood through college, establishing techniques and traditions that continue to define the sport today.

TAKING THE HELM AT NC STATE

In 1959 at the age of four, Cathy became the mascot for her father's football team, and cheer continued to be a part of her life through her college years at Akron University in Ohio. She started coaching her first team, Bantam League Cheer, when she was seventeen.

Cathy's husband, Dave, and his twin brother, Don, were football stars at NC State. Later, Dave became an assistant coach for the NC State football team, and the university needed someone to oversee the cheerleading team. In 1979 Cathy applied to be the cheerleading coach and was hired shortly afterward. What the university didn't know was the impact that Cathy would have on NC State cheerleading and the surrounding communities.

THE CHAMPION LEGACY

Although Cathy was the university's cheerleading coach, her pay was low, so the school encouraged her to offer camps to supplement her income. That's why she started Cathy Buckey Cheerleading Camps (CBCC). Her athletes staffed the camps, which allowed Cathy to train, lead, and instruct them throughout the summer. "I really didn't like having my name in the title," Cathy said, "so after a few summers I changed it to Champion Cheerleading Camps." She and her staff coached over

150 girls in that first camp, and that number eventually grew to thousands of athletes per summer.

In Ohio where Cathy grew up, cheerleading was more advanced than it was in North Carolina, so she took her knowledge and experience from her childhood and started Champion Cheerleading Competitions in Raleigh in addition to her summer camps.

Cathy transitioned the NC State cheerleading team into a powerhouse that earned her team one of only five invitations to compete in the first UCA Collegiate National Championships in Hawaii. Cathy continued teaching summer camps but took a break from hosting competitions to focus on the college team until the mid-1990s.

THE ICONIC WOLF WALL

The focus on her college team led to the iconic Wolf Wall pyramid, now performed by All Star and school teams across the country. "I think it took us five hundred tries to finally figure that pyramid out," Cathy said.

Her team's pyramid collapsed over and over until the Wolf Wall was perfected just in time to perform it in Hawaii. Because it took Cathy and her team months to successfully perform the amazing Wolf Wall, they continued to showcase it every year.

As more teams learned Cathy's pyramid, NC State remained one step ahead by adding a new element each year—the lean-back version, the ground-up version, and now the rewind into the Wolf Wall.

In 1986 NC State won its first UCA National Championship, putting Cathy, the school, and Champion Cheerleading on the map. Cathy and NC State added two consecutive championships in 1990 and 1991. During Cathy's tenure the NC State cheer team was the only one in the country to earn paid bids to attend college nationals every year, and her team never placed lower than fifth.

After winning that national title with NC State in 1991, Champion Cheerleading Competitions began providing college scholarships to cheerleaders that same year. All-Americans and Champion staff performed in the Hula Bowl and Pro Bowl in Hawaii, the Citrus and Capital One bowls in Florida, and various Thanksgiving Day parades. In addition, they performed on the sidelines and at halftime during the NC State football game designated as Cheerleader Day.

BUILDING A PIPELINE

In 1994 All Star cheer was growing, and Cathy started Champion Cheer Gym. She was excited about leading and instructing athletes year-round, training them to become the next generation of collegiate and NC State cheerleaders. Her program offered Twinkle, Youth, Junior, and Senior teams. From inception, NC State Cheerleading and Champion Cheerleading gym have been symbiotic.

Many NC State cheerleaders coached the teams, and Cathy was ecstatic to train her athletes year-round and see the impact the gym had on the local community. The two programs working in unison provided profound benefits to both parties. To have the opportunity to train kids from a young age all the way through college with the proper progressions was a dream come true. Champion's mission was to instill excellence in all aspects of cheer and to develop each person, including staff, to be the "best they could be."

Cathy has coached thousands of athletes, and many of her former athletes are coaching today. There is no doubt that her influence is still present today, especially in North Carolina and Virginia.

In 1996 the NC State Cheerleaders were selected to perform in the opening ceremonies at the Olympic Games in Atlanta, Georgia. That same year Cathy joined Jim Lampley to provide television commentary on the first NCA Collegiate National Championships in Daytona Beach, Florida.

In 2004 Cathy started the Champion Cup National Cheerleading Competitions for All Star. A few years later she began Cheers for Charity to benefit the Victory Junction Gang camps' nonprofit, year-round program for children with complex medical conditions or serious illness. In 2008 Cathy joined the USASF and began awarding Cheerleading Worlds bids at her event.

The ripples of Cathy Buckey's influence continue to spread throughout the cheerleading community, decades after she first stepped onto NC State's campus. Her legacy endures not only in the iconic Wolf Wall pyramid that teams nationwide continue to perform but also in the hundreds of coaches she mentored and who now lead their own programs and gyms. Through

Champion Cheerleading Camps, Champion Cheer Gym, Champion Cup National Competitions, and charitable initiatives, Cathy built not only organizations but also a "Tradition of Excellence," progression, and character development that has influenced thousands of young athletes.

Though officially retired from competitive cheer, Cathy continues to mentor cheer coaches and teams. Her return to coaching middle school highlights her enduring commitment to the sport. For Cathy Buckey, cheerleading transcended performances and championships. It was about nurturing confident, skilled individuals who would perpetuate her passion for generations.

> "Success is knowing that you helped kids learn and progress."– Cathy Buckey

EARNED WISDOM

★ **Success:** You're a teacher first. You teach your athletes everything from A to Z. Feeling successful comes from the look on your athletes' faces when the light bulb goes off, seeing the friendships they've built, the camaraderie, and the mental toughness.

★ **Wisdom:** Be a contributor to a "Tradition of Excellence" and remember to always "autograph your work with excellence."

- ★ **Gratitude:** Cathy is grateful to her father. He worked hard as a police officer, but she also watched him coach his football team at every practice, pushing them to strive to be better every day. She also attributes her success to her cheer coaches. She is grateful to cheerleading because it taught her many valuable lessons throughout her life.

- ★ **Cathy's Wish:** Cathy wishes that greed, politics, and evil would rid themselves of the cheer industry. As cash came in, people would steal money, and gyms would steal athletes and coaches. It all happened to her at various times. Cathy wishes everyone would realize there's room for everyone to thrive in the amazing All Star cheer and dance world.

- ★ **Mistakes:** Every mistake is an opportunity for something better. Embrace your mistakes and learn from them.

- ★ **For Gym Owners:** Hire individuals you absolutely trust to manage your finances and your athletes.

- ★ **For Coaches:** There are no shortcuts. Follow the proper progressions and teach your athletes correctly and safely. Remember: safety first, last, and always.

DID YOU KNOW?

★ Cathy's favorite part of cheer is pyramids. Her NC State teams invented the Wolf Wall and several variations over the years.

★ Her favorite routine was all of them, especially the ones she was coaching at that moment. So much was invested in each routine. The creativity, the blood, sweat, and tears were all poured lovingly into each routine with no detail left undone. "If you don't love it," she said, "how can you believe in it?" She also said the Top Gun coed teams coached by Kristen and Victor Rosario are the best. "To me," Cathy said, "they exemplify what coaches should be. I love their creativity, their ability to get the very best out of their kids, their humility, their knowledge, and the perfection that their routines always have! Many kudos."

★ Cathy has coached tiny teams, collegiate cheer, and everything in between.

★ She loves traveling, the beach, watching sports, thrifting, making bows, and creating things as a crafter.

★ Cathy loves animals and would have a hundred cats and dogs if she could. She's rescued many of both over the years.

★ Cathy said she's too old for superheroes.

★ As her animal, Cathy chose the ant, which symbolizes being group-minded, determined, patient, active, purposeful, united, self-sacrificing, and industrious. Cathy also said she was like the lion—fierce, protective, and loyal.

PAY IT FORWARD.

"I can do all things through Christ who strengthens me." – Philippians 4:13

DEBBIE LOVE

The Love of Tumbling – 1980

A PIONEER IN CHEER AND TUMBLING

In the realm of All Star cheer and tumbling, few names carry as much weight and respect as that of Debbie Love. A visionary whose technical expertise, educational methods, and steadfast commitment to athlete safety transformed an entire industry, Debbie's journey from backyard cartwheels to international recognition exemplifies how passion, mathematical precision, and an educator's heart can elevate a sport to new heights. Debbie didn't merely participate in the evolution of competitive cheerleading, she engineered it by introducing structure, safety standards, and scientific principles to a discipline that urgently required her guidance.

IN THE BEGINNING

Nine-year-old Debbie Love was training front walkovers and cartwheels with her father in the backyard, and from the instant she went upside down, she was hooked. Her father, a minister who grew up on a farm, was athletic. And Debbie took her father's athleticism with her as she participated in cheerleading, gymnastics, and track throughout her childhood and into college.

BREAKING BARRIERS

Debbie majored in math in college (1973-1977). As a fellow math major, I was curious what it was like for Debbie in the 1970s when most women chose more stereotypical female majors. It was clear that Debbie was determined and bold, even back then. She credited one of her professors, Dr. Hancock, for his encouragement and support throughout her college years. In addition to math, Debbie loved writing and minored in English and psychology. She also nearly earned a degree in kinesiology.

After graduating from Memphis State University, now the University of Memphis, she began teaching math at the Southern Baptist Educational Center in Memphis, and she also coached the cheerleading team. Two years later her husband graduated from optometry school, and they moved to her hometown of Lexington, Kentucky.

Debbie began working with several gymnastics and school cheerleading teams and, eventually, coached gymnastics at the Bluegrass Gymnastics Training Center, home to the Bluegrass Tigers, one of two All Star programs in Lexington. The other was CHEERS! Inc., owned by Dawn Duncan Walters.

Debbie's husband was Dawn's optometrist, and he kept encouraging Debbie to bring her kids to CHEERS! Inc. When Dawn sold her facility to Brian Elza and Craig Monte, the timing aligned, and Debbie finally made the move.

STANDARDIZING THE SPORT

As All Star evolved and event producers crafted their own rules and scoresheets, coaching grew increasingly challenging and frustrating because routines had to be adapted for each event. Debbie prioritized the sport's safety and longevity amid the chaos. She attended the NACCC and contributed to developing a standard set of rules that the USASF ultimately adopted.

Debbie dedicated many years to the USASF Board of Directors. She served on the rules committee and was instrumental in developing the first credentialing program. She has devoted her life to improving the sport, spending years working with the USASF. Debbie also played a key role in developing the prep, novice, and fundamentals programs. She brought vital awareness of technique and the physics behind the skills to the industry.

Her awareness and training inspired many coaches to follow suit, resulting in numerous technicians in the sport. "Conditioning leads to proper technique," Debbie said, "which leads to excellence in your skills."

In 2010 she was inducted into the USASF Hall of Fame.

THE MENTAL GAME

Debbie also highlighted the mental aspects of cheer and has helped thousands of athletes overcome mental blocks. She embodied a train smarter, not harder mentality, teaching the industry to use time wisely and train more efficiently. She educated coaches on injury prevention, conditioning, and effective warm-up techniques. Debbie Love's teachings are woven into the fabric of All Star cheer.

Debbie, technically retired, relishes every moment with her eleven grandchildren. She still teaches acro part time at a local dance studio and works with Off Main All Stars.

Debbie travels internationally, most recently attending the Australian National Cheer and Dance Competition. You can continue to learn from Debbie by visiting her website at theloveoftumbling.com.

Debbie has long been an invaluable resource for our sport. Her focus has been on putting athletes first and fostering growth in the sport. By implementing standardized rules, pioneering mental training, and applying physics-based skill development, she helped transform cheerleading from a mere activity into a respected athletic discipline. Countless athletes training safer, coaches teaching smarter, and organizations operating with greater structure all testify to Debbie Love's extraordinary legacy.

As cheerleading evolves globally, her foundational work and key principles will guide generations of athletes as a testament to her lifelong dedication to a sport she loves.

I believe our industry owes her tremendous gratitude. Thank you, Debbie, for anointing our sport with your greatness.

"Success is being able to produce your best when you're best is needed." – Debbie Love

---

EARNED WISDOM

★ **Success:** When everything you do is centered around your core principles, you don't compromise on them. Debbie laughed and said, "That gets me in trouble sometimes, but I don't think I can do anything with excellence if it is not centered on my core principles."

★ **Wisdom:** Character is your daily armor. Train your character every day. Debbie does daily Bible readings and works every day to become a better person. "I'm seventy years old," she said, "and I'm still getting better every day."

★ **Gratitude:** Debbie is grateful for the opportunity to have worked with wonderful people like Elaine Pascale and Kristen and Victor Rosario. She also values the time she spent working with Leroy McCullough on Team USA. He coached her daughters at Oklahoma State University. She adores him and Orson Sykes and appreciates the impact they've had on her girls. She appreciates the opportunity to teach tumbling at various All Star gyms. She has great respect for Morton Bergue and admires how he always stayed true to his philosophy.

★ **Debbie's Wish:** Debbie thinks the industry is score and competition driven. She wishes cheer would be driven by a growth mindset focused on growing a little bit each day and celebrating the incremental goals that each team or athlete achieves. She wishes that, as a sport, we could focus on the beginning of the year. Instead, we're always looking toward the post-season event we'll attend. She wishes we could collectively find a way to stay focused on the athletes as individuals, who are becoming better every day, and on our team becoming more cohesive and better each day. She would like to see our sport focus on both the individual athlete improving and teams improving, ensuring that each day is better than the day before, but not as good as the next day.

★ **Mistakes:** Have a growth mindset. Mistakes happen, and we learn from them. Your character is what will produce the core principles with which you align yourself.

★ **For Gym Owners:** Never compromise on your principles. You'll be miserable if you do. Don't try to become someone else just because you think you must. God made you a masterpiece. He gave you unique abilities, and you need to use those abilities to create the environment you want, not what you think someone else needs.

★ **For Coaches:** Don't compromise on progressions. If you do, you're guaranteed to have injured athletes.

★ **Lessons Learned:** Debbie learned early that she could not be a reactor. She learned she had to be a responder. She learned the art of pausing before responding to someone. Debbie said, "The art is very hard to learn." In her early years she thinks she reacted a lot, but now, when she doesn't know what to say, she just stays quiet.

DID YOU KNOW?

★ Debbie's favorite part of cheerleading is tumbling.

★ Debbie was a youth minister.

★ She participated in gymnastics and track, but she also plays piano and organ.

★ Debbie was a minister's daughter and had several ministers' kids in her wedding. She has been married for forty-seven years and has six children, all of whom participated in cheerleading.

★ She likes Wonder Woman because she would turn around furiously and be changed. She feels that quick changes equal strength.

★ As her animal Debbie chose the cow, which symbolizes love of home, community, contentment, joy, easygoing nature, patience, being grounded, and fertility.

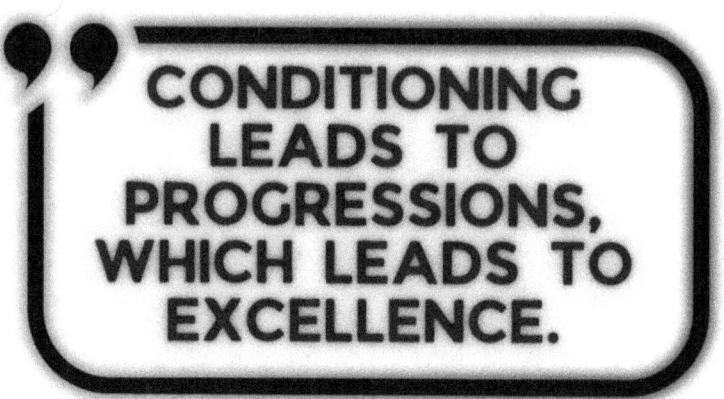

"Lack of preparation on your part does not constitute an emergency on my part." – Bob Carter

KEVIN JONES
NCA – 1981
America's Best – 2000

FROM RURAL MISSOURI TO NCA

It all began in 1981 in a small rural high school in Missouri. "I tried out for cheerleader, made the squad, went to an NCA summer camp, and was the only guy among 700 girls there," Kevin Jones recalled with a chuckle. "Lance Wagers was my head instructor."

That chance encounter would shape the next four decades of Kevin's life. Lance saw something special in the athletic young man who "could flip" and offered him an application to join the NCA staff. Two weeks after graduating from high school, Kevin embarked on his first summer of teaching NCA camps, the beginning of what would become an eighteen-year relationship with the organization.

Throughout college and beyond, Kevin worked at NCA's summer camps. In 1989 an opportunity arose in the form of a position at the NCA corporate office in Dallas,

Texas, where he worked alongside Lance and Carol Wagers. He's lived in Dallas ever since.

"I started out doing one-day clinics for NCA," Kevin said, "then moved into taking over the youth program, and then moved into doing all the special events."

During his tenure at NCA Kevin managed high-profile events including the Aloha Bowl, Hula Bowl, and the Macy's Thanksgiving Day Parade. His most significant contribution was yet to come when he recognized the need for All Star cheerleading to have its own distinct identity and competitive platform.

CREATING ALL STAR NATIONALS

For years, All Star teams competed in school divisions because that was their only option. All Star teams were mere afterthoughts in the cheerleading competition scene, so Kevin recognized that something needed to change. The All Star style was evolving differently than traditional school cheerleading, featuring distinct performance elements and expectations. As a result, Kevin made a game-changing decision to launch the NCA All Star National Championships in 1994 as a standalone event.

"I started The NCA All Star National Championship. I created the Gold Megaphone Trophy," Kevin said with pride.

The Gold Megaphone Trophy is still the iconic award presented at the NCA All Star Nationals. To create a clear difference between the newly formed All Star

Championship and school cheer competitions, Kevin added the production value of All Star. Even today, this is one of the major elements that separate All Star event production from school cheer event production.

The establishment of a dedicated All Star National Championship cemented the legitimacy of All Star cheerleading at a pivotal moment in its evolution. It marked All Star as more than a mere sideshow to school cheerleading and established it as a distinct discipline deserving of its own spotlight. In 1987 NCA introduced All Star divisions for competition, but it wasn't until 1994 that the event stood alone, thanks to Kevin Jones.

BUILDING AMERICA'S BEST

After Lance and Carol Wagers retired from NCA, Kevin seamlessly took the reins of all event production, including the newly independent All Star competitions. By 1999 Kevin was primed for a new challenge, so he left NCA and created America's Best Championships. "In 2000 I did host my first event," Kevin said.

In 2001 America's Best exploded to eight events, doubled to sixteen the following year, and ultimately soared to twenty-six under Kevin's leadership, an impressive growth during a pivotal era in All Star cheer. The landscape remained largely uncrowded with only a handful of companies hosting nationwide events. Kevin pointed out that the only other events happening then were CHEERSPORT with Kevin Brubaker and American Cheer Power with Regina Symons.

"NCA and UCA really weren't doing anything outside of their big national championships," Kevin said.

America's Best Championship events rapidly earned a reputation for quality and innovation. Kevin's time at NCA taught him that crafting a complete experience matters more than just competing. He recognized that building relationships with gym owners and coaches was just as crucial as mastering the technical side of running an event. "It's not just getting a bunch of people in a venue and throwing down a spring floor and running a competition," Kevin said.

INDUSTRY FOUNDATION

"I was one of the original board members of USASF with Jim Chadwick and Steve Peterson," Kevin said. But in an interesting twist, Kevin decided to step away from the board after that first formative year.

"I opted to step away from the board because I felt like it was really hurting my business at the time," Kevin said. "Not a lot of people knew about the USASF."

Though his formal role with USASF was brief, Kevin continued to shape the sport's development through various channels. He actively served on multiple rules committees, influencing discussions on divisions and competitive structures that would shape All Star cheerleading for years.

"I really helped to lay the groundwork," Kevin said. "I think the brands that I had in the industry really contributed to helping grow the industry."

BRINGING THE "BLING" TO ALL STAR

In 2003 Kevin launched Spirit Innovations, an All Star apparel company that revolutionized competition uniforms with a groundbreaking feature—sparkle.

"I was the first company to actually put sparkle on uniforms back in the day," Kevin said. "And, of course, that's really evolved over the past twenty years."

Kevin's desire to make All Star cheer visually distinctive sparked the innovation. With experience running a screen printing and embroidery business, he was well-versed in apparel production. Kevin recalled the early materials: "Back in the day, we used sequin dot material. It was awful." Yet those early designs marked the beginning of a visual transformation that would become integral to All Star cheer's identity.

The evolution of All Star uniforms mirrored the sport's own growth, relentlessly pushing boundaries and becoming increasingly elaborate.

TRANSITION TO NEW BEGINNINGS

By 2008 the competitive landscape was shifting, and Kevin sold controlling interest in America's Best Championships to JAM Brands. Four years later he negotiated deals that led to Spirit Innovations being sold to Varsity and JAM Brands acquiring his remaining stake in America's Best.

Kevin joined the Varsity All Star Fashion team but quickly realized it wasn't the right fit. "I did a little stint with Varsity All Star Fashion for about eighteen months before I decided it wasn't the place for me and kind of took some time off." The hiatus didn't last long.

His latest venture, The All Star Premiers, tackles a crucial need he identified during his decades in the industry. Before competition season, All Star programs hosted their own showcase events, but managing them added another burden on already overwhelmed gym owners and coaches.

"Whether they choose to do them in their gym or host them in a high school," Kevin said, "it's a lot for them to manage. We take care of everything for them. The gym just shows up, and we produce an elevated, preseason experience for the athletes, coaches, gym owners, and spectators."

SOMETIMES YOU NEED A CHICKEN TRUCK

Among Kevin's forty-four years in cheerleading, one story stands out as emblematic of the profound changes in the sport and the world.

Fresh out of college camp at the University of Tennessee in the early 1980s, Kevin got a message to call the NCA office. They wanted to place him in a camp in the Northeast. With no cell phones and little planning, Kevin set out on an adventure that seems unimaginable today.

"I took a taxi to the airport and caught a flight to Albany, New York," Kevin recounted. "From Albany Airport I had to catch a bus to go up to Schroon Lake."

But the bus driver missed Kevin's stop. Miles down the road, Kevin finally alerted the driver, who simply pulled over and opened the door. "I guess my suitcase and I are going to walk back to the campsite," he recalled thinking.

After an initial wrong turn that led him to what appeared to be a religious retreat, Kevin found himself walking along the road with his suitcase, hoping to eventually reach the right camp.

"I'm not kidding you, Stacy," Kevin said with a laugh, "a pickup truck pulled over that had chickens in the back, and the guy said, 'Do you need a ride?' And I said, 'Yeah, I'm going to Schroon Lake.'"

Kevin hopped into the back of the truck with the chickens. That's how he arrived at his camp.

Kevin's story, with its lack of cell phones, GPS, or safety protocols, represents a simpler era in cheerleading, one that contrasts sharply with today's highly organized corporate industry. Yet it also demonstrates the resourcefulness, adaptability, and determination that have characterized Kevin's approach throughout his career. Ever since his ride in that chicken truck, Kevin Jones has been finding his way forward, one step at a time.

As he continues to reimagine how All Star programs showcase their athletes through All Star Premiers, Kevin remains as passionate about All Star cheer as he was when he first stepped onto that cheer floor in Missouri. He continues to believe in the transformative power of the sport, not only in creating champions but also in fostering character, teamwork, and joy, values he hopes the next generation of industry leaders will uphold for the next forty-four years.

"Success is finding your path." – Kevin Jones

EARNED WISDOM

★ **Success:** Success is finding the path you want to be on and being happy about what you do. When you wake up every day with a purpose, that is success.

★ **Wisdom:** Give back to the industry you love.

★ **Gratitude:** Kevin gives credit to Lance Wagers, who saw something in him when he was a young kid. Lance opened doors for him and supported his outside-the-box thinking.

★ **Kevin's Wish:** Kevin wishes we could bring back some cheerleading fundamentals: Can we get a nice High V?

★ **To My Younger Self:** Do what you love. Love what you do.

★ **Mistakes:** Trying to prove something instead of doing what you love. But it's never truly a mistake if you learn from it.

★ **For Gym Owners:** Don't try to be everything to everybody. Find your lane and stick with it. Don't try to keep up with the people down the street. Do what you're good at.

★ **For Coaches:** Be nice. Find your coaching style and remember to treat your athletes with respect. You'll get more from them.

DID YOU KNOW?

★ Athletes' personal growth and lifelong friendships are Kevin's favorite parts of cheer.

★ Kevin loves to do yard work, and spring is his favorite time of year.

★ Fashion is Kevin's obsession. He has 225 pairs of shoes, fifty pairs of glasses, and about fifty belts.

★ He is an avid bike rider, enjoying both trail riding and Peloton.

★ His favorite superhero is Batman because he loves his mysterious look.

★ Kevin chose the ram as his animal because it symbolizes stoicism, sensitivity, perseverance, curiosity, imagination, new beginnings, change, and life force.

INSPIRE.
INNOVATE.
INCLUDE.

"Winning isn't everything. It's the only thing." – Red Sanders

HILDA McDANIEL
by KENDALL TYLER BATTLESON
Q94 Rockers – 1982

A MOTHER'S DEVOTION

Hilda McDaniel grew up with her two sisters in Richmond, Virginia. Reared by their mother, aunt, and grandmother, the three girls participated solely in ballet. No sports were allowed. Hilda went to college and had a blast, including learning to play the ukulele, but she dropped out after her first year. She fell in love and soon discovered she was pregnant with her daughter, Kendall. She and her partner eloped and married. But a few weeks later her husband was drafted into the Army. It was 1965.

After Hilda gave birth to Kendall, her father gained permission to bring his wife and daughter to Germany. For two years they lived off base while Kendall's father worked as a chauffeur to a colonel. Isolated and unable to speak German, Kendall was largely alone.

Upon returning to the United States, Kendall's father was often unfaithful and seldom at home. As a result,

Kendall was the center of her mother's world. Hilda was an attentive "stage mother," fully engaged in everything, and she always dressed Kendall beautifully. Kendall's tennis shoes perfectly matched her dresses, and her hair was always neatly styled in two pigtails adorned with large bows. Hilda would style Kendall's hair like a doll's and encourage her to put on a performance.

Kendall participated in a range of activities, from ballet to choir. Hilda wanted her to be a star. A neighbor told Hilda that a new cheerleading group was forming and thought that Kendall might be interested in joining. Hilda soon accompanied her daughter to register for the Tuckahoe Tomahawks. Kendall was among the earliest participants to register for Peewee cheerleading.

THE TUCKAHOE TOMAHAWKS

The first year Kendall participated in cheerleading was 1972. Hilda knew nothing about cheerleading, but she was curious, so she brought a lawn chair to each practice and sat on the sideline to observe. During each practice the ten girls on Kendall's team would learn sideline cheers and refine their competition routine. The girls wore black saddle Oxford shoes and knee-high socks paired with their homemade uniforms. Kendall's team sat in a circle and chanted, "We are the Tomahawks, the mighty, mighty Tomahawks!" She said they did that crazy chant and then ran off. The following year, the lady in charge of the program asked Hilda if she wanted to be an assistant. She was at every practice anyway, so Hilda said, "Sure, why not?"

Hilda began to coach Kendall's Tomahawk team, but she also wanted Kendall to be involved in other activities. She saw an ad in the paper for auditions at the Swift Creek Theater for *The King and I*. Kendall didn't know anything about theater, but she sang show tunes in the car with her mom all the time. She stood on stage at her audition and sang "Raindrops on Roses" and bam! she was cast in *The King and I*.

Of course, Hilda attended every practice and observed how the play was staged as the actors sang, danced, and entered and exited the stage. Kendall's role in *The King and I* led to an opportunity at the Children's Theater of Richmond. Once again, Hilda was perched at every rehearsal, learning about staging and choreography. Kendall was cast in a lead role, and she continued to sing her songs on the way home in the car with her mom.

FORMATION INNOVATIONS

Practice resumed with Tuckahoe in the Bird Middle School parking lot. The teams would split into lines and rehearse their chants. Hilda disliked the chants, so she began crafting her own catchy rhymes. She even created her own "Hello" cheers. Hilda aimed to include every girl, so she crafted long lines of pyramids for everyone to join in.

Kendall's acting career skyrocketed. She was cast in productions at Dogwood Dell, Richmond's sprawling outdoor theater, and she was selected to perform in radio commercials. She was having a blast. Kendall's father was usually absent, so Hilda worked forty hours a week in customer service for the phone company. In the evenings she coached the Tuckahoe Tomahawks and took charge as the program's director. Under Hilda's leadership the league expanded to 250 cheerleaders with teams of over fifty girls each. The uniforms remained homemade and featured a sweater vest with puffy white sleeves. Hilda also insisted that every girl wear matching hair ribbons.

Hilda brought her teams to the Eastern Cheerleading Association (ECA) Summer Camp at the University of Richmond, led by Janice Cutler, and insisted that her girls not only wear matching ribbons but also coordinated outfits. At that time no one else was doing that. A large group of Tuckahoe cheerleaders gathered on the campus and caught everyone's attention. Today, a cheerleader wouldn't dream of taking the stage without a bow or a decorative hairpiece.

As the program director, Hilda set to work designing uniforms for everyone. She collaborated with Cheerleader Supply, NCA's uniform company, to create her ideal uniforms. Hilda relentlessly pursued unique designs, determined to get exactly what she wanted. At one point she sought unique lettering that Cheerleader Supply couldn't deliver, so Hilda presented her idea to Varsity, and it crafted the exact lettering she had envisioned. She would constantly go back and forth between the two brands to get the best price for the design she wanted. One year Hilda sought a more affordable uniform for her youth team and asked Cheerleader Supply to add the lettering to the bodysuit beneath the vest—a skirt and a bodysuit—giving rise to the crop-top uniform.

Hilda and her Tuckahoe teams have always marched to the beat of their own drum. They only competed in Richmond, except for driving to Williamsburg, Virginia, once a year. Later, they clinched the national championship with ECA. Hilda crafted unique routines inspired by her daughter's performances on stage, incorporating her towering pyramids and rhythmic chants. She spent her nights drawing on paper to figure out how to move her army seamlessly around the floor. Hilda would kick off her season by covering all the sideline material in two weeks, then she would devote the rest of the year to perfecting competition routines.

As the weather turned cold, the Tuckahoe program was allowed to practice in the middle and high school gyms and auditoriums. As a result, they could practice more difficult routines. Hilda was adored by her girls, but she was tough on her teams. When she said "Get in line!" the girls got in line.

THE Q94 ROCKERS

Kendall was aging out of Tuckahoe, and when she didn't make her middle school cheerleading squad, she insisted she would not try out for the high school team. But Hilda was determined to find a way for her daughter to continue cheering. The stars aligned, and a parent named Jackie Shockley from a younger Tuckahoe team approached Hilda to create a cheer team. Jackie was forming a basketball team of disk jockeys from the radio station where she worked and wanted a group of cheerleaders for those games. In the 1980s almost everyone listened to the radio, because that's where the music was, so the disk jockeys were a big draw. They would go to a local school and play against the teachers for a fundraiser.

Hilda asked if she could choose the cheerleading team.

"Yes," Jackie replied.

"Well, can I pick the colors?"

"Yeah, I don't care."

Finally, Hilda asked, "Can I take them to competitions?"

Jackie shrugged and said, "I don't care what you do as long as you're at the games to cheer for the disc jockeys. And if we do a parade, I need you there for that."

It was 1982, and Hilda had her team, thanks to WRXL Radio and, later, she formed the Q94 Rockers.

Hilda took six girls to NCA summer camp for the first time where she met instructor Don Collins, who also coached the University of North Carolina cheer team. Hilda's squad received an invitation to attend the NCA High School Nationals in Dallas, Texas, so Hilda rented a bus for her team's trip, but the icy interstates were closed, so they had to turn around and go home.

In 1984 Hilda decided the team would fly to avoid icy roads and help guarantee their arrival. For most of the kids, it was their first time on a plane. Passengers smoked onboard, making it a memorable experience, according to Kendall. When they arrived at NCA High School Nationals they watched the teams perform. According to Kendall, the routines were simple: Teams lined up to perform a chant, moved to build a pyramid, returned to their lines for another chant, and then ran off the mat.

In contrast, the Q94 Rockers took the stage like a Cirque du Soleil production with their cheer raps in sync with three high pyramids that transitioned and moved. Everyone was stunned when Hilda's team, with pigtails and ribbons in their hair, won the title in their first year at nationals.

Hilda coached while continuing to work for the telephone company until her retirement. In 1998 she teamed up with Don Collins to launch USA All Stars in Richmond. Don ran the business while Hilda coached, bringing along her 300 Tuckahoe Tomahawks and Q94 Rockers. Kendall coached alongside her, earning the nickname "Mini Hilda."

Hilda and Elaine Pascale became friends and collaborated on designing creative uniforms that eventually were featured in the uniform catalogs.

A GLITTERING LEGACY

Kendall's daughter, Ashton, cheered for USA All Stars until her husband's job took them to North Carolina. There she joined Cheer Extreme, owned by Betsy Smith and Courtney Pope, and cheered in Kernersville for the remainder of her career. Kendall's son, Brennan, even participated on the Coed Elite team for two years and cheered with Derrick "Twist" Brown, a former athlete of mine. Cheer is a vast yet surprisingly intimate world.

Eventually, Hilda left USA and started her own cheer gym called Cheer Factory, adorned in pink and green. Hilda managed the gym and coached until her passing on March 19, 2011. Kendall was heartbroken at the loss of her mother and was uncertain about what to do with the gym. She was unable to run it from North Carolina. Desperate for a solution, she approached Courtney and Betsy: "I have a gym. I don't know what to do with it. It's fully operational. It just needs someone to be Hilda." Kendall entrusted them with the gym, leading to the formation of Cheer Extreme Richmond.

When Hilda coached Tuckahoe and Q94, the teams practiced wherever they could, leaving their awards without a permanent home. When Hilda passed, the trophies were stored in her attic. Kendall recalled the moment she opened the attic door. As her flashlight swept across the space it revealed a room that glittered with trophies—wall-to-wall gold.

"It was like King Tut's tomb," Kendall said.

In 2014 USASF brought Kendall to the Cheerleading and Dance Worlds to honor her mother with the USASF Pioneer Award. Kendall reminded me that I was on stage with her that same year as the recipient of the USASF Dance Coach of the Year Award, again underscoring how small the cheer community can be.

Hilda McDaniel was not just a coach, she was a visionary who transformed cheerleading from basic sideline chants into an art form characterized by precision, creativity, and pageantry. What began as a mother's devotion to her daughter blossomed into innovations that forever changed the sport, from the matching bows adorning every cheerleader's hair to the iconic crop-top uniforms.

Hilda's choreographic brilliance—born from observing theater and sketched out on paper late into the night—stunned the cheerleading world, setting new standards for competitive routines. Yet Hilda's greatest legacy wasn't the wall of gold trophies or the iconic uniform designs, it was the thousands of young women she empowered to believe in themselves.

Hilda built pyramids of confidence, inclusion, and excellence. Her story is a testament to how innovation often arises from unexpected places, in this case from a mother in a lawn chair who wanted the best for her child and, ultimately, created the best for an entire sport.

THE FAMILY CHEERLEADING DYNASTY

Today, Kendall has closets filled with uniforms from every era—Tuckahoe Tomahawks, Q94 Rockers, Cheer Factory, and her children's Cheer Extreme along with school and collegiate uniforms.

A few years ago she returned to Worlds to honor the second wave of Pioneer Award winners. But now Kendall has retired from cheerleading. Both of her children are married but have no children . . . yet.

Over the years, Kendall has been a cheerleader, coach, choreographer, music coordinator, uniform designer, judge, gym owner, and cheer mom. The only role she has yet to experience is that of a cheer grandma, which is coming soon. Her daughter is pregnant with a little girl who will be named Palmer. October will bring the newest addition to the lifelong legacy of All Star cheerleaders in the family.

Kendall has already decided that Palmer will be cheering as soon as she can walk, and she'll be teaching her the perfect High V motion before she can crawl. Kendall is beside herself with joy and can't wait to get back into the gym: "The cheer dynasty is back," she said. "Watch out world, because here we come!"

> **"Success is about standing out, creating opportunities, and inspiring those around you through hard work and determination." – Kendall Tyler Battleson**

KENDALL'S EARNED WISDOM FROM HILDA

★ **Success:** Success is not just about personal achievement. It is about making an impact and paying it forward. It's about the positive influence we have. It's about being confident and unafraid. Success is about embracing the spotlight and using it to inspire and uplift others. Challenge yourself and push boundaries. It's exhilarating. Success can come from daring to be different and thinking outside the box. Push your limits by constantly seeking ways to innovate and excel. Success is being remembered as someone who changed another person's life.

★ **For Coaches:** Continue to innovate. Push yourself to think of things you never thought you could do. Remind your team that they are all in this together. Push yourself to work with what you have. If you don't, you won't be able to create something amazing. "Don't listen to the parents; they are obnoxious," Kendall said with a laugh. "Keep smiling and be nice to everyone."

★ **Lessons Learned:** People often dismiss others before recognizing what they are truly capable of.

DID YOU KNOW?

★ Kendall's favorite part of cheer was the pyramids.

★ Kendall has many favorite routines from the early days of Q94 Rockers, but her absolute favorite routine was her son's Worlds team during his third year with Cheer Extreme when they earned a bronze medal at The Cheerleading Worlds.

★ One of the Tuckahoe Tomahawks' uniforms was among the first batch of uniforms produced by Varsity Spirit.

★ The first Q94 Rockers uniform resides in a shadow box at the USASF office in Memphis, Tennessee.

★ Kendall prefers DC Comics to Marvel. Wonder Woman is her favorite superhero.

★ Kendall has been recognized by the USASF as the first All Star cheerleader.

★ Kendall has been selling SAP services, a German software company for the last thirty-two years. You can find plenty of her interviews on YouTube under SAP PRESS Book Club.

★ She loves fast cars and owns a Maserati.

★ Kendall loves animals and has four dogs.

★ For her animal Kendal chose the goat, which symbolizes surefootedness, stubbornness, independence, diligence, being in the moment, aloofness, virility, and sturdiness.

A Q94 Rockers Cheer from 1989

Irresistible, unpredictable
Q x is x just much too much
Q x 94 x Rockers x x
Do it, do it, do it, do it x x again.

There's absolutely x positively x x no way x
We've seen your stuff it's not enough
We'll blow you x x away!

Hey x what out x
Here we come x
A thrill x a minute x there is no limit x
When it comes to competition x we'll win it!

Celebrate x generate x
Energy for 89 x
Virginia's best above the rest x
Rocker x perfection.

Maximum x potential x
Show 'um we're on top x
Hey x Rockers x
Give it all you've got!

Unique x alive x we'll say it once again x
Q x is no 1 x x
and we will win!

Total devastation x
We're the best in the nation x
Q x 94 xx ready to rock the floor!

"Some days come from the work you do today." – Ernest Hemingway

BILL SEELY
UCA/Varsity Spirit – 1984

FROM BASEBALL CLEATS TO CHEERLEADING SHOES

Bill Seely never planned to become a cheerleader, let alone help transform cheerleading into a global phenomenon. His journey began with a dare—and a cowboy hat.

"I started out as a college baseball player," Seely said with a laugh. "In high school I was a five-sport athlete—track, football, basketball, baseball, and even skiing on the European circuit while attending high school there [in Europe]."

After entering college on a baseball scholarship, Seely transferred schools and had to sit out a year due to NCAA Division I rules. During his break from baseball, an unexpected opportunity arose one night at a restaurant near Winthrop University in South Carolina.

"These girls came up and said, 'Hey, you should come out for cheerleading,'" Seely recalled. It was 1984. Seely and his roommate—another baseball player also sitting out his transfer year—showed up at cheerleading tryouts the next day, though reluctantly and without any preparation. The girls had come to wake them up at 7:30 in the morning.

"I told them, 'Um, we were just kidding. We don't want to try out.'"

But despite his protests, he soon found himself at the clinic wearing cut-off blue jeans, a tank top, white Chuck Taylors, and a cowboy hat because, as he put it, "I had hat hair."

In just one day Seely mastered a toss chair, a "Purdue up" (a now rare stunt technique), a back handspring, the school's fight song, and a cheer. But his jump skills were another story. The judges held their scorebooks in front of their faces, but Seely could see their shoulders shaking. "They were dying laughing," he recalled. Convinced they were mocking him, Seely decided to own the moment: "I ran up to the judges' table, jumped onto it, did a toe touch off the table, and then ran out of the room, screaming, whooping, and hollering."

Seely and his roommate returned to their dorm, certain they had failed the tryout. But when the roster was posted, they were stunned. They were listed as the top two male cheerleaders. There was just one problem: If their baseball coach found out they had joined the cheerleading team, they feared losing their scholarships.

A deal was struck with the cheerleading coach: She would temporarily remove the roster from public view if they committed to attending cheerleading camp in August.

"So we went to camp on August 4," Seely said. "After camp, she offered us full-ride scholarships. I only had a partial scholarship for baseball, so I thought, 'I'm going to be a cheerleader.'"

That fateful decision launched Seely on a journey that would revolutionize both his life and the entire cheerleading industry.

FINDING HIS PLACE AT VARSITY

After attending the 1984 UCA camp at Virginia Tech in Blacksburg, Seely was offered a position as an instructor. He later transferred to George Mason University in Fairfax, Virginia, where he was part of the 1990 national championship cheerleading team while completing his degree in sports management.

During his senior year Seely needed an internship to fulfill his degree requirements. He received offers from Nike, the Boston Celtics, and Varsity. While the first two might have seemed more prestigious, Seely made a strategic choice: "I felt like Varsity was small—really small back then—and I might be able to interact with some upper-level executives," he explained. "I met Jeff Webb at one of my camps, was super impressed with him, and listened to him during our staff training as he talked about how the company was built."

After completing his internship in 1990, Varsity offered Seely a full-time position. His early responsibilities were

"Everything. I stuffed catalogs. I worked out in the warehouse. I managed events. You name it."

It wasn't long before he identified an opportunity to streamline Varsity's business model. At the time Varsity camp staff handled school recruitment for cheer camps, but most staff members were college students who worked part-time for Varsity. Meanwhile, professional apparel representatives exclusively sold cheer apparel.

"I saw it as an opportunity to train our apparel reps on the camps," Seely explained, "since many of them came from the cheerleading world."

Seely's idea was bold, and Jeff Webb challenged him to present it to the board of directors. At just twenty-four, Seely found himself in a high-stakes meeting with influential figures like Bo Schembechler, the University of Michigan football coach, and Roy Kramer, the SEC commissioner.

"I walked out of that meeting with a sweat stain down to my belt loop," Seely admitted. "I was so nervous."

But the idea worked. His initiative to combine camp recruitment with apparel sales helped fuel Varsity's growth, and Seely became the company's first Southeast regional manager, just as cheerleading's popularity was expanding beyond traditional school programs, boosted by ESPN broadcasts.

WITNESSING THE BIRTH OF ALL STAR

As Varsity's school competitions expanded, Seely noticed a striking trend: Gymnastics centers were forming cheerleading teams primarily made up of students who hadn't made their school squads.

"These were the kids that weren't making the team," Seely said of those early All Star teams. "But they wanted to be on a team, they wanted to learn how to tumble and stunt, and so the gym owners put together a team and entered it into competitions."

Those gym-based teams evolved rapidly. "They became more and more of a presence at the events," Seely recalled. "And then they started getting really good. They started gaining crowd excitement, and they started to beat the school teams."

That success created tension with traditional school teams that complained the All Star programs had an unfair advantage by focusing exclusively on competition rather than game-day support and other traditional cheerleading responsibilities. The solution was to have separate competitions for All Star teams, with NCA leading the way.

"NCA was definitely the one that really embraced All Star," Seely acknowledged. "I think UCA, which is what I was a part of, was slow to that party."

As All Star cheerleading grew throughout the 1990s, so did concerns about injury rates. With more athletes participating and attempting increasingly difficult skills, insurance rates for schools began to rise, even though many of the injuries were occurring in gyms rather than in schools.

Simultaneously, the competitive landscape was becoming increasingly fragmented. Kevin Brubaker's CHEERSPORT had introduced a leveling system, but with dozens of event producers each running their own competitions with different rules and divisions, the result was often diluted achievements.

"You'd have maybe fifty teams," Seely said, "and twenty of them would be 'national champions' because there was no one else in their division."

Those challenges—safety concerns and competitive fragmentation—marked a pivotal moment in the evolution of All Star cheerleading.

CREATING STRUCTURE THROUGH USASF

By the early 2000s Seely began to view All Star cheerleading through a parent's lens. "If my daughters are going to be in All Star, and I'm going to watch this as a dad—let's say I don't know anything about cheerleading, but I know sports— how frustrated would I be if there was only one team in her division? She doesn't even get to compete against anyone."

The surge in injury rates and Seely's view of an unsustainable competitive structure convinced him, along with many others, that All Star cheerleading required governance and standardization to thrive for the long term.

"I worked with Jeff Webb and a few others," he said, "and that's when we came up with the idea of creating Worlds and the USASF."

The United States All Star Federation (USASF) was founded in 2003 and launched its inaugural Cheerleading Worlds competition in 2004. Seely was a founding board member who made several key contributions to the USASF.

"I helped establish the USASF—the credentialing program, the mission statement," Seely said. The original mission statement that Seely wrote was clear: "To increase the number of young people benefiting from the positive life experiences of All Star cheer and dance."

The emphasis on youth development highlighted Seely's profound personal connection to sports. "I grew up in a single-parent family. My mom was a secretary, and I know what youth sports does for kids. If it weren't for youth sports, I might not be alive today, as many of my friends from the tough neighborhood in New York where I grew up are no longer with us."

One of USASF's most important early initiatives was the safety credentialing program. Varsity had created proprietary partner stunt progression techniques through years of camp instruction, and under Seely's leadership this valuable intellectual property was disseminated within the broader All Star community to benefit all participants.

"A lot of people had gone through either NCA or UCA training, but there were a lot of people that didn't, and they didn't know about partner stunt progressions," Seely explained. "They didn't know how to take people through the proper stages of learning the skills. And that's where we found the injuries."

The creation of Worlds provided a prestigious end-of-season goal that helped standardize rules across the industry. "Teams didn't have to come up with another routine . . . Some competitions allowed two-minute and forty-five second routines, some allowed three-minute routines, some allowed two minutes, some a minute thirty . . . and so each week All Star teams had to change their routines," Seely said, "which added even more exposure to injuries."

BEYOND VARSITY: CREATING CROSSCHECK

In 2005, despite his integral role at Varsity and his contributions to establishing the USASF, Seely made the surprising decision to leave Varsity. His departure wasn't driven by disagreement or opportunities elsewhere but by a desire to address a pressing community need in Memphis, where he lived.

"The mayor cut funding for the community centers and youth activities," Seely said. "Growing up where I did, I understood how crucial that was for kids, especially those with moms working tirelessly to make ends meet. It's important for kids to have something to do."

So Seely founded Crosscheck, a youth sports organization that provided football, basketball, baseball, and now soccer to young athletes in the Memphis area. The program evolved into the largest youth sports organization in Shelby County, offering structured athletic opportunities to young people who would go without otherwise.

His four-year hiatus from Varsity underscores Seely's unwavering dedication to youth development through sports, an investment that spans beyond cheerleading to include all athletic activities that offer structure, mentorship, and valuable life experiences for young people.

INNOVATING WITH USA CHEER AND STUNT

While leading Crosscheck, Seely actively advanced cheerleading's development. Jeff Webb enlisted him to help create "a national governing body for all disciplines of cheer," leading to the founding of USA Cheer in 2007.

In 2009, after returning to Varsity, Seely became USA Cheer's first executive director and launched two major initiatives: Team USA, the national team program for international competition; and STUNT, a competitive format tailored to meet Title IX requirements in schools.

STUNT emerged as an innovative solution to a complex problem. Despite decades of advocacy, traditional cheerleading has yet to gain Title IX recognition, not due to doubts about athleticism but because cheerleading supports other sports. As I highlighted in my historical analysis, the powers that be dismissed cheerleading as a sport when Title IX was established.

"Name another sport where you have to support another sport," Seely points out. "There isn't one. All sports exist just for themselves. It's just baseball. All they do is play baseball. But traditional cheerleading is part of a school spirit program and has other responsibilities."

Only 20 percent of high school cheer programs compete nationwide, proving that traditional cheerleading's main focus never was competition, an element essential to meet Title IX's definition of a sport.

Rather than continuing the unproductive debate about whether cheerleading was a "real sport," Seely and his collaborators at USA Cheer created something entirely new. Bill Boggs introduced a competitive format centered on head-to-head matchups that assess compulsory skills, awarding points based on objective execution.

"We had to try to come up with something that was more objective," Seely explained. "Whoever performs the skills the best wins the points. It's not a two-minute-and-thirty-second routine; it's a forty-five-minute-to-an-hour game."

This groundbreaking approach has garnered considerable support. STUNT has been officially recognized as an emerging sport by the NCAA across Divisions I, II, and III, and it has already received approval from the NAIA. According to Seely, it's on track to become a full NCAA championship sport "within the next one to three years."

Importantly, STUNT was designed to complement—not compete with—All Star programs. "We wanted it to help All Star gyms," Seely explained. "Kids don't have much to do in the summer, and gyms aren't crowded. We thought a summer STUNT season could be a great offseason option. It would also teach kids to focus on technique and perfecting their skills, which helps reduce injury rates."

LEADING VARSITY SPIRIT TODAY

In 2017 Seely was elevated to president of Varsity Spirit, a role he continues to occupy. Under his leadership the company has diversified its offerings to include band services (since 2019) and yearbook services in addition to cheerleading and dance.

Seely's vision for band programming mirrors what he helped create for cheerleading: reconnecting performance with school spirit and community identity. After observing his son's high school band wearing unfamiliar uniforms instead of the school colors at a football game, Seely recognized an opportunity.

"Kids want to feel appreciated and valued," he said. "When the University of Tennessee takes the field, you're like, 'Yeah, here comes our band.' Ohio State, 'Here comes our band.' We've got to create a band on Friday night where everyone is proud of their school and their community, and the band's a big part of that."

To execute his vision, Varsity acquired a band uniform company, an accessory company, and a plume company (which produces the feathered components of band headwear), creating a comprehensive band division within Varsity Spirit.

HONORING TRADITION, EMBRACING INNOVATION

Throughout his career Seely has championed the need to recognize and celebrate every facet of cheerleading, from traditional school spirit programs to competitive All Star teams and collegiate stunt competitors.

"One of the missions for USA Cheer," Seely said, "and one of the missions for me at Varsity, is to make sure all of those disciplines, one hundred percent of those disciplines, are great for kids."

Seely views different cheerleading formats not as competitors but as complementary pathways that meet diverse needs and preferences. He defends traditional cheerleading's value, even if it isn't classified as a sport: "My experience as a traditional cheerleader is not diminished because it wasn't classified as a sport. I won a national championship. That championship was harder than any other sport I ever played. And I played at the most elite levels."

At the same time, he marveled at the evolution of All Star cheerleading. When All Star began, many teams were just "okay." But now, "They're flipping off-the-charts amazing," Seely said. "It's unbelievable what they do."

With STUNT, Seely developed a competitive format that preserves cheerleading's athleticism while aligning with Title IX and NCAA standards. This inclusive approach—honoring cheerleading's past while innovating for its future—has defined Seely's contributions to the activity that transformed his life. From an impromptu toe-touch off a judges' table to guiding cheerleading's largest corporate entity, his journey reflects the remarkable evolution of the field over four decades.

The five-sport athlete who accidentally became a cheerleader helped transform an activity once dismissed as peripheral into a respected athletic discipline. Under Seely's influence, cheerleading now boasts multiple competitive pathways, international recognition, and ever-expanding opportunities for young people to grow, not just as athletes but as leaders.

As Seely reflects on his own transformation—from a shy college student to a confident performer—he credits cheerleading for the change.

"It was cheerleading that made me face that fear and be able to stand up in front of people and lead," he said. This fundamental aspect of cheerleading—its power to build leadership skills, confidence, and character—remains central to his vision, regardless of which competitive format participants pursue.

Seely, father of four, proudly continues his role as president of Varsity Spirit today. His oldest daughter is an attorney, and his youngest daughter, Mckenna Bray, is an accomplished songwriter with Warner who recently released a new song. His son Hopper owns a local brewery, and Dequan, his youngest son, adopted when the child was eight, works for FedEx. Seely also has five grandchildren he adores.

"Success is making a difference." – Bill Seely

EARNED WISDOM

★ **Success:** You are successful if you have done something to make a difference.

★ **Wisdom:** God has a big plan for all of us.

★ **Gratitude:** Seely said that Jeff Webb was the most influential person in his journey. Webb placed him in situations he wasn't ready for, but it pushed him and accelerated his growth.

★ **Bill's Wish:** Bill wishes he could change all of 2020. He said solemnly, "That was a sad, sad time in my career."

★ **Mistakes:** When you have big ideas, you can share them but be sure to illuminate the path. Don't illuminate the entire path, just the next step, one step at a time.

★ **For Gym Owners:** Surround yourself with people who are smarter than you are and willing to help, people that genuinely care about you and love you, people who will tell you the truth, especially when something is not a good idea.

★ **For Coaches:** Illuminate the next step for your athletes. Be better than you were yesterday, but not as good as you'll be tomorrow. The work is in the day, so do the work today, and you'll be better off tomorrow. Basically, focus on getting better. Don't focus on the result. Focus on getting better, and the results will follow.

★ **Lessons Learned:** Stay on the path.

DID YOU KNOW?

★ Seely's favorite part of cheer is the confidence it builds in participants and the life skills they learn that benefit them long after they leave the sport.

★ Bill is dyslexic.

★ He is terrified of public speaking.

★ Bill got into a lot of trouble when he was a boy.

★ His favorite superhero is Superman.

★ As his animal Bill chose the eagle, which symbolizes divine spirit, sacrifice, connection to the creator, intelligence, renewal, courage, illumination of spirit, healing, creation, freedom, and risk-taking.

"Dream it. Believe it. Achieve it." – Tony Robbins

KATHY GAFFNEY
Clayton Valley All Stars – 1984

THE BIRTH OF WEST COAST ALL STARS

Kathy started as a youth league recreational cheerleading coach. Her daughter wanted to participate, so Kathy volunteered to coach her team. Kathy was paired with an extraordinary fifteen-year-old cheerleader named Diane Ahern. Kathy, Diane, and sometimes Lisa would travel to Southern California to watch cheerleading competitions so they could learn more about cheer. "If I was going to do something," Kathy said, "I was going to do it right." Together they clocked hundreds of hours watching cheerleading and teaching themselves to be the best coaches they could be.

They worked together for several years at Clayton Valley Youth Football in Concord, California, and mostly coached the same group of girls from the age of nine until they aged out. The team was talented and wanted to stay together as they transitioned to high school. Kathy and Diane were the perfect duo, Diane crafted dynamic and creative routines and Kathy drilled them into precision. Kathy said, "My daughter, Lisa, was so sharp and a great example of precision, which helped."

Kathy figured that other sports had all-star teams where the best of the best came together to play, so why not cheer? She decided to start the Clayton Valley All Stars, the first All Star team on the West Coast. According to Kathy, Herkie Herkimer told her Clayton Valley was the first All Star team in the nation, and that is where the name for All Star originated.

Kathy created a nonprofit for the group in 1986, and the team worked hard to fundraise to create opportunities so every girl could participate. "We called it fun-begging," Kathy said. "It was a challenge to explain to people that we were a cheer team that didn't cheer for anyone." They were athletes, but they were not in a traditional sport, so people were not quick to support them.

Kathy made the whole team work together to raise the funds needed to participate, including those girls who could afford it on their own. The team worked hard to ensure the entire team had the funds for uniforms, camp, competition, and travel. Kathy wanted to make sure that every kid who was a Clayton Valley All Star paid nothing to participate. "We fundraised for everything right down to their socks and shoes," Kathy said. "I believe it's why the girls are still close friends today." Through the several conversations we had, Kathy's passion was clear: She poured her heart and soul into her athletes and teams. She wanted to make a difference in her cheerleaders' lives. She wanted to help them succeed.

FROM LOCAL PARKS TO NATIONAL COMPETITION

Kathy, Diane, and the team practiced five days a week, usually at Cowell Park in Concord under the headlights of parents' cars. If the weather was bad, they'd practice in elementary school cafeterias. A few times they even practiced at a local bowling alley. Occasionally, they'd practice at the Concord Naval Weapons Station where the Marines had a nice gym, and they were kind enough to let the team use it when it was available.

The Clayton Valley All Stars attended their first NCA competition at Arroyo High School where they met Danny Kahn, who now owns Cheergyms.com. The team received a bid to NCA Nationals in Orlando, Florida, in 1985. All Star didn't exist at the time, so they competed in the Junior Varsity High School Division and earned ninth place, which was outstanding for a first attempt. Eventually Kathy and Diane added the Clayton Valley All Stars dance team, the first All Star dance team. They competed at Disneyland in Anaheim, California. They won their first year as the only team in the division and returned the following year to face several more All Star dance teams. In true Clayton Valley All Star fashion, they clinched first place again. Kathy sent me videos of her teams to review. Both cheer and dance teams were comprised of tremendous visuals and ripples, all performed with outstanding precision. It was impressive.

Eventually, NCA moved back to Dallas, and Clayton Valley's two routines were scheduled to perform back-to-back. They competed with their cheer routine in one area and had to run next door to an auditorium to perform their song routine. Kathy coached long enough for her daughter, Lisa Gaffney, to graduate and come back to coach alongside her. Lisa's attention to detail and knack for streamlining routines helped the team continue to succeed. Kathy also credits Danny Kahn, Rey Lozano, Bob Gaynor, Ray Jasper, Edd Taylor, and Cris Stuart with providing quality training, choreography, and innovation that helped her team. After a decade, Kathy and her daughter thought they had accomplished everything they had set out to do, including winning numerous NCA national titles, so they decided to retire.

What started as a mother volunteering to coach her daughter's team transformed into a pioneering movement that forever changed competitive cheerleading on the West Coast. Under car headlights and in makeshift practice spaces, Kathy and Diane didn't just build a team, they built a family. The Clayton Valley All Stars defied expectations, breaking new ground in a sport that had yet to recognize the potential of All Star teams.

Though the program ended when Kathy and Diane stepped away, its spirit lives on in twice-yearly dinners where former teammates gather, their bonds undiminished by time. Those reunions aren't just testaments to championship routines or competition placements, they are testaments to Kathy and Diane's greater vision that with dedication, inclusivity, and a little ingenuity, ordinary girls from a few small California towns could accomplish extraordinary things.

Kathy wanted to acknowledge the participants of the first and last Clayton Valley All Star teams, their hard work, and dedication to a sport that was new, different, and not understood. The team that started it all at Clayton Valley All Stars included the following: Shelly Ahern, Lisa Gaffney, Windy Mesquita, Dawn Zelinski, Jennifer Reed, Laurie Knight, Mary Ellen Seigel, Michelle Laidlow, Jennifer Aston, and Danielle Shullaw. The last team, which was a dance team, closed the Clayton Valley All Star chapter and featured Kristen Gandek, Marianne Kasemi, Kari Henriques, Kendra Archie, and Wendy Crabaugh.

> "It's the people who continue to work, believe in themselves, and refuse to quit who find success." – Kathy Gaffney

EARNED WISDOM

★ **Success:** Kathy told her athletes to always do their best: "You can't do more than your best. People are working as hard as you are. It's those who continue to work, believe in themselves, and don't quit who find success."

★ **Gratitude:** Kathy credits Rey Lozano for the team's success. After Diane created the routine, Rey would tweak it. Kathy referred to him as the "greatest innovator of choreography." She also said Rey was kind and helpful as he drove cheerleading choreography to where it is today. She believes he pushed everyone he worked with to be better. Kathy is also grateful for Lawrence

Herkimer and Steve Wedge for allowing her team to compete instead of turning them away. They figured out a way to fit them into their competitions and had the foresight to see what cheer could become.

★ **Lessons Learned:** You can't want it more than your kids do. Your athletes must want it for themselves.

★ **For Gym Owners:** Don't ignore the kids who are sitting in the corner. They can be your stars. Help them believe in themselves.

★ **For Coaches:** Believe in your athletes and teach them to believe in themselves. Don't let anyone tell you that you can't do it. Be honest with your kids. If they don't look good, they don't look good. Tell them the truth.

DID YOU KNOW?

★ Kathy loves to travel, and she previously lived in Wales.

★ She loves German shepherds and has two, one named Hazel and the other Hannah. Hazel's real name is Kissed by Charlie's Angel, but Kathy decided that was a mouthful, so she calls her Hazel instead.

★ Kathy worked in a psychiatric ward at a prison after spending most of her life working with adolescents.

★ Her father died when she was four. He was a paratrooper and was awarded a Silver Star and a Bronze Star.

★ Kathy's favorite superhero is Wonder Woman.

★ Kathy chose the alligator as her animal because it symbolizes maternal instincts, revenge, quickness, aggression, stealth, efficiency, and basic survival.

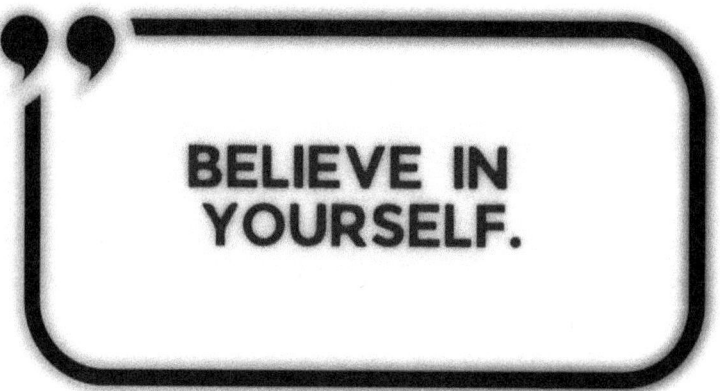

BELIEVE IN YOURSELF.

"You don't grow unless you're willing to step out of your comfort zone." – Regina Symons

REGINA SYMONS
American Cheer Power – 1985

THE HEART BEHIND THE POM-PONS

In the world of competitive cheerleading, few have made as profound an impact as Regina Symons. What started as a teacher's commitment to extracurriculars evolved into a powerful force that shaped modern All Star cheer. Her story shows how a passion for youth development paired with business acumen and steadfast principles can transform an entire industry.

Regina's cheerleading journey started in the classroom. "As a teacher for many years, I became involved in many activities such as cheer, dance, pep and drill teams," she said. "I saw how important those extracurricular activities were to the development of the social part of the individual and to the power they had on developing self-esteem."

Her fundamental insight—that cheerleading offered essential social development—became the cornerstone of everything Regina would later create. At New Caney High School in Texas she led the cheer team, drill team, and pep squad, opening doors for all students to participate, no matter their skill level.

"I think we often forget the importance of those activities," Regina reflected. "As a teacher, I witnessed children from diverse backgrounds, yet they all shared the same desire. They craved friendship and sought approval. Extracurriculars offer kids that opportunity."

FROM SCHOOL GYM TO INDUSTRY PIONEER

Regina's early ventures into competition organizing were modest—just two events per year, typically held in high school gymnasiums or, on one memorable occasion, at Northline Mall. Even then, her athlete-first philosophy was evident. "Most of the money I made went back to awards," she said, noting that she even provided thoughtful touches like corsages for the female coaches.

Those early competitions set the stage for what would become American Cheer Power, originally known as the Texas Cheerleading Association. "The timing was perfect," Regina recalled. "When we launched our company, gyms were just beginning to offer cheer classes and competitive cheer classes. Our business and All Star grew up side by side."

The path wasn't without obstacles. Regina openly recounted the tale of a disastrous early competition at Galveston College where the promised seating and parking failed to materialize.

"What a nightmare! What is it they say about learning from your mistakes? I can honestly say I have had quite a few of those instances," she laughed. "We charged five dollars to get in, and we gave five dollars back as people left when they could not find a seat. I said, 'Well, it's over for me!'"

But her husband, Ron, suggested they consider Moody Gardens as a potential venue. The following year they hosted a successful competition there, and American Cheer Power was on its way.

AN ATHLETES-FIRST APPROACH

What set Regina's approach apart was her unwavering commitment to putting athletes first, a philosophy that fueled key innovations and helped legitimize competitive cheerleading.

"We always had the mindset that the athlete was first," Regina said. "Our goal was to build confidence in every athlete who competed with us, helping them become successful adults." Her athlete-first focus led to a transformative decision to adopt skill levels for Texas. "Not everyone is a Level 5 athlete, and they don't have to be," she said. "This approach is the single biggest reason for the sport's growth."

Going beyond team performances, Regina introduced individual competitions. She believed it was a wonderful experience for athletes to gain confidence. "Can you imagine getting up in front of that kind of crowd?" she asked. Those opportunities helped participants develop poise and self-assurance that would serve them throughout their lives.

She also offered awards to every team. "Each team was recognized on the floor with a trophy," Regina said proudly, despite criticism from some competitive-minded colleagues. She also made a point of recognizing graduating seniors at the final awards ceremonies, complete with commemorative T-shirts, a tradition later adopted by Varsity.

THE ALAMODOME

The turning point for her company's success, Regina said, was a bold decision that illustrates her philosophy of growth through risk-taking: renting the Alamodome for a Halloween competition.

"One thing that brought us into the spotlight was renting the Alamodome for a Halloween competition when we definitely could not afford it. No other company had rented it before, and no one has rented it since. It was the most impressive place I had ever held a competition."

Her willingness to take calculated risks—to step outside her comfort zone—had become a hallmark of Regina's approach: "So if I could offer any advice to anyone it would be this: You don't grow unless you are willing to step out of your comfort zone."

CORPORATE EVOLUTION

In 2008 industry leader Varsity purchased American Cheer Power, but Regina continued to manage the company with her established philosophy. "They left me entirely alone to run my business with the same philosophy I had always had," she recalled, adding with characteristic humor, "even grandfathered in my dog Buddy to take to work every day."

Regina continued until the pandemic of 2020 when industry-wide disruptions and technological adaptations presented challenges. "It was all so fun until 2020 and the pandemic hit," she said. "Was I going to get on a Zoom call? I don't think so! Email me or call me." Her son, Ty, now runs the Southwest area for Varsity, continuing the family legacy in the cheerleading industry.

ADVOCATING FOR THE SMALL GYM

Perhaps Regina's most significant and lasting impact on the sport came through her passionate advocacy for smaller cheer gyms.

"I can say for sure that it was recognizing the importance of small gyms," Regina said. "They are the majority in the sport and, for so long, have been completely overlooked." This recognition led to the division of gyms by size, creating more equitable competitive opportunities.

Regina takes particular pride in her role in convincing Varsity to establish not just a Division I Summit but also a Division II Summit competition. "It took me a long while before convincing Varsity to hold a DII Summit," she said. She believed with her whole heart that every kid was going to be at the highest level. She believed that small gyms have a tough time competing against large gyms. She believed that every gym wanted the opportunity to succeed, not to win every time but to create an even playing field so they had the opportunity to win.

THE BITTERSWEET NATURE OF SUCCESS

In a heartfelt reflection, Regina recognized the irony that the remarkable success of her company ultimately rendered it impossible to uphold some of the elements she cherished most.

"How can I say my biggest regret was my success? No, certainly I can't say that. It was stunning to watch Cheer Power grow into a national company, one that eventually caught the attention of a huge cheer organization, especially considering it was run out of my house for so long."

But with growth came constraints, leaving Regina with little time for the things that mattered most to her as an individual—no time for parent teams, no time for individual competition, and no time for anything extra at awards except handing out the trophies.

A LEGACY OF OPPORTUNITY

Today, All Star Cheer has evolved into a thriving industry with numerous former athletes transitioning into roles as judges, gym owners, and successful professionals across many other fields. Regina's vision of providing opportunities for young people to build confidence, develop social skills, and feel valued has enabled countless individuals to grow, not only as athletes but also as individuals.

Her story serves as a reminder that behind every significant industry evolution are individuals motivated not only by business savvy but also by a genuine concern for the people they serve. In Regina's case, prioritizing athletes wasn't merely a slogan, it was a groundbreaking strategy that transformed cheerleading from a sideline activity into a respected competitive sport that continues to empower young people today.

As Regina herself might say with her characteristic blend of pride and humility, "The sport of cheer can be proud of this accomplishment."

Currently, she is retired in Conroe, Texas, but Regina likes to keep herself busy, so she's involved in community activities and occasionally catches up on cheerleading. She misses the coaches and athletes but is enjoying retirement.

> **"Success is keeping your family together."**
> **– Regina Symons**

EARNED WISDOM

★ **Success:** Success on a personal level must be about family and maintaining unity. As your kids get older it becomes a tough thing to do. Professional success is meeting the challenge and winning. For Regina, the challenge was starting a company in her house and elevating it to a level where athletes were proud to compete in her events and wear their championship jackets.

- ★ **Wisdom:** If it isn't fun, then it's not worth doing.

- ★ **Gratitude:** Regina thanks the coaches for their significant impact on her. They helped her succeed.

- ★ **To My Younger Self:** Never take yourself too seriously.

- ★ **For Gym Owners:** To be successful in business you need to have a good business manager, someone you trust to help you manage your money. Don't let the parents run your gyms. Don't be afraid to step out of your comfort zone.

- ★ **For Coaches:** Love your athletes. Don't look down on your lower-level athletes. Treat each of your athletes and teams with the same respect.

- ★ **Lessons Learned:** Never run from a problem. It will catch up with you eventually.

DID YOU KNOW?

- ★ Regina's favorite part of cheerleading was watching the athletes tumble and dance.

- ★ Her favorite routine was one that included the song "Who Let the Dogs Out," and there were quite a few that did.

- ★ Pyramids frighten Regina.

★ She relocated the Tournament of Champions, which had tanked in Houston, to Florida where it became highly successful.

★ Regina loves holidays—all of them.

★ Her favorite superhero is Superman. (She was afraid to answer because she thought it would reveal her age.)

★ Regina chose the mama bear as her symbol animal for its powerful representation of maternal energy, fierce protection, and nurturing strength. It also embodies courage, resilience, and intuition.

"To thine own self be true." – Polonius in Shakespeare's *Hamlet*

STEVE WEDGE
COA – 1987

WHEN ONE DOOR CLOSES

As Steve contemplated his journey into cheerleading, he remembered his strong aspirations to become a collegiate gymnast. Following high school he enrolled at The Ohio State University with dreams of joining its nationally acclaimed gymnastics team as a walk-on.

"I was a pretty good high school gymnast, but I was not that caliber to be a collegiate gymnast," he said candidly. A fellow club gymnast encouraged him to try out for cheerleading instead, and so he did. He made the team his freshman year and fell in love with cheerleading. Instantly, he had thirteen brothers and sisters.

During that initial year at Ohio State, the cheerleading squad won the Collegiate National Championship, igniting what would evolve into a lifelong passion and, ultimately, a career in competitive cheerleading. While in college Steve began teaching cheer camps for All-American Cheerleading, which was responsible for selecting cheerleaders for the Hula Bowl and, later, for the Pro Bowl.

THE ACCOUNTANT

After earning his accounting degree from Ohio State in 1985, Wedge launched his professional career at an engineering consulting firm. But cheerleading continued to be an integral part of his life as he began choreographing for high school, middle school, and recreation teams on the side.

Those side gigs ultimately resulted in an invitation to join the board of Songleaders and Cheerleaders of America, an organization that sponsored cheer camps and competitions. In 1987 the organization faced a crisis when its president abruptly resigned, leaving the company in financial distress, so the board turned to twenty-four-year-old Steve Wedge. "I was young and had a lot of energy," he said.

Despite having a full-time job, Steve agreed to take on the role. Using his accounting skills, he conducted a forensic analysis of the company's finances and discovered it owed significant amounts to various universities where the organization had held, or had planned to hold, camps. He had to figure out how they were going to pay the schools back with the little money in the organization's bank account.

BUILDING FROM THE GROUND UP

In a remarkable display of determination, Steve successfully organized ten regional cheerleading competitions for the fall of 1987, generating revenue and establishing qualifying events for the national championship in Nashville the following spring. Three of those events were on the West Coast where he encountered some of the earliest All Star cheerleading teams, including Kathy Gaffney's Clayton Valley All Stars.

He often would hop on a plane on Friday evening, fly to California, and host a regional competition. Then he would return on Sunday and be ready for his accounting job on Monday morning.

Despite the challenges, the organization successfully hosted its first National Championship at Opryland in Nashville during the spring of 1988, featuring around forty-five teams. After that accomplishment, Steve resigned from his accounting job in June of 1988 to dedicate himself full time to the cheerleading business, which he rebranded as Cheerleaders of America (COA).

GROWTH AND INNOVATION

Seeking to expand, COA moved its national championship to Jacksonville, Florida, in 1990. "When we moved to Jacksonville, our participation numbers doubled," Steve said, noting that many participants saw "Florida" in the address and were eager to compete there, even though Jacksonville sits just minutes from the Georgia border. The move coincided with the early 1990s explosion of All Star cheerleading, a pivotal moment when the separation of divisions began and demand grew to separate All Star from school cheer.

For COA, the shift was transformative. "The combination of the move to Florida and the explosive growth of the All Star marketing is what made COA grow exponentially," Steve said.

COA brought significant innovations to cheerleading competitions. Around 1992 Steve introduced "category scoring" at his COA events, a concept he adapted from his experience in the high school marching band. Category scoring means one person judges tumbling, one person judges building elements, and another person judges the overall performance. Steve's category scoring approach, which is now standard in cheerleading competitions, was revolutionary then.

COA also implemented safety judges. Teams could sign up for practice the night before a competition, and a safety judge would review their routine to ensure they didn't have any legal issues. The day of the competition, the safety judge would be on the floor during performances to monitor whether the participants' skills were legal under the competition rules.

BEYOND COMPETITION: THE SCHOLARSHIP FUND

While building COA Steve maintained the original Songleaders and Cheerleaders of America as a nonprofit organization that focused on scholarships. The organization has awarded over $400,000 in college scholarships to individual competitors. Eventually, Steve renamed the scholarship program the Shirley A. Wedge National Cheer and Dance Scholarship Fund after his mother who had supported the business in its early days by answering phones while Steve was at his accounting job.

INDUSTRY EVOLUTION

In February 2008, after two decades of building COA, Steve merged his company with JAM Brands. Although Varsity had reached out to him multiple times, including a last-minute offer on Christmas Eve 2007, he felt more at ease partnering with JAM Brands where he had already built relationships with other company owners who had previously merged with them. "It wasn't a financial decision," Steve said, "but rather my instincts told me that JAM Brands was the right choice."

The merger occurred just before the 2008 economic crisis severely impacted the industry, forcing gyms that previously competed ten times a year to reduce their participation to six or seven competitions. Despite the challenges, the company navigated the downturn, and by 2010-2011, conditions had begun to improve.

Steve stayed with the company for three years after the merger before retiring in June 2011. He maintained a 10 percent ownership stake for several more months before selling his remaining interest. COA continued under the JAM Brands umbrella until it was acquired by Varsity in 2015.

RETIREMENT

Now fully retired and dividing his time between Ohio and California, Steve stays engaged with the cheerleading community through his Ohio State endowment fund that offers scholarships to cheerleaders because they still lack athletic department funding, even though cheerleading is now recognized as a varsity sport.

Steve's most meaningful takeaway from his time in the industry hasn't been his own success in business but rather, he said, "What brings me the greatest joy is when I see the influence I have had on others' successes as a result of my time in the industry."

Steve's journey, from a gymnast who fell short of joining the college team to the founder of one of cheerleading's most influential competition companies, exemplifies what passion for cheer and for people can lead to. It also demonstrates how one person's vision and determination can transform an entire industry.

> **"Success is being honest and true to yourself." – Steve Wedge**

EARNED WISDOM

★ **Success:** Be honest and true to yourself, and you will be successful.

★ **Gratitude:** Steve is grateful to the coaches and gym owners who provided valuable insights to help his business grow and improve.

★ **Mistakes:** Not asking for help when he should have. Often, he had many people who were willing and able to help, but he didn't want to ask.

★ **Steve's Wish:** Steve wishes we could remove toxic social media from the cheer community as well as from society in general.

★ **To My Younger Self:** When things seem difficult, trust that you are exactly where you're supposed to be.

★ **For Gym Owners:** Focus on what you do best and keep doing it. You can't be concerned with what the person down the street is doing.

★ **For Coaches:** Be a sponge and learn from the best. That means not only the people in your immediate orbit, but also people from all over. Find great people and learn from them.

★ **Lessons Learned:** Know your limitations and ask for help. Trust yourself.

DID YOU KNOW?

★ Steve's favorite part of cheerleading is watching the seamless transitions that are choreographed flawlessly to the music.

★ His favorite routine was Ohio State's in 1985. "It was the one," he said, "that should have won."

★ Steve was a tumbling field commander in his high school marching band.

- He loves escargot.

- Steve loves to travel because it brings him great peace.

- His favorite superhero is Underdog because he loves a good underdog in life.

- The bee is Steve's animal because it embodies organization, industry, productivity, wisdom, community, celebration, fertility, sweetness, defensiveness, an obsessive nature, and a zest for life. The puma is another favorite because it is a companion on journeys to other worlds and exudes grace and silent power.

"For I'm the Lord your God, who takes you by your right hand and says to you, don't be afraid. I'll help you." – Isaiah 41:13

GWEN HOLTSCLAW
Cheer Ltd. – 1988

PIONEERING COACH EDUCATION

Gwen cheered as a child and continued her passion at Methodist College, now Methodist University, in Fayetteville, North Carolina. After graduating from Methodist College, she became the school's cheerleading coach in 1971.

As the coach she launched a residential camp for cheerleaders that she hosted on campus. During one summer camp she received a call from Charlie Adams, executive director of the North Carolina High School Athletic Association (NCHSAA), asking her to educate coaches.

The North Carolina Legislature planned to involve the state in cheerleading coach education to promote safety. Since cheerleading was not classified as a sport, there wasn't a specific safety protocol, and the NCHSAA recognized that some training needed to be offered to coaches, but they didn't want the state legislature to take control.

In 1986 Gwen hosted the first high school coaches conference at Methodist College with the support of the NCHSAA. That two-day workshop featured fifteen diverse classes. North Carolina had around 300 high schools, and the training attracted over 200 coaches who were excited and appreciative to receive the cheerleading education. Some state legislators attended the conference and informed the legislative committee that the NCHSAA had everything under control.

The following year, Charlie reached out to Gwen again and said, "I just got back from the National Federation meeting. My colleagues in Virginia and South Carolina are excited and want to participate in our conference. Can we expand to include them?"

Gwen agreed, and in May 1987 the conference became the National CheerCoaches Conference. The event was packed with coaches from across the country and from a variety of levels—college, high school, middle school, and All Star. As the conference grew, coaches began asking Gwen to teach camps nationally.

THE BIRTH OF CHEER LTD.

"I was an English major with a journalism minor," Gwen said, laughing. "I didn't know anything about business and, quite frankly, it sounded awful."

She thought she'd rather run through a plate glass window than start a business, but as a newly divorced mother of two she said, "I didn't want to be a bag lady, either. I guess I'll do business."

She had already turned the residential cheer camp at Methodist College into a sold-out event that attracted about 500 campers each year. Gwen launched Cheer Ltd. and started hosting private camps in 1988. As camps expanded nationwide, All Star team programs turned to Cheer Ltd. to bring their private camps to their gyms.

Cheer Ltd. expanded its reach by deploying staff to All Star programs and schools nationwide and by providing customized private camps. Cheer Ltd. and Gwen's residential camps not only honed cheerleading skills but also empowered cheerleaders to see themselves as athletes, a view Gwen strongly held. She believed it was crucial for cheerleaders nationwide to be recognized for their athletic skills.

As Gwen built her network within the All Star community, she launched CANAM, a Cheer Ltd. National Championship in Myrtle Beach, South Carolina, attracting All Star, high school, and college teams for fierce competition.

Numerous industry professionals hail from Methodist College and Cheer Ltd., including Abel Rosa from Premier Athletics and Varsity who is now with Deep South Spirit; Ricky Hill, a renowned coach, choreographer, and judge until his passing in September 2021; Leroy McCullough, head coach of Team USA and the University of Oklahoma cheer; Ben Pope, husband of Cheer Extreme All Stars owner

Courtney Pope; Tina Simms, Varsity Fashion executive; Serena Vance, Team Travel Source; me, Stacy Rowe; and many others.

Gwen is proud of what she and everyone else in the industry have accomplished. "As All Star and cheerleading professionals," she said, "we don't feed the hungry, provide houses for the homeless, or cure terminal diseases. But there's no question that we have enhanced the experience of young people. We have made them stronger and more competent, particularly women. We have made them problem solvers, and there's something very healthy about that."

From a passionate young cheerleader to a visionary, Gwen's journey embodies the spirit she instilled in countless athletes across generations. Her unwavering, pioneering belief that cheerleaders are athletes didn't just change minds, it changed lives. Through decades of dedication she created not just camps and competitions but a foundation upon which young people—especially women—could build confidence, discipline, and leadership skills that would serve them far beyond the mat.

The cheerleading world celebrates her bold leap into the unknown that turned an English major's hesitation into a groundbreaking business that lifted cheerleading to new heights. Gwen's impact still resonates in gymnasiums and on competition floors across America.

> "You are successful if you have found your joy. You can't achieve anything without it." – Gwen Holtsclaw

EARNED WISDOM

- ★ **Success:** Success is defined by joy. You are successful if you've found your joy first because you can't achieve success without it.

- ★ **Gratitude:** Gwen is grateful for her husband, Tim, and his business acumen. The encouragement Tim gave her to move forward and start the business together was exactly the push she needed.

- ★ **Wisdom:** No regrets. Every step is a part of your journey. Most of the time patience is the right decision. Trust in God's path, and He will guide you.

- ★ **Lessons Learned:** The sport would not be what it is today without the efforts of the original pioneers who sought to improve it. Don't be afraid to be the first and to be bold.

- ★ **Gwen's Wish:** All Star grew at a rapid pace, prompting gym owners and event producers to create fair and safe divisions. The unintended consequence of that was the development of too many divisions.

★ **For Gym Owners:** Often remind yourself to look in the rearview mirror. We must all remember where the sport originated. The history of the sport is important for everyone in All Star to know.

★ **For Coaches:** The athletes wanted better year-round training, and the staff provided that. Be sure to deliver.

DID YOU KNOW?

★ Gwen is an extraordinary cook, and she and Tim own a restaurant.

★ Her favorite dishes are ahi tuna with homemade marinade, spaghetti with homemade sauce, and pan-seared salmon with homemade marinade.

★ Wonder Woman, one of the first female superheroes, is Gwen's favorite. Wonder Woman doesn't embody the typical persona of a superhero. She is humble, smart, thoughtful, and always there when you need her.

★ For her animal Gwen chose the giraffe because it symbolizes beauty, gentleness, kindness, and wisdom. It also represents grace, patience, and the ability to see the bigger picture. People connected to the giraffe spirit animal are often seen as gentle, refined, and capable of reaching great heights, literally and figuratively.

"Change the way you look at things, and the things you look at will change." – Wayne Dyer

DAWN DUNCAN WALTERS
CHEERS! Inc. – 1988

FINDING HER PATH

Dawn started cheering in middle school. Although she wasn't selected for the team her first year, she tried out again in eighth grade and made it. During her early teenage years she began coaching in the junior pro leagues in her area, which sparked her enthusiasm for cheerleading. By the time she was sixteen and had obtained her driver's license, she was deeply involved in helping the teams and creating their choreography.

Dawn cheered in high school and graduated in 1983. She didn't participate in cheerleading her senior year, but she thought she might resume her cheer career in college at the University of Kentucky. At that time freshmen were not allowed on the cheer team. But the Dance Cats team had just been established, so Dawn joined the dance team as a freshman. Her cousin, Robert Brown, was an instructor for NCA, and he wanted to help her make the cheer team. They were going to start stunting together but, sadly, he passed away, so Dawn didn't try out.

"Back then," Dawn said, "you didn't train your entire life to become a college cheerleader."

Eventually, Holly Bankemper, the queen of University of Kentucky Cheer, took Dawn under her wing and urged her to team up with a new stunt partner. Dawn described her first day with the new guy as a comedy of errors.

She executed a front up to shoulder stand, also called a Purdue up, propelling her hips so high that she flipped over and landed on the mat, still gripping her partner's hands. She looked up at him and thought, "Yeah, I probably don't need to be a cheerleader."

Her partner pointed out where her feet should have landed on his shoulders, and they both burst into laughter. She tried out, made the squad, and that year marked the beginning of the University of Kentucky's twenty-four national titles.

Dawn was the first to join both the dance and cheer teams. While still in college she launched her first cheer camps with her roommate, Lori Gooch, calling it the Gooch and Duncan Camp. She went on to become a cheer instructor for NCA and began teaching her own camps through the University of Kentucky.

TAKING A GIANT LEAP

After graduation, Dawn's parents promised to help her open a gym if she was ready to take the leap. But she thought she wanted to use her degree in sports information and work for the Southeastern Conference (SEC) instead.

But when Dawn's mom found the perfect location to start a gym, things got real. Dawn was debating with herself . . . Do I get a real job, or do I go out on a limb and start a gym?

Deciding there would always be time for a real job, she seized the moment and launched DD CHEERS! Inc. Cheer and Gymnastics Center in the fall of 1988. (The "DD" stood for Dawn Duncan.) She was about to start a business unlike anything ever seen in Kentucky.

Starting a business wasn't the smooth and easy process she had hoped. The day she was supposed to receive her spring floor, a trucking strike began. As a a former gymnast herself, she knew the value of a spring floor, but it was stuck on a truck in Georgia. She opened her gym anyway with a large exposed concrete square in the middle where her spring floor was supposed to be. But she did have an inground trampoline and an inground pit, and she added a long wooden tumble strip.

She took her first team to the NCA All Star Nationals her first year after being open for only a few months. In Lexington, Kentucky, there was a rule that only one middle school team could attend nationals, but the city had two exceptionally talented middle school teams. Dawn used that rule to her advantage and put a team together quickly enough to compete. Dawn continued to coach and grow the gym for ten years.

In 1992 Dawn was pregnant with her son and had to miss nationals because her doctor wouldn't allow her to travel. She threatened to take a Winnebago because she knew her seniors were going to win. Her junior team had already racked up many national championships. But since she was unable to attend with her seniors, one of her cheer parents called on her cell phone so Gwen could at least listen to the routine. Her junior team won again, but her senior team came in second to Pro Cheer from Kansas, a group with ten guys on the team. The next year the Coed Division was added.

CHEERS! Inc. focused on developing techniques throughout all aspects of a routine. Dawn pushed her teams to be the best in every category on the scoresheet. She was determined to perform every aspect of the routine well. Her teams were known for throwing their basket tosses so high that the athletes appeared to soar into the rafters.

Dawn wanted time to raise her son, so she sold her facility to Brian Elza, but she refused to sell him the name, CHEERS! Inc. (She had dropped the DD.) Brian and Craig Monte assumed ownership of the gym and rebranded it as Kentucky Elite. They owned the gym until the early 2000s when they sold it to Premier Athletics.

Dawn went on to coach the University of Kentucky Dance Team for fifteen years before retiring in May 2024. She continues to evaluate the cheerleading and dance communities while enjoying her retirement.

A LEGACY OF INSPIRATION

From a determined middle schooler who failed to make the team on her first attempt to a pioneering entrepreneur who established one of the first cheer gyms in the country, Dawn Duncan Walters' journey embodies the true spirit of cheerleading—resilience, courage, inspiration, and the ability to lift others.

Her legacy extends well beyond the national titles she won at Kentucky and the countless athletes she coached at CHEERS! Inc. Dawn changed cheerleading in Kentucky from a sideline activity to a respected sport, breaking barriers as the first to participate in both dance and cheer teams and, later, mentoring generations of athletes who would carry on her techniques and passion.

Though she may have retired her official coaching whistle, the echoes of her "Throw it to the rafters!" continue to resonate in gyms nationwide, inspiring young cheerleaders and dancers to push their limits and believe in possibilities that never existed before Dawn dared to dream them.

> **"Success is knowing that I had a positive impact on the athletes I coached." – Dawn Duncan Walters**

EARNED WISDOM

★ **Success:** Dawn believes the relationships she developed with the kids she coached are what define success. She still has relationships with her athletes today. She formed beautiful relationships with the athletes and their parents, and she enjoyed helping others grow.

- ★ **Gratitude:** Donna Robinson, coach of Henry Clay High School and Dawn's cousin, played a significant role in encouraging Dawn to get involved in cheer. Donna shared her love for the sport and helped her learn and understand cheerleading when Dawn was in middle school.

- ★ **Dawn's Wish:** Dawn wishes everyone could keep the kids at the forefront of everything, because "that would be beautiful."

- ★ **For Gym Owners:** Make sure you know all the details required to run a gym. You can't just do it because you love coaching. You need to understand business, the rules, and the requirements. You need to understand parenting today, children today, and all the external factors that are necessary for successfully running a gym.

- ★ **For Coaches:** It's a tough role to be a coach in 2025. Talk to several other coaches who have been there and done that. Be realistic about your responsibilities and what that looks like in terms of your time and sacrifices. Give yourself a few years to stick with it before you give up. Learn and understand the variety of coaching styles. Most important, give yourself grace. You're not going to make everyone happy.

- ★ **Lessons Learned:** You must be true to yourself. Don't get caught up in what everyone else is doing. Do what you know is right, not what you think is going to feel good in the moment.

DID YOU KNOW?

★ Dawn has jumped out of a plane.

★ She's a big-time country girl. She was a pre-veterinary major when she started college.

★ Dawn has been scuba diving with sharks. She's been seventy-five to one hundred feet under the water.

★ Dawn's favorite superhero is Black Widow. She loves her fighting style and all the gymnastics she does. She is Marvel all the way.

★ Dawn chose the dragon and the dragonfly as her animals because the dragon and the dragonfly symbolize change, adaptation, and resilience. They also represent a connection to nature and the ability to see reality.

"Hell hath no fury like a woman scorned." – from *The Mourning Bride* by William Congreve

ERIC LITTLE

NCA STAFF - 1988
USA Staff – 1993
All Star Choreographer – 1996

DANCING INTO CHEER HISTORY

It started with a dare in 1984.

Eric, a naturally creative ninth grader with a flair for performance, found himself swept up in an unexpected proposition—his high school friends thought it would be a great idea for him to try out for cheerleading.

While his friends dismissed the idea as a casual joke, Eric had been quietly captivated by cheerleading since childhood. At nine he had been spellbound by a made-for-TV movie featuring Lauren Tewes from *The Love Boat* as a Dallas Cowboys cheerleader. Around that same time *Charlie's Angels* aired an episode on the kidnapping of LA Rams cheerleaders. Those pop culture moments planted seeds that later blossomed into Eric's remarkable career.

"The first cheer I ever learned was 'Let me see your Frankenstein,' " Eric said, laughing. "I couldn't help but want to be part of that."

When the opportunity to try out for cheerleading presented itself in high school, Eric jumped at the chance. His friends weren't as excited. After tryouts Eric was the only one who followed through when the JV cheer captain called during summer break. Just like that, he became the only male cheerleader at his school.

RISING THROUGH THE RANKS

By his junior year in 1986, Eric's natural talent was impossible to ignore. Though officially part of the JV squad, he was often placed in front of the varsity cheerleaders during games because, as he honestly put it, "I was better than everybody."

That same year Eric attended an NCA camp at UCLA, the largest camp on the West Coast. There he earned the coveted All-American designation. Though he unexpectedly lost the competition in his senior year because of a mistake during his cheer, he gained a valuable lesson in humility. The setback only fueled his momentum.

At just eighteen, Eric was hired by Carol Wagers to join the NCA staff. The early recognition launched him onto a path that would ultimately reshape All Star cheer. While at NCA he worked with none other than Ray Jasper, Morton Bergue, Danny Kahn, Lance Wagers, and Cenie Royal, who became his lifelong friends.

THE DANCE CONNECTION

After high school Eric's journey took him through Riverside Community College and then to Long Beach State University where he began to seriously develop his dance skills alongside cheer. His dual focus became his hallmark contribution to the sport.

The early 1990s marked a golden era for dance in Los Angeles with artists like Paula Abdul and Janet Jackson redefining creative boundaries. Eric fully immersed himself in that vibrant scene, taking classes from renowned choreographers such as Marguerite Derricks (known for choreographing *Showgirls*), Michael Rooney (son of Mickey Rooney), and Jerry Evans (*The Mask, The Scorpion King*). No doubt Eric's choreography was influenced by those amazing teachers. "It was a really good time to be in dance in LA," Eric said, "and I was around all of it."

Eric was nicknamed The California Kid. Although he never flew to the Dallas headquarters, he learned every bit of the NCA camp material, including the dances, which made people take notice and led to his nickname. As a result, he made friends with several USA staffers. After five incredible years with NCA, Eric wanted to focus more on choreography, so he transitioned to the California-based camp company United Spirit Association (USA). Eric continued with USA for eighteen years. He developed their curriculum and taught at their prestigious college dance camps.

BRIDGING WORLDS

In 1996 Eric received a pivotal call from Brad Vaughn of Spirit of Texas, a gym destined to become a powerhouse in the All Star world. Recommended by his friend John Peters, Eric began choreographing for the newly formed program, setting the stage for a transformative chapter in his career.

That same year Eric moved to Miami to assist with Cheer Factory in Broward County, Florida. Although the gym itself didn't last, it became an incubator for what would eventually evolve into two of the most influential programs in All Star cheer history—Top Gun and Miami Elite.

"Cheer Factory started, then Top Gun, and then Miami Elite came from there too," Eric explained. He detailed how Victor and Kristen Rosario of Top Gun and Alex Fernandez of Miami Elite all came from the same network of cheerleaders at Miami Dade Community College.

Eric's unique role as a choreographer with strong ties to both the dance and cheer communities enabled him to bridge the gap between those programs, despite the fierce rivalries among the gym owners.

"I was friends with everybody," he said.

TRANSFORMING ALL STAR CHEER

What set Eric apart in the emerging All Star cheer industry was his ability to seamlessly blend professional dance elements into cheerleading routines. Before time limits were imposed his dance sections could stretch to nearly a full minute of continuous movement to showcase the athletes' performance abilities beyond stunts and tumbling.

Eric's fusion of dance and cheer helped elevate All Star routines to new heights of entertainment and artistry. Programs that embraced this approach—like Spirit of Texas and Miami Elite, which won the first coed world championship—proved that dance could be a powerful competitive advantage in cheer.

Even as the sport evolved and dance sections were shortened, Eric's influence ensured that dance remained an integral scoring component, particularly at NCA events where dance was valued at up to ten points compared to just two points at UCA.

LEGACY AND LONGEVITY

Nearly four decades after that casual tryout in high school, Eric remains a sought-after choreographer in the All Star cheer world. His enduring success stems not only from his technical expertise but also from the relationships he has built throughout the industry. Eric still choreographs year-round.

"I don't know if it's because people just want me around, or if I still have an eye for it," he joked. But let's be honest—he still has an eye for it.

"I still love what I do," he said.

What began as a dare from friends who never showed up evolved into a career that helped shape All Star cheer as we know it today.

Blending cheer knowledge with professional dance training, Eric developed a signature style that has left a lasting impact by transforming dance into a core element of competitive cheer and influencing countless routines along the way.

> "Success is finding joy and happiness."
> – Eric Little

EARNED WISDOM

★ **Success:** Success is finding joy and happiness.

★ **Wisdom:** With time and growth you become better at everything.

★ **Gratitude:** Eric credits the two Brads, Brad Vaughn and Brad Habermel, for giving him his first opportunity in All Star.

★ **Eric's Wish:** Eric wishes we could have one universal scoresheet.

★ **To My Younger Self:** Don't make it about you. It's about the kids.

★ **Regrets:** Being irresponsible and not taking things seriously.

★ **Mistakes:** Missing too many flights.

- ★ **For Gym Owners:** Stay strong and focus on your little ones, because they are your future.

- ★ **For Coaches:** Be patient. Leave your ego at the door.

- ★ **Lessons Learned:** My body can't physically do what it once could. Now it is less about what I can do and more about directing the athletes and painting pictures with their movements.

DID YOU KNOW?

- ★ Eric's favorite part of cheer is, of course, dance.

- ★ Eric loves to cook.

- ★ He enjoys decorating houses. One time he decorated an Airbnb because he thought it was too empty. He purchased paintings, lamps, and other items from Marshall's.

- ★ A good state fair brings him tremendous joy. The Alaska State Fair is his favorite.

- ★ Batman is his favorite superhero because he is mysterious and only comes out at night. He also likes all his cool gadgets and amazing mask.

- ★ Eric chose the meerkat as his animal because it symbolizes community, precise vision, boundaries, liveliness, courage, intuition, and heart energy.

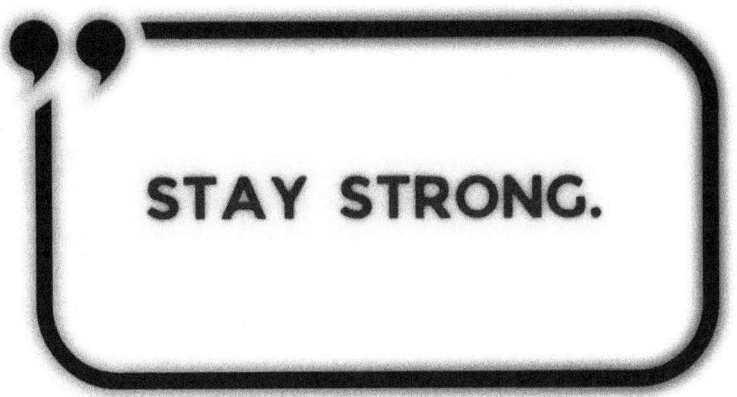

"Humility is not thinking less of oneself but thinking of oneself less." – C.S. Lewis

RAY JASPER

NCA | Choreographer – 1989
Action Spirit – 2015

FROM MARCHING BAND TO MEGAPHONES

From band nerd—his words, not mine—to cheerleading trailblazer, Ray's journey embodies the passion and creativity of All Star. It kicked off in 1988, his senior year at Serra High School in San Diego.

"I was doing back handsprings on the football field," Ray recalled, "and this girl asked me if I wanted to try out for cheer." Ray was quick to say no, because he didn't want to hold pom-pons and shout cheers on the sideline. But he quickly changed his mind when she explained that the team would be competing too. "I had no idea that cheerleaders competed," he said. "I was a band nerd."

That single fact—that cheerleading was competitive—changed everything. After watching a videotape of competitive cheerleading teams, Ray was hooked: "My mouth hit the ground. What is this? Are you kidding me?"

During his high school cheerleading career Ray competed against none other than Eric Little, a cheerleader at the rival high school. Although they were frenemies at the time, they pushed each other to bring the best choreography to the industry and became lifelong friends.

FROM ATHLETE TO COACH

After competing at the NCA High School Nationals in Dallas, Texas, Ray quickly transitioned into coaching when a cheerleader from another school recognized him at a party and asked for his help. He attended a practice to assist the team, which ultimately led to Ray coaching at Madison High School in Dallas. Like any self-respecting cheer coach in the early nineties, Ray took his team to NCA summer camp after his first year where he caught the attention of NCA staff.

"Morton Bergue saw how I was coaching the team and gave me an opportunity. He said, 'Hey, we want you to audition for NCA instructor next year.' I said, 'Yeah, of course I want to be an instructor.' So that's how I got my foot in the door to become camp staff for NCA." Ray worked with NCA from approximately 1990 to 1997 during which time he became a head instructor and built an extensive network in the cheerleading community.

THE BIRTH OF ALL STAR CHEERLEADING IN SAN DIEGO

All Star cheerleading began gaining momentum in the early 1990s when Ray joined San Diego's first All Star team, the San Diego Rebels. His experience and creativity were valuable assets, and he eventually created his own program called Champion Outlaws.

Among his early athletes were the three Emamjomeh sisters, including Tannaz, who later founded California All Stars, one of the most successful programs in competitive cheerleading. The connections and relationships formed during those years created a legacy that continues today.

"I have so much history with the Emamjomeh sisters and, of course, they've gone on to do great things," Ray said. "I got to see all that happen, which was pretty amazing."

HOLLYWOOD COMES CALLING

In 1999 Ray's reputation as a choreographer led to an unexpected opportunity when he was approached to work on a film called *Cheer Fever*, which later became the hit movie *Bring It On*. Despite his initial hesitation, Ray took on multiple roles in the production. He choreographed the routines in the movie as well as consulted. He helped select many of the cast members, because they had to be athletic and know cheerleading: "I was really trying to help them pivot every time they would do something negative or off about cheerleading."

The experience was exhausting as Ray juggled film responsibilities alongside his coaching commitments, but it was rewarding at the same time. The movie was released in 2000 and became a cultural touchstone for cheerleading.

After *Bring It On*, Ray briefly tried working in commercials before returning to the California All Stars from 2001 to 2004. Eventually, he made the crucial decision to focus exclusively on choreography.

ACTION SPIRIT: A NEW APPROACH TO TRAINING

About eighteen years ago Ray founded Action Spirit, a summer camp company that differentiated itself by focusing on customized choreography and training. The company was born from his frustration with teams that were unable to execute his choreography after he left. "A lot of them told me that after I left, they just couldn't hit the routine," Ray said, "or they didn't understand it, or it just wasn't working."

His solution was to create a camp that teaches the necessary skills and drills before the actual choreography is implemented. Today, Action Spirit employs approximately sixty instructors from around the world, including athletes from top college programs such as Navarro College, University of Louisville, Weber State, and Trinity Valley Community College.

BEYOND WINNING: THE TRUE LEGACY

Ray said his philosophy is to emphasize the life lessons he seeks to instill in his athletes rather than focusing on trophies and titles. "I try to teach the kids humility," he said. "I try to teach them that this is a sport and that it's not always going to go your way. It's competitive. You have to remember that it's great to celebrate all the wins, but if you fall short, you also need to acknowledge that." He worries that the modern focus on winning has overshadowed the valuable lessons learned during the journey.

At fifty-five and with decades of experience in the sport, Ray recently achieved unprecedented success at the Cheerleading World Championships with ten of his programs winning gold medals. Yet even in a moment of such triumph he said, "For me, it is about my relationships."

From a high school field in 1988 to the world stage in 2025, Ray's journey showcases competitive cheerleading itself, growing from a niche activity to a global phenomenon while maintaining the core values of creativity, dedication, and connection that make the sport special. His background in band, dance, and cheer gave birth to many of the picturesque routines we have become accustomed to with seamless transitions and levels galore. His creativity has captivated many, and it will surely continue to do so.

"Success is giving your all." – Ray Jasper

EARNED WISDOM

- ★ **Success:** Success is knowing that you've given your all and can walk away feeling proud of the work you put in.

- ★ **Gratitude:** Rey Lozeno, coach of Los Alamedos, has had a huge impact on Ray, along with Dave Marquez, coach and choreographer for Mater Dei.

Eric Little was a frenemy, but now he and Ray are super close.

- **Mistakes:** Reaching a state of burnout that led him to walk away, feeling as though he had burned a bridge or two.

- **Wisdom:** Do not burn bridges. You never know when you might have to work with someone again.

- **Ray's Wish:** Ray wishes that leaders in the industry—coach, owner, or event producer—would remember it's about the kids. It's not about us.

- **To My Younger Self:** Believe in yourself, and don't be afraid of the opportunities that may come your way. Take advantage of every opportunity and enjoy it.

- **For Gym Owners:** Remember, it's a process, and it takes time. Be patient and stay vigilant. You're doing this for the kids.

- **For Coaches:** Know your kids. They are not all the same. Don't generalize. Find out what makes each athlete tick and coach them accordingly.

- **Lessons Learned:** Stay true to your word and build strong relationships. Show grace.

DID YOU KNOW?

PIONEERS OF ALL STAR

★ Ray's favorite part of cheer is everything. He loves creating visual transitions.

★ His favorite routine was CheerForce Nfinity from 2015. The team was so connected, and that's why it's Ray's favorite.

★ Ray played clarinet in his high school marching band.

★ He was in *Bring It On* and performed with the Clovers and the Toros when an actor didn't show up.

★ Ray loves to shop.

★ His favorite superhero is Wonder Woman because he loves strong women.

★ The dolphin is his animal because it embodies harmony, balance, and playful joy, symbolizing the connection between intellect and instinct. Dolphins are also associated with protection, resurrection, and the importance of approaching life with humor. Dolphins also encourage teamwork, mutual support, and compassion.

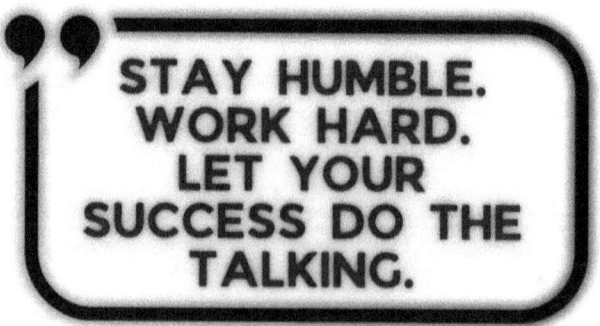

> STAY HUMBLE. WORK HARD. LET YOUR SUCCESS DO THE TALKING.

"The most beautiful thing you can wear is confidence."
– Blake Lively

DANNY KAHN

Diablo Valley Hawks – 1989
Pyramids Cheerleading Studio,
Cheergyms.com – 1995

THE ACCIDENTAL BEGINNING

Danny Kahn was a high school cheerleader at the NCA High School Nationals in 1985 when he bumped into Kathy Gaffney and the Clayton Valley All Stars. Realizing they were from the same general area, Kathy asked Danny if he'd be interested in helping her team. That's how Danny started coaching with the Clayton Valley All Stars where he stayed until approximately 1989 when he started his own team, the Diablo Valley Hawks. In only their second year, his team won the NCA All Star Nationals.

Danny continued to coach the Diablo Valley Hawks while teaching NCA summer camps for several years. Then he figured it was time to get a real job. But he was drawn to All Star, like so many others in the sport, and he couldn't walk away. As a result, he partnered with

Morton Bergue to open his first official All Star location in 1995, the Pyramids Cheerleading Studio.

The beginning was a struggle for Danny and Morton because they had to endure being among the first to educate people about what All Star competition was. There were no clear examples to point to, not just within cheerleading but anywhere. Club soccer was just emerging, and indoor basketball facilities didn't exist. Some parents even dismissed Pyramids Cheerleading Studio as nothing more than a glorified youth recreation program.

On the other hand, Danny said, "It was great fun." The kids were passionate, fully dedicated to building their teams and perfecting their routines. There was a unique excitement back then. Their teams won most of the competitions, but then they didn't face many quality opponents, often performing exhibitions because there simply weren't enough local teams to compete against.

BUILDING A BUSINESS

From the start, Morton and Danny chose to open a standalone facility, a bold move at the time. Not long after, many All Star programs began springing up within local gymnastics centers.

Danny didn't marry until the age of forty because he was immersed in coaching, dedicating every minute of every day to his teams. Coaching wasn't just a job for Danny, it was an all-consuming passion. But the sport itself eventually pushed him away as Danny struggled to keep up with the overwhelming inconsistency in levels, divisions, and rules. He laughed and said, "I blame Kevin Brubaker for that."

Trying to run a successful business and coach successful teams was far more challenging than Danny had anticipated, and he felt like he couldn't do both. Today, you practically need a PhD in All Star cheer to keep up with the rules and scoring.

Danny believes he coached during the golden era of All Star cheer, a time when the rules were simple—no stunts higher than two bodies and no trampolines. Beyond that, anything was fair game. Each team had its unique choreography and music, creating a diverse and innovative landscape.

A look of nostalgia softened Danny's face as he reminisced: "Do you remember sitting at NCA Nationals or Worlds and someone would say, 'Let's go get a hot dog'? The first thing you'd do was pull out your schedule, look down the list of teams, and say, 'Okay, after Stingrays.'"

The excitement of that is gone in today's All Star, because there isn't a team you can't see on YouTube. And there isn't as much surprise in the routines.

"Back then, you knew you were going to get something different from World Cup, something different from Stingrays, something different from Cheer Athletics, something different from Georgia," Danny said. "You knew you were going to see something that was just them, uniquely theirs. But now, it's all pretty much the same."

Today it feels like hardly anyone is paying attention when a team is performing. The fans of the team crowd into the priority viewing area to scream and cheer, but the rest of the spectators mostly seem uninterested.

Danny and Morton launched several locations, each sporting a unique name. They even met with Boog Potter and Mike Martinez of Premier Athletics with the idea of creating a corporate umbrella for all their websites.

As a result, in 2002 the corporate umbrella name Cheergyms.com was created. Social media was new and nowhere near the powerful marketing tool it is today. But websites were the hot item for promoting your business, so Danny thought Cheergyms.com would be a smart name during the dot-com boom.

Danny's innovative coaching and entrepreneurial spirit helped legitimize All Star cheerleading as both a competitive sport and a thriving business. His journey mirrors the evolution of the sport itself, from informal beginnings to structured competition. Yet his nostalgia for the days of unique routines and genuine spectator excitement serves as a poignant reminder of cheerleading's roots.

Though the sport eventually evolved beyond what Danny wanted to pursue as a coach, his legacy endures through Cheergyms.com and the countless athletes whose lives he shaped.

Danny and Morton still own the original Cheergyms.com gym along with Regina Kahn (Danny's wife) and Derick

Patterson. The business operates in the original building constructed thirty years ago. They currently have nine competitive All Star teams, over one hundred students, and train more than twenty school teams each year.

Danny and Regina have three children and one granddaughter.

> **"Success is being happy." – Danny Kahn**

EARNED WISDOM

★ **Success:** When Danny started pyramids, his mom gave him a mug that said, "Do what you love. Love what you do!" He's carried that saying throughout his life. If you work in cheerleading, you may not always have a lot of money, but you do it because you love the sport. Business ownership has its ups and downs, but you're successful when you find happiness through it all.

★ **Gratitude:** Danny credits Rey Lozano with getting him interested in cheerleading, first as an athlete and then as a coach and choreographer. Danny believes Rey was ahead of his time, and he says he learned a great deal from him. Danny also spoke highly of Victor Rosario for bringing so many innovations to the sport. Remo Medrano was his choreography partner for five successful years and, according to Danny, was one of the most innovative geniuses in cheer history. Two individuals who also deserve a ton of credit for their contributions to All Star Cheer in California are Ed Mari and Ronald Buccat. As leaders of The San Diego All Stars (1989-1999), their innovation was groundbreaking and highly underrated.

★ **Danny's Wish:** Danny wishes we could go back to the time when competitions provided special experiences. Each event producer had a different flair, creating unique experiences for the athletes. It was a time when event producers knew their customers and built relationships with them.

★ **To My Younger Self:** Ask for help. Although businesses like MotUS weren't around back then, you could have asked for help along the way.

★ **Mistakes:** Doing simple, ignorant math. For example, Danny thought if his rent was $3,500, all he needed was thirty-five All Stars paying one $100 each to cover the bills. Any smart owner knows that is naïve math.

★ **For Gym Owners:** Get help from experts like you find within MotUS, even if you think you know it all. Avoid making mistakes by getting help. Don't reinvent the wheel. There are many resources available now, so use them.

★ **For Coaches:** Open your eyes to the fact that you can learn something from anyone, no matter their age or experience. Never stop trying to learn. Ask yourself often, "Why am I doing this?" Do you want to be recognized as one of the best coaches? Do you want to support the growth of young athletes? What's your why? There's no right or wrong answer, but be honest with yourself and your employers about your reasons.

DID YOU KNOW?

★ Danny's favorite aspect of cheer is the ability of a choreographer to create a routine that ignites the crowd.

★ His favorite routines of all time were the 1992 North Garland High School team at NCA and the 2007 Top Gun Large Coed team at Worlds.

★ Danny played the accordion when he was six.

★ He didn't have his first child until he was forty-one.

★ Danny hasn't lived in the same house or apartment for more than four years, except for his childhood home.

★ Danny's favorite superhero is Batman. He wasn't much of a superhero guy, but he loved the Michael Keaton Batman movies.

"Let your faith be bigger than your fears." – Unknown

AMY TYLER
By ANNA LOVE LOGAN
Greensboro All Star Cheerleading – 1989

THE BIRTH OF A LEGACY

GAC wasn't always the resolute gym it is today. Founded by Amy Tyler in 1989, the gym had humble beginnings with practices held wherever space could be found—school gymnasiums, church fellowship halls, or the YMCA. Anna Love, with a hint of nostalgia, said, "I competed on quite a few wrestling mats myself. I remember how excited we were to get seven panels of carpeted foam!"

Before adopting the now-iconic blue and gold that define GAC, the gym operated under various identities. First, it was the Triad Tigers before becoming the Elite Spirit (which explains why the World's team is still called Elite today).

THE APPRENTICE

The wrestling mats were like concrete beneath her feet, nothing like the spring floors of today. It was 1997, and Anna Love had just been thrust into the world of All

Star cheer after another athlete had unexpectedly quit the team. "The coach asked if I could fill in for the first competition that was coming up," Anna Love recalled, the spark in her voice still evident decades later. "And that was it. I was hooked!"

Anna Love had grown up as a dancer and a swimmer before discovering cheerleading in middle school. Her younger sister had joined Greensboro All Star Cheerleading (GAC), which led Anna Love to take private tumbling lessons. But little did she know that one fill-in performance would change the trajectory of her life.

After competing at GAC from 1997 to 2000, Anna returned as a coach in 2002 while studying at the University of North Carolina at Greensboro. "I was so thankful that Amy provided me a chance to work at the gym," she said.

Following her college graduation in December 2005, Anna Love began working full-time at the gym alongside Amy, learning the intricate details of running a successful cheer program. The transition of leadership happened gradually, with Amy slowly stepping back while encouraging her protégé to move forward.

"In 2009 Amy sold GAC to me and some amazing business partners, Tricia Fodel and Cindy Ellis," Anna Love said. In 2016 Anna Love took the ultimate step by becoming the sole owner of GAC, carrying forward a legacy that had begun nearly three decades earlier.

"I continue to lean on Amy for advice and guidance after all of these years," Anna Love said. "She is a fantastic mentor and leader."

Today, GAC celebrates thirty-five years of excellence with fourteen teams spanning ages three to nineteen, including an exceptional athletes' team, a testament to the gym's commitment to inclusivity and growth.

LESSONS IN LEADERSHIP

What makes GAC special isn't just its longevity, it's the family atmosphere that permeates every aspect of the organization. Anna Love's family remains deeply involved in daily operations. Her mother works in the office, her sister runs the special needs program, and her father can often be spotted on the riding lawnmower, keeping the grounds in pristine condition.

Perhaps most telling is that they have ten coaches, including Anna herself, who were athletes in the program. "GAC is truly a family," Anna said, "and is built inside our four walls from the ground up."

This family commitment extends to her personal life. Phil Logan and Anna Love, longtime industry friends, now happily share a life and family as husband and wife. Anna Love's dedication runs so deep that, after marrying Phil, she relocated to Virginia, but she continues to make a weekly three-hour commute to Greensboro to lead the program she is passionate about.

A LOOK BACK

As the torchbearer of one of cheerleading's original programs—the first cheer gym in North Carolina and one of the first in the nation—Anna Love views her impact on the sport as "a continued legacy of an original in this sport." Looking back on her journey from fill-in athlete to gym owner, she reflects on the honor of walking alongside those she once coached, watching them grow in new ways and contribute not only to GAC but to the sport as a whole. She is proud of the regional and national accolades GAC has collected, including those earned at The Cheerleading Worlds over twenty-plus years.

The floors may have changed from wrestling mats to spring floors, but the spirit of GAC—built on family, consistency, and heart—remains as strong as ever, ensuring that GAC will continue to inspire for generations to come.

> **"Success is providing a safe space for athletes to grow physically, mentally, and emotionally." – Anna Love Logan**

★ **Success:** Watching your athletes achieve great things outside of cheer, knowing that you helped mold them into strong, independent, and caring individuals. When they continue to come back year after year to support the gym and even bring their own children to GAC, that's success.

★ **Gratitude:** Anna Love is especially grateful to Amy Tyler for entrusting her legacy to her. She said there are not enough words in the English language to express her appreciation and gratitude for Amy, who taught her so much about the sport and about life. Anna Love is also tremendously grateful to many amazing coaches and industry leaders who helped her and who continue to help guide her path.

★ **Mistakes:** Allowing the fear of failure to guide decisions and comparing herself to others rather than standing on the confidence of her choices.

★ **For Gym Owners:** Don't quit. Gym ownership can be a heavy load, but don't give up. Always offer the best version of your product that you can.

★ **For Coaches:** Be consistent, especially with your coaching, standards, and rules. Coach from the heart and with love, and you will always get the best out of your athletes. Also, don't get involved in drama. Stay professional.

★ **Lessons Learned:** You cannot please everyone. You can only make the best choices for yourself, your team, and your gym.

DID YOU KNOW?

★ Anna Love's favorite part of cheer is watching the athletes compete on stage. She said there's nothing better than seeing the athletes' pride that comes from hard-earned success. She also values the lasting relationships formed with athletes, families, and fellow coaches.

★ Her favorite routine was the Georgia All Stars Large Coed Team's doctor theme from the early 2000s.

★ Spending time with her family is Anna Love's favorite pastime.

★ She's a huge college football fan.

★ Anna Love enjoys traveling to new places.

★ Her favorite superhero is Spider-Man for his integrity, humor, and determination to help others. Plus, he's her son's favorite.

★ The wolf is her animal because it represents loyalty, perseverance, success, intuition, spirit, and an appetite for freedom, but it also can be a loner.

"You can't control everything that happens to you, but you can control how you respond to it." – John Wooden

JOHN NEWBY
Varsity Spirit – 1990

FROM CHEER UNIFORMS TO EXECUTIVE

John Newby didn't set out to become a cheerleading executive. He was working a management job in textiles near Clemson, South Carolina, when his wife, Mary, made a career move that changed everything. Mary was a high school math teacher and cheerleading coach at Walhalla High School when she quit those jobs to focus on selling uniforms for Varsity.

"All I knew was she spent a ton of money on gas and travel all over North and South Carolina," Newby said with a laugh. "She kept telling me, 'Just trust me. This is going to work out. This is a bigger opportunity than teaching school.'"

When Mary showed John her first commission check—roughly equal to what she made teaching—he was convinced. She was named Rookie of the Year and, before long, John quit his job and joined her to become a sales representative for Varsity. Together they covered the Carolinas. It was 1990, and neither could have predicted where their new career path would lead.

THE "WAIT, WHAT IS THIS?" MOMENT

Around 1992, while making their typical rounds to high schools, Newby encountered something different in Goose Creek, South Carolina. A mom whose daughter hadn't made her school's cheer team started her own All Star program at a local gym by recruiting kids from multiple schools around the low country.

"At the time we had youth recreational cheer," Newby said, "and we had high school and junior high, but that was really the first time I heard about All Star in our territory."

Soon, up in North Carolina, Charlotte Allstar Cheerleading became one of his biggest accounts, introducing him to the fledgling All Star world. What he didn't know then was that All Star cheer would eventually transform the entire industry and, with it, his career.

By 1993 Newby and other uniform sales reps had compiled a list of customer service headaches that needed to be addressed: shoe inventory problems, late uniform deliveries, and return issues. They nominated Newby to present the list to Jeff Webb, Varsity's founder, and his right-hand man, Kline Boyd.

Rather than getting defensive, Jeff and Kline looked at each other and said, "Yeah, those are all problems we need help in fixing. Why don't you and Mary move to Memphis and help us fix them?"

By 1994 the Newbys had packed up their three kids and relocated to Memphis where John stepped into operations management. He moved through various positions, including vice president of sales for Varsity Spirit Fashion. Then, around 2000, Webb approached him with a surprising offer.

Bill Seeley had decided he was going to start a youth sports nonprofit ministry in Memphis. Jeff's brother, Greg, decided to pursue other options, which created space for new opportunities.

"Jeff Webb came into my office one day," Newby said, "and asked me if I would consider taking over UCA." Despite never having been an instructor himself, Newby took over the UCA division, the summer camp business that was Varsity's original foundation.

EYE-OPENER: THE NCA ACQUISITION

In 2004 Varsity acquired its longtime rival, the National Cheerleaders Association (NCA). The purchase proved pivotal in opening Varsity's eyes to the potential of All Star cheerleading.

"NCA was way ahead of where we were in All Star at the time," Newby admitted. "There was such a rich tradition and commitment to the school space on the Varsity side that All Star was growing around us. NCA was kind of our first real recognition that All Star was here to stay."

The truth was more complex than a simple oversight. When asked whether Jeff Webb was anti-All Star, as some have suggested, Newby clarified the situation: "Jeff wasn't, but there were people inside Varsity that were anti-All Star. They saw All Star as a threat."

Meanwhile, NCA had embraced All Star cheerleading to differentiate itself in a market where Varsity was focused. "NCA was struggling," Newby said candidly. "All Star was an opportunity to set itself apart. And to its credit, All Star did just that."

NCA's approach influenced the style and composition of All Star routines, emphasizing dance elements and musical integration that would become hallmarks of competitive All Star cheer.

Once Varsity recognized All Star cheerleading's staying power, it moved quickly. Rather than building its own events from scratch, it acquired established companies that were familiar with the space.

"All Star was the wild west—anything goes," Newby said. "Divisions, rules—there were hundreds of national championships. We realized we couldn't just enter the space by creating our own events. There were already experts out there."

Newby became the first general manager of Varsity All Star around 2008-2009 and was tasked with creating a cohesive strategy for the newly acquired companies that had previously competed against one another.

When Bill Seely returned to Varsity, he took over the summer camp business. By then Varsity owned NCA, ACA, USA, and UCA. Seely worked to create cohesion among the camp brands while Newby focused on building an All Star team to develop a strategy for what Varsity would do with all the companies they had acquired.

THE VARSITY FAMILY PLAN

One of Newby's initiatives was the development of what became the Varsity Family Plan. The concept came directly from gym owners in the Premier Network who identified their biggest challenge: survival during the summer.

"The original purpose behind the Family Plan and the rebate," Newby said, "was centered around feedback from Premier Network Gyms that said they struggled financially during the summer."

Instead of offering discounts throughout the season, the program provided end-of-season rebates that helped gym owners keep their lights on during the summer when recreational participation declined significantly. It became a game-changer for gym sustainability.

THE SUMMIT: JOHN NEWBY'S LEGACY MOMENT

Perhaps John's most lasting contribution came from an insight that was both professional and personal. His daughter cheered for a Level 3 team at Memphis Elite because she didn't have the tumbling skills to advance to Level 5. This fact raised a crucial question: Why would athletes continue in All Star cheer if they couldn't reach the pinnacle event, The Cheerleading Worlds?

Working with Dennis Worley and Damianne Albee Steward, Newby developed a championship for teams that didn't qualify for the World Championships. When presenting the idea to Jeff Webb, Newby acknowledged that it was a huge financial gamble. Jeff thought for a moment and asked, "You really think this is going to work?"

"Jeff, I one hundred percent think it's going to work."

"Let's do it," Jeff said.

The first summit in 2013 faced challenges, including rain and lightning that forced the evacuation of competition tents. Newby vividly recalls Dennis Worley running between venues in the downpour, clutching an orange dress shirt.

Despite the weather drama, The Summit succeeded beyond expectations, evolving into a prestigious championship that spawned the Dance Summit in 2014 and the DII Summit for small gyms soon after.

When asked about Varsity's contribution to All Star cheerleading, Newby focused on its structure and legitimacy: "Our focus and commitment were on safety and trying to take a sport that was young and growing and organize it into a more legitimate sport than it was at the time."

Working with the USASF, Varsity, and other gym owners and event producers was crucial in establishing rules, safety measures, and division guidelines that provided structure and legitimacy.

Those efforts helped transform the wild west of All Star cheer into a more structured activity with clearer standards while creating career paths for athletes beyond their competitive years—as coaches, choreographers, music producers, and gym owners—and helping build All Star into a worldwide sport through connections with Disney, ESPN, and the founding of the US All Star Federation (USASF).

"My most significant legacy is probably leading the creation of The Summit," Newby said. "I believe that event helped spur growth in the industry and created opportunities for kids who, perhaps, didn't have the tumbling or building skills to reach Level 5 at the time, now Level 6. Those athletes are talented and deserve a chance to earn bids to Summit and go up against the best teams in their divisions from across the US and, now, the world."

Today, Newby is executive vice president and general manager of operations for events and camps at Varsity Spirit. He and Mary have been happily married for thirty-seven years. They have five daughters and eight grandchildren with a ninth on the way.

"Success is defined by achieving your goals."
– John Newby

EARNED WISDOM

★ **Success:** Success depends on how each person defines it for themselves and what their goals are. Success is achieving those goals.

★ **Wisdom:** The Duke University women's basketball coach said, "Things are going to happen to you, and it's never going to get easy. You just have to get better at handling hard."

★ **Gratitude:** Newby credits several people with having a significant impact on his journey: Jeff Webb for his evolving vision, recognizing All Star's potential, and elevating everyone around him; Jim Chadwick and the work he did to build the USASF; and Mike Martinez, Boog Potter, and Cole Stott for teaching the industry about hospitality and relationships in the All Star space. Newby also credits Jim Thorpe and Jeff Fowlkes with teaching him life lessons and Don Collins for being a breath of fresh air and daringly creative.

★ **Newby's Wish:** He wishes we could have a stricter image and appearance for All Star. If All Star is ever going to be in the Olympics, a more athletic look would be beneficial.

★ **Mistakes:** Throughout most of Newby's career he was successful in leading teams, building brands, creating cohesion, and developing innovations. When he took a new role with Herff Jones in Indianapolis, he inherited issues that cost the company a significant amount of money. That experience was the most humbling of his career and shaped who he is now.

★ **For Gym Owners:** Focus on developing all aspects of the young athletes in your care. Be patient.

★ **For Coaches:** Be kind. Kids are motivated by different things. Try to learn what each kid needs and how each kid is driven so they can get the most out of their talent and skills.

★ **Lessons Learned:** There are two sides to every story. Be sure to hear both sides before you react.

DID YOU KNOW?

★ Newby's favorite part of cheer is the pyramids. He loves the creativity, building, and teamwork it takes to nail a pyramid section.

★ Newby played defensive back and, occasionally, wide receiver in college.

★ He's the youngest of four children and has three older sisters.

★ Newby has five daughters and eight grandchildren.

★ His favorite superhero is Superman, because he'd love to fly.

★ For his animal Newby chose the eagle, which symbolizes divine spirit, sacrifice, connection to the creator, intelligence, renewal, courage, illumination of spirit, healing, creation, freedom, and risk-taking.

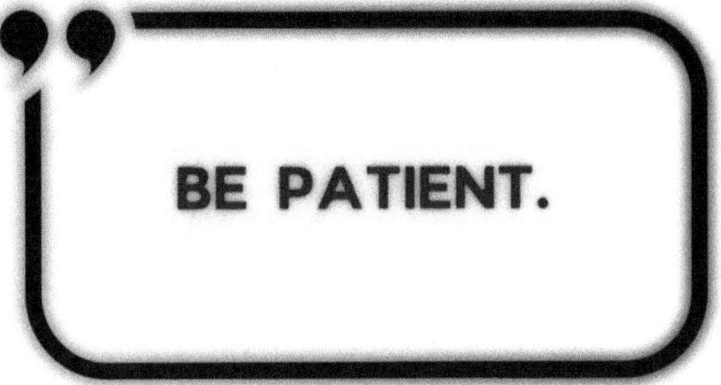

"The best predictor of future success is past success."
— Proctor & Gamble

JIM CHADWICK
NCA & VARSITY – 1990
USASF – 2003

AN UNLIKELY CHAMPION

Jim Chadwick didn't follow a traditional path to cheerleading leadership. "I was a Navy pilot and flew attack, close air support in Vietnam," he said. "When I got out, I went to work for Procter & Gamble as a brand manager. Later, I worked for PepsiCo in various roles before moving on to Seagram."

Jim's corporate and military background seem a universe apart from cheerleading mats and competition venues. But his connection to cheerleading ran deeper than most understood. He had been a cheerleader at the University of Utah in 1966, and his uncle was none other than Lawrence "Herkie" Herkimer, the man widely credited with founding cheerleading.

"I always thought cheerleading was a sport, a legitimate sport that deserved recognition," Jim said. "My uncle, Lawrence Herkimer, who started everything, viewed it as a business. He took cheerleading from being a backyard activity to a legitimate enterprise, but I never felt he took the next step." To Jim, cheerleading was more than just a business, it was a sport with untapped potential.

His conviction—that cheerleading deserved to be treated as a legitimate sport—would drive Jim's most significant contributions to the All Star cheerleading industry.

FROM CORPORATE AMERICA TO CHEERLEADING

After decades in corporate roles, Jim was working for Seagram in New York when an unexpected opportunity emerged. The company that bought NCA was headquartered just blocks from his office. That twist of fate gave Jim the chance to chat with the new owners. As a result, he traded his corporate life in New York City to join NCA in the early nineties. "It was time for me to leave that phase of my life," Jim said, "which was marketing, and go back to cheer and do something that needed to be done."

The timing was perfect because NCA was struggling financially under its new ownership. "It [NCA] was an airliner that had lost all of its engines," Jim said. "It was heading straight for the ground at warp speed."

Drawing on his marketing expertise, Jim helped keep the plane in the air. Eventually, NCA was sold to Randy Best & Associates, a merchant banking firm from Houston. During that transition, Jim observed the early development of All Star cheerleading. He recognized that Lance and Carol Wagers' Cheerobics gym—one of the earliest All Star programs—was primarily "a way for them to employ their staff during the offseason so they could employ them year-round."

But Jim saw greater potential in this emerging segment of the industry. He told Randy Best, "I really think All Star is going to be big." Jim believed All Star cheerleading had staying power. Unlike traditional cheerleading, which was often dictated by the preferences of individual counties, All Star had its own vision, one driven by creativity, competition, and athlete development.

Jim's comparison encapsulated the artistic and athletic essence of the evolving nature of All Star cheerleading: "I basically explained to them that All Star was like Cirque du Soleil."

THE VARSITY YEARS

After leaving NCA in 1996 due to disagreements with Randy Best over business practices, Jim joined Varsity, which was primarily focused on school cheerleading. As a senior vice president, Chadwick became a relentless advocate for greater investment in All Star cheerleading. During every meeting focused on the business's growth for the upcoming year, Chadwick sat in the back of the room, rooting for All Star.

Finally, Jeff Webb, Varsity's founder, asked Jim directly how he would like Varsity to become more involved in All Star cheer. Jim responded by requesting three months to develop a plan.

During that time Jim conducted an extensive tour of All Star gyms across the country, beginning with Morton Bergue on the West Coast. What he observed was a rapidly growing segment of cheerleading that lacked structure and standardization, a situation that many in the industry called the wild west.

All Star cheer had reached a point where its continued growth required standardization. "If All Star is really going to grow," Jim said, "you can't have 200 event producers hosting their own nationals with their own rules. It's just not going to work."

Jim presented his research during a Varsity brainstorming meeting, and the group decided that All Star cheer needed an organization to standardize and unify its rules and divisions.

THE BIRTH OF USASF

The concept of creating an All Star cheerleading organization faced immediate challenges. First was the question of who would control it. Another challenge was funding.

Jim convened a meeting of the top twenty event producers in Atlanta around 2002-2003, proposing that each contribute $25,000 annually for about five years to fund the organization independently.

"Guess how many checks I got?" Jim asked. "Zero. I tried everybody. I even asked Herkie."

This little-known attempt to secure industry-wide funding reveals a more complex reality about Varsity's role in establishing USASF than is commonly understood.

"Everybody wants to be in charge, but nobody wants to pay the bills," Jim said. "Finally, Jeff Webb said he'd fund it."

Jeff's involvement led to complaints that Varsity's funding would compromise the organization's independence. Meanwhile, a parallel effort at industry governance was taking shape through the National All Star Cheerleading Coaches Congress (NACCC), which was under the leadership of prominent gym owners including Elaine Pascale and Victor and Kristen Rosario. The NACCC championed coach-driven governance, a concept Jim respected, but he believed the leadership should come from event producers. It seemed more feasible to align the goals of thirty or forty producers rather than trying to achieve consensus among 10,000 coaches.

Jim's proposed solution was a balanced approach: "The USASF needed to be one-third coaches, one-third event producers, and one-third governing body, ensuring that no single group held a majority vote."

THE PHILADELPHIA DINNER

The tensions between USASF and NACCC came to a head when Jim learned that Elaine Pascale, a leading figure in NACCC, had made disparaging comments about him. Similarly, Elaine had heard that Jim was speaking negatively about her. Rather than allowing the rift to widen, Jim took a direct approach: "I called Elaine, and I asked her to meet with me."

She said, "I'm not coming to Memphis," so they met in Philadelphia. What began as a brief, tense encounter transformed into a breakthrough. Chadwick's polite, one-hour dinner evolved into a five-hour epiphany. They both recognized they were heading to the same place with the same heart. In the end, they forged a strong friendship and chose to work together.

That dinner marked a pivotal moment in the evolution of All Star cheerleading. Jim returned to Varsity and advocated for NACCC's approach instead of competing with it, upholding his vision of balanced governance where coaches have a powerful voice.

CREATING THE WORLD CHAMPIONSHIP

As the governance structure emerged, Jim saw that a single championship event was crucial to unify the sport's rules and establish a pinnacle achievement for teams to strive for. This change would encourage everyone to follow the same rules and allow teams to maintain consistent routines across events.

When Varsity acquired NCA in early 2004, Jim seized the opportunity to bring in Steve Peterson, an expert in running All Star competitions. Together, they conceived the idea of a world championship, known simply as "Worlds."

"We chose that name because there were already nearly 200 national championships," Jim said. "This event had to be bigger than those."

Thanks to Jeff Webb's ties with ESPN and Disney, Jim landed a venue at Walt Disney World for the inaugural Cheerleading Worlds. Jim initially planned to use a Disney sound stage for the competition but, upon inspection, realized it wouldn't work. The competition floor wouldn't fit widthwise, and there was a pillar in the way.

After a tense forty-five-minute wait for Disney executives to deliberate, they proposed a larger sound stage, one that was used to produce *Who Wants to Be a Millionaire*, one of TV's top-rated shows. Astonishingly, Disney moved the show to a smaller stage to accommodate The Cheerleading Worlds.

"That impressed me so much about Disney's vision for youth sports," Jim said, "because they could see what the future was going to bring."

The partnership with Disney would prove enduring, despite occasional suggestions that The Cheerleading Worlds should rotate to various locations. "We have the perfect location," Jim said. "We have a partner who was more visionary than we were."

THE FIRST WORLDS

The inaugural Cheerleading Worlds in the spring of 2004 was designed as a made-for-TV event. Sixteen top teams were invited, though only fourteen accepted, with all expenses covered. The competition featured two divisions: All-girl and Coed.

The competition itself produced a memorable moment that Jim believes legitimized the entire concept. The Maryland Twisters, widely considered the nation's top all-girl team at the time, delivered what appeared to be an unbeatable performance . . . until Cheer Athletics took the floor.

"At the end of their routine, honest to goodness, there was dead silence. Everybody's mouth dropped," Jim recalled. "What nobody knew was that Cheer Athletics was a huge program. They didn't take the team that had been winning everywhere. They had tryouts for all their teams and formed a superstar squad. And their routine was a killer." It showcased unimaginable skill combinations that left the audience, Jim included, in awe. "I just stood there with my mouth wide open," he said. "Everybody else did too."

That moment confirmed for Jim that Worlds would succeed in pushing the sport forward. "I told myself, 'That routine just made The Cheerleading Worlds legitimate. When you can compete with skills nobody's seen before . . . wow.'"

GOING GLOBAL

In the aftermath of that incredible competition, international cheerleading program representatives requested a meeting, prompting Disney to close an entire restaurant for around fifty All Star cheerleading teams from abroad.

"We were so arrogant," Jim said. "We only thought US teams were good enough."

Among the international representatives was an official from China's Ministry of Sport. When Jim asked which China he represented (Taiwan or the People's Republic), the young man swiftly presented his ID card. "He was from the People's Republic of China," Jim said, "the mainland central government Ministry of Sport." The Chinese official boldly declared, "We'll be competitive in two years. We'll win in three years."

Jim called it hubris, and the official shot back with a stinging rebuke: "No more hubris than you running a 'world championship' and not inviting any other countries but the US."

That exchange cemented Jim's dedication to transforming Worlds into a truly global competition.

BUILDING LEGITIMACY THROUGH STRUCTURE

For Jim, the ultimate goal was to legitimize All Star cheerleading as a sport through proper structure. That goal came into clear focus when he addressed a meeting in Texas of owners who ran small gyms. When asked why gyms should join the USASF, Jim asked a question of his own: "Do you want to have a business that you can leave to your kids or not?" Then he elaborated: "Here's the reality. If you're a member of a legitimate sport that has rules, guidelines, and cares about safety, that is something people will understand, because that's how all other successful sports are organized."

His pragmatic perspective—that legitimacy through proper standards would be essential for the sport's sustainability—drove Jim's approach to structuring the USASF along the lines of the United Nations.

"There's really no handbook for creating governing bodies," Jim explained. "Every governing body is different. Once you get into the Olympic spectrum, there are certain requirements. But if you're not seeking Olympic recognition, you can structure it however you want."

The USASF was established with a board that included both permanent and rotating seats. Several committees were established to handle specific responsibilities, such as the committee that set sanctioning standards and the committee that set the rules. In addition, members could vote and express their opinions on what they did or didn't want.

THE LEGACY

Looking back on the creation of USASF and Worlds, Jim emphasized the personal connections that made it possible. He had worked for both NCA and UCA and had relationships on both sides that enabled him to look into their hearts and bring the USASF together as a family for everyone's benefit. Jim credits two individuals as instrumental to the USASF's early success: Steve Peterson and Justin Carrier.

Steve, who managed all NCA competitions, was recruited by Jim at the first meeting after the NCA-Varsity merger. Justin, who Jim described as "a superstar," quickly became a driving force within the organization.

Justin initially worked directly for Jim for about six months, primarily providing information about All Star programs. "I didn't know the rules. I'm not a rules person," Jim admitted. "I just had a vision, and I needed Justin's help."

Justin was so invaluable that Varsity ultimately reassigned him to NCA, and that turned out to be a spectacular decision.

For Jim, the vision was always clear—transforming cheerleading from a business into a legitimate sport with proper governance, safety standards, and a pinnacle championship showcasing the highest level of performance. Despite facing resistance and navigating complex industry politics, Jim's marketing background, diplomatic skills, and deep personal connections across competing factions enabled him to chart a course for All Star cheerleading's future.

The Cheerleading Worlds event he envisioned has expanded from fourteen teams in two divisions to hundreds of teams from around the globe that compete across multiple levels and categories. Crucially, the governance structure he established, which continues to evolve, set the groundwork for All Star cheerleading to become the sophisticated sport it is today.

Jim Chadwick's unconventional journey—from Navy fighter pilot to corporate executive to industry visionary—has left an undeniable mark on the evolution of All Star cheerleading. By envisioning the sport's potential beyond the wild west, he transformed a scattered array of competitions and programs into a unified, global phenomenon.

Today, Jim is retired, but he's a commercially rated pilot and continues to fly his own plane. He also enjoys cycling and rides one hundred miles a week.

> **"Success is in the journey." – Jim Chadwick**

EARNED WISDOM

★   **Success:** Jim believes the journey is the destination, and when you understand that, you are successful.

★   **Wisdom:** The best predictor of future success is past success.

★   **Gratitude:** Jim credits Lawrence "Herkie" Herkimer and Jeff Webb for impacting his All Star journey. Herkie endowed him with a love of cheerleading that extended well beyond the financial and athletic benefits. Jeff fully supported his long-standing dream of making cheerleading legitimate.

★   **For Gym Owners:** Your passion for cheer will not put food on the table. Implementing a solid financial plan will.

- ★ **For Coaches:** Be the best cheer skill developer the world has ever seen.

- ★ **Lessons Learned:** Always be sure to have a rainy-day fund. You never know when you're going to need it.

DID YOU KNOW?

- ★ Jim's favorite part of cheer is the great people he met through the sport.

- ★ His golf game is terrible.

- ★ He received two Clio Awards for advertising excellence.

- ★ Jim is a commercial pilot with single and multi-engine ratings as well as an instrument rating.

- ★ His favorite superhero is Hondo from the 1953 film of the same name.

- ★ For his animal Jim chose the raven, which symbolizes introspection, self-realization, courage, transformation, messaging, magic, psychic abilities, and divination.

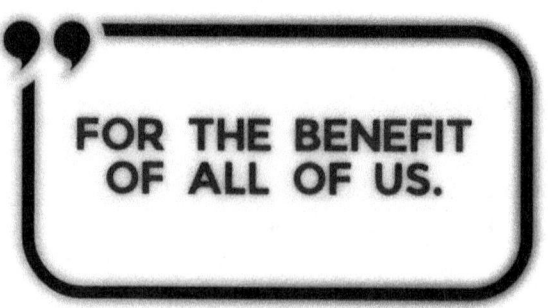

"FOR THE BENEFIT OF ALL OF US.

"Rejoice always; pray continually; give thanks in all circumstances, for this is God's will for you in Christ Jesus." – I Thessalonians 5:16-18

KEVIN BRUBAKER

Charlotte Allstars – 1990
CHEERSPORT – 1999
MotUS, CX Brands – 2022

BACK TUCKS TO BULLDOGS

Kevin Brubaker started gymnastics in fifth grade in Sheridan, Wyoming. He was eager to follow in the footsteps of his older brother, John, a collegiate gymnast at the time. He said his brother took only ten minutes to teach him a roundoff back handspring back tuck. Next stop, the Olympic Games.

Kidding!

In high school Kevin spent his fall playing football. He participated in gymnastics in the winter, track and field in the spring, and baseball in the summer. He excelled in gymnastics but planned to pursue football or baseball in college.

His mother was originally from South Carolina, and Kevin's aunt and uncle live in Matthews, North Carolina.

Kevin visited his aunt and uncle every summer and developed a deep affection for the time he spent with his family in North Carolina. When he was finalizing his decisions for college, he ended up at Wingate University in Wingate, North Carolina, largely because of the influence of his aunt and uncle, and because he thought it would be great if he no longer had to shovel snow.

When he arrived at Wingate in the fall of 1986, the school had a highly talented cheerleading program. Kevin was surprised to learn the college had filled two sixteen-member teams with eight guys and eight girls each. Not only did the school field full junior varsity and varsity teams, but they could also stunt and tumble. There were only two schools in North Carolina at the time that were better—Appalachian State with Scott Williams, Eddie Z, and Ransome Harper; and North Carolina State, coached by the legendary Cathy Buckey.

Although only knowing gymnastics, Kevin joined the Wingate cheer squad in his freshman year, fell in love with the sport, and continued it throughout his four years. Some of his best memories were at East Tennessee State University cheer camp with the big dog schools. He's proud that Wingate cheer held its own as a small school that no one had heard of. He also taught local school teams stunting and tumbling.

BUILDING CHARLOTTE ALLSTARS

After graduating from Wingate, Kevin wasn't sure what he wanted to do, so he decided to attend the University of North Carolina at Charlotte and cheer while studying for his master's degree in counseling, personal growth, and human development. He thought he would like to be dean of students at a college or university while he also coached cheerleading.

While attending UNC Charlotte, Kevin worked at Weyandt's Gymnastics, the largest facility of its kind in the Carolinas at the time. The gym was home to renowned coaches from East Germany and Russia, and Kevin quickly rose to assistant men's gymnastics coach, but cheerleading remained his passion.

Eventually, he taught all the tumbling classes while continuing to work with school teams, finally working with them inside the gym instead of outside on the grass.

Kevin competed in his first NCA College Nationals in Dallas, Texas, with UNC Charlotte. He was mesmerized by the event and the other collegiate teams competing. "We lost to Louisville," he said. "Imagine that!" Louisville continues to be a powerhouse coached by James Speed and Misty Hodges.

While at the NCA Nationals Kevin watched his first All Star team performance, a group from Midwest City, Oklahoma, and he thought he could do that. He knew he had plenty of talented athletes in every class and school he coached.

Upon returning to Charlotte, he launched the Charlotte Allstars with eighteen athletes. They faced off for the first time at an ECA regional in Winston-Salem, North Carolina, in the spring of 1991. The team competed for the second time at Carowinds in Charlotte and won. They had arrived and quickly became the best team in America. (Not really, but to themselves, they were.)

Charlotte Allstars continued to grow and, eventually, Weyandt's Gymnastics didn't appreciate the loud cheer music and the space that the cheer program required, so Kevin needed to find a new home. The East German gymnastics coach and preschool director, Julie O'Brien, Kevin's best friend, were leaving to start a new program. So in the fall of 1991, the three of them opened the International Sports Center that housed International Gymnastics, Charlotte Allstar Cheerleading, and about a dozen other sports including aerobics, indoor diving, Taekwondo, fencing, and a full dance studio.

The cheer and gymnastics programs ballooned to such an extent that the other sports gradually disappeared. Thom Glielmi served as the head boy's gymnastics coach until he moved to Minnesota to coach alongside Fred Roethlisberger where he trained three-time Olympian John Roethlisberger. Thom, the head gymnastics coach at Stanford for the past twenty-three years, remains friends with Kevin to this day.

The Charlotte Allstars' early triumphs at the NCA and UCA Nationals skyrocketed Kevin and his teams to fame, and that fame propelled his business and established him as a rising star in the sport. Kevin won national titles in Large All-girl at NCA in 1994 and UCA in 1995. Kevin invented the "full-up" and competed with it for the first time at NCA Nationals in 1994.

Most cheer programs only compete with one company, either NCA or UCA, but Kevin led the Charlotte Allstars to compete in both, and his team won UCA. For whatever reason, in the nineties UCA Nationals was the ESPN filler for every rained-out baseball game or other canceled event. As a result, Kevin said he thought Charlotte Allstars was on ESPN fifty times in one year alone.

THE BIRTH OF CHEERSPORT

In 1993 Kevin decided that Charlotte Allstars should host a competition for his All Star teams and his school teams. He hosted his first event inside the gym with eleven teams on his gymnastics spring floor, which everyone loved.

"The event ran on time, we had a couple of judges, and we didn't make any money," Kevin said, chuckling. "Wow! That was really fun." But even then he couldn't help but think of how the event could become bigger and better.

Around the same time, several All Star programs from North Carolina were coming together to start the North Carolina All Star Coaches Association. North Carolina was a growing hot bed for All Star cheer at the time.

Don Collins with Spirit Express, Cathy Buckey with Champion Allstars, a woman named Barbie who really pushed for them to come together, Sandye Teague Hicks from Wilmington All Stars, Amy Tyler from Greensboro All Stars, and Kevin from Charlotte Allstars worked together to form the association.

In 1994 they hosted the North Carolina Cheerleading Championship at the Charlotte Hornets training facility on a spring floor that Kevin built, drawing around thirty-five teams. Proceeds from the event allowed them to provide a few college and program scholarships, an early sign of their commitment to giving back.

Kevin hosted the North Carolina State Championship again in 1996 with teams from North Carolina, South Carolina, Virginia, Tennessee, and Georgia, because All Star teams were looking for places to compete. He thought the event could be even bigger, so he called all the gyms in those states to see if they would come back to compete in Charlotte. Most gyms outside the Carolinas said no. He laughed and said, "Okay, so where am I going to host this thing."

He settled on Atlanta with the foresight that someday it might become an event that people would fly to attend, and Atlanta was an airline hub.

In 1997 Kevin hosted his first event in Atlanta with partner George Shinn, owner of the Charlotte Hornets. They called it the United States All Star Cheerleading Federation Event. Thirty-two teams attended, and the event was the first to introduce spring floors and level play with intermediate and advanced divisions that eventually became Level 3 and Level 5.

In 1998 USACF became CHEERSPORT, and the event moved to a larger high school in the Atlanta area with seventy-five teams in attendance. That year Kevin and his team added two more levels, Novice and Elite, that would become Level 2 and Level 6.

In 1999 CHEERSPORT Nationals was held for the first time in its current location, Atlanta's Georgia World Congress Center (GWCC). It featured 150 teams. Top Gun came all the way from Miami, Florida, to attend, and CHEERSPORT was on the map. That same year Kevin and his team added a fifth level called Excel that became Level 4.

Back then, most teams didn't travel far to attend competitions, and most events were small, not even approaching 150 teams. For the diehard CHEERSPORT fans, the entire event took place in B5, which is now the Worlds Arena. Kevin rented a sound system from Shannon Smith, the owner of Carolina All Stars. The warm-up area was tucked into the corner behind a pipe and drape, and there was a small stage off to the side for individual competitors and stunt groups, complete with a lackluster backdrop. And that's how they ran CHEERSPORT Nationals in the third year.

After the event ended, the GWCC handed Kevin a bill far higher than he had expected. Security costs were higher, facility expenses exceeded the budget, the catering bill was overrun, and there were dozens of additional fees for first aid and other services. CHEERSPORT didn't have the funds to pay the bills. As a result, Kevin skipped a post-event meeting with the

Congress Center. Furious, the center vowed never to allow him back into the GWCC. Of course, eventually he did pay the bill. It took about three months, but he squared it away. Despite that rocky moment, CHEERSPORT continued to grow, and it expanded its events to Greensboro, Raleigh, and Charlotte, North Carolina.

The Atlanta competition moved to the Gwinnett Convention Center in 2000, which is currently known as Gas South Convention Center Arena. Ironically, Kevin's new event brand, The CX Brands, hosts an event there today.

CHEERSPORT grew to 225 teams and required two halls. Smaller teams competed in the auditorium while the main stage in the convention center was where the Side A, Side B concept was invented.

For those readers who haven't been to CHEERSPORT Nationals, this is when the curtain would open and a team would be facing Side A, ready to compete. Once they finished, the curtain would close. The team that just competed would exit while another team entered, facing the opposite direction, or Side B. This process allowed the event to move more quickly through the teams and added a new stage flair to the competition.

It also created priority viewing, allowing parents and fans to rush to the front of the stage to watch their team up close. Twenty-five years later, no other All Star event offers a curtain that opens and closes on the stage, but the curtain still exists at CHEERSPORT.

In addition, CHEERSPORT introduced a new division called Basix, spelled that way because it was the base of the six levels. It eventually became Level 1. Teams could then compete in Basix, Novice, Intermediate, Advanced, Excel, and Elite, offering a broader range of competitive options. (Those six original divisions became the levels 1-6 that we have now.)

This was a humongous development in All Star because it allowed for tremendous growth for gyms and event producers. The USASF didn't come along until 2003, but it adopted the principles and concepts from CHEERSPORT and the NACCC that make up the All Star cheer rules and divisions used today.

CHEERSPORT continued to grow like a weed, expanding from 300 teams to 350 and, eventually, to 450 teams. CHEERSPORT also was the first to introduce spring floors to All Star competition. Massive coed teams began to gather at CHEERSPORT Nationals to compete, including Top Gun, Kentucky Elite, Miami Elite, and ProCheer.

"They were destroying our springboards in warm-ups," Kevin recalled. "One year we had to run to Home Depot during the event to rebuild our tumbling runways in warm-up because the boards were just beat to death."

With the event continuing to grow in 2001 and 2002, they squeezed 450 teams into the Georgia International Convention Center, but the event was at capacity, and the only larger option was the Georgia World Congress Center (GWCC).

Kevin approached the GWCC, tail between his legs, seeking forgiveness and another chance to hold his event there. Initially, they refused him space. But when he demonstrated the event's growth and paid large deposits in advance, they finally agreed.

The GWCC welcomed CHEERSPORT back to its facility in 2003. The event was rescheduled for President's Day weekend in February where it remains a fixture on the calendar to this day.

CHEERSPORT was a pioneer in offering paid bids for teams to compete at The Cheerleading Worlds. One year the USASF bill for CHEERSPORT Worlds bids soared to $230,000.

During his CHEERSPORT days Kevin was a pioneer in sales by visiting over 1,100 gyms, forging relationships and learning how diverse business models thrived across the country. Between 2005 and 2014 he expanded CHEERSPORT to 1,200 teams, establishing it as one of the largest All Star cheerleadng competitions in the world for ten years in a row. At its peak in 2015, Kevin decided to sell CHEERSPORT to Varsity.

Kevin worked as the national sales director of new business development for Varsity All Star until he was let go during COVID in 2020. Currently, he has retired from coaching but still owns Charlotte Allstar Gymnastics and Cheerleading with his wife, Jenn Brubaker. The gym has grown significantly over the years and is home to 1,400 families involved in All Star cheerleading, gymnastics, recreation classes, preschool, tumbling, birthday parties, and summer camps.

In 2023 Kevin joined MotUS, a gym facility group that brings owners together to collaborate and grow participation in the sport with business partners Cole Stott, Casey Jones, and me, Stacy Rowe. This move led to creating a competition company in 2023, CX Brands, which organizes competitions nationally.

> "Success is being able to help and encourage others." – Kevin Brubaker

EARNED WISDOM

- ★ **Success:** The number one reason Kevin started CHEERSPORT and USACF was to provide more opportunities for his Charlotte Allstar coaches to earn additional income. He thought if he could host a cheerleading competition, he could pay his coaches more. Everything he and his gym have done has been to try to help people be better, whether it was the families in his gym, the athletes who came to the gym, or the coaches and staff.

- ★ **Gratitude:** Kevin lives his life by the acronym JOY—Jesus first, others second, and yourself third.

- ★ **Favorite memories:** Talking on the phone with all the coaches and gym owners before they attended CHEERSPORT was one of Kevin's favorite activities. He loved learning about their businesses and helping them succeed. (Do you remember receiving a phone call from Kevin?)

★ **Mistakes:** Kevin says his biggest mistake was not paying more attention to the business side of things early on. He wanted to grow at lightning speed, but he didn't have the business acumen he needed at the time.

★ **For Gym Owners:** Stay in your lane and do what you do best. Every gym owner starts out wearing a million hats, but be sure you make time to do what you're passionate about. Time is money, so have someone else do the things you aren't good at. Focus on what will help your business grow.

★ **For Coaches:** Knowledge is key. Know your strengths and weaknesses as a coach and work with people who complement you. Don't be afraid to ask for help or seek others' opinions. For example, Kevin told me a story about coaching with Robert Burns for eleven years. Robert is a creative choreographer and stunt/tumble technician. Kevin is Type A with tunnel vision, old-fashioned, and often resistant to change. But their differences complemented each other and helped their routines and friendship thrive.

★ **Lessons Learned:** There is great value in learning from and collaborating with others. From a young age, Kevin was fortunate to have wonderful mentors and coaches who helped guide him as a coach.

DID YOU KNOW?

★ Kevin's favorite part of cheerleading is the pyramids. He created some epic pyramids like the original "fall back" and the "scorpion flip."

★ Kevin worked on a cattle ranch in Wyoming between his junior and senior years in high school. He branded cattle, baled hay, moved sprinkler lines, and built fences nonstop every day. He said it was exhausting and the hardest thing he has ever done. It was an experience that encouraged him to go to college so he could figure out what else to do with his life.

★ He grew up in Sheridan, Wyoming, and during his time there he had the good fortune of meeting Kenny Rogers, the Queen of England, and Prince, who debuted his movie *Under the Cherry Moon* in Sheridan.

★ Kevin spent every summer as a kid in Myrtle Beach, South Carolina, with his uncle, a glorious break from the insane amount of snow in Wyoming. Ultimately, that is what led him to the Carolinas.

★ When he was a little boy, he thought it would be awesome to fly, so his favorite superhero is Superman.

★ Kevin chose Jesus as his symbol. The cross represents Jesus Christ, who died for our sins. Everything Kevin does with family, church,

Charlotte Allstars, MotUS, and the CX Brands is to love Jesus, love others, and to bring those two together.

"Live the life you've imagined." – Henry David Thoreau

"Yesterday is history. Tomorrow is a mystery. Today is a gift from God; that's why we call it the present." – Eleanor Roosevelt

BRAD PAGE & LADD LeBUS
Cheer Station – 1990
Cheer America – 1997

HUMBLE BEGINNINGS

Brad and Ladd met in 1987 at Baylor University in Waco, Texas. Brad, a college sophomore, and Ladd, a high school senior, spent the next few years teaming up at NCA summer camps.

Brad stayed at Baylor to finish business school while Ladd moved back to Austin, Texas, his hometown. The two had developed a relationship and didn't want to be apart, so Brad left Baylor and moved to Austin.

They had no money to pay rent, so they began to teach private cheer lessons. Initially, starting a gym wasn't on their minds. They taught private lessons in recreation centers, living rooms, and front yards. Any kid in town who wanted to make the high school team scheduled a private lesson with Brad or Ladd.

During the week Brad and Ladd traveled across the country choreographing routines while weekends were spent teaching private lessons back home. They operated out of three recreation centers—Central, South, and North—calling them stations, which inspired the name Cheer Station when they opened their first gym in 1990.

Initially, they focused on middle school and high school teams preparing for NCA Nationals, though they also worked with a few All Star teams. But the constant travel and packed schedule left them exhausted. They realized they couldn't sustain that pace, so they wondered if teams would come to them. That shift would allow them to continue offering choreography and private lessons without the constant travel. So they took a chance, opened Cheer Station, and continued using the three recreation facilities as part of their growing business.

BUILDING THE STATION

They visited every middle and high school in town and invited the teams to come to the station and work with them. "We told them we wanted to help their teams," Ladd said. "They could work with us as a group, or we offered private lessons." Brad and Ladd then hatched the brilliant idea of attending Friday night football games in the area. They would choose one standout cheerleader from the game as Cheerleader of the Week and showcase the cheerleader's photo and a brief promo in the newspaper. The kids thrived on the recognition.

At Central Station, Brad and Ladd launched their first junior All Star team, the Flyers, a name that still exists on one of their junior teams today. Starting with just nine athletes, the pair took the Flyers to NCA camp and NCA Nationals in Dallas, Texas.

In their second year they expanded to two teams, one Junior and one Senior. The growth led them to consider renting a building to consolidate the three stations under one roof. Young and without significant funds, they turned to their parents for help, but their parents' advice was blunt: "Go back to school!"

But Melissa Cook, who was in real estate, said, "You look hungry to succeed, and I believe in what you're doing. If you can pay double the deposit, I'll support your business."

Brad and Ladd worked twice as many choreography jobs the following year, and by the end of the season they had saved enough for the down payment. They moved into their new space, which was just big enough to fit seven carpet-bonded foam rolls. They grew from two teams to four and worked with nearly every school team in the area.

THE YES PROGRAM REVOLUTION

Many readers may remember the infamous case of Wanda Holloway, the Channelview, Texas, cheer mom who was convicted of hiring a hitman to kill the mother of her daughter's cheer rival. The story made national headlines.

So in a state where cheerleading had become its own special kind of crazy, Brad and Ladd created a junior high program where everyone could cheer, and they sold their program to schools across Texas. Parents hated it. They wanted their daughters to be stars. But principals loved it, because they were tired of the cheerleading momma drama. The program was titled the Youth Experience and Spirit (YES) Program.

YES allowed all sixth, seventh, and eighth graders to participate, just like in other school sports. In basketball, for example, anyone could sign up to be on the team, but only the best would play. But before YES, only the best seven girls, or the most popular seven girls, were selected for cheerleading, and everyone else was cut. In contrast, the YES Program was inclusive, but the best kids could still rise to the top.

By exposing so many new children to cheerleading, Brad and Ladd's new gym grew because the girls who wanted to be serious and make their high school teams needed a place to train, and Cheer Station was the only gym in town, making it a win-win. The YES Program also led to Cheer Station offering private summer camps across Texas, which meant Brad and Ladd traveled to bring their camps to school campuses.

In 2004 the two were among the first supporters of USASF. Cheer America was one of the first event producers to offer bids for The Cheerleading Worlds. Brad helped develop the scoresheet with Victor and

Kristin Rosario, who were in charge at the time. Brad also served on the rules committee, establishing standards and guidelines for All Star. He still serves on the rules committee today.

A LEGACY OF KINDNESS

Brad and Ladd's journey from teaching private lessons at recreation centers to establishing one of Texas's first cheer programs showcases their dedication, innovation, and passion for the sport.

What started in 1990 as a cash-strapped partnership between two college friends has transformed into a powerhouse cheer institution that has trained countless athletes. Despite economic challenges, industry evolution, and a global pandemic, their commitment to inclusivity and excellence has remained steadfast.

The Cheer Station legacy extends far beyond its gym walls. It lives in the eleven Austin-area gyms that sprouted from its influence, in the national standards it helped establish through the USASF and, most important, in the "kind Cheer Station demeanor" that defines its athletes.

Today, Cheer Station is in its sixth building, a testament to its growth and longevity. Katie Rebers serves as Brad and Ladd's right hand and currently manages their location. She switched from gymnastics to cheerleading when she was fourteen. She completed a work study program with Cheer Station, went on to college, returned to coach after graduation, and has been with them ever since.

Brad now focuses on the gym while Ladd oversees Cheer America alongside his business partner, Colleen Little. Cheer Station currently has around 200 All Star athletes, both Prep and Elite, and serves another 500 kids through its classes. They also continue to offer a wide range of summer camps.

Known for their strong sportsmanship, Cheer Station is proud of its cheerleaders and their signature kindness, a quality that clearly starts at the top. After interviewing Brad and Ladd, it's easy to see where their athletes get their warm, respectful demeanor.

"Success is being happy." – Brad Page
"Success is longevity." – Ladd LeBus

EARNED WISDOM

★ **Success:** For Brad, success means being happy and enjoying your job, making a living doing something you love. Wanting to go to work every day is a sign of success. For Ladd, success is maintaining what you're doing for the long haul.

★ **Wisdom:** Brad and Ladd love to win, but in the end it's more important for athletes to learn team values and to understand that they can push themselves. Teach them to face failure and how to redeem themselves. Make sure your athletes enjoy their journey with your program.

★ **Gratitude:** Carol Wagers was a tremendous influence on Brad and Ladd. She was his head instructor for years at NCA. Ladd said that Lance and Carol practically raised them. They spoke highly of Carol and the incredible woman she was.

★ **Wish:** Ladd wishes the rules didn't change constantly, because it makes it difficult for both owners and event producers. Brad appreciates the longer rule cycles and hopes they will be extended.

★ **Mistakes:** They wish they had invested in purchasing their building twenty-five years ago. They would no longer be paying a mortgage or rent today. On the flip side, they never took on investors and have done it all themselves.

★ **For Gym Owners:** Learn to delegate. Find people you love and trust and then let them do the job. Stay true to yourself. You don't have to be a powerhouse gym. You can have a successful business by finding your own niche and staying true to it.

★ **For Coaches:** Utilize your resources and learn to be a good listener. Humble yourself and learn lessons from each thing you do. Don't think you know it all. Learn from those around you. Both say they're still learning.

★ **Lessons Learned:** Brad and Ladd ventured into multiple locations several times, and each time they realized they were spreading themselves too thin. They learned that they weren't the best at delegating. They value all the lessons they learned, and they ultimately decided that no other single location could offer the best business model for their own situation.

DID YOU KNOW?

★ Brad's favorite part of cheer is tumbling while Ladd's favorite is pyramids.

★ Ladd enjoys baking. He makes delicious cheesecake and banana bread, but Brad doesn't love the smell of the ripening bananas.

★ Ladd enjoys yoga and anything outdoors in the sun. He doesn't like to watch television. He'd rather be outside all day.

★ Brad also enjoys yoga. He also likes to spend his spare time drawing and painting.

★ Brad loves dancing. He took tap, jazz, and ballet as a child. He took hip-hop classes in college.

★ Brad's favorite superhero, without hesitation, was Green Lantern, and Ladd's favorite is Aquaman.

★ Ladd chose a ringtail lemur as his animal because it symbolizes traits such as social cohesion and communication.

★ Brad chose the octopus as his animal for its intelligence, adaptability, and creativity. Known for blending into its surroundings, the octopus represents the importance of adapting to any situation and overcoming challenges.

> BE KIND.
> —Brad

> WE ARE THE MUSIC MAKERS, AND WE ARE THE DREAMERS OF DREAMS.
> —Ladd

"The sun will come up tomorrow." – Unknown

TAMMY SKINNER
Cheers and More – 1990
American Spirit Championships – 1993

FROM BACKYARD COACH TO ALL STAR CHEER

The summer sun blazed down on Tammy Skinner's backyard in Edmond, Oklahoma, where local high school cheerleaders were perfecting their stunts on the grass. A lucky opportunity struck when Tammy's father, a commercial real estate owner, offered her space in one of his buildings. The transition from backyard coaching to a professional facility marked a pivotal step in Tammy's entrepreneurial journey in the All Star cheer world. In the late 1980s private coaching sessions were about to evolve into something much greater, something that would redefine an entire industry.

In 1990 Tammy launched Cheers and More Training Center in Edmond with 250 students. The timing was perfect. The All Star cheer category was just starting to gain traction at the NCA High School National Championship in Dallas, Texas.

By August 1991 her program had expanded rapidly, leading her to establish two teams—a Senior team and a

Junior team—known collectively as the Edmond All Stars.

Though school-based cheerleading had existed for decades, independent, gym-based teams competing on their own was still a fresh concept. Tammy helped lead the charge in shaping All Star cheer.

CREATING AMERICAN SPIRIT CHAMPIONSHIPS

With her gym thriving, Tammy seized another opportunity in the booming All Star industry. In 1993 she and her husband founded American Spirit Championships (ASC), a competition and camp company that expanded opportunities for the growing number of All Star teams nationwide.

Tammy saw the need for an independent company to provide more competitions throughout the season and resort-style camps where athletes would stay in hotels rather than in college dorms. That decision illustrates her sharp business instinct for spotting market gaps and filling them.

The decision to launch ASC was not taken lightly, and it required courage. Tammy's husband boldly jumped from a stable job as an actuary at a major corporation to embrace her entrepreneurial vision.

"He quit his awesome job to help me start this new adventure in the competition industry," Tammy said. "We booked several arenas throughout the US and purchased all the production equipment. Bottom line—we were broke."

The early days of ASC thrived on passion and sacrifice, not comfort. The financial strain of launching a new business forced Tammy and her husband to cut corners at every turn.

"Our staff was so gracious to jump on board with us," Tammy said. "We piled our staff into a van and shared rooms, with some sleeping on the floor. We ate peanut butter and jelly for every meal because we couldn't afford to eat out."

Their bootstrapped beginning created a special bond among the ASC team and forged relationships that have endured. Many of the original staff still work for Tammy, and she's grateful to be able to treat them to steak dinners and their own hotel rooms. "But I will forever be grateful for their hard work and determination to help us succeed," Tammy said.

This entrepreneurial vision and team loyalty set ASC apart. While many competitions were tied to larger organizations, Tammy's independent approach allowed for greater flexibility and innovation. The resort-style camps offered a premium experience that both athletes and coaches appreciated. This new concept was a welcome alternative to the traditional college dormitory accommodations that had been the standard.

A LASTING LEGACY

Tammy's journey to All Star prominence was rooted in a strong foundation of traditional cheer. During her college years she spent summers working at NCA's renowned camps. Throughout the school year she balanced her studies with teaching cheerleading and tumbling at Creative Movement, a local gym owned by Meredith Wilbur.

After three decades in All Star cheer, Tammy's passion is as fierce as ever. She coaches and travels with ASC nationwide, witnessing the evolution of a sport she helped pioneer. "I continue this journey," she said, "because of the kids."

Her work's impact shines through at the end of each season. When she considers stepping away, the senior speeches at the end-of-season banquet remind her just how vital coaches are to athletes. "This keeps me going," she said. "I want to continue to make a difference as long as I can."

This sentiment captures why Tammy Skinner is a staple in All Star cheer. Her legacy transcends business success, competition victories, and trained athletes. It is defined by the countless lives she's touched and the positive impact she's had on generations of young people.

REFLECTIONS ON AN INDUSTRY TRANSFORMED

From backyard training sessions to today's elite All Star programs, Tammy has helped drive remarkable changes in the industry. What started as a spin-off of traditional cheerleading has transformed into a unique sport with its own identity, rules, and culture. All Star cheer now boasts hundreds of thousands of athletes nationwide who compete in top-notch facilities, including massive convention centers, with championships airing on major TV networks.

Amid all these changes, Tammy has stayed adaptable but firmly rooted in her core values of athlete development and positive coaching. Her dual roles as a gym owner and competition event producer have equipped her with unique insights into all sides of the All Star world, enabling her to serve the community she loves more effectively.

As the All Star industry continues to evolve, visionaries like Tammy Skinner remind us of the passion that has shaped this community from its inception. Her journey, from teaching in her backyard to impacting an entire industry, serves as a testament to what dedicated individuals can accomplish and how they can transform not only businesses but also the lives of countless young athletes.

As long as there are athletes to mentor and lives to influence, Tammy plans to build upon the legacy she established in that Edmond backyard more than thirty years ago.

> "Success is knowing that your athletes leave your gym with life lessons." – Tammy Skinner

EARNED WISDOM

★ **Success:** Success is defined not by wins but by the life lessons athletes take from our programs. How will it make them a better person?

- ★ **Gratitude:** Tammy credits Meredith Wilbur, coach of the University of Oklahoma and owner of Creative Movement, for helping shape her coaching philosophy and business approach, providing a template for successfully running both a gym and a coaching career.

- ★ **Tammy's Wish:** Tammy wishes she had kept her ASC summer camps. But she thought she and her staff needed a break after the competition season.

- ★ **Mistakes:** Thinking that quantity is better than quality. Cheers and More has been in over five cities during its thirty years, serving more than 1,000 students. Tammy prefers the smaller gym atmosphere where every student is learning to the best of their ability, and coaches can focus on quality.

- ★ **For Gym Owners:** Surround yourself with a positive staff and a supportive team mom for each team. Stay true to your beliefs and keep the kids first. Don't sweat the small stuff and choose your battles wisely.

- ★ **For Coaches:** Always remember that kindness wins.

DID YOU KNOW?

- ★ The all-girl divisions are Tammy's favorite.
- ★ One of her favorite routines was the year Lady Lightning performed the airline routine. The

choreography, costumes, and cleanliness of the routine were fantastic.

★ Tammy's favorite memory comes from the mid-1990s when her program drove from Oklahoma to Nashville for a competition despite a huge snowstorm. They left the Grand Ole Opry with national titles in both Senior All Star cheer and dance, and Tammy was named International Coach of the Year in both All Star cheer and dance.

★ Tammy owned an antique store.

★ She has two grandchildren.

★ She has been a co-songwriter on two albums.

★ Her husband is her hero.

★ For her animal Tammy chose the lynx, which is often associated with vision, intuition, and the ability to reveal hidden truths, embodying qualities of keen insight and deep understanding. The lynx is a symbol of grace, calculated decision-making, and choosing moments with care.

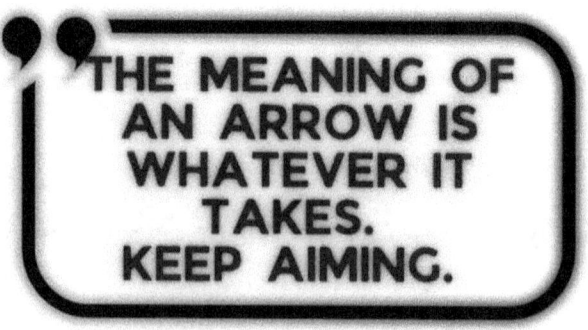

"THE MEANING OF AN ARROW IS WHATEVER IT TAKES. KEEP AIMING.

"Before you leave the house, look in the mirror and take one thing off. – Coco Chanel

JAMIE PARRISH
Georgia All Stars – 1990

FINDING HIS PATH

In the summer of 1986 a high school boy in Tifton, Georgia, watched the cheerleading squad gear up for camp. Jamie Parrish could do a "decent" back handspring. High school coach Ginger Brodie noticed Jamie's talent and swiftly invited him to join the Mercer University camp in Macon, Georgia, a transformative experience that would alter the course of his life.

Growing up in the 1970s under the guidance of his father figure, Ronny Kelly, Jamie had developed a foundation in gymnastics at South Stars Gymnastics in Fitzgerald, Georgia. But in the mid-1980s male cheerleaders were a rarity, especially in small-town Georgia. Although Jamie couldn't officially join the high school squad, his coach recognized his talent and passion, inviting him to choreograph routines for the team. Jamie eagerly created "little dances" that hinted at the creative vision that would later become his signature.

THE SPARK OF INSPIRATION

"I was watching TV one day and saw the UCA Collegiate National Championships," Jamie recalled. "That's when I saw Daryl Landy doing partner stunts, and I thought, 'Wow, I want to do that.'"

Determined to pursue his new passion, Jamie took a remarkably bold step for a small-town kid in the pre-internet era. He went to the local library, sifted through microfilm archives, and tracked down the phone number for the University of South Carolina. When he called, he reached Bill Boggs, the cheerleading coach.

"Bill told me I could be a cheerleader at the school," Jamie said, still sounding somewhat amazed at his own audacity.

In 1989 Jamie was admitted to South Carolina and simply showed up. Without even trying out he was added to the cheerleading squad. His leap of faith paid off, though perhaps not academically. After one year of poor grades, Jamie returned home and enrolled at Georgia State where he continued cheerleading for another year.

FROM ATHLETE TO COACH

In 1990 Jamie's trajectory took a turn when he joined the National Cheerleaders Association (NCA) staff. At NCA High School Nationals Jamie envisioned a transformation that would revolutionize cheerleading forever. He encountered a team at Nationals made up of students from various high schools, so Jamie thought they should start a club team division. When he pitched the idea to Lance Wagers, Lance said they were already thinking about doing that exact thing. This convergence of vision occurred at just the right moment. One team from Marietta, Georgia, was assembling a team named Cheer Tech Tigers, soon to become Pro Cheer, as the competitive landscape began to shift.

In 1991 Jamie launched Georgia All Stars and held tryouts on a local tennis court. He rallied a team of sixteen kids in the first year by promoting the opportunity at local high schools. Their practice conditions were far from ideal: They trained year-round on that same tennis court, dragging out wrestling mats at each session to accommodate more advanced skills.

TENNIS COURT TO GYM

Those humble beginnings forged lifelong bonds. The girls from that original team are still tight, with Jamie walking two of them down the aisle, officiating one wedding, and serving as godfather to many of their kids.

After two years in Tifton, Jamie's life took another turn when he met Kirk, who became his husband. Jamie applied for the YMCA gymnastics and cheer program director position in Augusta, Georgia, prompting the couple to relocate. Kirk was studying at the Medical College of Georgia. Remarkably, some Tifton girls were so committed to Jamie's coaching that they drove two hours to Augusta for practice. Jamie then expanded to two teams, Junior and Senior Coed.

Upon Kirk's graduation the couple relocated to Charlotte, North Carolina, but Jamie wasn't ready to hang up his coaching hat. He discovered Eve King in Atlanta, owner of Georgia Cheerleading Center (GCC), who let Jamie run his program alongside hers in her gym. During that time Roger Schonder left United to coach the all-girl Youth and Senior teams at GCC while Jamie concentrated on juniors and coed teams.

After a brief stint coaching at GCC, Roger moved to The Stingray Allstars, prompting Jamie to make another bold move. With a loan from Kirk's father, he established the first dedicated physical location for Georgia All Stars in Marietta. In 2008 Jamie entered a short-lived partnership with Casey Jones and Roger Schonder to create Stingrays Purple. But after only a year they recognized that their coaching philosophies differed, so in 2009 Jamie revitalized Georgia All Stars and made Roswell, Georgia, his base.

THE RHINESTONE REVOLUTION

Jamie's impact on competitive cheerleading goes well beyond building successful teams. He was a true innovator, infusing theatrical flair into a sport that had once merely supported athletic teams. The Georgia All Stars made a name for themselves with their themed costumes—doctors, nurses, *Grease* characters, wedding parties—and pioneered the use of rhinestones in cheerleading uniforms, introducing a dazzling standard that transformed the industry.

One of Jamie's most memorable innovations was the introduction of "carwash skirts"—uniforms that flipped and changed colors mid-routine, creating a captivating visual spectacle that thrilled audiences and impressed judges. Under Jamie's leadership the Georgia All Stars expanded to nine teams, and more than 300 of his athletes earned college cheerleading scholarships. Georgia All Stars also became a trailblazer on the global stage, becoming the first team to compete in the international division at the World Championships, helping establish what would become a major competitive category.

Jamie's choreography clinched multiple gold medals at The Cheerleading Worlds. He created unforgettable routines with high entertainment value. According to Jamie's record, he remains the winningest choreographer in the Large Senior division at The Cheerleading Worlds, having choreographed for legendary programs including World Cup Shooting Stars, Cheer Extreme Senior Elite, and Cheer Athletics Panthers. His own program, Georgia All Stars, also captured several gold, silver, and bronze globes. Jamie helped to transform cheerleading from athletic support into a vibrant, standalone art form.

BEYOND THE MAT

Jamie was a founding member of the National All Star Cheerleading Coaches Conference (NACCC), an accomplishment that would eventually earn him the USASF Pioneer Award, one of the highest honors in the industry.

His choreography portfolio extended beyond All Star. Jamie choreographed over twenty college football bowl games and even brought his signature flair to pop culture, choreographing scenes for the hit TV show *The Vampire Diaries*.

Today, Jamie may have retired from competitive coaching, but he remains a vibrant creative force. He continues to design and create costumes, occasionally works on commercial choreography, and has discovered a passion for cooking, which he now shares on his local Channel 5 television station.

"Success is positively impacting others." – Jamie Parrish

EARNED WISDOM

★ **Success:** Success is when someone names their child after you or asks you to be in their wedding. It's when someone asks you to give them away at their wedding or to be the godfather of their child. Success is knowing you've positively impacted others. It's also helping kids who couldn't afford to be part of the sport to participate anyway.

★ **Wisdom:** You can reinvent yourself.

★ **Gratitude:** Jamie credits Don Collins for having a vision of where All Star could go long before it arrived there. He gives high praise to Bill Boggs for being a great father figure and mentor. Jamie credits Rey Lozano with being the father of All Star dances. Ray created the levels, transitions, and use of picture-perfect moments that have become standard in All Star dances today.

★ **Jamie's Wish:** Jamie wishes the sport would abandon the rubric completely and revert to a more subjective, comparative scoring style.

★ **To My Younger Self:** You are extremely creative in many ways, so nurture that.

★ **For Gym Owners:** Be aware that when you sell your business, its value is determined solely by the worth of the physical assets. The numbers you have in your gym are not assets.

★ **For Coaches:** Jamie said that his answer would have been different twenty years ago. Don't bring your personal life into the gym. You need to learn to connect with your athletes as the coach version of yourself and leave the personal version of yourself at home.

★ **Lessons Learned:** You don't have to be stuck in one specific place.

DID YOU KNOW?

★ Jamie's favorite part of cheer is dance. He thinks it's what separates us from gymnastics and acrobatics.

★ Memphis University's pom routine from the year they performed with the clowns is Jamie's favorite. At the time it stood out as being on a completely different level than anything he'd previously seen.

★ He loves to travel and has explored every continent except Antarctica.

★ Jamie twice decorated the Oval Office for Christmas.

★ He grew up on a peanut farm in South Georgia.

★ Wonder Woman is Jamie's favorite superhero because, when he was little, he was stuck on a peanut farm in the middle of nowhere. The only channel his television received aired *Wonder Woman* with Lynda Carter. He painted red stars on some tinfoil that he wrapped around his wrist and did cartwheels all over the yard.

★ For his animal Jamie chose the rescue dog, which symbolizes loyalty, courage, and resilience, particularly the ability to overcome adversity and find love and acceptance after hardship. It also represents the qualities of a faithful companion and a source of emotional support.

"The greatest glory in living lies not in never failing but in rising every time we fall." – Nelson Mandela

JAMES SPEED

Gymtyme All Stars, Spirt Sports, Speed Camps – 1992
Head Coach,
University of Louisville Coed Cheerleaders

FROM FOOTBALL PADS TO CHEER MATS

James Speed was an ex-football player who had attended Western Kentucky University. He began his career on an academic scholarship but chose to move back to Louisville and take residence in his childhood home after his parents moved. That's how he ended up at the University of Louisville. He hoped to play football again and did his best to get in shape to earn a spot as a walk-on.

While pumping iron in the gym one day, a female cheerleader named Catherine Thomas interrupted his workout. She needed a partner to work on stunts for cheerleading tryouts, and James agreed to help.

He arrived at tryouts sporting long hair, a scruffy beard, and jorts to assist Catherine. When the tryouts ended,

James heard his name called. He scanned the gym and said, "I'm not here to try out. I'm here to help her." And he pointed at Catherine.

The coach smiled and said, "Well, I'm offering you a spot. Do you want it or not?"

That's how James Speed became a cheerleader.

Unfortunately, Catherine didn't make the team, but she was a great dancer. James helped her create the Ladybirds dance team at the University of Louisville, which continues to this day. While still in college, James began teaching at NCA summer camps.

In 1986, during James's senior year at Louisville, he was cheering at a game against the University of Kansas in Lawrence. At halftime the Kansas athletic director and spirit coordinator requested a meeting with James. "My coach said, 'We need to meet with you right now.' My heart sank, and I thought, 'Oh, my gosh, I'm in trouble.'"

But James wasn't in trouble. Instead, he was offered a coaching position with the Jayhawks' cheerleading squad and a chance to attend graduate school for free. James took the job.

After graduating with his degree in business marketing, he moved to Kansas and began coaching while working on his graduate degree. (He told me he received an actual paper airline ticket in the mail for his move, and we laughed.)

A few weeks after arriving in Kansas, James received a call from a man named Lamar Hunt. He wanted to meet with James about coaching a cheerleading team he wanted to start. James wasn't sure he was interested, but he took the meeting anyway. It turned out that Hunt was the owner of the NFL's Kansas City Chiefs. He wanted to start a coed cheerleading squad and needed a coach. Lamar told James that he would be responsible for pregame and halftime routines. "Can you do it at the pro level?" Hunt asked. "You have done it before, right?"

James smiled confidently and said, "No problem. I've done it before. I can absolutely do that."

He had never choreographed a routine in his life.

Still, he stepped up to the challenge, coaching cheer squads for both the Kansas City Chiefs and the University of Kansas for four years while completing his graduate degree in sports administration with a minor in sports psychology. In 1990 James led Kansas to its first NCA College National Championship in Dallas, Texas, where the Jayhawks won, defeating none other than the University of Louisville.

HOME SWEET HOME

A year after Kansas beat Louisville, James's former coach called him and said, "I'm retiring. Put in an application to coach at Louisville and come home." James's grandfather was seriously ill, and James wanted to help take care of him, so he applied for the job and accepted the offer without hesitation.

When he returned to Louisville in 1992 he quickly learned how difficult it was for the cheerleaders to find practice space. On several occasions his team rolled out the mats and, halfway through practice, someone would come in and say, "Okay, we're locking up. You've gotta go."

Frustrated by the limited gym time available for his team, James decided to create his own space where his team and others could practice. He named it GymTyme.

Starting small, he purchased twelve folding chairs and a table, borrowed mats from the university, and declared, "Now we can practice." Initially, GymTyme was intended as a rental practice facility for all sports needing extra time in the gym.

THE SPEED CAMP INNOVATION

James not only taught summer camps for NCA, but he also played a key role in developing its college camp curriculum. Bill Boggs was brought on to develop and expand the collegiate programs at NCA with James continuing to assist.

During that time James met and recruited Leroy McCullough to cheer for him at the University of Louisville. After transferring from South Carolina, LeRoy eventually became captain of the Louisville cheer team and competed on GymTyme's open All Star team. After graduation, LeRoy returned to Oklahoma to work for Twist-N-Shout All Star cheer facility and to coach the Oklahoma State University cheer team. Leroy is currently the brand director for NCA and coaches Team USA Cheer.

In addition to NCA camps and college camps, James started his own camp company called Speed Camps. "The truth was I hated doing motions," James said. "I hated teaching motions even more. But I loved stunts, and I loved teaching stunts."

He approached Andy McNeil, NCA president at the time, with his stunt camp idea, and NCA agreed to let James start NCA STUNT Camps. But just as the camps were about to launch, NCA canceled the project because it feared the new camps might negatively impact their summer camp business. But NCA did give James its blessing to conduct the camps on his own.

The model was for James to travel to All Star gyms and offer a skills camp focused on stunting. The All Star gym could invite local school teams to participate, and James would split the registration fees with the gym as a fundraiser for its athletes. It was a win-win.

The camps were initially called Skills Camps. James said that when he traveled to the gyms, there were notes in the office or on a bulletin board about James Speed Skills Camps. But the kids would refer to the camps as "Speed Camps," which is how the name originated. After years of teaching those camps on his own, he eventually came to an agreement to sell the camp company to Varsity. That's how NCA Speed Camps came to be.

GYMTYME ALL STARS

In 1994 James was in his second year of coaching at the University of Louisville. Several of his athletes wanted to participate in more competitions, so James put together an open team and, at age forty, he competed with them as the GymTyme All Stars. And they won. A few years later, when Kevin Brubaker created the Novice, Intermediate, and Advanced levels, James started more All Star teams out of GymTyme and stopped renting space to other sports.

In 1996 Misty Hodges and Brad Habermel were captains of the team, and Louisville launched the unmistakable big bows, big hair, and red lips that are still common among All Star cheerleaders today. Misty was the first freshman at Louisville to make the varsity squad. After graduation, Brad moved to Dallas, Texas, and became part owner of Cheer Athletics in Plano. Misty stayed on as the assistant coach at Louisville and, eventually, became James's business partner at GymTyme. That's when Louisville started its all-girl program. The coed team could field only a limited number of girls, most of whom needed to be flyers. Creating the all-girl team allowed James and Misty to create opportunities for girls of all athletic types—bases, back spots, and flyers—to cheer for the university. The all-girl team became a powerhouse too.

COMPETITION ANYONE? SPIRIT SPORTS

Christie, a former captain at the University of Louisville, approached James while they were at an NCA College camp and said, "Hey, I have someone I want you to meet." That someone was Shannon Smith, who talked to James about starting a competition company. He needed someone who had more connections in the industry than he had. James agreed to join the effort.

In 2000 Shannon and James launched Spirit Sports. They dove in headfirst, and the first year was a nail-biter. They hosted one event in Myrtle Beach, South Carolina, that was meant to take place on a baseball field, but Mother Nature failed to cooperate. A cold mixture of sleet and rain rolled in the day before the competition. Luckily, they were able to secure an exhibit hall at the Myrtle Beach Convention Center, and that's where the event is still held today.

Spirit Sports focused on delivering exceptional events in a few key regions across the country. James leveraged his network, connecting with former teammates and colleagues from his cheerleading days. One of those connections was Tanaz Kirichkow, a former Louisville cheerleader who had launched an All Star program in California. Seeing an opportunity, she reached out to James, urging him to bring an event to the West Coast. At the time, USA hosted events in the region, but there were few other companies offering similar experiences. In response, Spirit Sports established an event at the San Diego Convention Center, expanding its reach and solidifying its presence on the West Coast.

MODERN SCORING SYSTEMS

James and Shannon, through Spirit Sports, created the first level- and category-based scoring system. Until then, scores had been random. You could score eighty-nine one weekend and ninety-eight the next. There was no rhyme or reason to it. James said there needed to be a rubric, so he drafted some ideas, and he and Shannon worked out the kinks and implemented their ideas at Spirit Sports. Instead of just one score you were given separate scores for stunts, pyramids, tumbling, jumps, and so on. Those scores were based on the difficulty of the elements the team performed at its level.

Everything for James and Shannon stemmed from a coach's point of view. They also took scoring a step further by providing coaches the first opportunity to attend an event in person and inquire about their scores through the Accuscore Review, a process later adopted by Varsity that is now the standard at competitions throughout the United States and the world.

Those innovations elevated the Spirit Sports profile, leading to expansion that included events in Worcester, Massachusetts; Dallas, Texas; and Palm Springs, California. In 2008 James and Shannon sold Spirit Sports to Varsity. Both remained employed at Varsity while also managing Spirit Sports.

THE SPEED FACTOR

James Speed is single-handedly responsible for a significant number of key people in the All Star industry. He not only trained his athletes at Louisville to become successful competitors while earning numerous national titles, but he also instilled in them his love and passion for the sport. As a result, many have dedicated their lives to All Star. LeRoy McCullough, Matt Goto, Damianne Albee Steward, and Santwon McCary all currently work full time for Varsity Spirit and have dedicated their lives to growing the sport and creating meaningful experiences for athletes across the globe.

A few other notable figures in the All Star industry who have been influenced by James Speed include Rob Ulrich, owner of The Stingray Allstars in New York; Carrie Seller, an up-and-coming super model; Tanaz, Rana, and Neda, owner of California All Stars; Misty Hodges, owner of GymTyme All Stars and coach of the University of Louisville all-girl program; Brad Habermel, owner of Cheer Athletics in Plano, Texas; Lindsey Sitzlar Settlemyer, program director at Premier Athletics; and Drew Malone, owner of Top Gun Arizona. James's impact and passion for cheer run far and wide throughout All Star, school, and collegiate cheer.

James Speed didn't just lend his name to the innovative Speed Camps, he fundamentally accelerated the entire All Star cheerleading industry. His lightning-fast approach to problem-solving—creating GymTyme when practice space was lacking, developing specialized stunt training when traditional camps fell short, and revolutionizing scoring systems when competitions needed structure—propelled All Star cheerleading forward.

Through his mentorship, James ignited a talent development wave that still ripples through the industry with many of his protégés still involved in cheerleading today. James is one of the few coaches, if not the only coach, to have won the NCA High School National Championship (with DuPont Manual), the NCA College

National Championship (with the University of Louisville), and the USASF/ISASF World Championship (with GymTyme), all in the same competition season. He was recognized by the USASF and IASF as Coach of the Year in 2008. James was named one of the Top 25 Most Influential Coaches, Choreographers, and Gym Owners 2008 by *American Cheerleader Magazine*. He was Team USA's first coach, coaching both the Coed and All-girl squads during the inaugural year of Team USA.

James loves his family. He has two daughters, a son, and three grandchildren from his previous marriage. He is filled with happiness to have found his person and gained an extended family in Texas, including three additional daughters and two grandchildren. He travels back and forth from Kentucky to Texas to visit family. He is entering his twenty-fifth year of coaching at the University of Louisville, but he still owns GymTyme, which has grown to fifteen All Star teams and continues to be active in the All Star community with twenty-nine World Champion titles and counting.

> **"Success is giving yourself the opportunity to win." – James Speed**

EARNED WISDOM

★ **Success:** James said he likes to win just as much as the next person, but to him success is giving yourself the opportunity to win. Winning is just one form of success. One of the most important successes you can have as a coach is knowing that you've impacted an athlete's life in such a way that they are successful in their own life with whatever their chosen career may be. James is especially proud when he sees his former athletes succeeding in the cheer industry.

- ★ **Wisdom:** Be better tomorrow than you were today. If you've done everything you possibly can and made every adjustment but someone is still better, you still win because you've pushed and created the best version of yourself.

- ★ **Gratitude:** Sheryl Travis Zimmerman had a significant impact on James. She gave him a chance when he showed up for his first tryout with long hair, a full beard, and jorts. She selected him for the team, and that moment changed his life. "I had no idea what I was doing," James said, "but she believed in me."

- ★ **James' Wish:** James would love to see a revamp of the scoresheet. The scoresheet dictates the sport, and right now the athletes are required to incorporate so many skills in the limited time that it's making the sport too difficult. This type of push could lead to injuries and a decrease in participation. The scoring system could, if designed correctly, be used to more effectively promote coed style stunting in All Star cheer. One whole section of the population of potential All Star cheerleaders is being left out. All Star cheer took off in popularity because of its inclusivity of all types of athletes. It's important to avoid developing a scoring system that fails to recognize the talents of all types of athletes.

★ **Mistakes:** Once upon a time two guys approached James to start a competition company. One cheered for James at the university, and the other was the mascot. He helped them create a business plan and guided them as they developed their ideas. Ultimately, James declined to be their business partner because he wasn't ready at the time. Those guys were Aaron Flaker and Emmitt Tyler of JAM Brands.

★ **For Gym Owners:** Communication is key. You need to be completely upfront with your athletes and their parents. Don't try to form a Level 5 team when you have Level 4 athletes. Take your time and focus on one thing at a time so you can be successful. Happy kids mean happy parents. Parents are not your enemy. They are your partners. Tell them the reasons behind your decisions, make decisions objectively, never show favoritism, and the parents will support you or, at the very least, they will respect you.

★ **For Coaches:** Make sure you understand the importance of separating the skill from the person. What an athlete can do reflects their skill. Who they are is their character. Those are two different things. Coaches should be able to train skills and develop young athletes' character. Coaching is life skills training, so don't take it lightly. Coaches influence lives and create lifetime memories. Take advantage of every opportunity. When it comes to the team, as the coach you have the final say, but you can include input from the team. Let them become part of the process. They will learn to be individually accountable and learn that success is earned as a team through each individual doing their part.

★ **Lessons Learned:** You don't get anywhere without hard work, but hard work is easy when you're passionate about what you're doing. Remember that making money is a by-product of your passion and not the driving force behind your motivation.

DID YOU KNOW?

★ James's favorite part of cheer is stunting.

★ James and his friend and teammate Andre Lyons created the "Awesome" during one of their many stunt sessions. The team was struggling to hold one-arm libs, so James suggested the flyer try landing on both feet instead of one. It worked, and that launched the success of one-arm stunts across the country. James went on to be the first to perform a "Double Awesome."

★ In 1985 James was teaching at a college cheer camp in Texas when he met a cute girl with a thick, country accent. He was seriously flirting, but she was clueless and blew him off. He went back to camp the next year, hoping to work up the courage to ask her out, but she had a boyfriend, so he refrained: "I didn't want to be that guy." Thirty-seven years later, at Spirit Sports Myrtle Beach, a beautiful woman approached James and said, "You probably don't remember my name," to which James replied, "Kelly Cox." The two have been together ever since. He waited thirty-seven years for the love of his life to cross his path again. He has a renewed passion for cheer because he's working with a partner who loves it as much as he does.

★ James loves the countryside. As a kid he spent a lot of time at his great grandmother's house that she had built out of tarpaper and cardboard and that had dirt floors compacted so tight it was cold to stand on them.

★ He loves to hunt, fish, camp, and travel the world to see new places.

★ James loves to fix things. His father was a self-taught plumber, electrician, welder, mechanic, home builder, and all-around handyman. He passed those skills on to James by having him watch and help at a young age.

★ James's favorite superhero is Superman. He likes that he's strong, can do anything, and has a beautiful girlfriend.

★ James chose as his animal the eagle, which represents divine spirit, sacrifice, connection to the creator, intelligence, renewal, courage, illumination of spirit, healing, creation, freedom, and risk-taking.

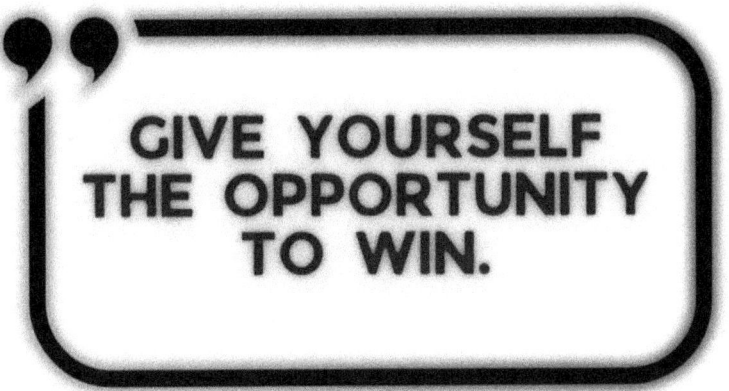

"Success is from the heart." – Unknown

COURTNEY POPE
Cheer Extreme All Stars – 1993

A FAMILY DREAM

Courtney Pope's cheerleading journey began with family at its heart. In 1991 she and her mother, Betsy Smith, started a recreational cheerleading program when Courtney's sister, Kelly (Smith) Helton, was in second grade. What began as a simple sideline cheer squad for elementary school basketball teams would eventually blossom into something much greater than anyone could have imagined. "I've loved every minute of doing what I love," Courtney said.

That passion quickly ignited a desire for a more challenging pursuit than recreational cheerleading. In January 1993 Courtney and her mother elevated their vision to a new level. They chose their twenty most talented girls, with Courtney's sister as the standout, and participated in their first All Star competition. The conditions were modest compared to today's standards. They showcased their talents on wrestling mats accompanied by music from cassette tapes, but the experience sparked a passion that continues today. Courtney's cheerleading empire has grown organically and with intention. "We grew gradually into the family empire we are today," she said, adding that it happened "one decision at a time."

Cheer Extreme expanded into various regions of North Carolina, recruiting the most talented athletes from across the state to join the organization at its main location. This strategy successfully propelled Cheer Extreme to the iconic program it is today.

Courtney's sister, Kelly, now owns and operates the Raleigh location where she has amassed numerous wins while nurturing her own athletes. Meanwhile, Cheer Extreme has eleven locations across Georgia, Illinois, Maryland, the DMV (DC and parts of Maryland and Virginia), North Carolina, and Virginia, serving thousands of young athletes chasing their cheerleading dreams.

Courtney said her philosophy is simple: "Coach with heart and create routines that move people emotionally."

This sentiment encapsulates what makes her programs special—technical excellence combined with emotional resonance. It's not just about executing difficult stunts or perfect synchronization, it's about creating performances that touch the audience on a deeper level.

> **"Success is making your mom proud."**
> **– Courtney Pope**

EARNED WISDOM

★ **Success:** If her mother was proud, she was successful.

★ **Wisdom:** Believe.

★ **Gratitude:** Courtney acknowledges that her mother has been her guidepost in life and in business. Her mom has a heart of gold, and Courtney strives every day to make her proud.

★ **Courtney's Wish:** To make All Star cheer more affordable.

★ **For Gym Owners:** Build your own facility and maximize every square inch. Don't rent.

★ **For Coaches:** Love the children above all outcomes.

DID YOU KNOW?

★ Courtney's favorite part of cheer is pyramids. You can witness her passion for pyramids firsthand in her routines.

★ Her favorite routine is the Senior Elite routine from 2023 and 2025. She also admires the routines of the Spirit of Texas Royalty every year.

★ Courtney is a mom to three children, and she loves the color teal.

★ Her favorite superhero is Spider-Man.

★ Courtney chose the sea turtle as her animal because it symbolizes longevity, ancient wisdom, emotional strength, and a deep connection to nature. It also represents protection, guidance, and the importance of slowing down and taking things one step at a time. Seeing a sea turtle can be a reminder to trust your path, embrace your unique journey, and find serenity in the face of change.

"Welcome to World Cup where cheerleaders are our trophies." – Elaine Pascale

"Analysis leads to paralysis." – Robert Herjavec

ELAINE PASCALE & JOELLE ANTICO
World Cup All Stars – 1994

COACHING HOOPS

In her early days, Elaine Pascale was a basketball coach at a private school in Jersey City. She moved to Greenbrook, New Jersey, in 1982. Her son, Anthony, started as a new student at St. Vincent de Paul, and Elaine was informed on the first day that every mother had to volunteer at the school. The options were bingo, lunch duty, or coach the cheerleading squad. "I don't like bingo," Elaine said. "I won't wear a hair net, so cheer coach it is. My daughter will do it."

Joelle was a freshman in high school at the time. Elaine served as the driver while Joelle stepped in as the coach and, together, the dynamic duo was born. They took a struggling team, affectionately dubbed the "Bad News Bears," and transformed them into champions. The nuns and priests were thrilled when the team won the Christian Youth Organization (CYO) Championship.

In 1992 Elaine and Joelle coached the Freehold Pop Warner Giants, the first Northeastern team to win the Pop Warner Nationals held in Jacksonville, Florida. Even back then, World Cup loved a good theme. Their routine had a USA theme, and they opened by spelling USA with their pom-pons.

Their victory earned them an invitation to President Bill Clinton's inauguration in Washington, DC, where the theme was, "Ask not what your country can do for you, but what you can do for your country."

So they spelled out USA with beautiful iridescent poms with red and blue metallic streamers in them. They marched down Pennsylvania Avenue while listening to President Kennedy's iconic 1961 inaugural speech and dancing to Neil Diamond's "Coming to America."

THE BIRTH OF WORLD CUP ALL STARS

The following year they took their Pop Warner team to San Francisco, California, and secured second place. Janee, Elaine's youngest daughter, was in eighth grade and would no longer be eligible to cheer. The team was excited to continue their journey together, so they didn't want their time as a team to end.

In 1994 Elaine and Joelle rented space from World Cup Gymnastics. In actuality, the team was directly funded by World Cup Gymnastics, and Elaine and Joelle volunteered their time as coaches. The girls on the team came from all over the area to be part of the team. A few moms talked to Elaine about forming an All Star team.

"Who do we cheer for?" Elaine asked. "Ourselves?"

There was a meeting with several of the moms and athletes encouraging Elaine to start the first Northeast All Star team. World Cup started out competing against high school teams. The team attended its first national competition with the Eastern Cheerleaders Association (ECA) in Virginia and was victorious.

Joelle laughed as she recalled, "People were like, 'Who are these World Cup people?' " She smiled and added, "We actually got our name from a gymnastics studio."

In 1995 World Cup competed at AmeriCheer Nationals in Orlando, Florida, and achieved another significant victory. As a reward, the team was given the unforgettable opportunity to ride in a convertible down Main Street, USA, alongside Mickey and Minnie Mouse. Janee was part of both winning teams making the victory's even sweeter. Elaine and Joelle said, "Wow! We're onto something here."

When they returned home they learned that World Cup Gymnastics would no longer house their teams. They immediately began to seek another facility for practice space. "We just won two national championships," Joelle said, "What are we going to do?"

A BLESSING IN DISGUISE

Elaine said, "It was a blessing in disguise" because they ended up moving into Ace Gymnastics with their three teams—Shooting Stars, Starlites, and Twinkles. They built a great relationship with the owner and his son George, who later worked at World Cup. As before, the athletes paid their fees directly to the gym, and Elaine and Joelle continued to volunteer as coaches. They worked full-time day jobs and coached on the side because they loved it.

They worked with other teams in the area to start the Eastern All Star Cheer Dance Coaches Association and hosted a scholarship event for local teams to come together and perform their routines. The kids would participate in a parade and a fifty-fifty raffle while the teams showed off.

World Cup revolutionized All Star cheerleading by infusing a deep connection between the routine and the music, using the soundtrack not just as background but as an integral part of the performance. This approach elevated the choreography, creating a captivating experience that resonated with audiences and set All Star cheer apart from traditional school cheerleading.

Beyond their innovative choreography, Elaine and Joelle added another layer of excitement by incorporating themes into each routine, making every performance a unique experience. Their influence extended beyond their own team as they became mentors, guiding other All Star coaches and program owners throughout New Jersey. Far from seeing these new teams as competition, they welcomed them with enthusiasm, thrilled to see the All Star community grow.

PIONEERS OF ALL STAR

Elaine is frequently referred to as the godmother, or fairy godmother, of All Star, a title I believe is deserved due to her selflessness in supporting other teams, coaches, programs, and owners. She has a passion for cheer and wants everyone to thrive.

But the influence of Elaine and Joelle reaches well beyond the confines of World Cup All Stars. As pioneers in the industry, their innovative methods in choreography, music integration, and themed performances have shaped generations of cheer programs across the nation.

Over four decades of commitment they have built not only championship teams but also a lasting community where athletes cultivate confidence, discipline, and lifelong friendships. Their eagerness to mentor fellow gym owners while upholding the highest standards of excellence showcases a unique blend of competitive spirit and generous leadership.

The story of Elaine and Joelle isn't just about building a successful business, it's about two visionaries who saw potential where others didn't, who persevered through challenges, and who helped shape the foundation of modern competitive cheerleading in America.

Elaine and Joelle started coaching together in 1982 and have been training All Stars together for forty-one amazing years. They are still the proud owners of World Cup All Stars along with Elaine's youngest daughter Janee, who manages the business, staff, coaches, and All Star directors. Elaine and Joelle are coaching Shooting Stars for the thirty-second straight year. For them it's World Cup All Stars all day, every day. Their business has grown to include four franchise locations, and they now manage forty staff members at their main Freehold location. Elaine has always felt that Joelle's accounting degree from Penn State University was a blessing to their business along with Janee, who graduated from the Fashion Institute of Technology in New York City in 2001. She has been a tremendous asset to World Cup through managing coaches, staff, and All Star directors.

Joelle has two children. Her son, Mikey, is twenty-six and plays baseball for the St. Louis Cardinals Triple A team in Memphis, Tennessee. He attended the University of Texas and was drafted in the eighth round in 2021.

Joelle's daughter, Gianna, is twenty-three and studies at Instituto Marangoni in Miami. She is now venturing out to start her own fashion line. Gianna was a Shooting Star who won Worlds in 2017, but she chose not to continue cheering in college after being bullied on social media. Since Gianna's experience, both Joelle and Elaine have educated their athletes on the importance of considering the words they use online.

"Success is when athletes wear beautiful smiles." – Elaine Pascale

"Success is seeing our alumni move on and become successful adults." – Joelle Antico

---

EARNED WISDOM

- **Success:** Elaine believes she is successful if the World Cup athletes wear beautiful smiles and have the support of their parents. Joelle believes success is when the athletes graduate, move on from the program, and go on to do amazing things. World Cup emphasizes education and the importance of a college degree.

- **Elaine's Wisdom:** Don't forget that the meaning of All Star forms a triangle. Everyone contributes. It's the efforts of parents, coaches and owners, and athletes working together as a triangle that create incredible experiences. Respect the triangle. All Star is a big family. Athletes need to realize that it's not the trophy that defines them but the thrill of the hunt that continues to stoke passion and success.

- **Gratitude:** NCA Dallas was a great experience during its early days. The event allowed them to see teams from Texas and California, and it helped them grow as coaches while also helping their athletes grow.

- **Elaine & Joelle's Wish:** Both ladies wish the NACCC still existed and that coaches had a larger voice in the safety of the sport. Or, at the very least, coaches would use the opportunities they do have to contribute to decisions in the industry.

★ **Mistakes:** Not purchasing or building their own facility. After all these years in business they are still paying an insane amount of money in rent.

★ **To Their Younger Selves:** Continue to develop an event brand. Elaine and Joelle started an event company called Infinity before Nfinity Shoes. The event boasted red carpets, Academy Awards, and loads of fun. Teams stopped coming because they didn't want to compete against World Cup. But the dynamic duo believes they ended up exactly where they were meant to be as they threw themselves into the gym, and their athletes were better for it.

★ **For Gym Owners:** Joelle encourages you to operate your gym as a business. Become a master of balancing success, money, and what is right for the athletes. Elaine encourages new gym owners to start with the younger, lower levels. Train the young athletes in your program and ensure you have a staff that will support their development. Level 6 teams present a challenge and a strain. It's difficult to work your way up to it, so don't start there. We are now in a conflicted industry; each day brings a new surprise. Home grown is the way to go.

★ **For Coaches:** Elaine urges coaches to make sure that training and coaching children is truly your desire. Don't coach just because you expect to win trophies. Do it to see your athletes' progress. Be respectful of your gym owner and other coaches.

Egos and personalities can be toxic. You need to be a good fit for the culture of the gym that you're at. Be the example you want to see in your athletes. Joelle encourages new coaches not to set their standards too high. Find your own niche and expand from there. If you don't have a passion for the sport, you'll burn out quickly. Last, most coaches can't make All Star their full-time job, so don't put your personal burdens on your gym owners.

★ **Lessons Learned:** You will be criticized day after day, but lions don't lose sleep over the opinions of sheep. Your future is determined by destiny. Give it to God.

DID YOU KNOW?

★ Elaine and Joelle's favorite part of cheer is the entire routine. They had to be experts at everything when they started, so they love it all.

★ Their favorite routine is the Shooting Stars' "Dancing With The Stars" performance, a memorable moment because Elaine's granddaughter, Gianna, was on the team that won gold that year.

★ Elaine was never a cheerleader, but she was a head basketball coach.

★ Elaine was the Women's A Flight Club Champion at Eagle Oaks Golf Club.

★ Joelle was Miss Yell in 1981.

★ Elaine is a huge fan of thoroughbred horse racing. Lucky for her, her son has secured a job working for FanDuel horse racing as an analyst and host. She enjoys visiting him in Louisville, Kentucky.

★ Elaine, Victor and Kristen Rosario, and Jamie Parrish started a sportsmanship camp called Hot Shots in Florida. They are celebrating their twentieth year offering Level 6 gym owners and their athletes a great experience.

★ Elaine was the recipient of the Lawerence B. Herkimer award, USASF All Star Pioneer award, Spirit Industry Hall of Fame award, USASF Top Cheer Coach award, and the USASF Lifetime Achievement Award.

★ No surprise, but both ladies are excellent Italian cooks.

★ Wonder Woman is Elaine's favorite superhero, but Joelle chose Road Runner because, she said, "That's our life."

★ Both Elaine and Joelle selected the lion as their animal. The lion symbolizes family, strength, energy, courage, guardianship, protection, ferocity, and authority. Elaine is a huge astrology fan, and being born a Leo makes her a natural leader.

"Hard work triumphs over talent when talent refuses to work hard." – John Wooden

"Attitude is everything." – Jeff Keller

VICTOR & KRISTEN ROSARIO
Top Gun All Stars – 1994

THE SPARK OF INSPIRATION

Victor Rosario attended his first college camp with NCA when he was a freshman at the University of Tennessee. James Speed was the head instructor, and according to Victor, James still had hair. Victor was amazed by the sport. He had only been participating in cheer since his junior year of high school. Excited to take advantage of every opportunity, he tried out for best tumbler, best jumper, and best stunter, and he won all three categories. NCA called the competition Top Gun.

When Victor returned to Miami, he told Kristen he wanted to start a team. His passion for the sport had only grown, and he saw it as an opportunity to not only pursue his love of cheerleading but also to help cover the cost of essentials like books and electricity as they navigated life on their own.

"I decided to call it Top Gun because, apparently, that signifies the best of the best," Victor explained.

BUILDING A DREAM FROM SCRATCH

In the summer, Victor taught NCA high school camps in the South Florida area. Anytime he noticed a standout athlete or one who was selected for All-American at camp, he would ask if they were interested in joining his team. He joked about how he would have to contact them or their parents using a rotary phone. After about two years of recruiting and explaining that he was putting together an All Star team, he assembled ten guys and ten girls to start his first team in 1994.

Victor and Kristen often joke that they were the first multilocation program. Their team practiced outdoors on the grass at Tropical Park in the Miami area. Practice ended when the park lights shut off or the rain turned on.

Eventually, they increased each athletes' monthly tuition by a few dollars so they could rent space for an indoor practice at least once per week. They cherish their memories of the inaugural team not only for its status as their first but also for the many challenges they overcame together.

When Top Gun launched, its team colors were black, red, and white. Top Gun fans must find that hard to imagine. Victor led his team to its first NCA camp sporting red Soffee shorts and a crisp white T-shirt emblazoned with "Top Gun All Stars."

Top Gun was the sole All Star team at the high school camp, yet it was more motivated than ever to compete. Victor developed a routine by essentially copying and pasting elements from his favorite high school and college cheer routines from his youth. Victor didn't know how to choreograph, and no one was teaching coaches how to design routines back then. You had to figure it out as you went. "We learned by trial and error," Victor explained. He cut the music himself using a dual cassette tape, and soon the team was ready to compete.

THE FIRST COMPETITION CHALLENGE

They set off for NCA Regionals with one goal: securing a bid to NCA Nationals in Dallas, and they succeeded. As Kristen and Victor prepared for the trip they meticulously checked everything: music, team, choreography, flights, and hotels.

But suddenly they froze, exchanged panicked looks, and spoke in unison: "We don't have cheer uniforms." The event was only a few weeks away, and every cheerleader knows that a few weeks isn't enough time to get a uniform. That hasn't changed in forty years.

Determined to have uniforms for their NCA Nationals debut, Victor and Kristen reached out to their coach at Miami-Dade Community College where they both were cheerleaders. They asked if they could borrow the college team's uniforms and, thankfully, their coach agreed.

The team competed in Miami Dade's striking black, white, and gold uniforms emblazoned with Jags across the chest. After finishing the event in second place, Victor and Kristen decided they couldn't return the following year in red, black, and white, so they kept the black, white, and gold colors permanently.

THE JOURNEY TO VICTORY

In the nineties, winning the NCA or UCA All Star Nationals was the pinnacle of the sport. From 1994 to 1999 Top Gun bounced between second and third place before finally winning its first NCA Nationals in 2000. Victor attributes their success to the many years of losing. "Failure makes you reflect on how badly you really want to succeed," he said. "Are you willing to invest the time, effort, and resources it takes?" He said those six years of trying to climb to first place helped build character and became a turning point for Top Gun All Stars. "If you're willing to give up and walk away because you didn't like the feeling of losing," he said, "then you never truly wanted it in the first place."

In 1997 Victor received a call from his former gymnastics coach telling him the gymnastics center had flooded, so he was in urgent need of additional revenue. Top Gun secured its first official home by partnering with Victor's former coach, successfully renting a 3,000-square-foot warehouse bay. Inside was an old trampoline and several pieces of mat that connected to form about seven strips of carpet-bonded foam.

Since the building lacked an office, Kristen worked in a space within the gym. As you may already know from reading the history portion of the book, her desk served as the starting point for the tumble track. Children would stand on the edge of her desk and leap off to begin their tumbling sequence on the tumble track. If they stumbled in the opposite direction or over rotated, her papers would scatter everywhere.

Ultimately, a ten-by-ten office space was constructed for her, complete with a small AC unit. Victor and Kristen appreciate their modest beginning, because it instilled the values of hard work and frugality. They learned to fully outgrow their space before seeking more.

Their single bay eventually expanded to one and a half bays and then to three bays spread throughout the warehouse complex. The program expanded from one team to two, then four and, eventually, to six.

CREATIVITY RISING

Victor clearly recalls that 1998 marked the creative turning point for Top Gun All Stars. He chose to push boundaries, innovate, and create routines that embodied his vision of what All Star should represent. He wasn't particularly concerned about how it would be received. He followed his gut and did what he felt was right. He believes that approach put Top Gun on the map and marked the beginning of its notoriety.

There is no doubt in my mind that Top Gun fueled the creativity in our sport, and Victor Rosario was—and continues to be—the force behind it. Year after year, Top Gun introduces something new, consistently challenging the status quo and driving innovation in cheerleading.

Kristen was a dancer who incorporated the graceful lines of dance into her cheer teams, insisting on clean body lines, an uncommon standard at the time. Her technique disrupted the norm and further advanced the sport. With Victor's creativity and keen eye for detail combined with Kristen's dance background that brought clean lines and purposeful transitions, a powerhouse was born.

Top Gun operated out of its three separate bays for years, but Kristen noticed a problem—parents weren't always stopping by to pay their bills or to collect important information. Instead, they would just drop off their kids and leave. As a result, Kristen and Victor agreed that they needed to consolidate everything under one roof.

In 2003 they made a significant move to an 8,500-square-foot facility that featured two full-size spring floors, a tumble track, a rod floor, and a trampoline. And Kristen finally had her own office.

In 2014 Top Gun established the facility where they continue to operate today. After twenty years the couple opened a state-of-the-art facility spanning 15,000 square feet on one acre of land. But to this day, the training area has no air conditioning.

Victor and Kristen credit the acquisition of such a facility to the wonderful individuals they encountered throughout their journey. One of the most impactful was a former parent and the mother of a current employee, Sean Guzman. She worked at a local bank and assisted the Rosarios in understanding the business, navigating the Small Business Administration, and securing loans.

Second was Carlos Velasquez, the former owner of the Miami Elite All Stars. Although Miami Elite was a local rival started by two former Top Gun boys, Victor and Kristen remained friendly with them. When Carlos left the All Star industry, he started a career in commercial real estate. He was Victor and Kristen's first call when they were looking for a new building. His experience in both the cheer world and real estate was integral in securing the right space and location.

Victor and Kristen earnestly conveyed their belief in the value of relationships: "It's important to show respect and be cordial to everyone."

After launching their new facility, they faced a substantial mortgage and sought new opportunities to expand their brand. After approximately two years of building a relationship with the owners of Orlando All Stars and Ohio Extreme to ensure they shared the same core values, they expanded the Top Gun name and licensed the brand to their first two locations.

Kristen and Victor share a wonderful relationship. They met when she was fifteen and he was sixteen, and they have cherished every moment together since. Many married couples argue about religion, finances, differing viewpoints, or household messiness. But Kristen and Victor said they only argue about cheerleading. They have been married for twenty-six years and are the proud parents of two wonderful children, Demi, twenty-four, and Jodi, twenty-two.

Top Gun started with one team in a park and, after thirty years, has expanded to twenty-two teams at the Miami location along with additional locations in Pennsylvania, Ohio, and Georgia plus three in Florida, two in Arizona, and one in the United Kingdom. The program started with Victor and Kristen handling everything and has expanded to employ over 130 staff members worldwide.

Victor and Kristen's impact on All Star cheerleading goes beyond just competitive success. From humble beginnings practicing on park grass to building an international powerhouse, they have fundamentally transformed the sport through their unwavering commitment to innovation.

Victor's creative vision pushed the boundaries of what competitive cheerleading could be, while Kristen's dance background elevated the technical precision and artistic elements of the performances. Their combined talents created a distinctive style that programs worldwide have sought to emulate.

Through three decades of leadership, Victor and Kristen have impacted the lives of thousands of athletes while establishing standards of excellence that continue to inspire the entire cheerleading industry. The Top Gun legacy stands as a testament to what determination, creativity, and a genuine love for the sport can accomplish.

> "Success comes from positively impacting the lives of others." – Kristen Rosario
> "Success is knowing who you are deep inside." – Victor Rosario

EARNED WISDOM

★ **Success:** Victor believes that success is knowing who you are deep inside and understanding your true identity. Success is when you have the courage to be that person every day, regardless of what others might say. Kristen believes that success comes from positively impacting the lives of others. She said, "I want to go to sleep at night and know that somewhere out there, somebody is a better person, or they were able to get through something difficult, because I was there." She feels blessed to have Top Gun as a vehicle to impact so many lives.

★ **Wisdom:** Surround yourself with people who share a similar mindset and vision for your life. Know that you can overcome anything that comes your way if you have faith in yourself. Victor also said it's vital to understand the business side of things. He was focused on training the athletes, and without Kristen, they'd probably still be in the park. She drove the ambition to operate like a business and acquire the first building, and each building thereafter.

★ **Gratitude:** Kristen credited two people with having an impact on her All Star career. The first was Victor. "I would not be here if it weren't for him," she said. "He taught me everything—literally everything—there was to know about cheerleading." Second was Elaine Pascale. Elaine is an iconic figure, but she is like a mother to Kristen: "She is truly the fairy godmother of cheerleading to me." Victor reminisced about his old times as a young collegiate cheerleader when he looked up to James Speed and aspired to stunt as brilliantly as he did. In addition, he spoke highly of Debbie Love. He respects the technical teachings and mental awareness that she brought to the sport. And they share a birthday.

★ **Victor & Kristen's Wishes:** Victor wishes the scoresheet wasn't so difficult: "The scoresheet dictates everything we do. There are so many skills that need to be jammed into a routine today." Kristen wishes the rules were less restrictive to allow for greater creativity. She'd love to be able to incorporate light and sound into their performances. She also wishes kids today could have a different outlet besides their phones. She would love for kids to have more social interactions.

★ **To Our Younger Selves:** You can achieve a lot more when you don't care who gets the credit. Parents can be your biggest allies if you create the right culture.

- ★ **Mistakes:** Victor said his biggest mistake was allowing his ego to drive his decisions. As a young, talented athlete who studied the sport intensely, he thought he knew it all. As an adult, he realizes he knows nothing.

- ★ **For Gym Owners:** Don't bite off more than you can chew. Start small and grow into your space. When you're busting at the seams, you grow a little bigger. It's easy to make the mistake of building a facility that is too large. Make sure you have customers for ten floors before you have a building with ten floors. People are going to come to your gym because of what you do for their children, not because of the size of your facilities or the amenities you offer. You're not in the business of cheer and dance. You're in the business of people. Recognize that and prove through your actions that you have the best interests of your athletes in mind, and they'll come. Surround yourself with people who are better than you at the things you're not good at. If you're trying to be the CEO, the janitor, the coach, and the choreographer, it can be overwhelming.

- ★ **For Coaches:** Believe in yourself. All good coaches question themselves. That's the hardest part of coaching. You may have great ideas, so don't doubt yourself. Give yourself a moment to prove that you're great at what you do.

★ **Lessons Learned:** Kristen struggled to find balance while raising her kids. As she attempted to step away from the day-to-day operations to raise her children, things slipped through the cracks. She said it was no one's fault. It just happened. The gym was growing, and they hired a lot of new staff, but she wasn't present as much to deal with things. She wouldn't trade it for anything, because her kids needed her, but she learned that you have to find a healthy life balance and put the right people in the right places to help you achieve that balance.

DID YOU KNOW?

★ Kristen enjoys watching all aspects of a routine, but her favorite parts of cheer when she was a participant were stunts and dance. Victor's favorite parts of cheer are stunting and tumbling.

★ Kristen was a dancer. She is extremely sensitive and empathetic. She also has crooked pinkies and is terrified of frogs.

★ Victor has a rare eye condition. He was on a dinner date with Kristen, and as he chewed, he kept winking at her. Kristen thought, "Why does he keep winking at me?" He later learned that his condition is called Marcus Gunn syndrome. A muscle in Victor's face is connected incorrectly to his jaw, so when he moves his jaw, his eye closes—he winks. I had the pleasure of witnessing this phenomenon in person during our interview.

- ★ The Top Gun athletes have the highest level of respect for Victor but are more afraid of Kristen. The kids say, "Let Victor be mad at me, but don't tell Kristen and let her be disappointed in me."

- ★ Kristen's favorite superhero is Iron Man. She loves that he is self-made and that his superpower is his intellect. As a child, Victor loved Spider-Man because he could climb walls. He said his mom would put her purse down, look around, and find Victor trying to scale the building.

- ★ Victor chose the honey badger as his animal because it symbolizes fearlessness, ambition, and a willingness to fight for its dreams.

- ★ Kristen selected the penguin because it symbolizes reassurance, loyalty, and the importance of community.

"Pressure is a privilege." – Billie Jean King

"Hard work beats talent when talent doesn't work hard." – Tim Notke

"Leadership and learning are indispensable to each other." – John F. Kennedy

THE THREE AMIGOS
ANGELA ROGERS, JODY MELTON, BRAD HABERMEL
Cheer Athletics – 1994

A PARK, TWO KIDS, AND A DREAM

In the spring of 1994, two passionate cheerleaders gathered at Bob Woodruff Park in Plano, Texas, poised to launch one of the most influential All Star cheerleading programs ever. Jody Melton and Angela Rogers waited with excitement and uncertainty, and only two athletes turned up for the first practice.

Most people would have viewed that turnout as a reason to rethink their venture. Instead, Jody and Angela made sure those two kids experienced "a glorified private lesson" they'd always remember. It was a modest start for Cheer Athletics, but the original duo pressed on.

Word of mouth spread, leading to the formation of a team of sixteen athletes called the Cheer Athletics Tigers. This inaugural team sported blue-and-gold uniforms, an early sign of the professionalism and polish that would define the Cheer Athletics brand. After that first year, Brad Habermel joined the team and the new trio —affectionately known by their Cheer Athletic (CA) family as "the three amigos"—forged their path to greatness.

Starting Cheer Athletics wasn't just about teaching cheerleading skills. For all three founders, it represented a genuine leap of faith at a time when All Star cheer program owner was not a recognized career path. Brad said his father was less than thrilled with his unusual choice. "There was no career path that anybody could see," Brad said, "because it had not happened. It was kind of a leap of faith for everyone who went all-in on the gym business." Since then, Brad's father has repeatedly said he's glad Brad didn't listen to him.

The three partners came from different cheerleading backgrounds but shared a common vision. Jody, who hadn't cheered until his junior year at Baylor University, met Angela through the National Cheerleaders Association (NCA) staff. Jody convinced Angela, who had been cheering since the age of five and was completing her cheerleading career at Southern Methodist University, to help launch the program.

Brad, a former cheerleader at the University of Louisville under the legendary James Speed, originally moved to Dallas to oversee the curriculum for NCA camps. When

Jody asked him to coach All Star, Brad was initially hesitant, but he eventually jumped on board. Their complementary backgrounds and personalities would prove to be their greatest strength.

GRASSROOTS GROWTH

Cheer Athletics' early days were marked by improvised training facilities and inventive solutions. After that first practice in the park, they rented space from various facilities including Lance Wagers' Cheerobics, Southwest Gymnastics, and the NCA Supercenter. In 1995, just one year later, enrollment surged from sixteen to fifty-eight athletes. By year three, the trio boasted eight fully rostered teams with no crossovers, a remarkable feat in an industry that was barely alive.

Though their growth was rapid, it was also methodical. "We wanted only the best coaches to grow with us," Angela said. "The whole culture from the beginning was fun, high-level training."

Modern cheerleaders might be surprised to learn about the training conditions in those early facilities. Brad vividly remembers the lack of air conditioning in the summer heat of Texas and the large industrial fans that tried to keep the teams and coaches cool. But despite the fans, athletes were sweating so much they seemed to be melting. Today's air-conditioned facilities with spring floors and in-ground pits were far from the norm in the mid-1990s.

It wasn't until their third year that the trio secured their first dedicated facility—a former batting cage in

Garland, Texas. The equipment was basic: carpet-bonded foam, panel mats, and a tumble track. There were no spring floors or in-ground pits.

RAISING THE BAR

From the beginning, Cheer Athletics set out to elevate the sport through professionalism and athletic excellence. "We wanted to be organized and treat it like a business," Jody explained. "The logo was clean and sharp and professional. The name was 'Athletic,' and we wanted that to be reflected in our routines."

Brad added, "Very early on we set a really high expectation for our athletes and for the people who were coaching at our gym." Cheer Athletics wanted to set the standard for the industry. CA wanted everyone to look toward them. That approach paid dividends at the inaugural Cheerleading Worlds in 2004. When given an all-girl bid without a specific team designation, they assembled an elite squad by combining their top female athletes. The resulting team, the Super Cats, claimed the first World Championship and, according to Brad, "sent All Star on its way because people could really see the athleticism behind the sport."

Rules were quickly amended after that championship to prevent such team combinations, but the impact was indelible. Cheer Athletics had established itself as an innovator that ultimately pushed the sport forward.

BEYOND THE TROPHIES

While championships were undoubtedly important in the early years, the Cheer Athletics' philosophy evolved to emphasize the overall athlete experience. CA made it a priority to focus on the importance of the everyday experience athletes had inside their gym and on the life lessons that were taught.

This revelation shifted their culture. When an athlete is thirty or forty years old, no one really cares what skills they might have. Cheer Athletics knew that what would matter long term was how well their athletes worked with other people, how they managed themselves in tough situations, and how they fought through the mud to get to the sunshine. The resilience that All Star taught the athletes became the most important aspect of training at CA. Their philosophy of inclusive excellence—"There is a spot for everyone in our sport," Jody said—

is captured in the message that greets visitors at their facility: "You Belong Here."

STRATEGIC EXPANSION

Unlike many successful gym owners who rushed to expand, Cheer Athletics maintained a single location for its first twenty years. The decision to grow beyond Plano primarily stemmed from a desire to create opportunities for their staff. "The only reason we even started to think about expanding," Brad said, "is because some of our most trusted and valued employees were like, 'Hey, what's next for me?'"

Between 2013 and 2014 Cheer Athletics expanded to five company-owned locations: the original Plano gym and new facilities in Austin, Charlotte (near San

Antonio), and Frisco in Texas plus Columbus, Ohio. But adding five locations was difficult and challenged their quality of life. "We just knew there had to be a better way," Angela said.

That better way turned out to be franchising. With the help of Chad Wright, director of expansion, Cheer Athletics transitioned to an official franchise model. Today, the three amigos only own the original Plano location. All the other gyms operate as franchises. The Cheer Athletics brand now encompasses over twenty locations across the United States and the United Kingdom, including specialty programs for dance and stunts.

THE THREE AMIGOS TODAY

After nearly three decades in business together, the three founders maintain distinct roles while fluidly sharing responsibilities. Brad continues to coach four teams, including three Worlds teams (Cheetahs, Panthers, and Wildcats) and the Level 5 Large Senior team, the Pumas. He also manages communication with staff and franchise owners, working behind the scenes to keep things running smoothly.

Angela coaches the Wildcats team and oversees brand consistency, vendor relationships, and often handles parent communications, drawing on her interpersonal skills to maintain the gym's culture.

Jody tends to handle technical aspects like website management, email systems, and facility maintenance as "the nerdy one," as he jokingly put it.

Their personal lives reflect their commitment to family. Brad married his husband, Jason, in 2015. Their eleven-year-old daughter cheers at the gym. Angela, a divorced mother of two daughters, eleven and thirteen, balances her gym responsibilities with her "taxi era" of driving kids to various activities, including cheerleading and softball. Jody married in 2002 and now has grandchildren who participated in Cheer Athletics programs.

ENDURING PARTNERSHIP

Perhaps the most remarkable aspect of Cheer Athletics is the lasting partnership among its three founders. In an industry where business partnerships often fracture under pressure, the three amigos have maintained their relationship for nearly three decades.

"We're blessed with the best partnership on the planet," Angela said proudly.

"We're really very different from each other," Jody said. "I think that makes it work. We have different strengths and weaknesses as well as very different personalities, but we've been together for a long time and trust each other completely." Through it all, their commitment to each other and their shared vision have remained steadfast.

LASTING PAW PRINTS IN THE SAND

From two kids in a park to thousands of athletes across multiple continents, Cheer Athletics has transformed countless lives and helped shape the evolution of All

Star cheerleading. CA's innovation at the first Cheerleading Worlds set new standards for athletic excellence. Its methodical business approach demonstrated that All Star cheerleading could be a viable career. The emphasis on inclusiveness and character development showed that competitive success and personal growth aren't mutually exclusive.

Today, as the three amigos gaze toward the future, they're driven by the same principles that united them in 1994: excellence, innovation, and the conviction that All Star cheer can transform lives far beyond the competition mat.

The words etched on their gym walls and reflected in every program, "You Belong Here," is a message not just for their athletes but for the entire cheerleading community, a reminder that this sport they helped pioneer has room for everyone.

"Success is waking up and being excited about your day." – Brad Habermel
"Success is waking up." – Angela Rogers
"Success is feeling good about what you're doing." – Jody Melton

---

★ **Success:** For Brad, success is being able to wake up every day and feel excited about the life you've created. Success is going to bed without stress or being at odds with your day. For Angela, success is waking up and having the ability to choose how you will move through your day. Success is having people in your life who support you, people who understand you, people who see you, and people who hear you. Success is feeling good about what you're doing and the impact you have on others.

★ **Gratitude:** James Speed and Cenie Royal had a significant impact on Brad's leadership. Angela credits Lance and Carol Wagers for their exemplary leadership and Kevin Jones, her college coach, for guiding her during her early journey. Jody also feels a debt of gratitude to Lance and Carol Wagers for their leadership. Brad, Angela, and Jody agree that they have guided and helped each other, and they are immensely grateful for their relationship.

★ **Their Wish:** All three amigos agreed they would wish for a single score- sheet.

★ **Mistakes:** Feeling like we had to control everything from the beginning. It wasn't until we gained some maturity that we learned to let others step in and help us grow.

★ **For Gym Owners:** Figure out what you're passionate about, do it well, and stick with it. Be open to possibilities and stay within budget. Don't let your parents influence your decisions.

★ **For Coaches:** Be a good human. Know that your words and body language will make a lasting impression on the athletes you coach. Continue to learn the scoresheet and the sport. Educate yourself more about people and how to communicate with them, both on and off the mat.

DID YOU KNOW?

★ Brad's favorite part of cheer is the creativity. Jody likes that anyone can be part of the sport, and Angela's favorite aspect is the lightbulb moments.

★ Their favorite routine was the 2004 Super Cats.

★ Brad loves yoga. He also won a special award at high school graduation because he was the only person in his district who didn't miss a single day of school from first grade through twelfth grade. And he loves dogs.

★ Angela played the piano for fourteen years. In addition to cheer, she was a softball player growing up.

★ Jody didn't cheer until his junior year of college. He completed a full Ironman, and his vice is drinking Mountain Dew.

★ Angela's superhero is Wonder Woman. Jody said his childhood favorite was Spider-Man, and Brad chose Aquaman.

★ Their animal is the tiger because it represents strength, courage, and determination, raw power, fearlessness, and the ability to trust your instincts. Culturally, the tiger is revered as a symbol of leadership, bravery, and protection.

"The problem is not the problem. The problem is your attitude about the problem." – Captain Jack Sparrow, *Pirates of the Caribbean*

BRETT HANSEN
Spirit of Texas – 1994

MATH TEACHER TURNED TUMBLING COACH

Brett began his All Star journey in 1991 when he met Amy Burrows when both were teaching NCA summer camps. Like Brett, Amy was from the Dallas-Fort Worth area. After teaching a few camps together they became great friends. She had two younger sisters who cheered for a powerhouse high school, and their mom was starting an All Star team. Brett said, "What's All Star?"

Amy explained that it was a new initiative involving a combination of athletes from various schools who competed together at the NCA High School Nationals. There was an All Star division then, but the event was still held in conjunction with the High School Nationals.

Amy noticed that Brett was excellent in and enthusiastic about tumbling, so she hired him as the tumbling coordinator for her sister's team, which her mom coached. Brett continued working on his degree in education with a concentration in mathematics. He was determined to work with children and teach math. While in college he decided to help coach Amy's sister's high school team, and he and Amy also started an All Star team together. They rented space from another All Star gym in Roulette, Texas, and coached the team until they graduated from college about three years later. Amy found a job right out of college and moved to Houston.

FINDING FREEDOM IN ALL STAR

Brett was heavily involved in school cheer but gravitated toward All Star because he appreciated the freedom it offered, including that he could choose his own team. He grew up doing competitive gymnastics and thought that All Star modeled that work ethic and excitement.

Brett stayed in Dallas and met Brad Vaughn, who was working at Rebel Cheer Company. The woman who ran the gym gifted them a senior team. "These older girls don't listen to me," she said. "I think they need somebody younger." She thought Brad's choreography combined with Brett's technical expertise would lead the team to greater success. The girls loved that combination, and the team's performance reflected that. The team went undefeated for most of its first season and broke into the top three at NCA Nationals.

THE SPIRIT OF TEXAS RISES

The next year Brad and Brett launched their own program. Brett came from Southwest Spirit, where he worked with Amy Burrows. Brad collaborated with the Rebel Cheer Company, which led to a rebranding as the Spirit of Texas Rebels. They boasted a small senior team alongside a new junior team based in Arlington, Texas, the largest Dallas suburb.

In their second year they added two more teams for a total of four and dropped the Rebels name to become simply the Spirit of Texas. They have grown every year since.

They eventually opened a second location in the metro area town of Coppell, just north of the DFW Airport, providing them with the opportunity to work with many new kids they wouldn't otherwise have encountered due to the longer drive.

Dallas had grown so large they decided to branch out. The business model at the original location was primarily based on school training, but when schools shut down due to COVID, school cheer shut down as well. To save money, they consolidated to the one location.

A DISTINCTIVE STYLE

Spirit of Texas introduced a clean, straightforward style to the All Star world, routines that were both challenging and entertaining yet easy to follow. Their choreography was designed with minimal distractions, allowing spectators to fully appreciate each detail. Brad and Brett aimed to create performances that resonated with everyone. As Brett explained, "We wanted everyone to root for us."

Every year they would fly to Worlds with their team, and they had a superstition that everyone had to be together. Standing at baggage claim with their team in tow in 2009, they received a call from a friend informing them that they had won USASF Gym Owners of the Year and were needed on stage at the Coaches Gala. Brett said, "Oh, my God, we aren't even on the magical express yet." Shocked and honored, they missed their big moment on stage and celebrated at the airport with their team instead.

Spirit of Texas has come a long way since its humble beginnings in 1994. They sold their original property in Arlington and, as noted earlier, transitioned to their new 65,000-square-foot facility in Coppell. That facility, larger than a football field, houses more than fifteen teams and a staff of over twenty. Brad and Brett continue to work together to pursue their passion and grow their business.

Brett Hansen's journey from a curious college student who went from asking "What's All Star?" to becoming one of the most influential figures in competitive cheerleading exemplifies the growth of the sport itself. What began as a chance meeting with Amy Burrows in 1991 blossomed into a lifelong passion that has shaped the lives of thousands of athletes. Brett's journey from a math education student to an influential cheer entrepreneur demonstrates how passion, vision, and adaptability can shape not just a career but an entire industry. As Brett and Brad continue their partnership at Spirit of Texas, their impact on the world of All Star remains as vibrant as their purple uniforms.

> "If you get up and go to work every day, and you feel happy with your job, then that is a success." – Brett Hansen

EARNED WISDOM

★ **Success:** Success is how you feel. If you get up, go to work every day, and feel happy with the job you do, that is success. Success for me is not measured by who has the most franchises, although that may be a form of success for someone else. I believe success is defined by how you feel and how you see yourself among your colleagues.

★ **Wisdom:** Coaching is a passion. There's a feeling deep in your heart when you see someone learn something, attain a goal, or push themselves further than they ever thought possible. I think there's an adrenaline rush from the feeling of helping others that keeps us coaching day after day.

★ **Gratitude:** Brett has tremendous respect for Lance and Carol Wagers. He is grateful to have had Lance as his boss and said that Lance and Carol were like second parents to him.

★ **Brett's Wish:** Brett's wish is simple: one scoresheet, please.

- ★ **To My Younger Self:** Don't place your trust in just anyone. Make sure the people you trust are worthy of that trust.

- ★ **For Gym Owners:** Be true to yourself and know your brand. Your brand can take on a life of its own.

- ★ **For Coaches:** Love every minute. Work with each athlete and help them love All Star cheer the way you love All Star cheer. Teach your athletes to believe in themselves.

- ★ **Lessons Learned:** The gym life can consume every minute of your day. Be sure to take time for yourself and know that it's okay to leave the gym behind once in a while.

DID YOU KNOW?

- ★ Brett's favorite aspect of cheer is difficult to pinpoint. He loves the whole package and is passionate about technique, whether it involves jumps, tumbling, baskets, stunts, or dance. He enjoys seeing the entire performance come together. Ultimately, anything done with excellence is his favorite aspect of cheer.

- ★ Brett loves to travel and is fluent in Spanish.

- ★ He has a mathematics degree.

- ★ Brett runs seven miles a day.

- ★ He loves bacon-wrapped meatloaf and egg salad.

★ Brett is a humongous Dallas Cowboys fan and loves to play fantasy football.

★ His favorite superheroes are the Avengers because even superheroes come up against circumstances they can't manage by themselves. He likes how they come together for the common good.

★ As his animal Brett chose the hummingbird because it represents a messenger, timelessness, healing, warrior spirit, energy, vitality, infinity, affection, and playfulness.

"When people show you who they are, believe them."– Maya Angelou

DON COLLINS
Spirit Xpress All Stars – 1994
All Star Challenge – 2000
UNC Charlotte Coach

THE COLLEGE YEARS

Don cheered at James Madison University (JMU) from 1979 to 1983. He continued as a student coach while obtaining his master's degree in higher education administration. While at JMU Don taught cheerleading camps for the Eastern Cheerleading Association. Through those camps he met Hilda McDaniel and the Q94 Rockers, who taught Don about All Star. Hilda and Don became friends, and she frequently asked him to be their camp counselor. In that role he would spend individual time with the team to help refine the skills they learned at camp.

In his first year at JMU, the UCA College camp commenced at Virginia Tech in Blacksburg, and JMU participated. While the team was preparing to leave for the airport, it encountered Jeff Webb. Jeff needed a ride, and the JMU coach kindly offered to give him a lift. She asked Don to move to the back so Jeff could sit in the front.

"I didn't know who Jeff Webb was," Don said. "I was a college kid." He laughed and said, "I refused to move. We didn't win a trophy at camp, and I was mad."

After his time at JMU, Don went on to establish a coed team at Slippery Rock University in Pennsylvania. The UCA Collegiate National Championships expanded to include competition for all colleges, not just Division I schools, and Slippery Rock claimed the Division III championship in the first year of that division. Don said the event was held outdoors in the sweltering sun of San Diego, California. "We had some carpet-bonded foam on concrete," he said.

After spending a few years at Slippery Rock, Don was hired to manage residence halls at the University of North Carolina (UNC) at Chapel Hill. Around the same time, the UNC cheer coach position became vacant, and Don was asked to step in. At that time the University of Kentucky and NC State, coached by Kathy Buckey, were the powerhouse teams that typically won the UCA College Nationals. But Don was creative and determined, and he brought a Collegiate National Championship to UNC Chapel Hill in 1994.

BREAKING BOUNDARIES

Don loved a good challenge and was constantly pushing himself, so he decided to see if his team could win the NCA College Nationals too. The NCA style was much different than the UCA style. A UCA championship routine wouldn't score well at NCA. UCA was a clean, crowd-oriented style that used signs. NCA, on the other hand, promoted creativity, encouraging teams to do whatever they could to impact the crowd.

Don took his team to the NCA College Nationals in Dallas, Texas, for a few years, but they failed to secure a victory. But in the 1996-97 season NCA made two changes to its event. It moved to the sunny shores of Daytona Beach, Florida, and changed the competition routine structure from a cheer and music style to a full music routine. That season Don and his UNC Chapel Hill cheer team won gold at NCA College Nationals, completing a sweep of both major collegiate events.

Don also enjoyed challenging the status quo. In addition to his cheer team, he coached the UNC Chapel Hill Dance Team. It was coed, which was unheard of at the time. NCA didn't have any rules barring men from dance teams, and Don's UNC team put on quite a show, earning second place with a routine choreographed by Rey Lozano.

THE LAUNCH OF SPIRIT XPRESS

To remain competitive, Don believed it was essential to cultivate a pipeline of athletes who were being trained to join the UNC squad, so in 1994 he started Spirit Xpress cheerleading. His new gym was the first in his area. Don had a goal to start his own business by the age of thirty-five, and he was determined to achieve it.

Once the gym was operating, Don brought in Mark Lyczkowski to manage the business. Mark graduated from the University of North Carolina Wilmington and was a cheerleader there, so he had extensive experience in cheerleading. Under Don and Mark's leadership Spirit Xpress evolved into Spirit Xpress All Stars before expanding to include Spirit Xpress Camps and, eventually, Spirit Xpress Competitions.

Although both UCA and NCA hosted camps at UNC Chapel Hill, Don, as the coach, had the authority to limit which camps were held on campus. He decided that only Carolina camps could operate on campus, which led to significant growth for Spirit Xpress Camps.

Don recruited the best of the best to teach his camps. Among them was Rey Lozano, owner of US Spiritleaders on the West Coast where the style was incredibly different from the style in other regions, so Rey brought something unique to Spirit Xpress Camps on the East Coast.

Life was great, and things were going well for Don, so he decided to shake things up and resigned from his residence hall job at UNC Chapel Hill to focus on choreography, Spirit Xpress, and coaching his UNC teams. He then took a position with NCA where Bill Boggs was starting a new collegiate division that would strictly focus on growing that aspect of the company.

Don eagerly seized the opportunity to collaborate with Bill on his new venture while launching yet another business, Spirit and Company. Don brought in Brown Walters, a former UNC Chapel Hill cheerleader, to run it. As cheerleading events and camps began to emerge nationwide, there was a growing demand for apparel sales at those sites. Spirit and Company provided a turnkey solution for event producers and camp organizers, offering on-site apparel sales.

Don and Brown set up a store and sold merchandise at the events, which gave Don firsthand insight into the evolving apparel industry. He observed numerous competitions, learning what worked and what didn't. Those events featured a diverse range of teams from school squads to Pop Warner teams to All Stars, each showcasing various cheerleading styles.

PUTTING THE "STAR" IN ALL STAR

"All Star was a show," Don said. "It was very different from all the other types of cheerleading. I decided that All Stars needed its own event that was just as showy and flashy as All Star itself."

He was headed to Hawaii to work the Pro Bowl, but he couldn't get the idea out of his head, so he decided to start a competition company. He began making plans and sketching ideas during the plane ride home.

In 2000 Don started the All Star Challenge, a competition strictly for All Stars. He contacted his friends from around the country, told them about his bold idea, and invited them to attend his first event on Jekyll Island, midway between Jacksonville, Florida, and Savannah, Georgia. Don wanted to host an event worthy of All Star competition, so he took inspiration from the Oscars, synchronized swimming, the circus, marching bands, and other outside-the-box ideas.

Don brought in gigantic balloon columns, new to events at the time. He created a special music mix for the event to enhance its ambiance. In addition, All Star Challenge was the first event brand to have a videographer on site to capture clips of the event and put together a compilation video to be played before the awards ceremony, similar to TV's "One Shining Moment" that leads into the NCAA basketball's men's Final Four.

Don organized a great team that featured Mark Lyczkowsi, Tim Morgan, Jim Paddison, Tanya Bowles, Brown Walters, and Kandy Gotwals to help bring his visions to life.

CREATING SPECTACULAR THEMED EVENTS

The event at Jekyll Island quickly reached capacity and, eventually, relocated to Jacksonville, Florida, marking the birth of themed All Star Challenge events. Clash of the Titans set the stage for the Jacksonville event. All Star Challenge elevated the competitive atmosphere with fully themed staging and elaborate decorations, transforming the event into a major spectacle.

Twenty-five-foot-tall Neptune statues towered over both sides of the stage where they dramatically spewed water. But when a Peewee team hesitated to perform, Don approached their coach and asked, "Why won't they go out?"

The coach sighed and said, "Because they think God is spitting at them."

Don couldn't help but laugh. "Lesson learned. We need to turn off the spewing water for the little ones."

Don and his team added a sports center for dads that included televisions that played live sports events and a bar that offered adult beverages. Other unique ideas were dinners at Hard Rock Café, awards ceremonies at the Boston Aquarium, and family-centered schedules to enjoy what each city had to offer.

With the addition of Dennis Worley and Bambi Nevel, Don eventually included Return to Atlantis, Battle Under the Big Top, King of the Jungle, and Queen of the Nile events. Each was extravagant.

The All Star Challenge provided an extraordinary and memorable experience. Don's team spared no expense, resulting in events that ignited a surge of excitement throughout the All Star industry. To keep things innovative, Don took his entire staff to Vegas for a retreat to brainstorm ideas for future events and to enhance existing event concepts.

Don wanted the scoring to be fair and preferred judges who understood All Star routines and the skills being performed by the All Star participants. He, along with Tanya Bowles and Dennis Worley, ultimately decided to hire only judges who either coached or owned All Star gyms. He believed that was the most effective way to have knowledgeable individuals on his judging panels. Don and his team also created the Thalia Awards, the industry's first specialty awards, which were based on the judges' choices rather than on scores. The awards frequently included the best choreography, the best music, the most enthusiastic fans, and similar categories. Don Collins and the All Star Challenge team brought the "Star" to All Star.

In 2011 Don retired from choreography because the All Star scoresheet had become so rigidly structured that it was challenging to find room for creativity. He prioritized creativity over cramming as many skills as possible into two minutes and thirty seconds.

Don Collins made significant contributions to the All Star cheerleading industry with his visionary approach that emphasized creativity, spectacle, and a holistic experience. His introduction of specialty awards, dedication to informed judging, and emphasis on the theatrical elements elevated recognition for teams beyond mere technical scoring. Don's readiness to challenge conventions—from establishing coed dance teams to creating competitions tailored specifically for All Stars—propelled the entire industry forward. Don Collins didn't merely take part in the All Star realm, he revolutionized it with a theatrical flair and a performer's insight into what constitutes an unforgettable experience.

Today, Don divides his year equally between North Carolina, San Francisco, and Provincetown on Cape Cod, where he also operates a bed and breakfast. Decorating his bed and breakfast brought Don great joy, and he loves welcoming his guests.

"Many famous writers have come through Provincetown over the years," Don said. "Tennessee Williams and Cunningham are famous for visiting the area. They'd find a quiet cabin and hide away and write for days on end."

> "Success is seeing those you taught succeed." – Don Collins

EARNED WISDOM

★ **Success:** Watching your former athletes or employees succeed in life is a true measure of success.

★ **Wisdom:** Things change, and although the industry doesn't look the same, perhaps it's where it needs to be.

★ **Gratitude:** Don is grateful to Hilda McDaniel, who showed him that All Star was possible; Rey Lozano, who taught him that creativity was essential; and the entire All Star Challenge team, who taught him that a team that understands the vision can leave a powerful legacy.

★ **Don's Wish:** Think of the amazing routines we're missing out on because we force All Star to fit into a specific box with a strict rubric to meet the scoresheet. Open the box!

★ **Mistakes:** Caring too much about other people's opinions.

★ **For Gym Owners:** You must have a business plan and know how to budget.

★ **For Coaches:** The most important thing is not your ego, it's the athlete's safety and growth.

DID YOU KNOW?

★ Don's favorite part of cheerleading is the creativity. Without it, routines are boring.

★ Don's favorite cheer routine is anything from Top Gun or Los Alamitos High School in the nineties.

★ His favorite memory was watching a cheer team of athletes from diverse backgrounds—White, Asian, Black, and Brown—working together to achieve their dreams. "My favorite memory was happening before my eyes," Don said, "and I didn't know it: inclusivity."

★ Don loves Korean dramas and enjoys reading the subtext. It makes sense to him.

★ He is an extreme introvert on the Myers Briggs personality test.

★ Don went from owning a cheer gym and event company to owning a bed and breakfast.

★ Don doesn't have a favorite superhero, but he'd love to have the power of invisibility.

★ Don selected the lion as his animal because the lion represents family, strength, energy, courage, guardianship, protection, ferocity, and authority. And he happens to be a Leo.

"A coach is someone who makes you do what you don't want to do so you can be who you want to be." – Tom Landry

ROBIN COE

Spirit Festival – 1994
Connecticut Spirit – 1999
Choice Events – 2018

FROM CORPORATE BUSINESS SUITS TO SWEATSUITS

"Can you build a state championship team?"

The question hung in the air as Robin Coe sat across from the nun interviewing her for a position as a high school cheerleading coach.

"I will certainly try," Robin answered cautiously.

The nun's response was swift and unforgettable: "That's not the answer I wanted to hear." She punctuated her words with a hammer-like strike on her desk, the sharp thud making Robin jump.

"Okay, I'll do it," Robin said, startled but undeterred.

Robin had no idea that moment would be the first of many pivotal points in a journey that would take her from the corporate corridors of IBM to a trailblazing force in competitive cheerleading across New England.

FINDING HER TRUE CALLING

Robin Coe never intended to become a cheerleading entrepreneur. As a cheerleader in high school, she originally aspired to become a teacher. Ultimately, she was persuaded to pursue a major in international business, which paved the way for her career at IBM. Cheerleading appeared to be a chapter from her past—until a pivotal volunteer opportunity transformed her life.

"My mother volunteered me to help one of her friends who was coaching at a Catholic school in New Haven," Robin said. What began as a favor quickly reignited her passion for coaching. "I ended up taking over because I truly enjoyed working with the kids."

That volunteer position was the spark that would eventually lead Robin to leave her corporate career behind. "I went from business suits to sweatsuits," she said. "It was a huge risk leaving IBM."

The transition didn't receive immediate support from everyone in her life. Her husband questioned the wisdom of leaving a stable corporate job, but her parents and brother strongly supported her decision. That family support would be vital as she began her journey into the world of cheerleading.

Robin's coaching career began in earnest when she took over a junior high cheerleading program. Her commitment to excellence led her to seek additional training through NCA camps where she connected with staff who would later become important contacts in her professional network.

Her success with the junior high team opened the door to a high school opportunity and that unforgettable interview with the no-nonsense nun. The principal had already built a state championship basketball team and aimed to do the same with cheerleading.

Robin fulfilled her promise, driving the Sacred Heart Academy team to multiple state championships. Her accomplishment was even more impressive in the context of her strategic approach. While coaching her high school team she engaged with the Archdiocese of Hartford and organized statewide competitions. Doing so enabled her to create what she called a feeder program by working with junior high athletes poised to join her high school team.

"If you're working with them and teaching them the basics at a young level," she said, "they're coming up with that talent into the high school." The results were undeniable: Her varsity team excelled, and her JV team was so well-trained that it competed in varsity divisions and consistently placed first or second.

Her success resulted in invitations to join various committees, including the Connecticut Association of Schools, where she played a key role in organizing the state championship. She took advantage of every opportunity.

THE BIRTH OF SPIRIT FESTIVAL

Robin's event production career began with a simple problem: Her high school wouldn't allow the cheerleading team to raise money to attend the NCA High School Nationals. Undeterred, she found a creative solution by establishing a 501(c)(3) nonprofit organization and started a cheerleading competition at the high school.

That was the birth of the Spirit Festival in 1994, which started as the Connecticut Spirit Association. What began as a fundraising event grew rapidly, soon outgrowing the high school venue and moving to Quinnipiac University in Hamden, Connecticut. The event continued to expand until it eventually found a home at the Mohegan Sun Casino in Uncasville, Connecticut.

The United States All Star Federation (USASF) was just forming, and Robin became the first event producer in New England to offer partial paid bids to The Cheerleading Worlds. The competition's success necessitated a change from nonprofit to LLC status because Robin was a good businesswoman, and the event was profitable.

CONNECTICUT SPIRIT: BUILDING A GYM FROM SCRATCH

Robin's journey into gym ownership began during a time of personal transition. Pregnant with her son in 1998, she found herself dealing with a new principal at the high school who didn't share the previous administration's enthusiasm for cheerleading. The new principal's preference for the Drama Department over the Athletic Department signaled a significant shift in priorities.

The situation at school, coupled with an angry parent who visited Robin's home and damaged her storm door because her daughter had failed to make the competition team, prompted Robin to resign from her high school coaching position. The timing aligned with discussions she had with Cheryl Thomes from USA Wildcats, who inspired Robin to launch an All Star team in her region.

In 1999 Robin joined Stars Academy, a gymnastics facility, to establish her first Senior All Star team. But she soon recognized that the values of the gym's directors did not align with hers. Robin's focus was on teaching life lessons and supporting kids while instructing them in cheerleading.

The philosophical differences led Robin to seek her own space, which turned out to be a volleyball facility she could rent three days a week. She bought seven mats and an air track with her personal credit card. She then situated the equipment on the side of the volleyball court. When space was limited, practices would move outside to a field.

In her second year she rented an end section of the facility and ingeniously divided it by using a twelve-foot fence and chloroplast sheets secured with zip ties to form a makeshift wall. A net was suspended from the ceiling to prevent volleyballs—and occasionally baseballs from the training facility at the far end—from entering her practice area.

Although it started modestly, the program—known as Connecticut Spirit—thrived. Robin utilized her connections with NCA and UCA staff, Pop Warner teams, and high school coaches to rapidly establish a significant clientele.

"My first year in business I had over 500 kids just starting," she said. "It was overwhelming to start with that many kids."

GROWTH AND CHALLENGES

By 2006 Connecticut Spirit had moved to its own dedicated facility and continued to grow. At its peak the gym boasted eighteen teams and over 1,000 students in tumbling classes. This success led to franchise inquiries, which Robin pursued, but she later regretted attempting to expand without a business partner.

"It was just me doing all of it," she said. "It was very difficult."

In 2011 she started a new gym with a fifty-fifty partner. Despite the challenges of expansion, Connecticut Spirit continued to thrive until 2017 when Robin relocated to Florida. She then sold the gym to her partner in 2019.

Throughout her career as a gym owner Robin faced numerous personal challenges that impacted her business. Taking care of her family while running multiple businesses stretched her thin.

"I had to be the mother, the daughter, the wife and try to take care of all of it," she recalled. "It was really difficult to have the gym and try to be that person while owning Spirit Festival and running two huge events."

TO SPIRIT FESTIVAL AND BEYOND

Aside from establishing successful businesses, Robin made substantial contributions to the development of the competitive cheerleading structure. She played a crucial role in implementing a scoring rubric created by her friend, Peggy Anderson, a Massachusetts principal who developed a more advanced evaluation system in the mid-1990s.

Robin presented the concept to the Connecticut High School Association and subsequently put it into practice at Spirit Festival. The system attracted the interest of various event producers, such as Dennis Worley from All Star Challenge, and played a significant role in the evolution of cheerleading scoring.

Robin played a crucial role in establishing the Prep Division in All Star cheerleading. The need emerged when she experienced an influx of eighty athletes transitioning from Pop Warner to All Star midseason. Due to the lack of a suitable category for these half-year athletes, Robin pushed for change before the USASF National Advisory Board.

"We led in the Northeast in trying to get a division for these kids," she explained. "That's how Prep was created." The concept later expanded nationwide, though with varying regional definitions.

In 2011 Robin sold Spirit Festival to Varsity and signed a three-year contract to keep the events running, but she realized the competition lost its spark under corporate ownership.

"There was no more personality," she said. Although she appreciated the overall efforts Varsity made throughout the industry, "It wasn't really something I wanted to be a part of anymore."

Who had the most significant impact on her All Star journey? Robin circles back to where it all began, her family. Her mother's influence forged her identity while her supportive family empowered her to take bold risks.

Most profoundly, her own children reshaped her coaching approach. Her son's brain injury and resulting ADHD taught her this: "You have to really learn how to coach each kid differently. Not everyone is receptive to one style."

THE WINNERS CHOICE

After taking a break from the cheer industry due to personal challenges and burnout, Robin was drawn back in while employed at Double Good Popcorn in 2017. She had watched her daughter flourish for years as an All Star cheerleader and dancer. Seeing the positive impact of the industry alongside the shortcomings of existing events inspired her to create something better. Her daughter believed in her mother's passion and ability, so in 2018 Robin contacted her friend, Don Collins, who had previously suggested she sell her business. But this time he encouraged her to reenter the industry.

Initially, Robin planned to develop technology for remote live competitions, even filing a patent, but she had to pivot when COVID hit. When she launched Winners Choice, she prioritized interactive experiences that kept audiences engaged throughout the event, addressing the gap she noticed in competitions where parents only attended for their child's performance. Winners Choice events are like an ESPN show—fast-paced and dynamic—and feature trusted judges dedicated to team success.

Robin now manages three distinct brands: Winners Choice, a globally recognized casino-themed event known for its high interactivity; Bring It, which emphasizes spirit and team colors while rewarding good sportsmanship; and Genesis Dance, dedicated to expanding dance participation and bridging the gap between studio and All Star dance. Robin's passion for advancing dance within the industry is evident. She played a key role in establishing dance representation on the USASF Board and created a dance advisory board to better understand and promote dance as a discipline separate from cheer.

Robin's story illustrates how the All Star cheerleading industry was forged not by corporations but by passionate individuals ready to take risks and prioritize athletes. Her bold shift from corporate success to entrepreneurial risk, along with her innovative strategies in competitions and training, transformed the cheerleading landscape in the Northeast.

"I had a huge supportive community making this happen," she said. "I feel really blessed."

In an ever-evolving industry, Robin Coe's journey echoes the passionate pioneers who built All Star cheer from the ground up, one mat, one athlete, one competition at a time.

Robin enjoys spending time with her family and working to build her new company. She also appreciates the continued opportunity to bring joy to the youth community through her work with Double Good. She also holds a seat on the USASF Board of Directors and continues to pour her passion into the sport she loves, making a positive impact on all the kids who participate.

"Success is helping other people be successful and watching them flourish."
– Robin Coe

EARNED WISDOM

★ **Success:** If you can have a positive impact on another person or positively impact an organization, then you've been successful.

★ **Wisdom:** Find a good community and get involved in it.

★ **Gratitude:** Robin's mom had a major impact on her life. She made Robin who she is, and she was supportive when Robin left her career with IBM.

★ **Mistakes:** Not finding a good work-life balance and running the business with your heart.

★ **For Gym Owners:** Start small and have a solid business plan. Pay attention to your finances from the beginning. In the long run you'll be better off growing at the right pace and not too quickly.

★ **For Coaches:** Be a good role model. Educate yourself and continue to level up so you can have a positive impact. Treat your athletes with kindness and teach them valuable life lessons.

★ **Lessons Learned:** My children have influenced my coaching style. Now I understand that you need to coach each athlete differently to help them succeed.

DID YOU KNOW?

★ Robin's favorite part of cheer is that it allows her to forge incredible relationships with people from all over the world. Some of her closest friends are in cheer, and it's reassuring to know that she can reach out to them anytime or visit them wherever they are. Having such a strong support system makes the experience even more rewarding.

- ★ Robin loves to parasail. She loves anything that's up in the air. For her next adventure, she'd like to skydive.

- ★ She drove a twenty-seven-foot box truck to events herself.

- ★ Robin had a corporate career at IBM. It took her ten years to part with her business suits because she wanted to make sure she wasn't going back.

- ★ Robin's favorite superhero is Wonder Woman because she gets hit with everything and handles it all.

- ★ Robin chose the butterfly as her animal because it symbolizes metamorphosis, transformation, balance, grace, the ability to accept change, lightness, soul, and vulnerability.

"Culture eats strategy for breakfast." – Peter Drucker

AARON FLAKER
JAMfest – 1995
JAM Brands – 2005

FINDING A NEW PATH

Aaron Flaker grew up in Louisville, Kentucky, and attended Louisville Male High School where he enjoyed playing both basketball and baseball. He also was co-valedictorian of his senior class in 1990. He then accepted a baseball and academic scholarship from Western Kentucky University in Bowling Green.

But Aaron's freshman year fell short of his hopes. His parents divorced, he missed his girlfriend, and baseball was wearing him down. He felt a persistent gut instinct that he was in the wrong place, so he transferred to the University of Louisville after his first semester. Though ineligible for a midyear scholarship, the Louisville baseball coach invited him to walk on.

A few weeks into February, Aaron decided it was time to retire his cleats. His heart was no longer in baseball. Aaron thought the game was telling him he wasn't good enough for the major leagues, so he should pursue academics.

Aaron eventually became friends with Dwight Clough who portrayed the Cardinal Bird, Louisville's mascot. Dwight was in his senior year and needed assistance with his appearances at women's basketball and community appearances.

"What the heck," Aaron said. "This might be a great opportunity to meet community members, business leaders, and Athletic Department personnel." So he dove in to assist Dwight with his mascot duties. Aaron also had switched his major to business, so the opportunity felt like a perfect fit.

The following year, 1993, Aaron was selected as the official Cardinal Bird and continued in that role until 1996. Being the Cardinal Bird helped Aaron stay close to athletics without being fully immersed in one specific sport. It was the perfect balance, and he loved it.

A few years into his time at Louisville, a new cheerleader named Emmitt Tyler joined the cheer team. He and his girlfriend (now his wife) transferred from Indiana State University in Terre Haute. Emmitt and Aaron became fast friends. They never roomed together at school, but they had tremendous respect for each other.

BIG BUSINESS IDEAS

One year the University of Louisville cheer squad, along with the Cardinal Bird, headed to Cincinnati for the NCA Kings Island competition on Labor Day weekend. After the performance Emmitt asked Aaron, "Hey, man! What do you think about running an event like this? We could take your business experience and community relationships with my cheer experience and contacts and put on a good event." Aaron thought about it before Emmitt continued: "I can worry about the cheer rules and details, and you worry about the business side."

Aaron had just graduated with a BS in Business and Marketing and was looking for his next steps, so he joined Emmitt in pulling off their first event. It was modeled after that NCA event at Kings Island. On July 24 and 25, 1995, the Pepsi Cheerleading Championships were held at Kentucky Kingdom in Louisville. The Pepsi sponsorship resulted from a relationship Aaron had developed as the Cardinal Bird. Aaron spent a lot of time working to attract additional sponsors and, ironically, Varsity was the apparel sponsor for that first event.

They managed to gather twenty-five teams, including Cheers! Inc., owned by Dawn Duncan Walters, but Aaron and Emmitt discovered the timing wasn't ideal for a cheer competition. Still, attendees loved the atmosphere—it took place inside a massive red-and-white striped pavilion-style tent.

JAMfest CREATION

Acting on customer feedback, the pair scheduled the second event for later in the fall and moved the competition to the Louisville Zoo. That competition attracted approximately 125 teams, a fivefold increase over the first year. Aaron and Emmitt also agreed that the second-year event required a sexier name. They knew they wanted to offer something unique.

NCA and UCA were the major competitors, but their focus was on championships. Their events offered little in terms of entertainment—minimal sound, basic lighting, and a straightforward setup. They essentially rolled out a mat and hosted a competition.

Aaron and Emmitt wanted their events to be family focused and fun with winning as a byproduct. They knew they needed a name that matched their vision, and championships sounded too official. "Festival" sounded more exciting, so they settled on JAMfest.

I think it's fair to say that JAMfest took cheerleading competitions and turned them into family-driven spectacles with people dancing on stage and throwing things into the crowd, like what you might see at other sporting events. Aaron drew inspiration from his baseball days and brought some of that into cheer. Even his mascot background came into play when JAMfest invented its own mascot, Jammy. The first Jammy was, of course, portrayed by none other than Aaron himself.

Between 2000 and 2003, JAMfest went regional by launching events in Evansville, Indiana; Gatlinburg, Tennessee; Dayton, Ohio; and Hot Springs, Arkansas. In 2003 Aaron and Emmitt hired their first official employees, Dan Kessler to focus on sales and April LaFramboise to plan the events. Eventually, Aaron Kendall was added to the team to oversee the warehouse and logistics. In addition, Aaron and Emmitt used subcontractors and every aunt, uncle, cousin, and nephew they could find to help on site at their events.

"My mom worked the gate to sell tickets," Aaron said. "It took a village." Aaron then chuckled and looked around as nostalgia washed over his face: "Ironically, I'm sitting in the original JAMfest building right now. The company I currently own leases space from me, Emmitt, and Dan. I'm back in the exact same space where JAMfest started its rapid growth phase."

VARSITY TAKES NOTICE

JAMfest was making waves across the country, and Varsity took notice. In 2005 Varsity approached the JAMfest team—then owned primarily by Aaron and Emmitt with Dan Kessler holding a minority stake—about purchasing the company. Negotiations led to the signing of a letter of intent. But the JAMfest leaders decided they weren't ready to sell after all. They still had more to accomplish. The company was thriving, hosting around fifty events annually, employing approximately twenty, and constructing a new building to support its continued growth. Things were moving in the right direction.

At that point Aaron not only had gained solid business knowledge but also had accumulated a decade of entrepreneurial experience. Varsity's potential acquisition became another learning experience that equipped him with insights he would carry forward.

Varsity had more money, staff, and resources than JAMfest did, but JAMfest was more agile and could maneuver quickly with calculated, swift decisions. It was a scary time. UCA and NCA, the two main powerhouses, merged, and Varsity owned the biggest All

Star national championships. Additionally, it enjoyed a great relationship with Disney. Varsity also had recently purchased Athletic Championships and recruited even more incredibly talented individuals. All that competition left Aaron and Emmitt to brainstorm how to stay relevant.

AND THEN... JAM Brands

With enthusiasm and passion, they established their parent company, JAM Brands, and collaborated with organizations that aligned with their cultural values. Their partnership model was designed to maintain their majority controlling interest so they could make swift decisions while ensuring the companies remained invested in the venture. They believed that permitting people to retain some equity in the company would be attractive. Essentially, if individuals wished to sell their entire company, JAM Brands would facilitate that, but they also encouraged people to retain some equity.

Tammy VanVleet, owner of the Golden State Spirit Association, was the first to join JAM Brands, which gave the company a strong presence in California. She also ran the Aloha Cheer and Dance Championships, thus giving JAM Brands an event in Hawaii.

Coastal, owned by Serena Andrews, jumped on board next, followed by COA, owned by Steve Wedge, and then the Great Lakes Cheerleading Championships. JAM Brands then added America's Best and Spirit Innovations, both owned by Kevin Jones. JAM Brands quickly learned that Spirit Innovations, the uniform company, was out of their wheelhouse, and if they didn't deliver uniforms on time, it reflected poorly on their events, so they eventually sold Spirit Innovations to Varsity.

The addition of new businesses across the country created seven separate offices, each with significant overhead. JAM Brands went from about twenty employees to fifty to ninety, which sounds impressive, but managing and overseeing everything was a massive undertaking.

"We were really good at managing things that were closer to home," Aaron said. "We quickly realized that managing seven offices and a uniform company that we knew nothing about was not our strength."

JAM Brands decided it was wise to consolidate warehouses, and it eventually brought everything back to the main office in Louisville. Consolidating offices also allowed the company to share resources, staff, and facilities.

"2005 to 2011 were some of the most stressful years because we grew so much so fast," Aaron said. "And guess what else happened during that time— the Great Recession."

In those trying times Aaron's mother frequently asked him, "Honey, when are you going to get a real job? You're a valedictorian with an MBA. You work in cheerleading, for God's sake. Go work for a large corporation or something."

Aaron spoke affectionately about his mother, but he had a vision and knew he was crafting something special alongside Emmitt and Dan.

SWING BATTER... THE MAJORS

The JAM Brands team knew it needed to do something spectacular to draw people to its events. Travel was declining due to the recession, event participation was down, and they needed something fresh to keep their business alive. And so JAMfest hosted the first Cheer MAJORS event in Indianapolis, Indiana, in 2012. The event remains as prestigious today as it was then.

The MAJORS is a highly competitive event exclusively for Level 6 Senior All Star teams, and participation is by invitation only. The inaugural event included only nine teams. In 2025 The MAJORS hosted twenty-seven of the top Level 6 Senior teams from across the country.

In 2015 JAM Brands decided it had accomplished everything it had set out to do, so it was finally time to sell to Varsity after being asked three times. It was time to part ways with the company Aaron and Emmitt had built from an initial investment of $600, half of which had gone to pay incorporation fees. Twenty years later, JAM Brands ranked second in All Star cheerleading and was valued at millions of dollars.

JAMfest's impact on the All Star cheer industry cannot be overstated. Its innovations—from dynamic lighting and sound to interactive mascots and audience participation—raised the bar for the entire industry, forcing even the largest competitors to evolve. By prioritizing the athlete and spectator experience over purely technical judging, JAMfest made All Star cheer more accessible and appealing to a broader audience.

The company's partnership model also created pathways for smaller regional event producers to thrive rather than be absorbed, thereby preserving the diverse character of cheer competitions nationwide. Today, the entertainment-focused approach pioneered by JAMfest has become the industry standard, a lasting testament to Aaron Flaker and his partner's vision of transforming cheerleading competitions from mere evaluations into memorable experiences for all involved.

Today, Aaron is still a lover of life, along with his wife Ashley and their two children, Braxton and Tyce. Aaron now serves on the Louisville Baseball Club Board of Directors and has been out of the cheerleading industry for many years.

After JAM Brands, he turned his attention to Athletx Sports Group, which he cofounded in 2016. Athletx Sports Group is an event production company that, according to its website, has brought multiple brands together under one banner, including Baseball Youth, Softball Youth, Game Day USA, Youth Baseball Nationals, Youth Softball Nationals, Pastime Tournaments, Mid-America Baseball, Youth World Series, New Year's BaseballFest, and TravelBall Select.

Collectively, Athletx Sports Group brands represent over 600 team-based and individual player events across the nation that feature more than 15,000 teams, 194,000 players, 38,000 coaches, and 371,000 spectators.

> "Success is surrounding yourself with the right people and believing in those people."
> – Aaron Flaker

EARNED WISDOM

★ **Success:** To be successful you need to have a vision and believe in what you're doing. Success is surrounding yourself with the right people and believing in them.

★ **Wisdom:** Treat people with respect, no matter their job or the money they make. Build relationships.

★ **Gratitude:** Aaron is grateful to James Speed, who introduced him and his business partners to the world of All Star cheer. Aaron is also grateful to Varsity for the opportunity to sell JAM Brands. He's equally grateful to them for being good stewards of his employees. Many have worked for JAM Brands for years and still work for Varsity today.

★ **Mistakes:** Trying to do things we weren't knowledgeable about. Aaron said, "We didn't know anything about running a uniform company." Be sure that if you're going to branch out into new ventures, you're prepared.

★ **For Gym Owners:** You need to have a passion for the gym business, or your chances of being successful are slim. You don't pour your blood, sweat, and tears into something that you're moderately happy doing.

★ **For Coaches:** Aaron graciously declined to answer this question because he said he never actually coached cheerleading.

★ **Lessons Learned:** Be great at what you're doing at a particular time and don't be distracted by trying to be or do something that you are not. Slowly and steadily make your climb.

DID YOU KNOW?

★ Aaron's favorite part of cheer is hosting events.

★ Aaron was never a cheerleader. He played baseball and performed as his college mascot, the Louisville Cardinal Bird.

★ He was co-valedictorian of his high school class.

★ Aaron survived colon cancer.

★ Aaron's favorite superhero is Superman. He loves his clean-cut persona and strength. Clark Kent was just a normal guy, but when you needed help, he became Superman.

★ Aaron selected the fish as his animal because it represents gracefulness, slyness, open-mindedness, quickness to change its mind, fertility, good luck, and happiness.

S. R. Fabrico

"Be happy!" – Morton Bergue

MORTON BERGUE
Pyramids Cheerleading Studio,
Cheergyms.com – 1995

DANCE AND CHEER, HAVE NO FEAR

Morton Bergue loved to dance, so he took dance classes in high school. And a few girls in those classes begged him every year to try out for the cheerleading squad. The girls were relentless. Finally, during his junior year, Morton gave in. He coaxed his friend, Joel, into trying out with him, and they both made the cheer team at Analy High School in Sebastopol, California. Morton and his team attended the NCA summer camp, where he was recognized as a superstar and given an application to join the NCA staff.

He filled out the application, attended a staff meeting, and was selected for the camp staff. He began teaching in the summer after his senior year in 1981. While teaching at camps he met Danny Kahn, who was assisting the Clayton Valley All Stars coaches, including Kathy Gaffney, and who would eventually become his best friend and business partner. Morton hired Danny to teach NCA summer camps with him.

In 1985 Morton accepted an opportunity with NCA and relocated to Dallas, Texas, to establish Cheerobics, the city's first cheerleading facility. Carol and Lance Wagers sought to establish a cheer-only facility, and they hired Morton to manage it. The facility served as a fitness center during the day and transformed into a cheer training venue for local high schools at night. Unfortunately, both of Morton's parents were experiencing health problems, and Morton decided it was best to return home to assist them.

GOING BACK TO CALI: BUILDING PYRAMIDS TO LAST

Morton relocated to Concord, California, and began coaching the cheer team at College Park High School, one of the best teams in the area. He continued working for NCA and helped hire staff for the West Coast. He also assisted with the development of camp curriculum and choreography for summer camp materials.

Danny was coaching at Clayton Valley High School alongside mutual friend Pat Relth, who coached Concord High School. They coached the top three high schools in the area. They wanted their team to win, but valuing their friendship, they united their resources to open a cheer gym.

Morton recalled the moment clearly. Danny called him and announced, "We're opening a cheer gym."

"We're opening what?"

"One of those cheer gyms," Danny clarified.

And just like that, Morton said, "Okay."

In 1995 Pyramids Cheerleading Studio opened its doors.

The gym opened in October, too late to launch an All Star team, so Morton and his crew concentrated on boosting classes and strengthening their school teams. Meanwhile, Morton kept judging and assisting NCA with its All-American events.

All-Americans were selected at NCA summer camps. With the honor came the invitation to attend several events throughout the year. An athlete could participate in one or all of them. Morton helped organize the cheerleaders and chaperones for those events that included the Macy's Thanksgiving Day Parade, the Cotton Bowl, the Hawaii camp and event, and the Aloha Bowl. During the winter Morton spent most of his time coaching his former high school team, Analy, and teaching exercise and dance. During the summer he continued to teach at NCA camps.

(Fun fact: I attended an NCA All-American event in Hamburg, Germany, and Morton was my chaperone.)

In the summer of 1996, Pyramids assembled the inaugural All Star team of twenty-five cheerleaders from the surrounding communities. It was the first dedicated training facility on the West Coast to have its own building. While other All Star teams practiced at gymnastics centers, Pyramids Cheerleading Studio also was the first dedicated exclusively to cheer and All Star. As the focus shifted to the gym, Morton retired from NCA. Between 2000 and 2010 Pyramids opened eight additional locations under various names, making it the first company on the West Coast to open multiple locations. That decision led to a rebrand under the name Cheergyms.com, Inc., which is still used today.

Morton received a degree in communications with a minor in dance from Cal State Fullerton where he cheered and danced. He never expected to do cheer for life, but opportunities kept popping up, and he took advantage of them. He loved cheer and appreciated that he could make a living following his passion.

Morton is a true ray of sunshine in the cheer world, radiating joy and boundless energy. His contributions to the industry have been significant, leaving a lasting impact on athletes and coaches alike by serving as a pillar of continuity in All Star since the eighties. He also has mentored, coached, and guided countless athletes for decades. He was a founding member of the NACCC and served on the original USASF Board from 2004 to 2015. He also has served on numerous committees and has helped with The Cheerleading Worlds since its inception. In addition, he has been involved in judging the USASF Scholarship from the beginning.

Morton Bergue's journey from a reluctant high school cheerleader to an industry pioneer exemplifies the impact one passionate individual can have on an entire sport. His infectious enthusiasm, unwavering dedication, and visionary leadership have helped shape All Star cheerleading. Through decades of coaching, judging, and mentoring, Morton has touched countless lives while building foundations that will support the cheerleading community for generations to come. Morton remains what he has always been, a beacon of joy, excellence, and innovation in the world of All Star cheer.

Currently, Morton lives near Sebastopol, California, where he grew up. During the week he takes care of his mother as she struggles with Alzheimer's. He still owns the gym with Derick Patterson and Danny and Danny's wife, Regina. On weeknights and weekends Morton continues to coach, judge, choreograph, and engage in all things cheer and dance.

> **"Success is the positive impact you have on those around you." – Morton Bergue**

EARNED WISDOM

★ **Success:** Success is a funny thing. As a young person you may think the amount of money you acquire defines your success. As you get older, you learn that success is the positive impact you have on those around you. When a former cheerleader asks you to walk her down the aisle at her wedding or a coach calls you because they trust your opinion . . . that is success.

★ **Gratitude:** Morton is grateful to Danny Kahn for encouraging him to start their gym. Elaine Pascale had the best interests of the kids at the forefront of her decisions. She was never afraid to stand by her beliefs. Morton was grateful for Jim

Chadwick's input and experience and for offering him a seat on the USASF Board. Morton was grateful to Lawrence Herkimer for starting the cheer industry and for encouraging him, both as an athlete and as an NCA instructor.

★ **Morton's Wish:** Morton wishes the industry were easier to understand. He thinks the intentions are good, but it has become difficult for athletes, coaches, parents and, especially, new customers to understand.

★ **To My Younger Self:** All Star will grow faster and farther than you could ever imagine, both nationally and internationally. You'll have the opportunity to travel the world. Cherish it all.

★ **Regrets:** Morton was a founding member of the NACCC, and when Jim Chadwick asked him to be on the USASF Board, he jumped at the chance. In the end, it all worked out, but he regrets not being loyal to his friends at the NACCC.

★ **For Gym Owners:** When you first start, don't try to be the most competitive gym in your area. Take the time to get to know the business side of things and discover your passion within All Star.

★ **For Coaches:** Do it for the kids, not for the money. Once you prove yourself to the parents, athletes, other coaches, and the All Star world in general, the money will come. Your success will be determined by the respect and love that people have for you.

★ **Lessons Learned:** Put your true friendships ahead of career advancement.

DID YOU KNOW?

★ Morton's favorite part of All Star is dance.

★ Morton is a neat freak.

★ He makes hundreds of funny faces that make kids laugh.

★ Morton is an expert gift wrapper. If you need that service, he's your guy.

★ Morton doesn't have a favorite superhero, but he mentioned Superman because "Superman seems selfless."

★ Morton's favorite routine was the Cheergyms.com All-American Level 5 routine called "Cheese" at the 2008 All Star Worlds.

★ His favorite memory of All Star is walking into his gym for the first time, knowing it would change his life.

★ Morton chose the otter as his animal because it represents playfulness, friendliness, dynamism, joy, helpfulness, sharing, a love of youth, and sensibility without suspicion.

S. R. Fabrico

"It's a dog-eat-dog-world, and I'm wearing Milk-Bone underwear!" – Norm from *Cheers*

JUSTIN CARRIER
NCA & Varsity Spirit – 1995

IT'S ABOUT TO GET RAMMY

"I got into All Star because, as a junior in high school, I was the school mascot," Justin Carrier said. "I wanted to be a cheerleader, but I was too afraid."

Before emerging as one of All Star cheerleading's most iconic voices, Justin spent his high school days hidden inside the Rocky Ram mascot costume. Too shy to audition for the cheerleading team, he took a different route into the world of spirit, sweating inside a furry ram head at football games. But that wouldn't last long.

FROM MASCOT TO ALL STAR TO NCA

By 1994 girls from Justin's high school team in Houston were discussing a new opportunity, All Star cheerleading, at a local gym named Acrocheer All Stars. He attended open gyms and, ultimately, tried out for the Coed team his senior year and made it.

Like many cheerleaders of his time, Justin viewed college cheerleading as the pinnacle of the sport. When his All Star coach, Randy Lyons, encouraged him to cheer at the University of North Texas in Denton, Justin chose to pursue that opportunity. "When he told me he believed I was good enough to cheer in college," Justin said, "that was all the motivation I needed."

His connection to Randy would prove pivotal and set Justin on a career trajectory that would touch the lives of thousands of cheerleaders over the coming decades. Justin began teaching NCA camps during the summer of 1995, straight out of high school, and he continued through his college years.

In 1999 he started working part time at the NCA office by answering phones. Before the widespread adoption of email, the customer service line was constantly ringing with coaches seeking information and guidance.

"I answered the phone lines through the rest of college and then joined NCA full time," Justin said. His official start date was initially set for September 11, 2001, but it was postponed by one day due to the tragic events of that morning.

THE VARSITY-NCA MERGER

While working at NCA and coaching evenings at Cheer Athletics, Justin accidentally landed at the perfect intersection of school and All Star cheerleading. When Varsity acquired NCA just before the February 2004 All Star Nationals, it sparked an unexpected opportunity.

At that time, Varsity had minimal traction in the All Star market.

"When Varsity acquired NCA and we started having meetings as a company," Justin said, "I was the only one coaching All Star at a gym, which gave me a credible insider perspective on what was happening in All Star."

His unique positioning elevated Justin's role within the newly merged companies, but it also highlighted fundamental differences in how the two organizations approached All Star cheerleading. "Jeff Webb admitted he miscalculated the role of All Star," Justin said. "But at NCA, we were struggling financially and saw All Star as an opportunity to revive our business."

The contrast in philosophy was stark. Varsity was accustomed to calling the shots while All Star coaches were used to having control. "At NCA," Justin said, "we listened to the coaches, understood what they wanted, and tried to provide it. Back then, UCA's approach felt more like, 'Here's what cheerleading should be.'"

Despite initial fears that Varsity might shut NCA down—a "conspiracy" many NCA employees had dreaded—Justin saw something entirely different at the first post-merger meeting with Jeff Webb.

"Jeff stood up and asked, 'Where do we want this to go? Where do we want to be in five years?'" Justin recalled. "At NCA we weren't having those kinds of conversations. We were just trying to survive, focused on whatever was right in front of us."

The difference, as Justin saw it, was more than just financial, it was philosophical. "What set Varsity apart from everyone else in the industry was its genuine, sincere sense of responsibility for how the sport looked and evolved," Justin explained. "Having deeper pockets allowed leadership to take a step back, think long term, and take some short-term risks, all of which were aimed at growing the activity."

SHEPHERDING THE COMPETITIVE SPIRIT

As more All Star event producers joined the Varsity family, Justin's unique position shifted. Companies like Athletic Championships, which included Premier Athletics and Spirit Sports, brought their own expertise and connections.

Justin carved out his personal niche, focusing on nurturing a healthy competitive spirit within All Star cheer. Over time he grew concerned about an overwhelming focus on winning at all costs, a relentless competitive drive from coaches without an environment that taught teams how to handle losing.

"I saw too many coaches storming off when their teams lost," Justin explained. "And I thought, 'No, no, this is when your team needs you the most. This is when you coach.' " His passion for proper sportsmanship and perspective led Justin to write his viral blog post, "I Hope You Lose," challenging coaches to reconsider what success means in All Star cheer.

"My coach was awesome," Justin said. "My coach in All Star opened the year by saying, 'It's a two-and-a-half-minute routine, but what you're going to take from this season is so many great memories and this team you're sitting with. This is your family now.' " Justin recounted. "We wanted to win, but success wasn't about that. Success was never going to be measured by that."

OVERGROWN CHEERLEADERS

When reflecting on his career and the industry, Justin offers a perspective that many veteran All Star professionals likely share: "I think there's a huge group of us that aren't really professionals. We're just overgrown cheerleaders that have stuck around."

This sentiment—of passionate people who found a way to extend their connection to an activity they loved—captures the essence of All Star cheer. It wasn't built by business professionals who saw market opportunities but by cheerleaders who couldn't imagine leaving.

"I'm not a professional," Justin said. "I have zero idea where I would go or what I would do if I wasn't in this sport. I only know how to work on something that I love."

From a shy high school mascot to an influential voice shepherding All Star cheer growth, Justin Carrier's journey parallels the evolution of the sport itself, from school sidelines to worldwide competitive NCA stages. And like many of his peers who helped build this industry, Justin remains, at heart, the same cheerleader who fell in love with the sport, just one who never left the gym because "the work is worth it."

> "Success is any forward momentum that gets you closer to your goal." – Justin Carrier

EARNED WISDOM

- **Success:** The goal may change frequently, but in the process of striving to reach it, we often find ourselves in a better position than we were before.

- **Wisdom:** One of the greatest aspects of All Star is how it allows female athletes to embrace their femininity while being athletes. Oftentimes, those two characteristics are siloed in other sports.

- **Gratitude:** Justin lists several people who impacted his All Star journey. His coach, Randy Lyons, instilled values that went beyond winning. Industry leaders, such as Jeff Webb and John Newby, provided business structure. And pioneering gym owners including Jody Melton, Brad Habermel, and Angela Rogers at Cheer Athletics showed him how to build sustainable businesses while maintaining the sport's core values.

- **Justin's Wish:** Justin believes we could benefit from a reset of the style and culture of the floor routines.

- **To My Younger Self:** Understand the responsibility you have and the role you play in this world and in our sport.

* **Mistakes:** The creation of the term "image policy" is one dimensional. The truth is that appropriately covering our athletes involves their safety, mental health, and well-being. It is much more than just about image and what others think.

* **For Gym Owners:** Don't try to be everything to everybody. Offer the best products that you can believe in and know that you may not be everyone's cup of tea. And that is okay.

* **For Coaches:** The way you speak to or handle a child will often be more impactful to them than how they interact with their parents. Don't take that responsibility lightly. As much as you expect from them physically, the world will expect you to help them become better people and prepare them for the real world. My All Star coach changed my life, and now you can do the same with your athletes.

DID YOU KNOW?

* Justin's favorite part of cheer is the stressful yet exciting moments of standing in the opening formation before the coach presses play.

* His favorite routine was Top Gun from 2007 or 2008. That routine changed the standard.

* He has a twin brother.

* Justin has Tourette's syndrome and is an ambassador for the Tourette's Association of America.

* He stuttered as a child and had significant self-esteem issues.

* Justin's favorite superhero is Superman because he flies, and sometimes Justin flies in his dreams. He would like to fly in real life.

* Justin chose the quail as his animal because it represents group work, teamwork, the creator of harmony and group tolerance, and protection, especially of children.

"The fleas come with the dog." – Ralph McGill

ORSON SYKES
Twist & Shout – 1996

GYMNASTICS ROOTS

Orson Sykes grew up in Memphis, Tennessee, and spent his childhood as a competitive gymnast who dreamed of performing in the Olympics. In his senior year of high school he received scholarship offers from smaller schools like Kent State and James Madison University. But he wasn't particularly excited about them. He wanted to compete at a bigger school.

He had a friend on the men's gymnastics team at the University of Oklahoma (OU), and Orson asked his friend to show the coach his tape. The coach invited him to Norman, and in 1989 Orson entered OU to major in communication and fight for a spot on the gymnastics team as a walk-on. In 1991 he competed with OU's national championship team and was the Big Eight Conference Champion in the vault.

Orson continued at OU as a graduate assistant and then as assistant coach for the men's gymnastics team. During this time the cheerleading coach asked Orson and a few other male gymnasts to try out for the cheerleading team. Cheerleading was not recognized as an NCAA sport, so there were no eligibility rules, which paved the way for Orson and his friends to join the team.

"The cheerleaders practiced in the gymnastics gym," Orson said, "so we assumed cheerleading was on a spring floor. We had no idea it was on a hard floor until we rolled out wrestling mats for practice one day." Seeing that made him laugh, and he asked, "We need to throw a double back on this wrestling mat?"

NATIONAL CHAMPS TO JAPAN

In 1993 the OU team headed to the NCA College Nationals in Dallas, Texas. "Me and my friends had just won the national championship in gymnastics," Orson said, "so we didn't really think cheerleading was any big deal." But when they arrived, they were awestruck by the TV cameras and the number of spectators.

"We knew then," Orson said, "that this thing was the real deal." Orson's team won the collegiate championship, and at that time the winning team traveled to Japan for a couple of weeks to teach at camps and perform at the Jal Cup, the Japanese High School National Championship. Orson's OU team visited Tokyo and performed at the competition and at Disneyland in Tokyo.

Orson was completely hooked, and when he returned from Japan his cheer coach connected him with a local gym owner in Edmond, about thirty minutes from the OU campus. The gym had carpet-bonded foam and a few mirrors, but there were no crash mats, no cheese wedges, and no panel mats. He was shocked that people paid for classes without any equipment, but he started teaching lessons and fell in love with it.

Over time Orson built a rapport with the athletes in his tumbling classes and in his private lessons, and he built a following. There was a gym on the other side of town that was going out of business, so Orson thought about going out on his own. But he was young and didn't have any money, so somebody else purchased the gym.

A little discouraged but not ready to give up, Orson went back to teaching classes. Soon he reached out to Dynamo Gymnastics run by Steve Nunno, coach of Shannon Miller. Orson called Steve and asked if he could start a tumbling program out of his gym. Steve's response was simple: "Cool."

And just like that, almost overnight Orson launched a tumbling class at Dynamo Gymnastics with approximately eighty kids. It was 1994.

TWIST AND SHOUT: IT'S A SHOUTER SPIRIT THING

Orson's tumbling program continued to grow, and one day a parent said, "Hey, man, I think you need your own place." That parent not only provided Orson with the funds to kickstart the program but also coined the name Twist and Shout.

In 1996 the first Twist and Shout facility opened. The parent said, "If it works, you pay me back. If it doesn't, then I made a bad investment."

They needed seventy-five kids to break even, and Orson had 150 in the first week. After four months he bought out the parent and owned the business himself. The same banks that had previously denied him were willing to do business now that he could prove the business's potential.

Orson initially launched his gym with a focus on tumbling and a small power tumbling team. But in 1997 he expanded into All Star cheer, starting with three teams. "In all my wisdom I took my brand-new teams to the NCA National Championship for their very first competition," Orson recalled, shaking his head. "I thought we were doing the right thing, starting at the biggest and best All Star competition. We placed fifty-third out of fifty-five." He laughed, his self-deprecating humor shining through, and said, "But I told my kids we got thirty-sixth because it sounded better."

Despite the rough start, Orson's love for All Star cheer only grew. Determined to improve, he began studying the sport obsessively, applying his gymnastics background to enhance his team's strength and tumbling. And he never stopped learning.

RISING TO THE TOP

Orson didn't come up through NCA camps or teach at them. He wasn't part of the established network. He didn't know anyone, and no one knew him. Instead, he built his business from the ground up. He taught classes and coached teams while his wife, Marketia, managed the front desk. It was the two of them against the world, and Orson was determined to rise to the top.

Eventually, his teams started to win big competitions like NCA, and Twist and Shout became one of the best programs in the country.

Orson was eventually asked to join the NCA Board, joining other industry professionals, including Victor and Kristen Rosario and Elaine Pascale. Elaine invited him to participate in the NACCC, which carried over into the USASF. As Twist and Shout grew, Marketia noticed that not every kid and parent wanted to travel all over the country, but they still wanted the All Star cheer experience. In response, Twist and Shout started a limited travel program they shared with the USASF, and that program eventually evolved into All Star Prep.

From double backs on the wrestling mats at OU to the national championship stage, Orson Sykes' journey exemplifies the power of perseverance and passion. His influence on All Star cheer extends far beyond the three Twist and Shout locations that Orson and Marketia have built. As an architect of the All Star Limited Travel (Prep) program, Orson helped make All Star accessible to families with varying resources and levels of commitment. His background in gymnastics brought technical expertise to All Star cheer, elevating the sport's athletic standards. Through decades of determination, Orson evolved from an outsider with a dream into an industry leader. His greatest contribution may be creating spaces where young athletes grow as performers and as individuals of character and faith, an enduring legacy that twists, shouts, and inspires.

Orson and Marketia still own Twist and Shout and strive to develop not just skilled cheerleaders and tumblers but also strong men and women of God. They have three Oklahoma locations: Edmond, Norman, and Tulsa. Theirs is a highly decorated program that grows each year.

> "Success is impacting young people in a positive way." – Orson Sykes

---

EARNED WISDOM

★ **Success:** Success is the positive impact you have on young people. It's very important to have a positive impact on the athletes who walk through your doors.

★ **Wisdom:** If nothing changes, then nothing changes.

★ **Gratitude:** Spirit of Texas and Cheer Athletics had a significant impact on him. He learned from what they were doing and went home and got better.

★ **Orson's Wish:** Orson wishes cheerleading could be a single division without a DI and DII split. He feels it detracts from the legitimacy of the sport.

★ **Mistakes:** Orson was young when he started, and he thinks he made many mistakes in the beginning—leadership of staff, management of the business, and financial oversight. In the end, they were all valuable lessons.

- ★ **For Gym Owners:** Be sure to plan properly. Figure out what you need to start your business and do that twice. Make a plan and then review the plan. Figure out what you're going to offer in your area that is unique. Be authentically you.

- ★ **For Coaches:** Decide what is important to you. Is it more important to win The Cheerleading Worlds while taking your athletes' heart and soul? Or is it more important for you to get the most out of each athlete, training them to reach their potential and helping them prepare for life?

- ★ **Lessons Learned:** Listen to parents. Over the years, Orson learned that lesson. Often, parents just want to be heard.

DID YOU KNOW?

- ★ Orson's favorite part of cheer is watching the routine develop from the beginning of the season to the end. Every year and every team represents a different journey.

- ★ His favorite routine was the Twist and Shout routine from 2010 performed at NCA All Star Nationals.

- ★ Orson barks at practice whenever his athletes excel. (He actually barked at me during his interview—quite a spectacle!)

- ★ He loves spending time with his family, and he's a huge movie buff. His favorite movie is *I Am Legend* with Will Smith. He also loves *Cast Away* with Tom Hanks.

- ★ Orson loves being a dad. He enjoys going to his son's games and watching him play basketball.

- ★ Orson's favorite superhero is Superman because he downplays his abilities in front of others. He saves his powers for when people need him.

- ★ Orson chose the lion as his animal because it represents family, strength, energy, courage, guardianship, protection, ferocity, and authority.

"The secret of change is to focus all of your energy not on fighting the old but on building the new." – Socrates

TATE CHALK
American – 1996
Nfinity – 2004

A BAD BREAK OR A GREATER PLAN?

"Sometimes you think God's working against you," Tate Chalk said. "He actually has a much greater plan for your life."

If not for a broken shoulder, Tate might have become an officer in the US Army. Instead, that injury sent him on a winding path that would forever transform the cheerleading industry. His journey from college athlete to Hollywood actor to founder of Nfinity, one of cheerleading's most iconic brands, is a testament to resilience, faith, and the power of unexpected opportunities.

FROM FOOTBALL TO FLYERS

In 1987 Tate Chalk was a freshman football player at Furman University in Greenville, South Carolina, with dreams of military service . . . until a devastating shoulder injury derailed those plans.

"I was on an Army scholarship. I mean, gung-ho, the whole bit," Tate said. "I was ready to go, and then I broke my shoulder. Of course, I couldn't go to jump school, and I couldn't do a bunch of things that I wanted to do."

After his injury Tate returned home to Columbia, South Carolina, and took a job at a local fitness gym. It was there that a chance invitation changed everything.

"A girl I worked with—Ann Watkins—stopped me one day," Tate said, leaning back with a smile. "She goes, 'Hey, we're practicing at the gymnastics center tonight.'" He chuckled as he remembered the scene. "Ann cheered at the University of South Carolina, and she asked if I wanted to come along. I hesitated and said, 'I don't really know.'"

But Ann wouldn't take no for an answer. "Oh, just come," she insisted, waving off his doubts. "It'll be fun. There's a bunch of guys and girls—you'll love it."

One practice was all it took. "I think my first stunt was a toss to hands extension or something," Tate said, his eyes lighting up at the memory. "I remember coming home thinking, 'Stunting is the greatest thing ever.'"

But the hard part was breaking the news to his traditional South Carolinian parents. Sitting across the kitchen table, Tate took a deep breath and said, "Hey, Mom, Dad, guess what? I'm going to be a cheerleader."

His dad's fork paused midair: "You're going to be what?"

"I'm going to be a cheerleader."

The room fell silent—until his dad's skepticism melted away the moment he realized the perk. "Wait . . . does that mean free season tickets to the games at the University of South Carolina?"

"Yep."

And just like that, the decision was a little easier to swallow.

What began as a casual invitation from a coworker became a turning point. That single request changed Tate's life and, eventually, would impact millions of cheerleaders around the world.

FROM SOUTH CAROLINA TO KENTUCKY

Tate cheered at the University of South Carolina for three years. When his teammates decided not to return, he received an unexpected call from the renowned coach of the University of Kentucky cheerleading program.

"I got a phone call from T. Lynn Williamson at Kentucky. He said, 'Are you interested in coming to cheer at Kentucky?' And I said, 'Yes, sir.' He said, 'Well, tryouts are this weekend. Get on an airplane.'"

The risk paid off. Despite fierce competition, Tate earned a spot on Kentucky's elite squad. "They're calling out the guys in no particular order . . . two more guys were left. Me and Jim Lord are standing there, and I remember looking at him and thinking he was so much better than me. And then they called my name, and then they called his." Tate smiled and said, "I thought it was amazing."

His Kentucky experience wasn't without drama. During nationals, after years of unchallenged dominance, the team suffered what became known as "The Great Kentucky Crash" or "The Great Cat Catastrophe."

"We're out there doing the Kentucky run," Tate said, "and as goofy as that was, you're just like, 'We got this' . . . and three eight-counts before the end of the music our pyramid—it was a ground up, basically connected two-and-a-half-high at the elbows—somebody tipped over, and the whole thing just crumbled, and I mean it crumbled. And in one beat of an eight-count, I thought my life was over."

The setback taught Tate resilience. After Kentucky, he returned to South Carolina as a graduate assistant coach under Bill Boggs, recruiting future cheerleading notables such as Pat Wedge and Jamie Parrish.

BUILDING GYMS AND BREAKING GROUND

After graduating with a degree in criminal justice, Tate was on track to join the US Marshals Service. "I finished in the top one percent on the marshal's exam. I was physically fit and excelled in all areas of the assessment." But fate intervened again when the federal government implemented a hiring freeze.

With his law enforcement dreams on hold, Tate took a coaching position in Florida before receiving a call from Eddie Zegarra, a friend who had been coaching at the

University of Georgia. Eddie invited him to work at American Cheerleading in Atlanta.

"I loaded up my used Honda Prelude, because I was fancy like that, with my one bag of clothes and headed to Atlanta," Tate said. "I remember it was 1995, because above the overpass was the countdown to the 1996 Summer Olympics."

"The gym was modest—the tiniest cheer gym you could possibly imagine. I think it was forty feet wide by a hundred feet long. It was one of those old industrial flex spaces where people just sort of threw a floor down, and you tumbled all the way up to the wall."

Tate bought into ownership of the gym and helped expand American Cheerleading to multiple locations, eventually serving nearly 4,000 kids weekly across all the gyms. The operation provided him with invaluable experience in the business of cheerleading, but it also taught him hard lessons about profitability.

Despite generating over $2 million in revenue, Tate realized that the gym business model didn't suit him: "The profit margin just wasn't there." He transitioned out of gym ownership, helping place trusted colleagues like Randy Dickey and Casey Jones in leadership roles at various locations before moving on to his next challenge.

FROM PRODUCT EXPERT TO HOLLYWOOD

Tate's journey took another unexpected turn when he began consulting for athletic companies. One client, Power, proved to be especially significant.

"I took them from a four-hundred-thousand-dollar company to a three-million-dollar company in eighteen months," Tate said. When the company couldn't meet the financial terms it had originally agreed upon, it offered Tate severance instead.

With the severance money in hand and at a crossroads once again, Tate made what may have been his boldest move yet by relocating to Los Angeles, California, to pursue acting. "I've learned that this is a wild ride called life, so all you can do is white-knuckle this thing and hope the bugs stay out of your teeth."

His Hollywood adventure got off to a rocky start. He arrived in LA with just a bag of clothes and $1,500. After crashing on friends' couches and facing roommate drama, Tate ended up in a pay-by-the-week motel just as the September 11, 2001, attacks rocked LA and the nation.

"I don't know that I've ever felt or could explain the loneliness of that morning. Everybody remembers 9/11 distinctly. I was four thousand miles from home. I had no idea what I was going to do next."

Yet, true to form, Tate persevered. A chance encounter with a cheerleader-turned-bartender named Mac Jackson led to stable housing. To make ends meet, Tate leveraged his cheerleading expertise and traveled for hours every day to coach teams throughout Southern California.

While almost everyone else was waiting tables, Tate ran around doing choreography as far out as San

Bernardino, about sixty miles from LA. His cheerleading background eventually intersected with his Hollywood aspirations when he was hired as a cheerleading coordinator for the 2004 comedy *Dodgeball*, starring Vince Vaughn and Ben Stiller.

"I met with them, and they had no idea what a cheerleading coordinator was," Tate said with a laugh. "So I told them, 'Look, I'll make you a deal. I'm not asking for the part—just give me an audition.'"

His gamble paid off. Tate landed a role in the film as a referee and even choreographed the Dodgeball Dancers. That experience led to another opportunity, working on *Coach Carter* with Samuel L. Jackson when a young Channing Tatum made his debut.

Despite his successes, Tate felt unfulfilled in Hollywood. At thirty-one—significantly older than most aspiring actors—he grew frustrated with the industry's flakiness and longed for something more meaningful.

FINDING DIRECTION THROUGH FAITH

Throughout his journey, faith played a central role in Tate's decision-making. Before moving to Los Angeles, he had sought divine guidance. "God, here's the deal," Tate prayed. "I'm moving to LA. But without hurting me, I need you to either close that door or show me another opportunity." In essence, he asked God for a clear answer, a yes or a no. If no obstacles appeared, he'd take it as a yes. With that resolve, he bought himself a one-way ticket to LA.

During the flight a friend left him a voicemail with a Bible verse from Joshua 1:9: "Be strong and courageous. Do not be afraid; do not be discouraged, for the Lord your God will be with you wherever you go."

Four years later, feeling his Hollywood chapter coming to an end, Tate once again turned to prayer: "I went to church that Sunday and said, 'God, I'm really done here. If you're done with me here, I don't know what's next, but this isn't for me.'"

Three days later his phone rang. It was Mike Pare, who Tate had once taught to tumble. Mike left this message: "Tate, call me. I've got a great opportunity for you."

Initially skeptical, Tate returned the call only to learn that Mike and several partners wanted to start a cheerleading shoe company, and they wanted Tate to lead it. They had seen his success at Power Athletics and believed he was the perfect fit. Stunned, Tate replied, "I'm going to have to call you back."

To Tate it felt like a divine answer. "I prayed on Sunday and got my answer on Wednesday. My mind was blown."

THE BIRTH OF NFINITY

Tate sold most of his possessions, shipped what remained to Florida, and embarked on building what would become Nfinity Athletic. The start wasn't smooth. Their first year saw a staggering 30 percent product defect rate compared to the industry standard of 1 percent, but the innovative concept resonated with cheerleaders.

"We had the world's worst marketing line ever," Tate admitted with a laugh. "But it got the point across." The line was simple: "The world's first and only spring floor cheerleading shoe."

"No ad agency would ever greenlight something with that many syllables," he continued, shaking his head. "But the kids understood it, and it worked."

Early on, industry experts doubted Nfinity's premium pricing strategy. Tate priced the Nfinity shoe at $65. Even Varsity insisted that its research showed only 0.3 percent of cheerleaders would pay more than $35 for a pair of shoes. Less than a year later, those same people were calling to get in on the Nfinity phenomenon.

Unlike many of his peers, Tate resisted selling to Varsity Brands. "From the early 2010s, even after Karen created Rebel, I was the only one of my friends who didn't sell to Varsity," he explained. "Let me tell you, that was a hard choice."

Instead of selling, Tate established Nfinity on fundamental principles, prioritizing "Brand before all" as the foremost value, followed by "Be impeccable with your word," a concept inspired by one of his favorite books, *The Four Agreements* by Don Miguel Ruiz. The company transitioned from specializing in shoes to offering a comprehensive array of cheerleading products and services, but Tate viewed Nfinity as more than a brand.

"We owned the club membership. When kids wear the Nfinity logo, even to this day, it's different than wearing some other logo. Wearing the Nfinity logo says, 'I'm a cheerleader, and I take this sport seriously.'"

Tate takes pride in Nfinity's inclusive values and the strong leadership team he's assembled, particularly the women in executive roles. "It's very important to have strong female leaders in my company," he emphasizes. "Three of the five top executive leaders in my company are women. And that's something unusual, especially in our sport."

FULL CIRCLE MOMENTS

Looking back on his winding path—from injured football player to cheerleader, from gym owner to Hollywood actor, from consultant to brand founder—Tate sees purpose in every detour.

"When you think your whole world is upside down and the universe is turned against you, sometimes you think God's working against you," Tate said. "He actually has a much greater plan for your life."

That broken shoulder didn't just change Tate's life, it changed cheerleading shoes forever. And through all the ups and downs, the couch-surfing and uncertainty, Tate found what he was looking for, both professionally and personally.

"The person that's had the most impact on my life is probably Grace, my wife," Tate said. After years of hoping, searching, and creating a manifestation list of the qualities he desired in a partner, Tate found Grace in 2006. She matched almost every item on his list. He prayed and prayed and prayed for her. Grace has been the constant. Out of nowhere, she came into his life, and they built Nfinity together. She's his ride or die.

From that first cheerleading practice in 1987 to building one of the industry's most respected brands, Tate Chalk's story exemplifies how life's unexpected twists often lead us exactly where we're meant to be. As Tate puts it, "God works in mysterious ways."

> **"Success is anything that leaves you truly content." – Tate Chalk**

EARNED WISDOM

★ **Success:** As people pursue success, they tend to be content with fewer and fewer things. Successful people are rarely "there." They are always looking ahead to what's next. Tate wants to strive to be content while still working to make something better.

★ **Wisdom:** God always has a plan, even if you can't see or understand it. Trust that there is a plan.

★ **Gratitude:** Tate is grateful for his wife, Grace. Tate believes he doesn't always know how to execute the big ideas in his head. Grace's insight and ability to turn complex ideas into a clear plan have guided the way. Tate says he prayed for her and that they were meant to be. After talking back and forth for a while, they went on their first date on a Thursday, moved in together four days later, and have been together ever since.

★ **Tate's Wish:** Tate wishes he could go back in time and start over with the end in mind. He would love to create a genuine pathway to a world championship and ensure total transparency.

★ **Mistakes:** Tate said he has made so many mistakes it's hard to know where to start. Step 1: Do whatever you can to make it right. Step 2: Don't waste your mistakes. They are the best teachers to prepare you for what is ahead. Step 3: Failure isn't final. Learn and keep going.

★ **For Gym Owners:** Take a long-term view of your business. Don't just go for short-term gain. Be sure to have good mentors and guidance from attorneys and accountants. Remember that winning doesn't pay the bills. Diversify your business.

★ **For Coaches:** You have to love it. Your passion for what you do is what will get you through the hard times. Have a great plan and stick to it. Then you'll succeed. Be dependable.

★ **Lessons Learned:** The key to success in All Star is staying power. It's a marathon, not a sprint.

DID YOU KNOW?

★ Tate's favorite part of cheer is witnessing things he's never seen before.

★ Tate was an actor.

★ He attended Harvard University and received a degree in criminal justice.

★ Tate loves dogs and riding horses.

★ He is fluent in sign language.

★ He is drawn to heroes who don't have special powers. I told him that Iron Man was my favorite, so he said, "Okay, you can have Iron Man, and I'll choose Batman."

★ Tate chose the wolf as his animal because it symbolizes loyalty, perseverance, success, intuition, spirit, and an appetite for freedom, but it also can be a loner.

"WINNING IS IN THE LITTLE THINGS.

"Always remember you're lucky to have the opportunity to coach kids, not the other way around." – Randy Dickey

RANDY DICKEY
ACX Jags – 1996

A CHANGE OF DIRECTION

Like many boys, Randy Dickey aspired to be a college athlete, a wrestler to be precise. But his dreams were crushed when he suffered a significant shoulder injury in his junior year of high school. Randy played football too, but he was passionate about wrestling. He was strong-willed and determined to find an activity that would keep him in top shape during the offseason, so he began working out at a gymnastics center where, by chance, he watched a VHS tape of a UCA summer camp and thought, "I bet I could do that."

The next day he approached the cheerleading coach at his school, Central Gwinnett High in Lawrenceville, Georgia, and asked if he could join the team. The coach did what any self-respecting coach would do and said, "Sure, I'll let you try out if you can get a few more guys interested." And thus, a cheerleader was born.

Randy went on to earn a scholarship to Georgia State University in Atlanta that combined wrestling and cheerleading. He began teaching UCA cheerleading camps the summer before he started college. During school he taught private lessons at Pro Cheer where he met Casey Jones and Heather Bartlett. (Heather would later become Casey's wife.)

Randy planned to become a chiropractor, so he envisioned attending Georgia State for four years before moving on to a clinician school for three years at Palmer College of Chiropractic in Davenport, Iowa. But in 1994 Randy decided to drop out of college at Georgia State and devote himself to cheerleading full time. His parents were less than pleased, but Randy was convinced that cheerleading was his desired career. He and Casey had begun working at American, which was owned by Kirk McElreath before Tate Chalk purchased it.

THE MOVE TO SOUTH CAROLINA

Randy was focused on teaching private lessons at American when Tate offered him the opportunity to run a gym in Irmo, South Carolina, in 1996. Tate wanted to expand and needed people to help get his new locations off the ground. Randy was supposed to move to Irmo, start the gym, and then return to Atlanta after six months. Randy's girlfriend stayed in Atlanta when he moved to Irmo.

Randy was tasked with finding a location and starting a program under the American name. He struck a deal with the owner of a gymnastics facility and paid rent per athlete, which was a great arrangement for a new business. Randy fell in love with Irmo and decided it would be a fantastic place to raise a family, so he stayed, and only eight months later he had outgrown the gymnastics center and needed a new location.

Excited to begin his next adventure, he moved his operation into a warehouse space shared with another business. The warehouse had supplies on shelves, forklifts, and workers, but there was a large open area in the center. That space was just big enough for a workout floor. Despite the one-hundred degree temperatures, lack of air conditioning, and additional tenants in the space, Randy's business thrived.

In 1998 Randy sought a more suitable space and new equipment, but Tate was managing multiple locations and couldn't dedicate time and financial resources to assist Randy with the Irmo site. Tate proposed that Randy buy him out, and they parted ways amicably. Randy secured a loan to buy the business and worked for another year to save enough money for a down payment on a new building for his current gym business, the ACX Jags.

REAL ESTATE MISADVENTURES

Negotiations began, and a contract was signed for construction of the new space. With a bright new future and a beautiful building on the horizon, life was good. Randy did what most anyone would and excitedly drove by the site frequently to check on the progress of his new building. But after four months without any visible progress, he grew concerned. Finally, he contacted the builder, who sounded surprised when Randy raised his concerns. "I'm not sure what you mean," the builder said. "The building is looking great. Things are coming along nicely."

"No, I'm standing here right now, and it's an empty lot. Nothing's been done."

The builder paused before he said, "The concrete's been poured. The framing is complete, and the metal was just delivered. It should be sitting out front right now."

Randy's frustration grew: "Well, I'm standing here, and I don't see any of that."

The builder said, "Where are you?"

A stunned silence followed. Eventually, the truth came out. The real estate agent had shown Randy a beautiful lot along the main highway. But the general contractor was constructing the building a few miles away from that site. Randy described the situation as being sold a Corvette and receiving a Camaro. At just twenty-three years old and a little green, he was furious. He exchanged some choice words with the realty group and walked away from the deal entirely.

FINDING A PERMANENT HOME

The builder was stuck with a building suited for a cheerleading gym that no one wanted to buy. He eventually reached out to Randy, and they agreed that Randy would lease the facility. Technically, he had already outgrown the new space at that point, but he didn't have a better option. He moved into the new

7,000-square-foot building and continued to save for his next facility.

Eager to grow and provide a larger space for his athletes, he soon built a 20,000-square-foot facility three buildings down from where his business is located today. He sublet his current facility and struggled with four different tenants during that three-year period. Many real estate lessons were learned during that time. Despite the many challenges, Randy said he'd do it all over again.

Now he enjoys working with the local schools and coaching the All Star teams. He takes pride in knowing that he has influenced the lives of the athletes who have walked through his doors.

Randy Dickey's journey from an injured wrestler to a successful cheerleading gym owner demonstrates the power of adaptation. What began as a creative way to stay fit during wrestling's offseason transformed into a lifelong passion and a thriving business. Through college transitions, cross-state moves, warehouse practices, and real estate challenges, Randy never lost sight of his purpose—creating opportunities for athletes to grow and excel. His willingness to take risks, learn from mistakes, and continually expand his vision has not only built a successful business but also has touched countless young lives along the way.

Randy still runs his gym and mixes music. He also enjoys watching his daughter thrive in college and spending time with his wife.

"Success is being able to provide for my family." – Randy Dickey

EARNED WISDOM

★ **Gratitude:** Find joy in coaching younger, lower-level athletes. Nothing is more gratifying than taking a group of kids who don't know anything about cheerleading and turning them into a competitive and winning team. When those same athletes go on to receive college scholarships and you receive letters of thanks, you can't help but feel pride in the small part you played in their success.

★ **Mistakes:** Randy's biggest mistake was not saving earlier. He encourages the younger generation to continue reinvesting in themselves and their businesses.

★ **To My Younger Self:** Focus more energy on your community and the grassroots of cheerleading. Kids walking in off the street cannot immediately join an elite team. Make sure to offer various options that can include beginners.

★ **For Gym Owners:** Do your homework. Know your demographics and ensure you understand the business aspects of opening a gym. Being a good coach doesn't necessarily mean you have what it takes to be a successful business owner. If you partner with someone, ensure that the relationship is sustainable. Plan your exit strategy, just in case.

★ **For Coaches:** Coaching is about teaching new skills. Every athlete needs to be coached differently. Read their body language and demeanor. Learn how to connect with your athletes mentally and emotionally.

★ **Lessons Learned:** Bigger is not always better. Randy's gym had reached a certain level of growth in a small building, and he felt that he needed to expand. A larger facility requires more revenue, which in turn requires more athletes, more staff, and more classes. But more potential issues can arise. Sometimes, it's not better to go bigger. He also dabbled in multiple locations and decided it was not a good idea for him. Learning to replicate and manage several locations under one brand requires specific skills.

DID YOU KNOW?

★ Randy plays the piano and has a baby grand in his home. He was never classically trained, but both his parents were musicians.

★ He raced BMX bicycles and won several state, national, and grand national championships as well as the High Point Winner award in the National Bicycle League.

★ Currently, Randy trains in Jujitsu.

★ His favorite cheerleading memory was winning CHEERSPORT, NCA, and Summit for the first time.

★ Randy doesn't have a favorite superhero, but he's a gigantic Rocky Balboa fan: "Hey, yo, Adrian!"

★ For his animal Randy chose the jaguar, which represents chaos, shape-shifting, aggressiveness, power, confidence, and manifestation.

"Eat, drink, and be merry." – Benjamin Franklin

GEORGE "BOOG" POTTER
Premier Athletics & Athletics Championships – 1997

FROM CUMBERLAND COLLEGE TO GRADUATE SCHOOL

Boog Potter attended Cumberland College, now the University of the Cumberlands, in Williamsburg, Kentucky, for his undergraduate studies. There he met his best friend and future business partner, Mike Martinez. Boog and Mike both cheered at Cumberland.

After graduating, Boog enrolled in the MBA program at the University of Tennessee. He was dedicated to earning a dual concentration master's degree in finance and entrepreneurship. Although Mike had two more years left at Cumberland, he and Boog taught summer camps for COA before teaching camps for UCA.

While he was in Kentucky for his undergraduate studies, Boog visited a new cheer gym in Lexington. After moving back to Knoxville to start graduate school at UT, he heard about another cheer gym in Memphis, and there were rumors that one was going to open in Nashville. Cheer gyms were just starting to become popular.

"It was awesome," Boog said. "It was exactly what I wanted to do."

He loved teaching summer camps and wanted to own his own gym. As a graduate student in business, Boog was especially focused on business growth, which led him to the idea of opening a family of gyms that could benefit from economies of scale.

He used his idea for his graduate thesis, specifically focusing on the concept of a cheer gym in Knoxville that included vertical integration and growth across multiple locations in several cities. "At the time," Boog said, "this was a brand-new concept, so trying to explain to my professor and to other students what a cheer gym was took up 95 percent of the project."

Boog conducted significant research before returning to Lexington to visit the Bluegrass Gymnastics Training Center, home of the Bluegrass Tigers. He'd spent plenty of time in gymnastics gyms, but he wanted to get a feel for a cheer gym. He wanted to learn about the layout, how to tumble, how to design a gym, and which equipment would be best. "I kind of fell in love with my project," Boog said, "and decided this is what I wanted to do with my life." After graduation in 1993 Boog was offered a job in the City of Knoxville's Finance Department. It was a stable job that paid well. In fact, he said the salary would have been the equivalent of $75,000 today.

TAKING RISKS

Boog thought about the offer, but he still wanted to start his own business. He told his parents he had decided to turn the job down. Instead, he was going to work for the Knoxville Gymnastics Training Center (KGTC) for $8 an hour. Boog's dad was angry. He thought his son was crazy for walking away from a great job with the city, but Boog did it anyway.

Before starting at KGTC, Boog and his friend, Barry Garner, spoke to the owners, Phil and Lisa Savage, and they agreed to work together to start a cheer program. Barry was a former cheerleader at the University of Tennessee and was just as eager as Boog to start the program. They focused on school team classes first. The classes grew rapidly, and Phil and Lisa quickly learned that Boog had a good business sense, so they hired him to manage the entire facility, the bookkeeping, accounting, scheduling, and marketing.

By then Mike Martinez was graduating from college and planned to move to Memphis and teach Spanish. Boog convinced him to forgo that opportunity and move to Knoxville to run the cheer program while Boog managed the gym. The plan was to eventually start a cheer gym together. Mike agreed, and they started their first All Star cheer team, the Knoxville Sharks, in 1994 at KGTC.

BUILDING THE FOUNDATION: KNOXVILLE SHARKS

The San Jose Sharks hockey team had just started play in the NHL in 1991-92, and Boog thought their logo was really cool, so he adopted the name for his team of twelve girls formed from the high school teams who had been practicing at the gyms. The Knoxville Sharks attended several local competitions and a COA national event in Jacksonville, Florida, where they competed against eight other teams in the Senior Division. There were no levels, and the Sharks won.

That victory springboarded their program, and the following year they had twenty-five girls on their Senior team and were able to start a Junior team. Mike continued to run the cheer program while Boog helped coach here and there, but he was focused on managing the entire business and trying to purchase the property in front of the gymnastics center so they could move the cheer program into its own facility and start their cheer gym.

The cheer side continued to grow, and with the help of Phil, Lisa, and Boog and Mike's parents, they were finally able to purchase the property and start construction of the new cheer gym. It was Boog's first construction project which, ironically, is mostly what he does every day now.

PREMIER ATHLETICS: THE FIRST MULTILOCATION CHEER BUSINESS

Boog was excited and loved what he was doing, but he wanted to open more facilities. Phil and Lisa didn't share his vision, so Boog bought them out of the single facility in Knoxville, and a new partner joined Mike and Boog.

Bill Asp, a non-cheerleader business entrepreneur, loved Boog's concept and jumped on board. In 1997 Premier Athletics became the first multilocation gym business when it opened three more Tennessee locations: Knoxville, Nashville with friend and University of Tennessee cheerleader Bill Noffsinger, and Asheville with Ben Pope, also a friend and former University of Tennessee cheerleader. Ben also had cheered at Methodist College with Abel Rosa, who started a Premier Athletics gym in Wilmington, North Carolina. Abel went on to coach at Methodist College where he coached me (Stacy Rowe), and that's how I became part of Premier Athletics and, eventually, one of the owners. In addition, LeRoy McCallough, coach of Oklahoma State University and Team USA Cheer, cheered at Methodist College alongside Ben and Abel.

Premier was the original name. Boog mentioned that when they were selecting a name for the business there were so many Elites and Extremes that they wanted to be different, so they decided on Premier. Athletics was added later. Cole Stott was soon hired as the Premier Athletics Knoxville and regional manager.

The business struggled at first, but the gyms eventually took off. Because Boog had some early success, he wanted to continue expanding. "That was our biggest mistake," Boog said. "Several times we just grew too fast. You know, 'We've got this thing figured out. Let's triple in size.' " But somehow they always managed to make it work.

GROWING PAINS AND NEW VENTURES

Premier attended the CHEERSPORT Nationals run by Kevin Brubaker. Boog and Mike had several gyms in eastern Tennessee by then, and they thought they'd like to start their own competition. As a result, they decided to host an event in Chattanooga. So in 2000 they took the Athletic part of Premier Athletics and renamed the event the Athletic Championships. Mike was still coaching while Boog handled most of the planning and logistics to get the event scheduled at the convention center, but the center didn't want to give them the time of day.

The second year was a different story. They had ninety teams, which was huge for those days. The city was ecstatic, and the event still takes place at the Chattanooga Convention Center today.

Two short years later the event boasted over 200 teams. The success allowed the gyms to grow, and in true Boog and Mike fashion they expanded rapidly by adding facilities in Florida, Alabama, Kentucky, Indiana, and Michigan as well as in Atlanta and South Atlanta. They also started two locations in North Carolina, one of which I ran. Boog and Mike also added several more events in Atlanta, Georgia; Tunica, Mississippi; and other cities.

Simultaneously, Boog and Mike started the Premier Network, a group of gyms that cooperated to obtain discounts from event producers, apparel companies, shoe manufacturers, and uniform suppliers. Boog focused more on the gyms, growth plans, and new opportunities for the gyms while Mike concentrated on the Athletic Championships and event expansion.

In 2004 Cole Stott was offered a seat on the newly formed USASF Board of Directors where he met Jim Chadwick. Jim was impressed with Cole and the Premier model, and he wanted to spread the word about the newly formed USASF, so he set up a meeting with Boog, Cole, and Jeff Webb.

THE VARSITY CHAPTER

At Boog's first meeting with Jeff Webb, Jeff said, "Varsity is late to the All Star party, but we want to help All Star cheer grow, and we want to do it right."

Jeff was impressed not only with Boog and Mike but with Cole and several other members of the Premier Athletics team. He appreciated what they had built, but he also recognized their business owner mentality.

Varsity went on to purchase Athletic Championships and Premier Athletics in 2005, but Mike and Boog both continued to work for Varsity for a time. Cole continued to oversee the gyms and, eventually, he became president of the Varsity Knoxville office, which managed the gyms and eleven event brands that hosted fifty All Star competitions per year.

Athletic Championships helped springboard Varsity into the All Star space and guided them through decisions and growth in All Star. The Premier Network turned into the Varsity Family Plan, which helped send money back to the gyms when they needed it most.

When Boog and Mike's three-year contract ended, they decided to leave the company and went on to start new business ventures. "Varsity was great to us," Boog said. "It gave us a lot of flexibility and allowed us to do other things."

Jeff wanted them to move to Memphis, but Knoxville was their home, so Mike and Boog stayed for a few months as consultants, but they eventually moved on. Cole had already taken over most of the operations, and things were left in good hands.

FULL CIRCLE

What goes around comes around. Mike and Boog, along with their partners Cole Stott and me (Stacy Rowe), eventually bought Premier Athletics back from Varsity. "It's really cool," Boog said, "that we own the original gyms again."

Boog has bought and sold several additional businesses, including a few marinas in the Knoxville area and Concord Title. He is semiretired and loves spending time in Florida when he isn't in Knoxville. He's also the proud father of teenage twins who are about to start their college careers.

Boog Potter stands as a visionary pioneer in the All Star cheerleading industry. From humble beginnings at Cumberland College to building Premier Athletics, the first multilocation cheer business, Boog transformed how cheer programs operate nationwide. His innovative business model, combining vertical integration with strategic growth, created a blueprint that countless cheer organizations have followed.

Beyond his business acumen, Boog's passion for cheerleading education, commitment to athlete development, and willingness to take calculated risks fundamentally shaped the competitive landscape. By establishing strong foundations, expanding Premier Athletics across multiple states, creating Athletic Championships, and eventually reclaiming ownership of his original gyms, Boog's entrepreneurial journey embodies the spirit of the All Star cheer world: determination, teamwork, and the relentless pursuit of excellence.

I am personally indebted to Boog for the opportunities he provided me early in my career. In addition, he taught me a great deal about business and people. He brought me into the Premier Athletics family, and I'll be forever grateful.

> **"Success is parenting awesome kids. Success is also friendship." – Boog Potter**

EARNED WISDOM

★ **Success:** He looks at his kids every day and thanks God that he hasn't screwed up parenting them thus far. He also says "success is beyond money, beyond business, beyond everything. It's knowing that you helped raise great kids."

- ★ **Gratitude:** Boog has great pride in and appreciation for his father. He was a firefighter who worked hard and moved up the ranks. Boog grew up poor, but things improved as he got older. His dad was always working multiple jobs. Boog attributes his work ethic to his father: "Looking back, I grew up a poor kid who ended up building and selling pretty big companies in a few different industries. I know I inherited that from Dad and his example."

- ★ **Wisdom:** If you have children, cherish your time with them. Work hard to grow your business, but make time to spend with your family.

- ★ **To My Younger Self:** Slow down.

- ★ **For Gym Owners:** Grow wisely and methodically, and don't let your eyes get too big. Feeling excited about your business and your future is fantastic. You can feel those emotions but still be smart and grow in a way that works for you. Don't get too far ahead of yourself. You can save yourself a lot of pain and anguish if you slow down occasionally.

- ★ **For Coaches:** Don't let your highs get too high and your lows get too low. There will always be good days, and there will always be bad days. Learn to appreciate the days in between.

- ★ **Lessons Learned:** Through business you can build tremendous friendships. Value each one.

DID YOU KNOW?

★ Boog's favorite part of cheer is the friendships he's made.

★ Although he has never lived in Texas, Boog has been a loyal Dallas Cowboys fan since he was six.

★ He's an avid golfer.

★ Boog is president of the booster club at his children's high school.

★ Captain America is his favorite superhero. Boog thinks that when the Avengers start to fall apart, Captain America is there to bring them back together. He's a great leader.

★ Boog chose the bear as his animal because it symbolizes industriousness, instinct, healing, power, sovereignty, guardianship of the world, watchfulness, courage, willpower, self-preservation, introspection, and strength.

LET KIDS BE KIDS.

"It is not the critic who counts; not the man who points out how the strong man stumbles, or where the doer of deeds could have done them better. The credit belongs to the man who is actually in the arena, whose face is marred by dust and sweat and blood; who strives valiantly; who errs, who comes short again and again, because there is no effort without error and shortcoming; but who does actually strive to do the deeds; who knows great enthusiasms, the great devotions; who spends himself in a worthy cause; who at the best knows in the end the triumph of high achievement, and who at the worst, if he fails, at least fails while daring greatly, so that his place shall never be with those cold and timid souls who neither know victory nor defeat." – Theodore Roosevelt

MIKE MARTINEZ
Premier Athletics & Athletics Championships – 1997

FROM FOOTBALL FIELD TO CHEER FLOOR

In 1987 Mike Martinez was a sophomore at Cooper City High School in South Florida. Like many teenage boys he played the traditional sports, basketball during his freshman year and football during his sophomore year. The football experience was less than stellar. "We were historically terrible," Mike recalled with a laugh. "We hadn't won a game in seven years. We were this big 7A school out in the suburbs playing against all these inner-city Miami teams that would just crush us."

That spring an unexpected opportunity appeared when Mike's math teacher, Ms. Sexton, who also coached the cheerleading team, approached him and several other boys: "I want to start a coed cheer team next year. I'd love for you all to be part of it. I'll even pay for you to come to cheer camp with us. If you like it, you can join the team. If not, no pressure."

The boys weighed their options, and the choice seemed obvious. So ten boys joined fourteen girls at an NCA camp at Camp Wildwood outside Orlando in the summer of 1987. "The best thing that could have happened, which is the genesis of my cheer story, is the fact that the University of Miami male cheerleaders were super cool," Mike explained. "They saw ten high school guys, saw we were athletic, and they taught us how to stunt."

The Miami cheerleaders took the high school boys under their wing, and those relationships would prove pivotal in Mike's cheerleading journey. By his senior year of high school in 1988-89, Mike and his teammates were serious about competition. With choreography from Mark Chakin, a University of Miami cheerleader who would later found his own event company in Florida,

Mike's Cooper City team qualified for the NCA High School Nationals in Dallas, Texas, an especially exciting accomplishment because they hadn't competed the year before.

"We went to NCA High School Nationals and, at that time—December of 1988—there were seven Coed teams in our division," Mike recalled. He chuckled and added, "I think we got third or fourth. We weren't the greatest team, but we could toss the hell out of some girls."

It was at that competition when Mike discovered All Star cheerleading. As he watched another team take the floor, curiosity got the best of him: "There was an All Star division," Mike explained, "and I remember asking, 'Man, what's that?' Someone told me, 'They're all from different schools, just put together to compete.'"

He shook his head, still amused by his initial reaction: "I thought, 'That's the most foreign thing I've ever heard.'"

FROM KENTUCKY TO KNOXVILLE

Mike wanted to continue cheerleading in college. Though accepted to Florida State and the University of Miami, he set his sights on Kentucky, the recognized hotbed of collegiate cheerleading at the time.

"I wasn't good enough to make the University of Kentucky team," he admitted, "but I figured if I could be on a good coed team in Kentucky, I'd improve and have access to where the action was."

Mike landed at the University of the Cumberlands (then Cumberland College) in Williamsburg, Kentucky, which offered athletic scholarships for cheerleading. During his freshman year in 1989 he attended UCA camp at East Tennessee State University in Johnson City where he met George "Boog" Potter, who would become his business partner and lifelong friend.

"Boog was a junior, and I was a freshman," Mike said. "We hit it off from the beginning. We were partners in crime."

The pair competed at UCA Nationals in San Antonio that year, and while their team wasn't particularly successful, Mike was hooked. The following summer he and Boog worked for the Cheerleaders of America (COA), using Columbus, Ohio, as their home base while traveling to various camps.

After Boog graduated from college, he briefly considered joining the University of Kentucky's renowned cheerleading program, but he followed his father's advice to attend business school at the University of Tennessee instead. That decision would prove fateful for both Mike and Boog's future.

BUILDING THE SHARKS

During his senior year at Cumberland College Mike found himself at another crossroads. He had been accepted to law school, but he was drawn to the entrepreneurial path that Boog was forging in Knoxville. The duo began working with Phil Savage at the Knoxville Gymnastics Training Center (KGTC) where they learned the operational side of running a gym. Mike would drive an hour from Williamsburg to Knoxville several times a week to teach classes. After graduation, he moved to Knoxville permanently, and they formed their first competitive All Star team, the KGTC Sharks.

"We were terrified," Mike said. "This was our livelihood, so we took it seriously." Mike's tough-love approach in coaching paid dividends quickly. "That first KGTC Sharks team, we coached them so hard and we made them so good," Mike said. "Out of nowhere, this little team from Knoxville was good, and everybody's like, 'Holy cow, who are these guys?'"

The Sharks won the COA Nationals in 1994 and repeated the following year with a junior team. Their aha moment came when they defeated established powerhouses World Cup and Top Gun at a WCA competition in Nashville.

"That was a big deal. That was pretty special," Mike said. "That still gives me goosebumps when I think about it."

THE BIRTH OF PREMIER ATHLETICS

Success breeds ambition. "We wanted to make a career out of it," Mike said. "We said, 'This is working in Knoxville. Why can't we put gyms in other places?'" The operation grew organically. KGTC added a cheer annex called the Knoxville Cheer Center (KCC), which it quickly outgrew. In 1997 Boog and Mike built a dedicated cheer facility on the lower part of the property and brought in Bill Asp, who left his medical sales career to join the business. That marked the official beginning of Premier Athletics.

With Bill's business acumen complementing Mike, Boog, and Cole's cheer expertise, Premier expanded rapidly. Their first wave of gyms included locations in Asheville (managed by Ben Pope), Nashville (managed by Bill Noffsinger), and Johnson City (operated by Renee Fontana) in the Tri-Cities area of Tennessee while Cole Stott oversaw the Knoxville location and managed several other locations in the region.

A second wave followed, including Wilmington (managed by Abel Rosa), Somerset, and Evansville. That expansion marked an unprecedented shift in the All Star cheer industry, a multilocation business model with standardized systems and shared resources.

VERTICAL INTEGRATION AND ATHLETICS CHAMPIONSHIPS

By 2001 Premier Athletics had cemented its status as a legitimate cheer gym organization in the country. With numerous locations and hundreds of athletes, Premier had the power to explore vertical integration strategies. "Let's run a really good event that all our gyms can support," Mike said, "and make it a great experience for our athletes."

His idea led to the creation of Athletic Championships. Rather than reinventing the wheel, they simply identified what they liked and disliked about existing competitions. "We kept the event experiences we liked," Mike said, "and we pieced together what we didn't like and made sure we did it better."

Premier also leveraged its scale in other ways, creating shared services like TeamLeader for uniforms and negotiating better pricing on shoes and other products for all its locations. This business model—using gym ownership as a foundation for broader industry ventures—would later be adopted and expanded upon by Varsity Spirit.

"Leveraging scale to help the gyms be more profitable" is how Mike described it. "I feel like that's also the kind of model that Varsity used. I feel like they took everything Premier was doing and then just compounded it across the industry."

CORPORATE EVOLUTION AND LEADERSHIP LESSONS

As Premier grew, Mike, Boog, and Bill Asp began to have differing visions for the company, so by 2002 they decided to restructure. Mike took full control of Athletic Championships while Boog, Bill, and Cole continued with Premier Athletics for another year until Bill eventually departed. The separation wasn't just a business decision, it became a valuable lesson about the cheer industry, one that continues to resonate today.

"Bill was a smart guy," Mike said. "He had his MBA and was successful, but he didn't have cheer in his DNA." Mike argues that the gap between standard business logic and the passion-driven world of cheer is why Bill ultimately left the industry. "We're selling a product or service where price and quality aren't the only things that matter," Mike said. "There are other factors involved."

THE VARSITY ACQUISITION

In 2005 Jeff Webb and Varsity met with Athletic. Sensing an opportunity to gain All Star expertise, Varsity proposed acquiring both companies as a package deal. The acquisition closed in May 2005, just a month after Mike's twins were born. Both he and Boog joined Varsity at the executive level where Jeff positioned them as his All Star experts.

"To Jeff's credit," Mike said, "he brought us in at the executive level and plopped us right in the middle of his management team and said, 'All right, here are the All Star experts. Let's figure this out.' "

"I'll be forever grateful to Jeff," Mike said. "We were all used to being small business owners in flip-flops. We went to Subway at lunch, made a decision, and then went back to work and implemented it. He taught us how to think through our decisions and implement them on a grander scale."

Jeff mentored Mike on corporate politics and executive presence, even taking him to high-level meetings with major venue partners. "Being exposed to that level of executive and being in those meetings really polished me," Mike said.

FULL CIRCLE: THE LEGACY OF PREMIER

In an ironic twist, after leaving Premier to focus on the event side of the business and then selling to Varsity and joining its corporate structure, Mike eventually found himself back as a silent owner of Premier

Athletics following Varsity's divestiture of gym ownership.

"Did I ever in a million years think I would own Premier again? No," Mike said, and he laughed. "But did I ever think there'd be a pandemic that made everybody walk around with masks on? I didn't think that either." Looking back on Premier's impact on the industry, Mike sees its primary contribution as bringing business professionalism to All Star cheer.

"Nobody gets into cheer to get rich," Mike said with characteristic candor. "People have carved out a very comfortable life for themselves and have done extremely well. But I think, at its core, when you take that first step across the line to enter the industry you do it because you have a passion for it."

Today, Mike continues to be involved in multiple aspects of the cheerleading industry, including apparel, through his All Star Outfitters. When asked why he remains engaged after all these years, his answer revealed the same passion that led him to choose cheerleading over football as a high school sophomore. "Number one, it's in my DNA," he said. "Number two, I've developed a group of people that I work with that I dearly care for and that I want to see fulfill their dreams." But perhaps most meaningful to Mike is the positive impact that cheerleading has on young people, particularly on girls.

"To be able to work in an industry where you're making a positive impact on females—there's not very many positive things that teenage girls can lean into," he says. "Think of that moment for the little twelve-year-old girl.

Who knows what she's dealing with? She puts on that uniform, looks in the mirror, and feels a sense of self-worth and pride. We play a small part in that, and I think that's pretty cool."

> "Success is making a difference."
> – Mike Martinez

EARNED WISDOM

★ **Success:** Success is gainful employment at a place where you believe you're making a difference while earning enough money to support your family so they can do the things they love.

★ **Wisdom:** Slow and steady wins the race.

★ **Gratitude:** Mike believes that attending the NCA High School Nationals in 1989 had the biggest impact on him. The event showed him what was possible.

★ **Mike's Wish:** Mike wished we could replace the current model with that of USA Gymnastics or USA Volleyball where the clubs run the events and are supported by the NGB.

★ **Mistakes:** Making decisions out of fear or anger.

★ **For Gym Owners:** Start at the bottom of the pyramid and work your way up. Don't worry about senior teams. Fill your gym with recreational kids and younger All Stars and develop it from the younger ages up.

★ **For Coaches:** Treat coaching as a profession and strive to become a professional. Continue to educate yourself and hone your craft. Conduct yourself professionally.

DID YOU KNOW?

★ Mike's favorite cheer memory was beating World Cup and Top Gun in 1996 at the World Cheer Association in Nashville.

★ His favorite routine was Premier Sharks 1996.

★ Mike is Cuban. His wife, Holly, and daughter, Willow, were both cheerleaders at the University of Tennessee and his son, Walker, played football in college.

★ Mike still has a passion for coaching.

★ His wife, Holly, was also a gym owner in Tennessee for ten years.

★ Mike's favorite superhero is Batman. Mike appreciates that Batman's core desire is to help people, but he is internally conflicted about the right way to do it.

★ Mike chose the turtle as his animal because it's shy, protective, patient, strong, innocent, enduring, and symbolizes longevity.

S. R. Fabrico

"Winners win." – Keith Lee Johnson

COLE STOTT

Premier Athletics – 1997
The CX Brands, MotUS, Stage 8 Dance Brands, Cheerfest, Prime Alliance

BORN INTO THE GYM BIZ

Cole Stott was born into the gym world. His mother owned two facilities in Ohio, one that focused on gymnastics and dance, and the other that focused on gymnastics, but it added cheer classes by the time Cole was 10.

Cole was a gym rat growing up, and he participated in gymnastics. During his senior year of high school he was persuaded to participate with his cheer team in a competition. His mom, Linda, was thrilled. Cole participated in a single competition and was then invited to attend the Hula Bowl (at that time a college all-star football game) in January 1993 with All American cheer in Honolulu, Hawaii.

FROM OHIO TO TENNESSEE: A COLLEGE CHEERLEADER

While in Hawaii Cole met Joy Postell, the University of Tennessee cheerleading coach who was judging the competition. She offered Cole a full scholarship. Cole never had thought about cheering in college. He didn't even know cheerleading offered scholarships.

He went home and talked to his parents about the possibility of attending Tennessee on a cheerleading scholarship. His parents were supportive. Cole had to participate in the tryout process in May, but he made the team and cheered for four years at UT. He met his wife, Kristy, who was from southern Georgia and who also cheered at UT.

Cole's freshman year was the first time the University of Tennessee competed at the UCA College Nationals in Orlando, Florida. He and Kristy also participated in the collegiate partner stunt competition and performed just before Kristen and Victor Rosario. Cole never was a member of the UCA College staff, but he often took part in the college demos that kicked off the UCA camps, which is how he came to know Jeff Webb.

THE PREMIER ATHLETICS BEGINNING

While in college Cole was hired by Phil Savage to teach classes at the Knoxville Gymnastics Training Center (KGTC) where Boog Potter was the manager, and Mike Martinez coached the cheer team. KGTC eventually transformed into Premier Athletics, and Cole attended the first staff meeting in Premier Athletics' history.

The gym was doing great, so Premier started to expand. Cole became a regional manager, overseeing three of Premier's first locations. Cole vividly remembers the beat-up Honda Accord he drove to visit those locations.

By the early 2000s Premier had expanded to twenty-one locations, and the Premier Network quickly grew to include over 150 gyms. The idea for the network was born at the United States Association of Gymnastics (USAG) Congress where Cole and Boog attended a session led by Jeff Metzger, a successful gymnastics facility owner.

Inspired by Metzger's insights, Premier broke down key percentages and identified the brands it wanted to include in its network. From there, Premier developed a strategic plan to expand and connect gyms under a unified network. For the next five years those original percentages and the family-centered approach remained the foundation of the Premier network's growth.

Cole was invited to join the National Advisory Board for CHEERSPORT and NCA where he began networking and building industry relationships. Because of his position in All Star, Cole also was offered a position on the USASF Board of Directors. The only companies that were part of the USASF at the time were UCA, CHEERSPORT, and JAMfest. All other event producers were part of the NACCC. Through the USASF Cole built a relationship with Jim Chadwick who introduced Cole and Premier Athletics to Jeff Webb.

In 2003 Cole started One Up out of Premier Athletics. After the company sold to Varsity in 2005, Cole became more involved in Athletics Championships. When Boog and Mike officially left their positions at the company to explore new opportunities, Cole assumed the role of president of Premier Athletics and Athletic

Championships, which ultimately evolved into the Varsity Knoxville office.

Shortly after, Spirit Sports joined the scene with James Speed and Shannon Smith in addition to World Spirit Federation with Craig Davis and George Carillo and Spirit Festival with Robin Coe. Abel Rosa managed the Premier Athletics location in Wilmington, North Carolina, and in 2008 he moved to Knoxville to oversee all Premier Athletics' locations because Cole was increasingly focused on the events side of the brand.

EXPANDING INTO DANCE AND EVENTS

In 2010 Cole hired Sabina Salter to create The Groove Experience from the Varsity Knoxville office, which was the first true All Star brand dedicated solely to All Star dance. Prior to Groove, dance events were hosted by cheer event producers as an add-on to generate additional revenue. In addition, Cole started the first All Star advisor team, which was based in Knoxville, to promote and sell the twelve brands operating out of the Knoxville office.

In 2011 Cole moved me, (Stacy Rowe) to Knoxville to help Abel run Premier as the director of gym operations. In addition, he added Cheryl O'Brien, now Cheryl Passalacqua, to the team to run the Groove dance brand and oversee dance sales. Premier purchased Kentucky Elite and hired Brian Elza to move to Knoxville and run Athletic Championships because Mike was no longer the face of the brand.

BUILDING A LASTING LEGACY

Cole continued to use his visionary prowess to elevate Varsity Knoxville by managing twelve event brands that hosted sixty-eight events. He grew the office and an extended family along with it to include Athletics Championships, WSF, Groove, Spirit Sports, Cheerlebrity, One Up Championships, Double Down, FlipFest Gymnastics Camps, VROC All Star, Encore Cheer and Dance, Spirit Festival, 180 Pro, PURE Technique Camps, ATC, Premier Athletics, and several other brands. Premier Athletics brought a sense of business and professionalism to All Star and set the precedent that All Star cheer could be a successful career. Cole, through Premier Athletics, also brought a sense of community and structure to All Star and helped organize and streamline the event processes from the Knoxville office. In addition, Cole is responsible for creating the first dance-only All Star brand and the One Up Cheerleading Event brand.

Throughout his remarkable journey from gym rat to industry pioneer, Cole Stott has consistently demonstrated an extraordinary ability to envision possibilities others cannot see and, more important, to bring people together to transform those visions into reality. His unique talent lies not only in building businesses but also in building relationships that endure.

Cole's leadership style combines strategic brilliance with genuine care for the people around him, creating environments where innovation flourishes and individuals are empowered to reach their highest potential. What distinguishes Cole is his gift for recognizing talent, fostering collaboration, and nurturing a culture of excellence that elevates everyone involved.

As a visionary, Cole continues to look toward new horizons, always with an eye for opportunity and a heart for the relationships that make the journey meaningful. His legacy isn't just measured by successful ventures but by the countless lives he has touched, the careers he has launched, and the enduring partnerships—both professional and personal—that continue to inspire and transform the industry he loves.

He remains a highly influential figure in All Star cheer. As part owner of Premier Athletics, he continues to shape the industry. More recently, he cofounded The CX Brands, a new cheerleading event company, alongside business partners Kevin Brubaker, Casey Jones, and me, Stacy Rowe. The group also launched MotUS, a gym networking organization that now includes over 200 gyms, all working together to support each other's growth. Most recently Cole and his team formed the Prime Alliance to partner with several independent event producers who align with the common mission to grow All Star and keep the kids at the center of every decision. The Prime Alliance launched the Prime All Star Finale, a prestigious annual event for teams to celebrate their season.

In addition to his event ventures, Cole and his partners cohost The MotUS Edge Podcast every Wednesday where they share insights and stories from the industry.

Cole's passion for dance led him to partner with Cheryl Passalacqua to launch Stage 8 Dance Brands, a dance-only All Star brand that is only the second company to focus exclusively on dance.

Cole is happily married to Kristy, and they have two boys in college. Their oldest, Mason, is in graduate school and teaches physics at UT. When Maddox is not in school, he manages the X-Shop Apparel store at The CX Brands events.

> "Success is being able to live the life you want to live." – Cole Stott

EARNED WISDOM

★ **Success:** Success is happiness and the ability to live the life you want.

★ **Wisdom:** "Every day" means you don't do things sometimes, you do them every day. For example, I'm not going to work hard sometimes. I'm going to work hard every day.

★ **Gratitude:** Cole credits Brian Allan with mentoring him during his college years and throughout the early stages of his business. Boog Potter, Mike Martinez, Carl Glass, Lynn Youngs, and I (Stacy Rowe) helped Cole grow his business. Cole thanks Roger Schonder and Casey Jones for their influence on the coaching aspects of cheer. They hung out all the time when they were coaching. Cole said that coaching a team in the large All-Girl Senior Division allowed him to build great relationships with Elaine and Joelle, Victor and Kristen, and Brad and Angela. As routines evolved and performances elevated, Cole credits his wife Kristy and Chris Sipes.

★   **Cole's Wish:** Cole wishes the industry were on one scoresheet and that All Star wasn't so fragmented. He believes a unified industry would foster even greater growth.

★   **Regrets:** He didn't compete in the Ironman. He trained for two years, but when his wife got pregnant, he didn't compete. But he wouldn't change it because he wouldn't want to miss his son's birth.

★   **Mistakes:** Cole said there were so many that it was hard to choose just one, but he did. He said he was offered a five-year agreement to hold annual events in Nashville's Music City Center, but he didn't sign it. Then Nashville exploded, and the following year the rental price was five times as much.

★   **For Gym Owners:** Bigger is not always better.

★   **For Coaches:** Don't push your athletes beyond the level they are capable of. Mistakes create a lot of bad cheerleading.

★   **Lessons Learned:** Keep things in perspective. Remember what's important in life and what you value.

DID YOU KNOW?

★ His favorite part of cheer is stunting.

★ Cole's favorite routine is from the University of Tennessee in 1997. He's a die-hard Vols fan.

★ Cole claims to have defeated my husband, Chris Rowe, in golf. (I said "claims," because I don't quite believe he actually defeated my husband.)

★ He participated in an Olympic distance triathlon, a 1.5-kilometer swim, a 40-mile bike ride, and a 10-kilometer run.

★ Cole is a twenty-plus year cancer survivor. His grandfather owned a large ranch in Montana, which is where Cole's roots are.

★ Cole's favorite superhero is Iron Man.

★ Cole chose the lion as his animal because it represents family, strength, energy, courage, guardianship, protection, ferocity, and authority.

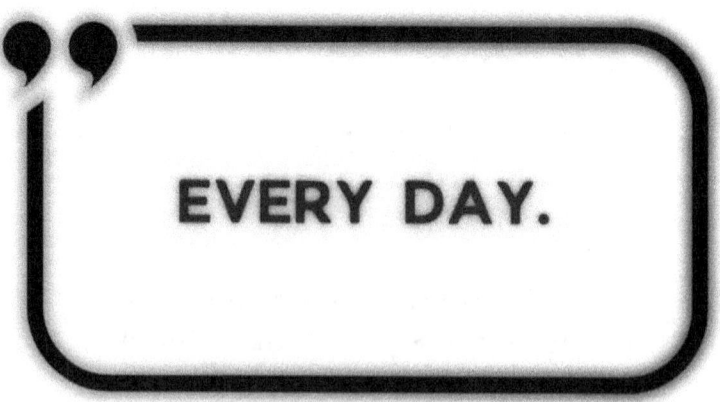

"You can't fix a broken brain with a broken brain." – Unknown

CASEY JONES

The Stingray Allstars – 1998
MotUS, The CX Brands,
Prime Alliance, Cheerfest

CHEER WITH A SIDE OF BUSINESS

"I felt like I could truly run it as a business." This statement captures what makes Casey Jones and The Stingray All Stars one of the most influential programs in All Star cheerleading. Unlike many gym owners who entered the industry driven solely by passion, Casey fused his cheerleading expertise with a thirst for business knowledge to revolutionize the sport by developing a program that embodies both competitive excellence and operational sustainability.

Casey's journey from the American Cheerleading Academy to the powerhouse Stingray Allstars shows how a commitment to professionalism can transform an entire industry.

AN UNEXPECTED INVITATION

Like many men who found their way to cheerleading in the late 1980s and early 1990s, Casey Jones didn't seek out the sport, it found him through a pretty girl.

"I knew nothing about cheerleading," Casey said. "I went to Georgia Southern [in Statesboro], and I lived next door to a cheerleader. She was really pretty and nice, so I always liked to be around her." But despite her persistent encouragement to try out for the cheerleading team, Casey rebuffed the idea: "That's not for me. That's silly. Why would I do that?" But one day at the pool she began demonstrating stunts, and something clicked, so Casey decided to try out. This common recruitment tactic—already established female cheerleaders seeking athletic males to join the team—launched countless cheerleading careers during that era.

Casey made Georgia Southern's JV team in the fall of 1990. Despite having minimal gymnastics experience his natural athleticism made him a quick study when it came to partner stunts. But what accelerated his development the most was the team's close-knit community.

"Officially, we practiced twice a week," Casey said, "but the reality was we practiced seven days a week because our community was so strong within our team that literally we met every single afternoon to stunt."

FROM ATHLETE TO INSTRUCTOR

During his sophomore year at Georgia Southern, Casey met a freshman cheerleader named Heather who would later become his wife. When Heather wanted to transfer closer to her home in the Atlanta suburb of Smyrna, Casey followed. The couple moved to Atlanta to cheer at Georgia State where they received scholarships, an opportunity that Georgia Southern didn't offer then.

The move to Atlanta connected Casey with Tommy Martin, the owner of Pro Cheer and coach at Georgia State. Tommy offered Casey a job at his gym, despite Casey having zero coaching experience. "He gave me a bunch of classes," Casey said. "I had never even taken a gymnastics class, much less taught one. So I would literally line my class up beside one of the other instructors and just emulate what he was doing and say what he was saying."

Despite this inauspicious beginning, Casey developed a passion for teaching. "I fell in love with coaching and started to study every aspect and really tried to get better every day," he said.

Pro Cheer was one of Atlanta's first dedicated cheerleading gyms, alongside American Cheerleading, and was later purchased by Tate Chalk. While the experience was valuable, Casey witnessed firsthand the challenges of balancing passion with business viability. "Tommy was a great friend, and we had an awesome time," Casey said. "He gave me a job and taught me a lot about business."

LEARNING THE INDUSTRY

When new management took over Pro Cheer and changed the pay structure, Casey moved on to assist with the opening of a gym owned by Jim Ledford on Atlanta's south side. As the only employee, Casey had to build the program from the ground up.

"When we opened, we had zero students," he said. "I would go to the grocery store, to the local mall, and pass out flyers. I begged people to come take a stunt class or tumbling class."

His hustle paid off as the program grew to a couple of hundred kids, but the commute—an hour and a half each way in Atlanta traffic—became unsustainable. After a brief stint at another small gym, Casey found his way to American Cheerleading in 1996 where Tate Chalk had recently taken over.

"That's where I got to really see how a gym was run more like a business," Casey noted. "They had good things in place. They had a front desk staff, and they had a lot of good instructors."

At American Casey met Randy Dickey and other future industry leaders while learning about the operational side of running a gym. Though he valued the experience, Casey increasingly felt the pull to strike out on his own. "I felt like I wanted my own gym," he said. "I felt like I could truly run it as a business."

His opportunity came when Tate decided to exit the gym business and sell off American Cheerleading's locations.

Casey expressed interest in buying the Marietta facility, but Tate insisted on selling both the Marietta and Norcross locations together. There was just one problem: Casey could hardly buy lunch, much less a gym.

THE INVESTOR WHO CHANGED EVERYTHING

Despite his financial limitations, Casey was determined to find a way. He approached Kathy Arnett, a cheerleading parent whose daughter, Sonny, had taken private lessons from him for years.

"I told her I wanted to buy the business," Casey said. "I asked her if she could help me put together a business plan so I could take it to the bank."

For six weeks Kathy "put me through the ringer," as Casey phrased it, making him develop budgets and analyze every aspect of the potential business. Casey discovered that Kathy wasn't a lawyer, as he had assumed. But she did own a law firm. She had previously worked as a secretary before buying the practice from the lawyers who couldn't manage their finances.

When Casey's business plan was complete, Kathy delivered unexpected news: "It would be a waste of your time. They're not going to loan you any money. You don't have any assets." Before Casey could process his disappointment, she added, "But I will. I believe in your business plan, and I believe in you."

Casey initially resisted, saying he didn't want a partner. "If I can't do it on my own, then I kind of think that's God's way of saying I'm not ready." Kathy then clarified her offer: "I'm not trying to be your partner. I'll never run the business. You run the business the way you want to run it. I'm going to be the bank, and I'm going to make money off you. Instead of paying interest to the bank, you'll pay me back with interest."

With that, Kathy loaned Casey $100,000, a staggering sum for him at the time. "I was flabbergasted that someone was going to give me that amount of money. And I was also scared to death."

The loan came with a seven-year term, but Casey's determination to clear the debt led him to pay it off in only three years. True to her word, Kathy never interfered with the business operations, asking only for free private lessons for her daughter.

AMERICAN CHEERLEADING ACADEMY TAKES SHAPE

In 1998 Casey purchased the Marietta and Norcross gyms from Tate. He immediately closed the Norcross location, even though six months remained on the lease. "I could barely run one," he admitted, "much less two." Rather than trying to escape the obligation, Casey sold the equipment and continued paying rent on the vacant space. "I knew what I was getting into. I agreed to it, and I was going to honor that."

The remaining Marietta gym operated as American Cheerleading Academy until 2001. Casey worked seven days a week, supported by a small but dedicated staff that included Susie Dufresne, who had briefly worked for Tate before becoming Casey's office manager.

"If I didn't have Susie in my life to teach me business and to hold me accountable, I don't think there would be Stingray's today," Casey said. "She was like my boss and my mother rolled into one. She made sure things ran smoothly, but the most important thing she taught me was that she loved people." Susie loved kids, she loved the customers, and she was all about customer service and fairness. She instilled all that in Casey and ingrained it in those who worked at American. And that's what set its culture in stone.

Despite his commitment, Casey's program continued to be smaller than competitors such as Georgia All Stars and United Cheerleading, particularly in All Star. Rather than trying to compete head-on for top talent, Casey developed a different strategy.

Georgia and United were looking for top-level kids. They worked with the school teams that won the state championship each year. Casey, in contrast, worked with ten schools that had no chance of winning, so his goal was to improve their ranking. If they placed eighth the previous year, he did his best to help them move up to at least seventh.

Taking that approach allowed Casey to build a sustainable business model that wasn't dependent on All Star success. "We had a building with about a floor and a half," he said, "and we had ninety All Stars and 600 class kids and school teams practicing everywhere. I would go to Cartersville on Friday afternoon and work with two schools at a time, just hustling to get all this business that, seemingly, no one else wanted."

While competitors speculated that American might go out of business due to its small All Star program, Casey knew better. "We weren't in jeopardy," he said. "It was a tough business, but we weren't just barely surviving or on the brink of going out of business, as some thought."

THE BIRTH OF THE STINGRAY ALLSTARS

A significant shift occurred in 2001 when Casey was approached by retired Home Depot executives who wanted to create a multisport center. Their vision included cheerleading alongside baseball, soccer, and even golf simulators. They proposed buying out Casey's business with him staying on to run the cheerleading division.

Around the same time, Casey had a late-night conversation at Waffle House with Roger Schonder from United Cheerleading. Roger was planning to leave cheerleading to become a pilot but, in the meantime, he was looking for a bridge opportunity. Roger proposed that he help Casey with the new venue. He could run the All Star side of the business while working on his pilot's license. This plan would help Casey get the new facility off the ground and, in a year, Roger would have his pilot's license. But Roger had one condition: "I'd really like to bring that Stingray mascot name. I think it's unique." Casey agreed, adding, "He loved the color blue, and I love green, and that's kind of how our blue and green was born."

The Home Depot executives purchased Casey's business, creating a complex called Coliseum Sports. The new venture brought unprecedented resources and marketing power to the cheerleading program. "There were billboards lining the way with pictures of cheerleaders advertising our tryouts, taking things to a new level that we never had the money to do," Casey said. During the first season at Coliseum Sports, The Stingray Allstars worked with 225 athletes and nine teams, which was ginormous at the time.

But the multisport concept soon exposed a significant imbalance. While cheerleading flourished, other areas of the 65,000-square-foot facility struggled to draw participants. "We would come in and walk through the baseball side and, literally, there were crickets," Casey said. "If it was a nice day, everybody was playing baseball outside."

The owners had made costly investments in high-end equipment that wasn't generating returns, and discord among the partners led to financial troubles. About nine months in, the paychecks stopped.

TAKING BACK CONTROL

Facing a crisis with unpaid staff and no salary for himself, Casey made a bold decision: "I bought myself out." But the terms were steep: $50,000 for the cheerleading equipment plus three months' worth of back rent on a massive facility.

"I dug myself into a hole pretty quickly and, once again, I felt like I was right back where I had started. It took every dime I had to pay the bills and to make payroll." Casey didn't share the full extent of the financial strain with his staff. He had many employees who had left other jobs and careers to work for him at The Stingray Allstars. "I internalized all of it," Casey said, "and I told myself I had to make this work."

The next phase brought even greater challenges. Casey relocated to a 20,000-square-foot facility, but it had no heating or air conditioning, and there was no way to install either one. "It's funny now," Casey said. "Sometimes our parents will complain the gym is too hot, or if it's cold outside, that it's chilly in the gym.

I'd buy propane for the grove heaters—like patio heaters—and set them up beside the tumble track and the floors." During winter practices teams would go full out on their routines and, when they finished, the coaches would gather the kids under the grove heaters to discuss the routine, keeping them from shivering in the cold.

Eventually, Casey secured a developer to create a custom facility across the street that he purchased during the 2008-2009 real estate crash. Despite the economic downturn, Stingray thrived, ultimately needing extra space six miles north to accommodate the overflow.

THE STINGRAY IMPACT

The Stingray Allstars infused All Star with a professional edge in business, coaching, and skill quality. Stingray revolutionized the sport by insisting on clean, safe, and flawlessly executed skills from every athlete, regardless of competition level.

Casey struck a balance—fueling the sport's passion while implementing solid business principles—that defines the Stingray approach. Roger Schonder, who never did become a pilot but who still coaches today, revolutionized All Star's competitive edge by standardizing systems across all age levels.

"His idea was to create all teams equally," Casey said. "If we're going to have a team, then let's make sure that team is competitive. Early on, we were followers of Jack Welch from GE, and he had said, 'If GE is going to make something, they want to be number one or two.' So we were like, 'Hey, if we're going to have a team, we want them to be number one or two wherever they go.'"

That commitment to excellence extended to every aspect of The Stingray All Stars and rippled throughout the industry. Perhaps the most remarkable aspect of the Stingray story is the longevity of its staff. While many gyms experience constant coaching turnover, The Stingray Allstars has retained its core team for decades. According to Casey, those people helped shape Stingray into what it is today.

THE STINGRAY ALLSTARS TODAY: A LEGACY OF EXCELLENCE

What started as the American Cheerleading Academy with ninety All Stars has grown into one of the sport's premier programs. Today, The Stingray Allstars' Marietta location operates in two facilities that total 50,000 square feet and that house thirty-two elite teams with over 1,000 athletes as well as eight half-year teams with approximately 225 athletes. It still works with approximately forty school teams as well.

Beyond Marietta, Casey has expanded the Stingray brand through licensing arrangements with twelve locations. This approach evolved after he realized the challenges of directly owning multiple gyms. "It quickly became apparent to me that a person that's best suited to run a gym is the person that owns the gym," he said. "It's really difficult to get directors or managers that are going to run and manage it like they own it." One of those licensing arrangements holds special significance for Casey, a way to honor Kathy Arnett's instruction and pay it forward.

"I had an awesome guy who grew up in our coed program," Casey said. "He didn't have anything, much like me. He didn't have family money or anything like that to be able to start a business, but he was a fighter. He went to college, graduated, came back and was running the Cartersville gym, and I was able to finance that location for him, much like Kathy had done for me."

Today, that former athlete owns the gym while Casey owns the building, a win-win arrangement that continues the legacy of support that made The Stingray Allstars possible in the first place.

From its humble 1998 origins to its rise as an industry leader, The Stingray Allstars exemplifies the power of passion fused with professionalism. Casey's transformation from a hesitant college cheerleader to a powerhouse gym owner is a powerful journey that everyone can admire.

Recently, Casey has expanded his businesses to include MotUS, The CX Brands, and the Prime Alliance with business partners Cole Stott, Casey Jones, and me, Stacy Rowe.

> "Success is being comfortable and happy."
> – Casey Jones

EARNED WISDOM

★ **Success:** For Casey, success is pretty simple. Are you comfortable enough to buy yourself a cheeseburger? And are you happy most of the time?

★ **Wisdom:** Invest in yourself, your business, and your people.

★ **Gratitude:** Casey is grateful for the many people he has encountered. Kathy Arnett for helping him get started, Susie DuFrain, his long-term office manager, for helping him through decades at Stingrays, and Roger Schonder for the growth and competitiveness of The Stingray All Stars.

★ **Casey's Wish:** Casey wishes the industry could reach a point where everyone could work together. He believes that if we help each other succeed, we all succeed.

- ★ **Mistakes:** As a business owner you make hundreds of blunders. Learn from each of them and move forward.

- ★ **For Gym Owners:** Focus on your business systems. Don't go into this focused on the wins. The wins, whether they be trophies or the size of your bank account, will come, but you have to run a good business no matter what.

- ★ **For Coaches:** As a young coach you are most likely getting into All Star to feed your ego, and that's normal. But you won't stick with it if you don't quickly realize that you should be doing it for the kids. Put your ego aside and learn from those around you.

- ★ **Lessons Learned:** Loving cheerleading isn't enough. You need to learn about business and become a good businessperson if you want to succeed as a gym owner.

DID YOU KNOW?

- ★ Casey's favorite part of cheer is stunting.

- ★ His favorite routine was Orange 2016 when his daughter, Emily, was a senior.

- ★ Casey has no rhythm.

- ★ He has five children who range in age from eleven to twenty-seven, all with his amazing wife, Heather.

- ★ Casey loves endurance sports and recently climbed Mount Tremblant, the equivalent of climbing Mount Everest.

- ★ Casey's favorite superhero is Superman. Casey was a gigantic Guns N' Roses fan, and Axl Rose had a Superman tattoo on his shoulder, which made him love Superman even more.

- ★ Casey chose the cow because it represents love of home, community, contentment, joy, a relaxed demeanor, patience, being grounded, and fertility.

"Do your job." – Roger Schonder

ROGER SCHONDER
The Stingray Allstars – 1998

ROGER SCHONDER'S JOURNEY

Roger Schonder and The Stingray Allstars have become influential in the All Star cheer world due to their unwavering commitment to fundamentals, precision, and consistency, setting a standard that others inevitably follow. Their approach shuns flashy trends and gimmicks, yet the results—both in competition and in establishing one of the industry's most enduring programs—speak volumes.

Roger's transformation from a hesitant college cheerleader to a respected All Star cheer coach shows that the best leaders in the sport arise not from lofty ambitions but from a passion for developing athletes and an unyielding drive for excellence.

ANOTHER ACCIDENTAL CHEERLEADER

Like many male cheerleaders of his generation, Roger Schonder never set out to be involved in the sport. In fact, his introduction to cheerleading came entirely by chance during his time at the University of Georgia in the early 1990s. "I knew nothing about cheerleading," Roger recalled. "I was cheering at Georgia, then started doing stunt privates."

His first exposure to All Star cheer came around Christmas of 1993 when he began working with an All Star team and traveled to WCA in Nashville for a competition. Unlike many coaches who began as gym owners or former All Star athletes, Roger entered the All Star world with collegiate experience, bringing a unique perspective to the emerging sport.

What started as casual involvement quickly developed into a deeper commitment. "I was kind of that guy that just showed up to practice and then didn't leave," Roger joked. By the 1994-95 season, he was all in with All Star cheer.

BUILDING FOUNDATIONS IN ATLANTA

Roger's early coaching experiences took place at Pro Cheer in Marietta, Georgia, where he met key figures who would influence his career path, including Casey Jones, who taught tumbling privates at the facility. This small circle of coaches—Roger, Casey, and John Dabbs (now a chiropractor in North Carolina)—taught private lessons on weekends and hung out together, forming the professional relationships that would later prove pivotal in Roger's career.

After some time at Pro Cheer he began coaching at a gym called Georgia Cheerleading Center while balancing a real job as a wine salesman for Ernest and Julio Gallo. "I was just coming back from Athens on the weekend and coaching the All Star team," he said. But when the gym owner posted debt lists at the entrance, publicly shaming families who owed money, the situation quickly spiraled out of control. Roger's group ultimately departed and wrapped up the season training at a gymnastics gym.

THE BIRTH OF UNITED STINGRAYS

In 1997 Roger took a bold step by teaming up with friends from the University of Georgia cheerleading team to launch United Stingrays in Kennesaw, Georgia. This new venture marked his departure from the corporate world.

Roger's motivation for a career change speaks volumes about why he has remained in cheerleading for over three decades. The turning point came when he received a promotion at his wine sales job, one that drastically altered his quality of life. "My promotion was, 'You're going to make less money, but you're going to work three to four times as many hours,' " he recalled, still shaking his head in disbelief.

The demands of the corporate job became crushing: "I had to be out of Costco by 6 a.m., which meant I had to be there by 4:15, which meant I had to leave my house in Athens by 3:15." Between those early morning shifts and late evenings at grocery stores, Roger found himself with barely enough time to sleep on weekends, much less enjoy life. He wasn't making any money, he was working an absurd number of hours, and he was miserable.

When an opportunity arose to coach high school and middle school teams for a modest monthly sum, Roger did the math and realized that a career change might improve both his finances and his quality of life. His decision—trading corporate stability for uncertainty but gaining the freedom to coach cheerleading—would ultimately lead Roger to become one of the sport's most enduring figures.

THE STINGRAY ALLSTARS PARTNERSHIP

After running United Stingrays for five years, Roger found himself at another crossroads. He had been planning to attend flight school—a three-month program costing around $50,000 that would advance him from a private pilot's license to commercial certification—but a conversation with Casey Jones, who had by then purchased American Cheerleading from Tate Chalk, changed everything. "Over the course of that fifth year is when Casey and I hatched The Stingray Allstars plan," Roger said. The timing coincided with a group of former Home Depot executives who were looking to create a complex to house several sports, and they wanted cheerleading to be one of them.

The venture seemed promising enough that Roger put his flight school plans on hold to help run the All Star program, and it took off. "Hey, this is a pretty good gig we have," Roger said. "I was going to do it for one year just to see how it went," Roger admitted with a smile. What began as a one-year commitment to help launch The Stingray Allstars evolved into a two-decade career.

And his interest in flying faded. "I've flown exactly twice since then," he said. "Twenty-plus years later, only twice." He laughed, still amazed at how his life had changed.

STINGRAY'S APPROACH: EXCELLENCE THROUGH CONSISTENCY

"I don't think of myself as an innovator at all," Roger said modestly. His humility perfectly reflects the Stingray philosophy that Roger has helped cultivate. Instead of chasing trends or striving to be cutting-edge, The Stingray Allstars built its reputation on consistency, precision, and results.

"I've never looked at things in terms of how they affect the industry," Roger explained. "I focus on what's best for our kids, our teams, and our parents within our building." And true to his approach, he keeps his focus on practical outcomes. "I'll stick with my plan and do what I think is best. I'll tell you in a year if it worked."

His inward focus of concentrating on excellence within his own program rather than comparing it to others has been a hallmark of Stingray's success. It stands in contrast to Roger's approach while serving on the USASF Board of Directors where he had to consider the broader industry impact of his decisions.

"When I was on the USASF Board, it was not that way," he said. "I was very much in favor of a logical response for the industry—not in favor of Stingrays but in favor of, 'Hey, this makes sense, and if we're going to make All Star as a whole grow, then we should do this.'"

During his time on the board from 2005 to 2009 and again from 2012 to 2016, Roger was involved in some of the sport's key standardization efforts, including the transition from classifications such as Novice, Intermediate, and Advanced to the numeric level system (Levels 1-6) that is now standard across the industry. "It's way more logical to call it by number, so we're all going to call it the same thing, and numbers just made sense."

STINGRAY'S REMARKABLE GROWTH

Perhaps the most surprising aspect of Roger's journey has been witnessing Stingray's extraordinary growth since its founding in 2002.

"When we started Stingrays, our first season brought in 223 kids," he recalled. "At the time that felt huge, but compared to Cheer Athletics and some of the other gyms, we were still much smaller."

Fast forward to the present, and the numbers are staggering. "This year we had 1,100 kids that tried out for All Star teams in Marietta," Roger said. "Our growth this year was about 25 percent over last year, so we grew this year by the amount The Stingray Allstars started with."

This remarkable expansion has surpassed anything Roger could have imagined when the program began. "I remember when someone had four floors in their gym, and I thought that was the craziest thing. I couldn't even fathom it," Roger recalled. But today his perspective has completely changed. "Right now we have ten floors, and it's still not enough."

REFLECTIONS ON THE WHY

At the heart of Roger's three-decade commitment to cheerleading is a simple but powerful motivation: the opportunity to make a positive impact while doing something he enjoys.

"I have an opportunity to do something that is fun, and I get to work with the best kids," he said. "These kids are smart, they're athletic, they're very driven to get to the level they're at. They love doing this. And so it's very rewarding to work with this group of kids."

Roger's priorities have shifted throughout his career. "At one point," he said,

"I wanted to be the best coach in All Star cheer. Now, I don't care about that at all. It's not about me winning. I want the kids that I coach to win. I know what it feels like, and I want them to have that winning feeling."

This evolution—from personal ambition to focusing entirely on athlete development—mirrors the journey many of the sport's most steadfast leaders have taken. For Roger Schonder, what began as an escape from corporate drudgery has become a lifelong mission to build not just champions but young people with the resilience, work ethic, and character to succeed in all aspects of life.

Through his partnership with Casey Jones at The Stingray Allstars, Roger has helped create one of All Star cheers most respected institutions, a program known not for flashy innovation but for consistent excellence, athlete development, and unwavering standards. Sometimes, it turns out, the most revolutionary approach is simply doing the fundamentals exceptionally well, day after day, year after year.

> "Success is when you can look back and know that you did everything you could."
> – Roger Schonder

EARNED WISDOM

★ **Success:** Success is when you do your best and put in the work over time to reach your goals. Success is when you can look back and say you did everything you could to create opportunities for yourself to be successful.

★ **Wisdom:** Don't let what strangers write on a piece of paper diminish the work you've done or the amazing feeling you had on stage when you performed a routine.

★ **Gratitude:** Roger credits Casey Jones for his continued presence in the industry today. If they hadn't worked together, Roger would have gone on to be a pilot and left the sport altogether.

★ **Roger's Wish:** Roger wishes the rules in cheerleading wouldn't change so frequently. The rules for other sports largely remain the same year after year. He also wishes it could be acceptable for competitions to only award the top three places. Everyone doesn't have to receive a trophy.

★ **To My Younger Self:** You don't have to control everything. Trust others to do their jobs.

★ **Mistakes:** Not recognizing my own limitations sooner and allowing others to help complement my weaknesses.

★ **For Gym Owners:** Focus on how you want to run your business, not on how everyone else is running theirs.

★ **For Coaches:** Focus on how you want to coach and what works for you and your teams. Do your job and stay focused on your athletes.

★ **Lessons Learned:** Sometimes, people aren't a good fit for your business, or they simply aren't a good fit for coaching. Don't hold on to them for too long. Let them go.

DID YOU KNOW?

★ Roger's favorite part of cheer is stunting.

★ His favorite routine is Orange 2005 when they won NCA after finishing second three years in a row.

- ★ Roger climbed Mount Tremblant, equivalent to climbing Mount Everest.

- ★ He is fascinated by wildlife. He loved seeing elk and bison when he visited Yellowstone.

- ★ Roger loves his dog and is a huge fan of the Georgia Bulldogs.

- ★ Roger appreciates all the Marvel superheroes, but he likes Iron Man the best. He enjoys his sarcasm and quick wit.

- ★ Roger chose the eagle as his animal because it represents divine spirit, sacrifice, connection to the creator, intelligence, renewal, courage, illumination of spirit, healing, creation, freedom, and risk-taking.

IT'S OKAY TO FAIL.

"For I know the plans I have for you, declares the Lord, plans to prosper you and not to harm you, plans to give you hope and a future." – Jeremiah 29:11

BRIAN ELZA

Kentucky Elite – 1998
Varsity Spirit – 2007
Liberty Spirit Championships – 2021

FROM BACK TUCKS TO COLLEGIATE CHAMPS

Brian Elza's entry into the cheerleading world started with a simple act of brotherly support—driving his sister and his girlfriend to gymnastics practice. It was 1992, and the sixteen-year-old basketball player and track athlete had no idea how dramatically his life was about to change.

The girls' gymnastics instructor was Dave Harvey, a former University of Kentucky cheerleader who would later become an All Star cheer judge. One fateful day Harvey asked Brian, "Hey, why don't you come out here? I'm going to teach you how to flip." Brian, already an experienced diver, took to tumbling immediately. Ten minutes into his first lesson he was executing a standing back tuck on his own. Excited to show off his new skill, Brian demonstrated his back tuck for his parents in the backyard later that evening. But his landing came up a bit short and resulted in a broken ankle, an inauspicious start to what would become a remarkable cheerleading career.

THE KENTUCKY CONNECTION

Despite the injury, Dave Harvey saw potential in Brian and began recruiting him to cheer at the University of Kentucky. Though initially resistant—"I planned to play basketball in college"—Brian couldn't shake the tantalizing thought of cheering at Kentucky, not because he thought it was so cool to be a cheerleader, but because it meant sitting in the front row at every game.

In 1993 Brian accepted Harvey's invitation to watch a Kentucky cheerleading practice. The program had just won its second national championship, and Brian was immediately struck by the camaraderie between "super fit, super athletic guys" and "amazing, athletic, gymnast-style girls." But what set Kentucky apart was its tumbling requirements. "At the time," Brian said, "I think we were probably the only college in the country that required full squad participation in tumbling." Every male cheerleader needed at least a standing tuck, a round-off back handspring tuck, and a standing back handspring tuck.

Brian joined the JV squad at Kentucky in his freshman year and filled in for the varsity team when needed. By 1995 he was a full varsity member, helping Kentucky secure national championships in 1995, 1996, and 1997.

THE BIRTH OF KENTUCKY ELITE

In 1997 Brian's college roommate, Doug Stithem, who had experience with Pro Cheer in Kansas, approached him with the idea of starting an All Star program. Their original goal wasn't to build a powerhouse gym but to create a feeder system for colleges like Kentucky, Morehead State, and Louisville.

The duo spent that summer teaching UCA camps while scouting for talent. "If we saw a girl that had a full twist or a double full twist," Brian said, "we would give her an information flyer with the message, 'We're starting the very first coed team in the state of Kentucky, and we'd love for you to be part of the team.'"

By the time their first Kentucky Elite clinic arrived, they had recruited about fifteen girls, almost all of whom had double full twisting skills, which were rare at the time. But they had a major problem. They were building a large coed team, but where were they going to get the boys? They scrambled to find male athletes from local area high schools, eventually opening their first practice with seven boys and fifteen girls.

Originally named the Kentucky All Stars, the program also lacked its own facility. The team practiced wherever it could find space, including unofficially at the University of Kentucky and in a rented area at a local gym known as the Pep Club.

By 1998, with growing interest and approximately sixty girls trying out for fifteen spots, Brian and his partners decided to expand. They reached out to Dawn Duncan

Walters, the owner of a gym called CHEERS! Inc., and effectively acquired her business by taking over the lease, equipment, and welcoming her roster of fifty athletes. That moment marked the official birth of Kentucky Elite, which would become one of the premier programs in the nation over the next decade.

GROWING PAINS

The late 1990s were formative years for All Star cheer with programs across the country helping shape the emerging sport's structure and competitive format. When Brian entered the All Star world, the divisions were remarkably simple: "We had Youth, Junior, and Senior—and that was it." NCA and UCA did use slightly different naming conventions—NCA favored terms like Junior Prep while UCA used Youth—but the fundamentals remained the same.

But everything changed when Pro Cheer from Kansas brought its coed team to compete against all-girl teams. As Brian recalled, "Pro Cheer strolled in there with these twelve big, football-player-looking dudes going up against these all-girl teams, and they wiped the floor with them. And that was how large coed was invented."

This led to the creation of separate divisions for all-girl and coed teams, followed by debates about whether having male athletes truly provided a competitive advantage, a debate that continues to this day.

As a gym owner in Kentucky, Brian faced unique regional challenges. Kentucky and Tennessee boasted strong high school cheerleading traditions, often putting

All Star programs in direct competition with school coaches. The biggest struggle for All Star in those states emerged from a conflict with the high school coaches who were concerned about their star athletes competing with All Star teams on the weekends. Talented athletes recognized that participating in the All Star experience could greatly enhance their chances to secure spots on collegiate teams at Kentucky, Morehead, or Louisville.

Financial considerations also impacted participation as families weighed the costs of travel to major competitions in Dallas or Orlando against local options. Despite the challenges, Kentucky Elite grew to approximately 350 athletes at its peak, fielding competitive teams across all age groups and skill levels.

THE BIRTH OF WORLDS

One of the biggest milestones in All Star cheer history was the creation of the World Championship, which Brian witnessed firsthand. The inaugural event, which included both a Coed and an All-girl division, faced initial resistance from several prominent programs. "I'll call them the NCA tribe," Brian said, "Jamie Parrish, Elaine Pascale, and a few others." Those leading programs refused to attend the first event, having just formed the NACCC and choosing not to support the USASF.

That decision created an opportunity for other programs to shine. Miami Elite won the Coed Division while the Maryland Twisters took home the All-girl title. As these teams gained prominence as world champions, programs around the country took notice. "It was neat to see all these incredible programs say, 'Okay, we better go to Worlds because it's a big deal,'" Brian said.

The international growth of the World Championships has been particularly impressive. In the first few years there were a couple of Japanese teams and a few from South America, "But it was a totally different game of cheer," Brian said. "You had Americans doing amazing routines. Everyone clapped for the other countries, but at the time they were just beginners."

That gap has closed dramatically. "To watch the growth over the years has been remarkable," Brian said. "Now international teams can out-stunt American teams. Some can even out-tumble them. It's pretty impressive."

THE VARSITY ERA

Wanting to have a bigger impact on All Star across the country, Brian sold Kentucky Elite and moved to Knoxville, Tennessee, where he worked in the Varsity Knoxville office. He started by breathing life into the Athletics Championships, a brand that, as I stated previously, was once owned by Mike Martinez and needed to be revitalized. Through that opportunity and his experience, including working under Cole Stott, Brian was offered the position of sales manager for the Varsity Knoxville office. His main goal was to grow all the brands within Varsity Knoxville.

With exceptional leadership in Knoxville and a fantastic team in place, the Varsity Knoxville office experienced rapid growth and set the standard for innovation within All Star during that period. Brian's career took a significant leap forward when he was offered the role of general manager at Varsity All Star, which required him to relocate to Memphis. "The opportunity was too huge to pass up," Brian said, "although I never saw myself raising my family in Memphis."

NEW COMPETITIONS, NEW OPPORTUNITIES

After parting ways with Varsity in 2020, Brian was not ready to abandon the sport, so he established the Liberty Spirit Championships and became engaged in the emerging Open Championship Series, which was primarily created by independent (non-Varsity) event producers. Brian said, "Every Apple Inc. needs a competitor. They came in and offered a great product with a great location, a great venue, and it's worked out really well."

ALL STAR CONTRIBUTIONS

Looking back on his contributions to All Star cheer, Brian takes pride in the innovation Kentucky Elite brought to the sport, particularly through the expertise of his business partner, Craig Monty. "One of the best all-girl stunt instructors out there," Brian said of Craig. "We would just go out with some of our younger teams and perform stunts that, at the time, weren't even being done at the high school or collegiate level."

Beyond running successful teams, Brian served on the board of directors for the USASF, helped shape rules and judging criteria, and has attended every World Championship since its inception. He's been a coach, an announcer, and an event producer.

From that initial back tuck (and broken ankle) to creating a talented and respected program in All Star, Brian's journey parallels the sport's evolution from simple divisions and local competitions to a global phenomenon with complex structures and international champions.

Today, through the Liberty Spirit Championships, Brian continues the philosophy that has guided his career: "I try to treat everybody on an equal playing field, and my staff at our events and the people who come there, they constantly comment that they can't believe how we go out of our way to make sure that everyone is happy, that everyone's having a good time."

For the basketball player who once sought only a front-row seat at Kentucky games, cheerleading evolved into a lifelong passion and profession.

> **"Success is creating great experiences."**
> **– Brian Elza**

EARNED WISDOM

★ **Success:** Success is in the people around you. Are they happy with what you've provided them? Success is creating great experiences for the athletes so they want to come back year after year.

★ **Gratitude:** Elaine Pascale has had a significant impact on Brian. They spent years on the USASF Board of Directors and many hours arguing over scores. She is a mother figure for the entire industry. And he appreciates Jeff Webb for ensuring the sport would be sustainable for years.

★ **Brian's Wish:** Brian wishes All Star could have one scoresheet.

★ **To My Younger Self:** Listen to your elders.

★ **Mistakes:** Putting all his eggs in one basket when it came to his career.

★ **For Gym Owners:** Diversify your offerings at your gym. All Star is great, but you must have additional sources of revenue.

★ **For Coaches:** Coach every age and every level each season.

★ **Lessons Learned:** Never have less than four revenue streams.

DID YOU KNOW?

★ Brian's favorite part of cheer is stunting. He wasn't a great tumbler, but he did win the NCA Collegiate STUNT Championship in his senior season.

★ His favorite All Star routine was Top Gun Large Coed in 1997. "They were so much fun to watch."

★ Brian grew up playing basketball. That was his main sport.

- He didn't start cheering until his freshman year of college.

- Brian was born and raised in a small town in Kentucky with a population of 4,000.

- Brian's favorite superhero is Superman, because who wouldn't want to fly?

- Brian chose Tony the Tiger as his animal. The tiger embodies strength, courage, and primal instincts, representing willpower, personal strength, and the ability to trust yourself. It also symbolizes raw power, independence, and focused energy, encouraging individuals to be more flexible and spontaneous.

"CTFO." – Warriors

HAPPY HOOPER
ACE Cheer Company – 1999

IT'S ALL ACES

Many people stumble into the world of All Star cheer. Others are born into it. Happy Hooper falls firmly into the latter category. "I do not remember my life ever having a day without cheerleading," Happy explained, a hint of pride in his voice. "My mom was a cheer coach, my dad was a football coach, and I was on the sideline with pom-pons."

Even as a toddler, cheerleading was woven into the fabric of Happy's existence. His mother would bring him to practice, and he would sit in a baby rocker while she coached. By the time he was three or four, he was already memorizing cheers, often reciting them better than the high school cheerleaders themselves. His early immersion would shape not only Happy's future but also the landscape of All Star cheer in the Southeast.

Happy's program, ACE Cheer Company, grew from modest roots to become one of the industry's most recognizable and respected brands. But that success was years away when a young Happy Hooper was fluffing pom-pons on the football sidelines in Alabama.

EARLY VENTURES

Happy's journey as a coach began in Roanoke, Virginia, in the spring of 1996, shortly after his time competing with Snead State at the UCA College Nationals. He founded the Cheer Force Panthers, operating out of the Roanoke Academy of Gymnastics.

"We were blue, silver, and black, and we thought we were amazing," Happy recalled with a laugh. "We were not that good." The silver in their uniforms was especially exciting: "It sparkled, and it was the only way to get sparkle," he said, noting how even small details like uniform materials were vastly different in the industry's early days compared to today.

Despite his enthusiasm, Happy admitted he was operating largely on instinct: "I had no idea what I was doing other than I loved cheerleading." Yet, somehow, that passion was enough. The program eventually morphed into what would later become Cheer Extreme Roanoke.

In 1999 Happy returned to Alabama to coach at the University of Alabama at Birmingham (UAB). He also surveyed the All Star landscape in Birmingham and saw an opportunity. There were few All Star gyms in Birmingham at the time, and Happy thought he could build a program that would get things done.

A DREAM FROM CHILDHOOD

What happened next revealed just how deeply cheerleading ran in Happy's blood. He didn't simply decide to start another gym, he brought to life a vision he had carried since childhood. "I'd had the idea for ACE in fourth grade and had created the colors and logo and everything," Happy said.

While choreographing for one of the existing All Star gyms in Birmingham, Happy pitched his vision with all the bells and whistles. Fortunately, they bought in, and Alabama Cheer Elite (ACE) was born in 1999.

The name Alabama Cheer Elite wouldn't last long. After competing in its first event in the fall of 1999, Happy was served with a cease and desist order. "I was sued for using 'Alabama' and 'cheer' in my business name because someone else had Alabama Cheerleading Center and cheerleading in their name," Happy said. "That's fine. No skin off my teeth. The uniforms say ACE, so we'll just be ACE."

What could have been a setback turned out to be a blessing in disguise, simplifying the brand to the three-letter acronym that would soon be recognized across the cheerleading world.

FROM THE GROUND UP

ACE's first season featured three teams: "A little baby team, a junior team, and a senior team," Happy said. By the second year, ACE expanded to six teams and continued to grow. This was before the days of specialized divisions and level distinctions. In the early 2000s, teams competed based solely on age brackets with minimal subdivisions. ACE quickly developed a reputation for strong coed teams. ACE averaged thirteen to eighteen boys on its junior coed team at a time when male cheerleaders often remained with the same program, unlike today's landscape where they frequently travel between gyms or states to compete.

The program's early operations reveal the scrappy, resourceful nature of All Star cheer's pioneers. ACE quickly outgrew its space at the gymnastics center, but it didn't immediately move into its own facility. Instead, ACE created a patchwork of practice spaces across the community. "We had trailers on the back of cars with rolls of mats," Happy said, "and we rented space at some church gyms."

Practice locations varied, depending on space and availability. On Tuesday, practice may have been at Rocky Ridge Methodist Church while Thursday's practice might have been at Springville Baptist. Sunday practices were usually held at the gymnastics center.

Communication in those pre-smartphone days was equally inventive. Happy and I laughed as we reminisced about phone trees. "We used this thing called a phone tree," Happy said. "We'd call and say, 'Hey, today junior coed is going to practice at Rocky Ridge Methodist.' Click, send message, press two, and it would go out to everyone's phones." That was the more advanced version.

The original method involved each team member having a contact list. To get a message out you'd call the first person on the list, relay the message, and they'd call the next person, passing the message down the line, one call at a time.

Each practice required setting up and breaking down the entire space. Before practice the teams would have to move all the tables and chairs against the wall. The trailer of mats would arrive, and the athletes and coaches would roll them out. After practice, they'd roll the mats back up, carry them to the trailer, and reset the tables and chairs back to the way they were. It was exhausting work, but as Happy put it, "We loved cheerleading."

BUILDING A BRAND

Around 2002 ACE finally moved into its own 13,000-square-foot cheerleading facility in Birmingham, Alabama. The program continued to expand, and by the 2006 season Happy was operating multiple locations. "We started doing multilocations because kids were driving so far to be on our team," he explained. Sometimes those distant athletes would train at other local gyms for tumbling, creating tension with the owners of those gyms. Happy's solution was straightforward: "Let's work together: Become an ACE gym." This model allowed ACE to expand its footprint significantly. At its peak, the program boasted twelve locations, but Happy has scaled back to six. The decision to reduce the number of locations reflects his commitment to quality over quantity. In 2017, the original Birmingham location found a new home in its current 41,330-square-foot facility.

COMPETITION AND SUCCESS

ACE quickly made its mark on the competition scene. In its first season at UCA Nationals, ACE placed second, an impressive feat for a new program. "Memphis Elite beat us," Happy said, recalling the beginnings of what would become several program rivalries over the years.

Those early competitive experiences were quite different from today's highly structured divisions. Happy and I recalled competing against each other at the US Spirit event at Universal in Orlando, Florida. The event hosted individual competitions where single athletes would perform a routine against each other, adding an extra layer of rivalry. Happy and I laughed as we recalled the boys from our team getting into a passionate debate at the competition because they were competing against each other in the individual competition.

The All Star routines were different too. Happy remembered when teams had forty-eight athletes on the floor at once. There was no maximum. Skills were added organically as athletes learned them. When a new athlete acquired a skill, you sometimes had to rearrange the routine to find a safe way to incorporate it due to the lack of floor space. Happy's solution was charmingly simple: "The music came on, and he did his back handspring. Then he grabbed for a basket toss. That's just how it was. You get a skill, we're going to add it."

Those without tumbling skills or the best stunting skills weren't excluded. Instead, they were incorporated differently by dancing in front of the pyramid. Sometimes they may have been great stunters, but they were even better dancers. The pyramid dance was a standard feature of routines during that era.

Over the years the balance between athletic skill and entertaining performance helped establish ACE's identity in the competition world. Meanwhile, its multilocation model, although not entirely unique to ACE, was implemented with a focus on maintaining quality across locations, a challenge that Happy acknowledged had become increasingly difficult.

The ACE story represents a fascinating microcosm of All Star cheer's evolution. From hauling mats in trailers to managing multiple locations across states, from teams with no skill divisions to the highly specialized competitive structure of today, Happy Hooper has witnessed—and helped create—the modern All Star landscape.

What began as a fourth-grader's dream has become one of the most recognizable brands in cheerleading. And through all the expansions and evolutions, one constant remains—a genuine love for the sport that has been part of Happy's life since before he can remember.

> **"Success is having peace." – Happy Hooper**

EARNED WISDOM

- ★ **Success:** Success is having peace, peace in knowing that you're doing a good enough job, peace that your staff feels loved and appreciated, peace that your families are having success in different facets, not just winning but wanting to be part of your gym.

- ★ **Wisdom:** Surround yourself with incredible people who are much better than you.

- ★ **Gratitude:** The Georgia All Stars had a significant early impact on Happy when he saw them at a WCA competition. He aspired to be as good as the Georgia All Star teams.

- ★ **To My Younger Self:** Your dreams can, and will, come true.

- ★ **Mistakes:** Trying too hard to remain a large coed team for longer than we should have.

- ★ **For Gym Owners:** Go into ownership with an open heart. Take care of your clients, take care of your staff, and take care of your families.

- ★ **For Coaches:** Be relentless in everything you do. If you need to tell your kids one more time, then tell them one more time. Happy credits this lesson to his friend, Theapia Best.

DID YOU KNOW?

- ★ Happy's favorite routine was Warriors 2004. It was a country theme with a thirteen eight-count dance to "Little Warehouse in Texas."

- ★ His favorite All Star memory was beating the Georgia All Stars at WCA in 2004 with his favorite routine.

- ★ Happy's full name is Claude Cornelius Happy Hooper III.

- ★ His business manager has been with him for so long she still has her original ACE Cheer Elite backpack.

- ★ He loves to play tennis.

- ★ Happy loves going to the movies by himself. He completely zones out and creates cheer routines on the screen while the movie is playing.

- ★ Jesus is Happy's superhero, because everyone needs a little Jesus in their lives.

- ★ Happy confidently said his male spirit animal is Post Malone and his female spirit animal is Kesha.

> DON'T GET CAUGHT UP IN THE CHASE.

"Learn as if you will live forever, live like you will die tomorrow." – Mahatma Gandhi

SEAN TIMMONS

World Cup All Stars – 1999
Premier Athletics – 2014
Nfinity – 2021

FROM VOLUNTEER TO FULL-TIME PROFESSIONAL

When an answering machine message changed the trajectory of Sean Timmons' life in 1999, he couldn't have predicted the decades-long career in cheerleading that would follow. At the time he was simply a junior in college who had been coaching Pop Warner cheerleading for a few years. "I had come home from class, and we had an old answering machine with those mini tapes," Sean said. "I had a message asking me to come down to World Cup and interview for a job."

That message—from cheerleading pioneers Elaine Pascale and Joelle Antico—led to a $14-an-hour coaching position that marked the beginning of Sean's professional journey in All Star cheer, a journey that, twenty-five years later, would include multiple world championships, leadership roles at major cheer companies, and a seat on the USASF National Advisory

Board. But Sean's cheerleading story begins well before that fateful phone call in the volunteer-driven world of Pop Warner cheerleading in New Jersey.

THE POP WARNER DAYS

Sean began coaching Pop Warner cheerleading in 1996. Like many coaches of that era, he was drawn to the sport by a genuine love for cheerleading rather than by career ambitions. He had cheered in high school and wanted to stay connected to the activity.

Working alongside a dedicated group of parent volunteers in Toms River, New Jersey, Sean helped create a successful program. His core group was Margie Miller, the owner of a dance studio; Lori Meehan (Muccia); and Joe and Marianne LaDuca, who would go on to become lifelong friends. "We had an incredible group of people who were some of my greatest mentors from the start," Sean said.

The team's success came quickly. In Sean's second year of coaching, his team finished second at the Pop Warner Nationals. The following year his team made cheerleading history. "We made it all the way to Pop Warner Internationals, and we won," Sean said with pride. "We were only the second program to win from the state of New Jersey."

That victory was merely the beginning. His team went on to win the national title again in 1999 and 2000 becoming, as Sean put it, "The first three-peat in Pop Warner history." Those achievements were recognized within the cheerleading community, particularly by

Elaine Pascale and Joelle Antico, who were developing their World Cup All Stars program into one of the most renowned cheerleading gyms in the nation.

BEYOND THE SEASON

While Sean and his coaching team were creating championship-winning Pop Warner programs, they faced a common challenge: The season ended in December, leaving athletes without structured cheerleading practice for months. "We were looking for an outlet to have our athletes continue in the offseason," Sean said.

The solution was to create an All Star program called the Toms River Twisters in 1997. With royal blue, silver, and white uniforms featuring the popular flyaway skirts, the team competed in ECA competitions. That decision allowed Sean to keep the team together a little longer.

This pattern of Pop Warner programs launching offseason All Star teams was playing out across the country, fueling the rapid growth of All Star cheer. What set Sean's path apart was his early connection to one of the sport's pioneering programs, World Cup All Stars.

THE WORLD CUP YEARS

When Sean joined World Cup All Stars in December 1999, the program had recently moved into its first dedicated facility. Previously, it had rented space in a gymnastics center called World Cup Gymnastics, which was the source of their name. "They hired me at $14 an hour, and I was killing it," Sean joked.

He was hired to coach the first satellite team—what is now called a prep or half-year team—designed for athletes who wanted to join midseason after their Pop Warner or school cheerleading seasons ended. Although Sean hadn't previously worked with the World Cup, he was familiar with the program. As a high school cheerleader, he competed in many of the same competitions as the World Cup's Shooting Stars team. In fact, one of his high school teammates had a sister who was an original World Cup Shooting Star.

Sean's competitive experiences before joining the World Cup reflect the nascent state of All Star cheer at that time. In 1997 he recalls competing at the NCA Spring Spirit Classic in Myrtle Beach, South Carolina, where divisions were not even separated by program type. High school teams competed directly against All Star teams. "My high school competed against the Georgia All Stars large coed team," Sean said. His team warmed up in one of the bars at Broadway at the Beach and performed on a stage in front of the big pyramid that housed the Hard Rock Café. "We performed outdoors," Sean said with a smile, "and we beat Georgia All Stars large coed with my high school large coed."

Such a scenario would be unimaginable in today's highly structured competitive environment where program types are strictly separated and dedicated venues are the standard.

BUILDING CHAMPIONS AND CREATING MOMENTS

Sean's coaching career at the World Cup spanned fifteen years, during which he guided numerous teams to national and world championships. When asked about his favorite routines, Sean became nostalgic for the days when All Star routines featured popular music instead of custom mixes: "I think it's sad that we can't use real music in cheerleading anymore," he said. "The songs created moments that really defined what All Star cheerleading is."

His coaching style combined technical instruction with creative motivation. In one memorable instance he promised his team he would swim in the hotel fountain if they hit their routine and won at a COA competition in Jacksonville, Florida. "They hit, and they won, and sure enough, I was backstroking in a hotel fountain waiting for security to kick me out," Sean said, and then he laughed. "Three of us were swimming around in there. One of the parents went out and got us the hair cap and the goggles, so we're in there with caps and swimming goggles, and we are literally backstroking and breaststroking around in a hotel fountain."

Those moments of celebration and team bonding were as much a part of Sean's coaching philosophy as the technical aspects of skill development. Creating memorable experiences for athletes was a priority, one that would continue to influence his career decisions.

RUTGERS UNIVERSITY: RETURNING TO HIS ALMA MATER

While coaching at the World Cup, Sean furthered his influence in the cheerleading community by returning to his alma mater, Rutgers University, in 2006. Recruited as an assistant coach, he swiftly won everyone over with his expertise and commitment to the sport. In 2008

Sean became the head coach of the All-girl team, signifying a major change in the program's direction.

Under Sean's leadership, the Rutgers cheerleading program transitioned from competing in NCA competitions to UCA competitions, a strategic decision that resulted in impressive outcomes. The team established itself as a consistent contender, reaching the finals in the D1 All-girl division each year during his tenure. Their dedication culminated in an impressive third-place finish in 2013, solidifying Rutgers as a respected name in collegiate cheerleading.

"Going back to coach at Rutgers was like coming full circle for me," Sean reflected. "Having the opportunity to build a nationally competitive program at the university where I had been a student was incredibly meaningful."

BEYOND COACHING: LEADERSHIP AND INDUSTRY INFLUENCE

Sean's pinnacle coaching moment came in 2009. "Winning a World Championship on my thirtieth birthday in 2009 was pretty awesome," he said. But Sean's contributions to cheerleading extended far beyond coaching championship teams. In a significant industry milestone, he became the first coach-only professional (not a gym owner or event producer) to be elected to the USASF National Advisory Board. When asked about his contributions to the sport, Sean said, "I was glad to show people that you didn't have to be a gym owner to have a voice."

His achievement helped pave the way for other nonowners to take leadership roles in the sport's governance, ensuring that those working directly with athletes had representation at the highest levels of decision-making.

After his long tenure at World Cup, Sean seized an unexpected 2013 opportunity that would propel his career in a new direction. After teaching a summer camp for Premier Athletics he was offered the All Star director role for all ten Premier Athletics locations in Tennessee.

"The greatest part was that I didn't have to go to my current bosses that I worked for fifteen years and talk to them, because the company that hired me did that for me," Sean said. "They called to make sure it was okay for them to offer me the position before they even offered me the position."

Sean took the role and dedicated the next eight years to Premier Athletics. He and I worked closely together as we built a camaraderie and healthy competition among Premier Athletics' All Star Program. Sean worked tirelessly to train coaches and athletes and to elevate the program.

FRANKLIN HIGH SCHOOL: A RETURN TO SCHOLASTIC CHEERLEADING

Despite his commitments to All Star cheerleading and Premier Athletics, Sean wasn't done with scholastic cheerleading yet. In the summer of 2014, after thinking he had left coaching behind for good, he accepted the challenge of leading Franklin High School's cheerleading program in Franklin, Tennessee.

"I thought I was done with scholastic cheerleading, but the opportunity at Franklin was too good to pass up," Sean said. The program had struggled in recent years, failing to make the finals at High School Nationals for three consecutive seasons. Sean saw potential where others might have seen obstacles. His impact was immediate and transformative. By his second year at the helm Franklin surged back into contention, claiming an impressive fourth place in the Small Varsity D1 Division. This remarkable turnaround marked the start of sustained excellence. Under Sean's guidance, the team finished in the top five for seven of nine years, cementing Franklin as a consistent contender.

To create more opportunities for athletes, Sean launched a junior varsity team in 2017. The new team swiftly triumphed, clinching the Small JV division in 2019 and solidifying Sean's reputation as a coach capable of building winning programs at any level.

INNOVATION AND ADAPTATION

Throughout his career, Sean has contributed to numerous innovative projects in the cheer industry. One he proudly highlights is 180 Pro, a venture he describes as "One of the greatest things I've done in my career." Premier Athletics was tasked by Varsity to create a program to help gym owners, and that's what 180 Pro did. Its series of educational resources and recreational programs for gym owners helped its businesses grow.

The ability to create and adapt has been a hallmark of Sean's career. From coaching championship teams and helping lead major cheerleading companies to creating new concepts and ventures within the industry, he has continually found ways to reinvent himself while maintaining his core passion for the sport.

In 2021 Sean's career took a different direction as he moved into event production with Nfinity, further expanding his influence in the cheerleading industry. And in early 2024 Sean made a significant personal transition, stepping away from coaching for the first time in twenty-seven years. That shift led him to reflect on why he remains in the cheerleading industry: "I continue to do this because our industry has changed so much . . . some things for the better, some things for the worse," he said. "I do it because I have a passion for the sport, and I have a passion for the athletes."

Though his role has changed, his commitment to giving back to the activity that has defined his life remains steadfast: "The sport gave me so much that I need to keep working to do that for the next generation and generations to come." From volunteer Pop Warner coach to world champion All Star coach and industry leader, Sean Timmons embodies passion, commitment, and the drive to create meaningful experiences for athletes.

Looking to the future, Sean embraces past lessons and remains committed to an industry that, despite its challenges, offers endless opportunities for growth, achievement, and connection.

"Success is growth." – Sean Timmons

EARNED WISDOM

★ **Success:** Success is growth. Sean's motto is that if you leave something better than the way you found it, that's success. Are we moving in the right direction? Is it better than it was? If you can answer yes, then that is success.

★ **Wisdom:** Sometimes your greatest losses are your greatest wins.

★ **Gratitude:** Elaine Pascale had a significant impact on Sean's career. He credits her with molding him into a great coach. "She was a tremendous mentor and motivator," Sean said. "She told me when I was being a fool."

★ **Sean's Wish:** Sean wishes for one unified scoresheet that includes international teams. There are too many scoresheets now.

★ **To My Younger Self:** You never know when opportunity will knock. Always put your best foot forward.

★ **Mistakes:** It's only a mistake if you don't learn from it.

★ **For Gym Owners:** Give your athletes as many opportunities as you can. Don't put yourself in a silo.

★ **For Coaches:** Listen and learn before you speak. There is tremendous science and body mechanics in what we do now. Learn it and continue your learning every day.

★ **Lessons Learned:** There is a difference between being a coach and being a teacher. The greatest coaches are a beautiful balance of both.

DID YOU KNOW?

★ Sean's favorite part of cheer is stunting.

★ His favorite routine is the Starlites routine from 2001: "The music was fantastic." He also loved the Shooting Stars Latin-themed routine.

★ Sean has an identical twin brother.

★ He has a niece who is almost his age.

★ Sean has three dogs, and he's obsessed with plants.

★ Superman is Sean's favorite superhero because he's all business and then all hero.

★ Sean chose the octopus for his animal because it's often associated with intelligence, adaptability, resilience, creativity, and intuition, representing the ability to navigate challenges with flexibility and to embrace change.

"Don't make someone a priority in your life when you're merely an alternative in theirs." – Maya Angelou

DENNIS WORLEY
All Star Challenge – 2000

THE HIGH SCHOOL DAYS

"If we make it to Nationals and we're on the cover of that catalog, I don't want to be just BHS." The insistence that Broughton High School's cheer team would always clearly identify itself with its full name became Dennis Worley's first unwritten rule in cheerleading. It was a small but telling detail that reflected his approach to everything that followed. He was deliberate, distinctive, and refused to be lost in the crowd.

Dennis Worley's journey into All Star cheer began unconventionally. Already an accomplished high school coach at Broughton High in Raleigh, North Carolina, he was invited to judge the CHEERSPORT Nationals in 1999 after his team claimed its third state championship. This introduction to the All Star world came after he had already established himself in the scholastic realm where his transformation of the Broughton program had become legendary.

"When I first went to coach there, I attended the North Carolina High School Coaches Conference," Dennis recalled. "Tanya Bowles showed a video of what not to do, and it described the team that I had just inherited." Rather than taking offense, Dennis introduced himself to Tanya, acknowledging, "That's my team, and you're correct. That's what not to do."

That encounter would spark a friendship that would later prove pivotal in the industry. Dennis took that struggling Broughton High program and turned it into a competitive powerhouse, coaching there from 1997 until he was ready to pass the torch to another coaching talent. "I begged Marge Elvers to leave Harnett Central and come to Broughton," he said. Marge has led the program for twenty-three years, building on the foundation Dennis established. "She's much more of an amazing overall program coach than I ever was. I was good at establishing a routine and creating a product. She's good at that and great at interpersonal things."

THE ALL STAR CHALLENGE ERA

Dennis's talent for choreography and legal expertise—he was practicing law full time—caught the attention of Don Collins, who was developing what would become the All Star Challenge. Dennis joined the company around 2002 as both the creative director and legal counsel. Don had already started the brand with a themed event called Clash of the Titans. But when Dennis came on board, the brand expanded to offer additional experiences such as King of the Jungle and

Return to Atlantis. Eventually, Queen of the Nile and Motown Showdown were added.

What set the All Star Challenge apart was its commitment to theming, and not just in name but in every aspect of the experience. Each competition had a distinct identity and carefully chosen locations. "Queen of the Nile was in Cincinnati on a river," Dennis said. "That's why I picked it. Lone Star Roundup was in Texas." The themes weren't arbitrary; they were strategically connected

"All Star Challenge was an anomaly because of the people who were there," Dennis said. "It was our unique ability among that small team to do many things." Most of the All Star Challenge team members had three or four jobs, because they couldn't provide the customer experience at the price offered without everyone on the team going above and beyond.

The themed competitions quickly became favorites in the industry. Parents and athletes alike embraced the opportunity to immerse themselves in the experience, sometimes dressing in togas for the Clash of the Titans or in jungle-inspired attire for The King of the Jungle. The announcer, John Avery, became legendary for incorporating themes and engaging parents in ways that made every competition memorable, win or lose. "We wanted people to be part of what we were doing," Dennis said, "and it really worked."

That approach—celebration over strict competition—became the hallmark of the All Star Challenge. In an industry increasingly defined by cutthroat competition,

Dennis and his team created events that emphasized joy alongside excellence.

TAKING THE CHALLENGE TO VARSITY

By 2008 the competitive landscape was changing. Varsity's Family Plan, which allowed gyms to receive rebates for attending events from the same producers, was reshaping competition attendance patterns. So All Star Challenge, despite its popularity, faced tough decisions regarding its future. "The writing was on the wall for us," Dennis said.

Rather than fight what seemed inevitable, Dennis represented Don Collins in business negotiations with Varsity, which ultimately led to the acquisition of All Star Challenge. The transition wasn't seen as a defeat but as an evolution: "We knew that was the route we had to go," Dennis said. "And it was great." The acquisition opened new doors for Dennis, whose position was reclassified under the Memphis office to become the first creative director of Varsity All Star. His role coincided with Varsity's International All Levels initiative, an ambitious virtual competition.

Dennis proposed a virtual competition that would culminate in a televised results show, and it was revolutionary. The first attempt was memorable, though not for the reasons Dennis had hoped. "The biggest failure was the first All Levels results show," Dennis admitted. "It was the first time that we attempted to do a reveal at the end of a competition where we would announce the winners and have a graphic, the things we now think are commonplace." The technology wasn't quite ready back then, and the execution fell short of the vision. "I was lying on the floor, sobbing in a studio in Fort Worth, Texas," Dennis said. "It was a disaster."

But Dennis persevered and improved the following year. His willingness to experiment and risk failure would become a defining characteristic of his career.

CREATING THE SUMMIT

In 2012 Dennis received a simple directive that would reshape the landscape of All Star cheerleading. It was a sticky note that read, "We need a game changer." So Dennis immediately went to work on what was initially called Cheer Project Number Seven. While others jumped ahead to discuss colors and names, Dennis stayed focused on the core concept. "We don't even know if we're going to do this yet," he said. "Let's not get bogged down in color choices."

His methodical approach led him to identify four guiding principles for the project: It had to be innovative, competitive, prestigious, and unforgettable. Those touchstones still appear in The Summit's official materials today.

The Summit was created to fill a gap in the competitive landscape by providing a championship opportunity for teams below the World Championship level. The inaugural Summit in 2013 was meticulously planned. The event was intended for 457 bids, and 456 were accepted. But the real indicator of success emerged the following year: "The success was the next year when thousands of people wanted those 457 bids," Dennis said, revealing his definition of success: "Success is when anyone wants to see something again."

The Summit also achieved another milestone in cheerleading history. It became the first cheerleading competition to be televised live when it aired on ESPN2. This achievement required special accommodation for ESPN's sports broadcast model. "ESPN insisted that the scoring be contemporaneous with the performances," Dennis said. "They wanted a scoreboard."

BRINGING JOY BACK TO THE JOURNEY

In 2021 Dennis partnered with industry veteran Robin Coe to launch her new company, Winners Choice Championships. Robin had developed an innovative concept and patented technology that enabled live competition between teams participating in various remote locations. Not virtual, but truly live. As the pandemic subsided, coaches and athletes were eager to travel and compete in person. Robin astutely pivoted and tasked Dennis with transitioning the brand to brick-and-mortar, in-person events, a vision that came to life as *Winners Choice Live!*

The brand represents a return to the values that once made the All Star Challenge special, only now on a much larger and more complex scale. Operationally, the *Live!* format demands one of the most ambitious traveling productions in the industry. The highly scripted and intricately coordinated blend of the team performances, multimedia presentation and graphics, live interviews, and educational and entertaining prerecorded segments create the overall experience

Dennis calls "the Winners Choice difference." And the experience includes an original theme song written by Dennis himself.

"Winners Choice is a boutique brand," Dennis said. "I want people to love it, even if they lost."

The focus on experience over outcomes is reflected in unique touches like the Hit Zero Celebration Zone where teams that execute error-free routines receive special recognition, regardless of placement. "For many people, that might be the highlight of their year," Dennis said, "and it's okay. We want to celebrate it with them."

This perspective stems from Dennis's understanding of competitive realities. He understands that if your sole focus is to be a World or Summit champion, you're most likely not going to be successful. The odds are against you simply by the sheer mathematics of it.

His newest venture, Bring It, is dedicated to celebrating all participating programs and recognizing the value of every teams' performance, regardless of age or skill level. The brand draws inspiration from the heyday of All Star Challenge, incorporating a blend of the nostalgic and the innovative—something old, something new, something borrowed, something blue. This philosophy is reflected in the brand's evolution from a black-and-white aesthetic to a vibrant blue color scheme. The goal is to recapture the magic that made those early events memorable while exceeding today's standards. Dennis continues to pursue his guiding principle of finding "joy in the journey" in his current role as chief creative officer at Robin Coe's Choice Events.

BUILDING BACKWARD

Perhaps Dennis's most significant contribution to All Star cheer isn't a specific event but a methodology, what he called "building backward." Dennis's greatest successes are defined by his ability to envision the entire experience and then reverse engineer it. "Whenever you have the opportunity to start from nothing and you do it correctly, the story will tell itself," Dennis said, "and everything associated with it will just play out."

This methodical approach and his unique blend of legal expertise, creative vision, and industry knowledge has allowed Dennis to shape All Star cheer at pivotal moments in its development.

From a high school coach determined that "Broughton" would always be prominently displayed to being the architect of themed competitions fondly remembered decades later, Dennis has consistently found ways to make All Star more than just a competition. In his hands it became an experience, a story and, most important, a journey worth taking.

"Success is when you create something that people want to see again."
– Dennis Worley

EARNED WISDOM

★ **Success:** You are successful when you can break the mold.

★ **Wisdom:** When you compete, it's not your choice to be the winner. All you can do is prepare and give a performance that "could be" the winner. If you put yourself in a position to win, sometimes you win, but if you're never in a position to win, you never can. It's about effort. Those with potential but no effort are "could-have-beens." Instead, be a "could be."

★ **Gratitude:** Dennis credits Don Collins with impacting his career. Dennis values creativity and is driven to innovate unique experiences for All Star. He appreciates the space Don gave him to grow and, most of all, he appreciates what he and the All Star Challenge team created together.

★ **Dennis's Wish:** Dennis wishes we could return to a single scoresheet for All Star and bring real music back to the routines.

★ **To My Younger Self:** Don't settle.

★ **Mistakes:** We made many mistakes back in the day. We were making it up as we went along. We learned from each mistake and improved. That's what matters.

★ **For Gym Owners:** Be able to articulate what your gym has to offer and make choices that support those values. Stay the course during rough times.

★ **For Coaches:** Study the teams you admire and choreograph what your team can achieve by Christmas. Dress the team you have, not the team you wish you had.

★ **Lessons Learned:** Circular management is when no one person is in charge. But where my world intersects with your world, I better not change anything without telling you.

DID YOU KNOW?

★ Dennis's favorite part of cheer is pyramids.

★ Dennis was the assistant attorney general for North Carolina and represented the state in two cases before the United States Supreme Court.

★ As a coach, Dennis is a credentialed member of the USASF.

★ Dennis loves boating and has his captain's license from the US Coast Guard.

★ His favorite superheroes are the Wonder Twins. He loves that they can become anything they want, but they have to do it together.

★ Dennis chose the lion as his animal because it represents family, strength, energy, courage, guardianship, protection, ferocity, and authority.

"Sometimes it is better to lose and do it right than to win and do the wrong thing." – Tony Blair

DAMIANNE ALBEE STEWARD

Prodigy All Stars | Spirit Sports – 2000

Varsity All Star – 2008

POP WARNER BEGINNINGS

The path to becoming a cheerleader isn't always straightforward. Sometimes it begins with heartbreak, a pair of white Keds sneakers, and a mother willing to step up so her daughter can follow her dreams.

"I did not make middle school cheerleading and was devastated," Damianne said of her seventh-grade disappointment. The sting of rejection could have ended her cheerleading aspirations before they began. Instead, it sparked a determination that would shape her cheerleading career.

When her family moved from Maine to New Hampshire in 1990 for her eighth-grade year, she saw an opportunity to reset her cheerleading journey through Pop Warner, a youth football and cheerleading organization. There was just one hurdle—the team needed a coach. "I convinced my mother to coach the team so I could cheer," she said with a laugh, remembering their basic uniform of "white Keds, black leggings, and a hideous gold Champion sweatshirt with maroon lettering."

Those early days in Pop Warner, despite the questionable fashion choices, laid the foundation for a lifelong passion and career in cheerleading. The girl who hadn't made her middle school team would go on to cheer in high school and college, though her collegiate cheerleading career would end earlier than expected.

THE ALL STAR OPPORTUNITY

Around 1997, after stepping away from college cheerleading, Damianne found herself working at a local gymnastics gym teaching classes and hosting birthday parties on weekends. It was there that an unexpected opportunity emerged. "Danny Harris, who coached at one of the local middle schools, offered me an opportunity to start an All Star program," Damianne said.

All Star cheer was still in its infancy. The structure, divisions, and standards that define the sport today were still evolving. Damianne's motivation for accepting the offer was practical: It was her dream, and it gave her the chance to earn more money. What she couldn't have known then was how that decision would set her on a path that would lead her to the forefront of the cheerleading industry. "Never did I think that it would lead me to where I am now!" Damianne said.

BUILDING A PROGRAM

The turn of the millennium brought another pivotal moment in Damianne's cheerleading journey. After a brief move to Alabama where she worked at a facility called Gym Tech, she maintained connections in North Carolina, returning occasionally to provide choreography services. During one of those visits, around 2000-2001, a father approached her with a proposition that would bring her back to North Carolina permanently.

That father offered her a position as a special education assistant at his high school, a job she would hold for six years. Meanwhile, an opportunity arose to establish a "true program" with Danny Harris, the same person who had initially introduced her to All Star cheer. The program operated out of a gymnastics facility for its first year before moving to a standalone facility. What made the arrangement unique was her position within it. "I was the program director who had complete autonomy over the program and facility," Damianne said, "so basically, he was a silent owner, which was great! I was able to do what I wanted and how I wanted, which I now realize is bananas, but also how lucky I was!"

That unusual arrangement—creative freedom without financial risk—allowed her to develop a distinctive program during a critical period in All Star cheer's evolution. Under her leadership the Prodigy All Stars built "strong teams in multiple ages and levels" despite operating in a competitive market that included established powerhouses like Cheer Extreme, Charlotte Allstars, and Victory All Stars who were "across the interstate from us for most of our existence."

Her ability to carve out an identity for her program amid such competition wasn't accidental. It stemmed from the relationships she had cultivated throughout the industry, including her work with Shannon Smith and James Speed at Spirit Sports as well as her efforts to maintain positive connections with local gyms.

CONTRIBUTING TO THE SPORT'S EVOLUTION

Many in today's cheerleading community would recognize Damianne for her more recent contribution to All Star: "I think that I am most known to today's generation for The Summits," she said.

As stated in the history, The Summit Championship, introduced in 2013, filled a crucial gap in the competitive structure of All Star cheer. While The Cheerleading Worlds has provided a prestigious end-of-season championship for the highest-level teams since 2004, the majority of All Star athletes—those competing in levels 1 through 5 and Junior Level 6—had no equivalent culminating event.

The Summit changed that by creating a championship experience accessible to a broader range of athletes and programs. Its impact on the sport has been profound, providing thousands of athletes with a championship to aspire to and helping standardize expectations across those levels.

"I think I have consistently brought an integrity and fairness to our sport," Damianne said. "I think that anyone who knows me knows that I may be tough, honest, or even curt, but I am always fair and consistent."

Her commitment to fairness has characterized every role she has held in the cheer industry, whether coaching, running team camps, operating Spirit Sports, or in her current position at Varsity. She said she applies those principles "not only to our customers but also with our internal team."

In an industry that has experienced rapid growth and significant changes over the past few decades, Damianne's consistency of character and commitment to integrity represents a valuable contribution in itself.

THE JOURNEY CONTINUES

From the middle school rejection that led her to Pop Warner to the development of The Summit Championship, Damianne's cheer journey spans more than three decades of the sport's evolution. She has experienced All Star cheer from nearly every angle—as an athlete, coach, program director, event producer, and industry executive.

Throughout those transitions she has held onto the perspective and principles shaped in her early days of white Keds and ugly gold sweatshirts. Her disappointment in missing the middle school team taught her the crucial lesson of creating opportunities for athletes at every level. Her role as a program director, coupled with unique creative freedom, shaped her insight into what gym owners and coaches need to thrive.

> "Success is being able to do what you love with people you care about."
> – Damianne Albee Steward

EARNED WISDOM

★ **Success:** Success is being able to do what you love with people you care about in an industry that has made a huge impact on your life, being able to wake up and work in All Star cheer every day.

★ **Wisdom:** Everything happens for a reason.

★ **Gratitude:** Damianne credits her high school coaches in New Hampshire, the Donaldsons, for sparking her love for the sport and for creating the foundation for the person she became as a coach.

★ **Damianne's Wish:** Damianne wishes to see more humility and care for the wonderful industry in which we have the honor to work. Too many people take it for granted.

★ **To My Younger Self:** Take school more seriously.

★ **For Gym Owners:** You will never make everyone happy, so know your why before you start and lean into that wholeheartedly. You'll need to keep circling back to your why when things are difficult. Whatever challenges you face, your why will be your guiding light.

★ **For Coaches:** Loyalty, integrity, and hard work go a long way. Do your time without complaint and learn everything you can. No one owes you anything. You have to earn every bit of it.

DID YOU KNOW?

★ The deeply rooted relationships and friendships she continues to make are Damianne's favorite part of cheer.

★ Damianne's father is a published author.

★ "Reality television trash" and true crime are her obsessions.

★ She has visited all fifty states.

★ Her favorite superhero is her father.

★ Damianne chose the wolf as her animal because it symbolizes loyalty, perseverance, success, intuition, spirit, and a strong appetite for freedom, but it also can be a loner.

ALL STAR STRONG.

"Never give up." – Winston Churchill

TRES LeTARD

Athletic Championships – 2001
Varsity Spirit – 2005
Allstar World Championships – 2024

FOUNDATIONS IN MOVEMENT

In the world of All Star cheer, some figures shape the sport from the sidelines rather than from center stage. Tres LeTard is one such architect who helped transform cheerleading from a passion-driven activity into a structured business. His path highlights the evolution of an industry that grew from scattered gymnastics gyms into a massive enterprise.

"My sport growing up was gymnastics," Tres said, a slight smile playing across his face as he recalled his early days. "I did gymnastics through high school." It was at the Knoxville Gymnastics Training Center (KGTC) where Tres first encountered cheerleading. The gym had launched an All Star program called the KGTC Sharks, which later evolved into Premier Athletics. This unexpected intersection would alter the course of his life.

By his own admission, Tres wasn't "the best gymnast that ever did the sport," which led him to explore other options once he reached college. A chance observation changed his path: University of Tennessee cheerleaders practiced at his gymnastics gym, and all of them were on full scholarships. "That sounds like a pretty good way to go to college," he thought, pivoting from his gymnastics to cheer. With determination—and help from the cheer program's leadership—Tres learned to stunt and mastered the basics. His effort paid off when he made the University of Tennessee cheer team in 1997.

FROM ATHLETE TO BUSINESS MIND

While cheering at UT, Tres balanced academics with coaching and teaching tumbling classes and private lessons at local gyms to earn extra money. His side hustle eventually expanded to coaching All Star teams, giving him insight into the operational side of cheer. His undergraduate studies in biochemistry initially pointed him toward medical school but, like his shift from gymnastics to cheerleading, Tres found himself drawn to a different path.

"I was trying to become a physician and pivoted to business school," he said matter-of-factly, summarizing years of soul-searching in a single sentence. During his transition period Tres seized the opportunity to manage Premier Athletics' Atlanta location, Premier Bears. The gym had been acquired in what Tres now recognizes as a challenging transition. The experience proved to be a valuable lesson in gym culture and management. Premier's initial franchise model attempted to standardize everything so each location operated identically, like McDonald's. But Tres discovered that such an approach didn't translate well to the cheerleading world.

"I don't necessarily think that [McDonald's approach] works a hundred percent in the All Star gym space because of the personalities, the culture, the individual intangibles that exist within a gym," he explained. And the Atlanta gym required a different approach, specific to the needs of its customers. Tres carried this lesson with him throughout his career: "Flexibility is important when managing business challenges and personalities."

Against the odds, and with the help of some incredible people who are still part of the All Star industry today, namely Greg Green of World Class Athletics in Panama City, Florida, Tres managed to form three teams that first season—"Bad News Bears teams" as he jokingly called them in a nod to both the gym's name and its underdog status. But he persevered, and the gym began to recover. Though Tres eventually returned to Knoxville for graduate school, the Atlanta experience provided valuable insights into the business side of cheerleading.

EVENTS: LIGHTS, CAMERA, ACTION!

Back in Knoxville, a new opportunity emerged. Premier had started a competition branch called Athletic Championships, but ownership decided to split its focus. While Boog and Cole led the gyms, Mike Martinez focused on the events business and invited Tres to help it grow. The offer aligned perfectly with Tres's new focus on business. Despite being enrolled in a full-time MBA program where students weren't supposed to hold jobs, Tres made it work. "I would be in class from eight to four every day, then go straight to the office," he said. His schedule complemented the cheerleading business cycle because he could call gym owners after his daytime classes ended.

Under his leadership, Athletic Championships expanded dramatically from just three events to eighteen before being sold to Varsity in 2005. As competitions grew, Tres gradually became the face of the organization with Mike Martinez mentoring him to take on more responsibility. "Mike would be in one city, I'd be in the other city," Tres explained, describing how they managed simultaneous events. As Mike focused more on family, Tres took greater control of the business.

THE CORPORATE EVOLUTION

The industry was transforming, and Tres found himself at the center of it. After Varsity acquired Athletic Championships—its first acquisition of an All Star business—Tres stayed on and became a key architect of Varsity's All Star strategy. "I feel like I was kind of the architect of the Varsity All Star structure," Tres said, "really developing the Family Plan and marketing positioning."

His influence extended beyond the rebate program. He also created Varsity's first sales team dedicated to All Star events that initially focused on promoting the Family Plan. As bid events like The Summit began to take shape, Tres was part of the strategic team that brought those innovations to market.

PRIVATE EQUITY AND CHANGING PRIORITIES

Throughout his years at Varsity, Tres witnessed multiple ownership changes as private equity firms became involved. He notes distinct differences in how each owner approached the business. Early private equity groups, like Leonard Green & Partners, were relatively hands off, trusting Varsity's leadership. Herf Jones maintained that approach after acquiring Varsity, and even the smaller firm, Charlesbank Capital Partners, "leaned heavily on the leadership team," Tres said. The watershed moment came in 2018 when Bain Capital took ownership of Varsity.

The pressure to grow intensified, particularly on the All Star division that had become Varsity's primary growth vehicle. School cheer programs maintained steady yet modest growth, but All Star was expected to deliver double-digit increases. With market participation nearing saturation, price increases and cost reductions became the primary growth strategy. Then COVID-19 hit in 2020, shutting down events and forcing massive cuts.

NEW BEGINNINGS

After leaving Varsity in July 2020, Tres stepped away from the cheerleading industry for nearly four years before joining The Open Championship Series, host of Allstar World Championships in April 2024. In his absence, the industry landscape shifted dramatically.

While Varsity shut down during the pandemic, smaller event producers found opportunities. Companies like

Redline, Deep South, MCDA, and Gold Rush (now part of The Open Championship Series) filled the void by running events when Varsity couldn't. "It probably opened their eyes to this bigger opportunity," Tres reflected, noting how those companies created alternatives to Varsity's Summit event, partnering with Universal Studios to create a rival championship, The Allstar World Championship (ASWC).

Today, ASWC boasts over 1,600 teams, making it larger than either of Varsity's individual Summit events. For Tres, that represents a positive development for the sport—more opportunities, more pathways for athletes, and a healthier competitive landscape.

Throughout his career Tres LeTard has witnessed—and helped shape—the transformation of cheerleading from an activity driven purely by passion to a structured business enterprise with all its triumphs and growing pains. While some may criticize the commercialization of the sport, Tres views the business structure as necessary for cheerleading's growth and sustainability. In his eyes, the business of spirit isn't about diminishing the heart of cheerleading but about creating sustainable frameworks that will allow the sport to flourish for generations to come.

> "Success is living life on your own terms."
> – Tres LeTard

EARNED WISDOM

★ **Success:** Success is living life on your own terms with the people you love most.

★ **Wisdom:** Participating in All Star events and being part of a team are among the most impactful and potentially life-changing experiences for a young person.

★ **Gratitude:** Tres credits Mike Martinez for giving him his first opportunity and guiding him into cheerleading. He also acknowledges the impact that Boog Potter and Cole Stott had by taking him under their wing. He also recognized Jeff Webb for teaching him a great deal later in his career.

★ **Tres' Wish:** Tres wishes for fun to return to All Star like the years prior to private equity and corporate influence.

★ **Mistakes:** Spending too much time on things that don't matter. Determine what is most important to you as soon as possible and focus your energy on that. If you play a stupid game, you tend to win stupid prizes.

★ **For Gym Owners:** Focus on building a community of passionate fans. Nurture relationships with key people in your community. Don't define your success by the wins and the losses. Focus on the fundamentals.

★ **For Coaches:** Listen to the people around you and ask lots of questions. If you see something at an event that you appreciate, reach out to the coach and tell them. They'll most likely be excited to connect with you and share ideas.

★ **Lessons Learned:** All Star cheer provides the greatest opportunity for participation for the largest number of young people, making it unique.

DID YOU KNOW?

★ Tres's favorite part of cheer is pyramids because they are what separate All Star cheer from other sports, such as gymnastics and acro.

★ Tres was a competitive snow ski racer, earning second in Tennessee.

★ He loves traveling around the United States with his wife to attend rock concerts.

★ On New Year's Eve in 2000 he rang in the millennium at New York City's Times Square.

★ Tres's favorite superhero is Superman because he's a classic superhero while the others seem like posers.

★ Tres chose the wolf as his animal because it represents loyalty, perseverance, success, intuition, spirit, and an appetite for freedom, yet it also can be a loner.

S. R. Fabrico

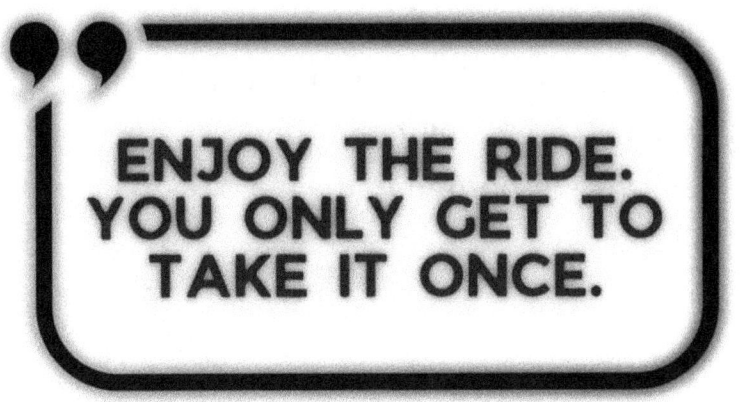

"A hundred years from now it will not matter what my bank account was, the sort of house I lived in, or the kind of car I drove. But the world may be different because I was important in the life of a child." – Forest Witcraft

BECKY HERRERA
CheerForce – 2001

THE CHEERFORCE STORY

Some of life's most significant journeys begin with unexpected detours. For Becky Herrera, founder of CheerForce, that detour came in the form of a broken toe. "After graduation, I was auditioning for local studios to get work as a teacher, and during an audition I broke my toe," Becky said. "That led to a couple weeks with my foot up, unable to do much but check the want ads. This was 1997. What internet!"

That seemingly minor injury would redirect Becky from her original plan of opening dance studios to becoming one of All Star cheer's pioneer gym owners in Southern California. While nursing her injury, she found a job teaching recreational cheer and dance classes, a stopgap that would evolve into a lifelong passion and a successful business.

Becky's connection to cheerleading wasn't entirely new since she had cheered in high school from 1989 to 1992. "I grew up dancing, but I was inspired by the Dallas Cowboys Cheerleaders and finally got to try out for cheer when I got to high school," she said. Her high school cheerleading experience culminated in her selection as team captain her senior year.

After high school Becky's focus shifted back to dance. She studied entrepreneurship at the University of Southern California with plans to open and franchise dance studios. "Dance was my passion," she said, "but I didn't have any capital to start a studio right out of college."

LEARNING THROUGH TRIAL AND ERROR

When Becky's recreational cheer classes gained popularity, the program owner approached her with a proposal to start a "competition team." And so they formed small teams in their respective cities—Becky in Simi Valley and her partner in Ventura, California. Without dedicated facilities, those early teams practiced in public parks and at the local Boys and Girls Club.

Becky's first team of fourteen attended its inaugural competition in 2000 at the Kern County Fair in Bakersfield, California. The experience was humbling yet formative: "I remember we got a zero out of ten in tumbling," Becky said. "We really didn't know what we were doing. We placed fourth out of four on the NCA scoresheet." That inauspicious competitive debut might have discouraged less determined individuals, but for Becky and her team, it sparked their competitive drive:

"But we did know that we were hooked and wanted to learn more."

The following season (2001-2002) marked the official beginning of Cheer Force, initially two separate words, with Becky and her business partner each running teams in their respective cities. The program reflected the transitional nature of All Star cheer at that time, incorporating elements that would eventually fade from the sport. "Routines still had music and cheers," Becky said, referencing the cheer segments that were once standard in All Star routines. Becky was pregnant with her first son during that early season, which gave rise to a team ritual. "We had a tradition of kissing my belly for good luck," she said.

BUILDING CHEERFORCE

After the first year, growing interest in Becky's classes and team coincided with business tensions. Becky is grateful to her partner because, without her, she may never have started her gym owner journey. But after a short time they decided to dissolve their partnership. The dissolution led to the rebranding that created the now-familiar single word "CheerForce" when Becky reapplied for her business license.

The program's growth accelerated, allowing Becky to finally secure a dedicated facility, albeit a modest one. "We doubled in size," she said, "and finally had enough cash flow to open a very small facility." The space was large enough for four strips of carpet-bonded foam that were partially covered by a twenty-foot tumble track. After just nine months, she outgrew the space and moved to a location that could accommodate a full floor in 2003.

What's particularly notable about CheerForce's early growth is that it occurred organically. "We did very little marketing, but parents were enjoying themselves," Becky said. "By word of mouth, we quickly grew to 150 students." Such growth reflects the program's quality and the positive experiences of its athletes and their families.

As the program expanded, so did its professional infrastructure. Becky began adding coaches to her staff and hiring choreographers. By 2006 CheerForce had outgrown its second facility and moved to a 14,000-square-foot space, a substantial upgrade that coincided with a major competitive achievement. "During that time we had a team compete at Worlds for the first time, winning bronze in 2006. It was like a dream." The rapid trajectory from recreational classes to a World Championship in less than a decade exemplifies the explosive growth that characterized All Star cheer in the early 2000s.

NAVIGATING CHALLENGES

CheerForce's journey, like that of many successful All Star programs, has been marked by resilience in the face of significant obstacles. When the 2008 economic crisis hit, Becky and her team had to make difficult decisions to ensure the program's survival. "In 2008 the economy took a dive, and we had to figure out how to keep our business alive," Becky said. "We ultimately moved to a smaller facility to ease up our expenses and started developing Prep and Novice teams."

That pivot toward more accessible and less expensive program options proved crucial. Diversifying allowed CheerForce to gain new customers and continue growing. This adaptation not only saved CheerForce but also established a model that many gyms would later follow, that of offering multiple entry points and commitment levels to broaden the customer base.

In 2012 Becky boosted her cheerleading involvement by taking on a coaching role at her local high school, a position she recently retired from. This connection to school cheerleading created greater stability and a dynamic exchange of ideas between the scholastic and All Star realms.

When the COVID-19 pandemic caused another major disruption to the cheerleading industry, CheerForce faced yet another facility challenge. After COVID, its facility was sold, and CheerForce had to move again. The program secured a new 19,000-square-foot home in 2021. "God truly blessed us," Becky said. "It's a unique space, but it works for us and the needs of our customers."

CONTRIBUTING TO THE INDUSTRY

Beyond creating her own successful program, Becky has made significant contributions to the wider All Star cheer community. She and her husband have shared their business knowledge through articles in industry publications and speaking engagements at coaching conferences. "I would say, having been through big economic changes," Becky said, "we've been able to teach other owners from our mistakes and how to pivot and diversify." That generosity in sharing hard-earned wisdom has empowered many gym owners to tackle their business challenges.

Becky also has dedicated herself to serving the sport through various leadership roles. She volunteered as a USASF Connection Leader and became the committee chair in 2020. She also serves as a USASF Board member. In these positions, she works to create opportunities for club owners, advocate for safe rules, and helps ensure that member feedback reaches those making key decisions.

This commitment to service reflects Becky's understanding that the sport's continued growth and sustainability require gym owners to contribute beyond their individual businesses.

A FAMILY LEGACY

Throughout CheerForce's journey, one constant has been Becky's family. She met her husband during her junior year of high school when she temporarily stepped away from cheerleading to focus on band, and he's been her partner for thirty-three years, throughout the CheerForce adventure.

Their three sons have grown up alongside the business with significant program milestones often coinciding with family ones. The first season of CheerForce featured the ritual of kissing Becky's pregnant belly for luck, and the move to their largest facility came shortly after the birth of their second son.

This intertwining of family and business reflects a common theme in All Star cheer where many successful programs are family operations. The sport's demanding schedule and unique culture often require the understanding and involvement of entire families, creating businesses that reflect deep personal values and commitments.

FROM BROKEN TOE TO INDUSTRY LEADER

What began with a broken toe and a job found in the want ads has evolved into a program that has touched thousands of young lives. Becky's willingness to adapt, learn from mistakes, and share knowledge has made CheerForce not only a successful business but also a model for sustainability in the volatile world of All Star cheer.

As the sport continues to evolve, programs like CheerForce—built on passion, resilience, and genuine care for athletes—will continue to form its backbone. The personal stories remind us that behind the glitter and spectacle of modern All Star cheer are entrepreneurs and educators who built something remarkable, often starting with nothing more than enthusiasm and a willingness to learn.

Becky Herrera and CheerForce continue to write new chapters in a story that began with an unexpected detour but that found its way to exactly where it was meant to be.

"Success is when your athletes come back to visit." – Becky Herrera

EARNED WISDOM

★ **Success:** Success is when your athletes become happy, well-adjusted adults. Receiving invitations to weddings or announcements of graduations or baby showers years after they have left feels so good. Knowing you impacted your athlete's childhood in a positive way by teaching them who they can become is what matters.

★ **Wisdom:** Cheerleading is just a pathway to learning life's best lessons.

★ **Gratitude:** Tammy Van Vleet and Morton Bergue inspired the early stages of Becky's coaching. Later, Karen Wilson and Kathy Penree helped Becky remember there was much to learn. Their friendship and guidance brought Becky to the USASF just before COVID hit, and those relationships are what kept her going during the hardest part (so far) of running a business.

★ **Becky's Wish:** Becky wishes she could go back and be firmer about having the tough conversations necessary to remove the "bad apples."

★ **To My Younger Self:** Focus less on placements. It's a moment in time. Look ahead and find the moments in the moment.

- ★ **Mistakes:** Allowing customers or staff to stay when they were no longer contributing to the positive culture.

- ★ **For Gym Owners:** Be sure to become a master of the business or hire someone you can trust. Understand and monitor your budget and cash flow. Remember, event outcomes are not the most important focus.

- ★ **For Coaches:** A passionate coach does not guarantee a successful business. A great athlete does not necessarily make a good coach. You are invited to be a part of a person's childhood. The memories you create will stay with them forever. What kind of memories will they hold?

- ★ **Lessons Learned:** Being married to your business partner is one of the most challenging aspects of Becky's journey. Over time the married couple learned to intentionally separate their emotions from work and home. Working together and being married requires effort, commitment, and communication.

DID YOU KNOW?

- ★ Having the opportunity to make a positive impact on young people is Becky's favorite part of the sport.

- ★ Becky's dad was a preacher, and she is an only child.

★ As a child she was a junior handler in dog shows. (A junior handler is an adolescent who is judged on how they show their dog.)

★ Becky was the fourth runner-up for Miss California in the 1996 Miss America competition. Becky won the talent preliminary for her ballet piece, "The Swan."

★ Her favorite superhero is Wonder Woman "because she rocks."

★ Becky said she is a combination of a swan and a whale. Together they represent grace, balance, innocence, soul, love, beauty, elegance, transformation, dreams, wisdom, provider, intelligence, kindness, deeper awareness, nurturing, navigator, and communication.

"See a need, fill a need." – Mr. Bigweld in *Robots*

LEON REYNOLDS
Alaska Athletics – 2003

THE LAST FRONTIER

In a state known for its rugged wilderness, extreme climate, and isolation from the Lower 48, competitive cheerleading might seem like an unlikely pursuit in the small community of Wasilla, Alaska. But it was in that town of 7,148 that Leon Reynolds would plant the seeds for a cheerleading revolution destined to transform Alaska's athletic landscape and produce teams capable of competing with the nation's best.

Leon's journey to becoming an All Star cheer pioneer began, ironically, with a firm rejection of the sport. As a competitive gymnast in Alaska he had amassed numerous state and regional titles before burnout set in during his senior year of high school. "Too much time, too much work, not enough fun," Leon recalled of his decision to step away from gymnastics.

But even without formal training, Leon couldn't resist showing off his tumbling skills, performing flips off "anything and everything" at school and, occasionally, tumbling during halftime at basketball games "to get a rise from the crowd." Despite frequent invitations to join the cheerleading team, Leon remained steadfast in his refusal—until Yvonne intervened. "Yvonne was the stereotype cheerleading captain with blonde hair, athletic body, bubbly personality, and she was dating the hockey captain," Leon said. Everyone had a secret crush on Yvonne, so when she asked Leon and three of his friends to try out for the high school cheer team, they couldn't refuse.

That fateful invitation led Leon to an NCA high school camp where he made the All-American team and was selected to apply for a staff position. That first exposure to organized cheerleading opened doors he never imagined existed. He used that opportunity to springboard into college with scholarships being plentiful in the late 1990s.

After college, Leon's career took an unexpected turn into Alaska's oil fields where jobs were lucrative and coveted. "The oil fields are very rough, very dangerous, and I loved it," he said of his time as a roughneck. The job schedule—two weeks on, two weeks off—allowed him to coach cheerleading at his previous high school during his off time. Under his guidance, both the JV and varsity teams went undefeated in state competitions for three years.

When his first son was about to be born, Leon faced the dilemma familiar to many oil field workers: Remain a "two-and-two dad" or leave the lucrative job to be present for his family. He chose family, returning to his roots at his parents' gymnastics business one month before his son's birth.

THE FIRST ALL STAR TEAM IN ALASKA

Though Leon had stepped away from high school coaching due to time constraints, his impact on his athletes lingered. Three particularly dedicated athletes that Leon had nicknamed "the Three Musketeers," weren't ready to lose their coach. They proposed a stunting class where they could continue training with him. "I started a one-hour class and opened it to all local high schools," Leon said. "Before I knew it, there were nine stunt groups from different schools."

The turning point came during a practice when all the stunt groups hit a heel stretch in unison. Leon turned to his mother, also a cheer coach, and said, "You know what this is? This is the state's first All Star team."

The following season Leon held his first official tryout, and seventeen athletes attended. The diverse group included high school athletes, gymnasts that Leon coached, and complete newcomers to the sport. Among them was Jessica Deckard, whose story exemplifies the unique character of Alaskan cheerleading. "Jessica Deckard was an athlete who showed up with the most ripped arms I had ever seen on a girl," Leon said. "She lived out in the sticks of Alaska, had no running water, and had to cut firewood with an ax every day for heat. She had never been in a gym, taken a class, or participated in any sport." After confirming she could do a handstand and a bridge, Leon welcomed her to the team.

"Everyone who had a pulse and a desire to learn made the first team in the state," he said. "It was awesome." Thus, Denali Allstars was born, Alaska's first All Star cheerleading team, named after North America's highest peak.

BUILDING THE PROGRAM UPSIDE DOWN

Unlike most small gyms that start with lower levels and build upward, Leon took the opposite approach. "We started with our top team and built our way down," he explained. "Next team added was a Junior team, then a Youth, and then leveling the teams when that became an option."

The pioneering program found immediate success, and word spread throughout the state. Athletes began commuting the forty miles from Anchorage, Alaska's largest city, three days a week to train. By 2008 the commute had become so common that Leon decided to open a satellite location in Anchorage. Not much time passed before the tiny gym in Anchorage was larger than the Wasilla location. In 2012 Leon made Anchorage his main location for cheer and rebranded from Denali All Stars to Alaska Athletics.

Today, Alaska Athletics offers a comprehensive range of programs beyond cheerleading that include tumbling, summer camps, after-school care, ninja warrior classes, preschool and, coming soon, a licensed daycare facility.

HOMEGROWN EXCELLENCE

What makes Alaska Athletics' accomplishments particularly impressive is its isolation from the mainstream cheerleading community. With no other in-state All Star programs to compete against during those early years, Leon's teams trained year-round for a single competition, the nationals in Texas.

Despite the challenges, Alaska Athletics has consistently performed at the highest levels of the sport. "We've had many top ten finishes at Worlds," Leon said proudly, "and years ago we even placed third at US Trials in the International Coed Division. Cheer Athletics was first, Spirit of Texas second, and Alaska Athletics third. Not bad company."

Leon attributes his success to the program's approach to athlete development. "Something I am very proud of for our staff of eleven—we train each and every athlete from the bottom up," he said. "We are a small gym in the middle of nowhere, Alaska, and are able to compete and win at the highest level of our sport."

FILLING THE COMPETITIVE VOID

Leon not only launched Alaska's first All Star program, he also played a vital role in advancing the state's cheerleading scene by launching competitions. Alaska's geographic isolation and limited cheerleading population deterred established event producers from holding events. "Varsity has tried, not to return, as well as Pacwest Spirit Group prior to the Varsity buyout," Leon said. "All of them failed, as they could not make it profitable."

Recognizing that competitions are essential to the sport's growth, Leon embraced the philosophy of "See a need, fill a need." That's why he created the Top of the World Championships, Alaska's first spring floor event. "This event has flourished through the years," Leon said, "and we now offer three in-state events, bids to ASW [All Star Worlds], and bring up amazing judges to not only judge but work hands-on with teams to help overcome our sport's isolation." Without Top of the World Cheer, there would still be no in-state events in Alaska to help grow the sport and provide healthy competition.

FAMILY TO THE CORE

Leon was the first with Alaska Athletics, but now there are several All Star cheer gyms in the state, and the sport is growing each year. Leon's journey through cheerleading has always been intertwined with his family. His parents took over his childhood gymnastics club, laying the foundation for his eventual cheerleading program. His mother coached cheerleading alongside him. Now, he has built his own family through connections formed in the sport.

He met his wife online while they were living in different states. Before meeting in person, they read *Jonathan Livingston Seagull* together, a 1970 book about a seagull striving to achieve the impossible, and Leon frequently shares anecdotes from the book with his senior athletes. The seagull became such a meaningful symbol that Leon incorporated it into his marriage proposal on January 13, 2020, creating a wooden plaque with "Will you marry me?" hidden beneath painted-over tape on the back.

As Leon continues to build Alaska Athletics and grow cheerleading throughout the state, he remains guided by the values that have defined his journey: family, legacy, and the courage to pioneer new paths in unexpected places. From the gymnast who reluctantly joined cheerleading to the oil field worker who chose fatherhood over financial gain to the coach who built a nationally competitive program in America's most isolated state, Leon Reynolds personifies a pioneering spirit.

In the same way that Alaska represents America's last frontier, Leon's program embodies cheerleading's frontier spirit, proving that with dedication, innovation, and heart, excellence can flourish even in the most unlikely environments.

"Success is legacy." – Leon Reynolds

EARNED WISDOM

★   **Success:** Defining success was easy for Leon: legacy. Teaching athletes where true value exists is his greatest success. Those lessons are how his legacy will live on long after he's done with the mat.

★   **Wisdom:** Leon often exercises with his athletes. He has the team sit in a circle and close their eyes. The objective is to recall, in detail, a trophy they won—the color, height, inscription, and weight. Most people cannot recall a single trophy or award with clarity. Considering the work that goes into earning awards and the excitement athletes exude when they receive them, it's odd they can't remember them. Leon then asks his team about their best accomplishment, funniest moment, or the hardest challenges they faced in a prior season. He asks them about something they are proud of. His athletes will talk his ear off to answer those questions. They relive the good, the bad, and the lessons learned. In time, the trophies and awards are forgotten, but the lessons will stay with them for years to come.

★ **Gratitude:** Leon credits his father and Cathe Rhodes for their impact on him. His father was his main gymnastics coach, teaching and training him in the sport. Cathe was his high school cheerleading coach and a great role model. She offered him a loan to help pay for his first semester of college. "Money isn't going to hold you back," she said. "This is a loan. You'll pay me back." Leon repaid every penny, and her kindness has stuck with him to this day.

★ **Leon's wish**: Leon wishes he could have removed the idea of what a cheer gym was sooner. Cheer gyms should offer cheer, but a good business model is strong because it provides additional services such as classes, after-school care, summer camps, and preschool.

★ **For Gym Owners:** Stress is spelled D-E-B-T. You don't need the best equipment or specialty training equipment to be successful. You only need a strong work ethic and fantastic leadership for teams, athletes, and staff. Start humbly and reinvest your earnings.

★ **For Coaches:** This life isn't easy. It will challenge you, frustrate you, break your heart, and make you doubt yourself at times. The coach's calling is a hard life to live. It also will be the most rewarding experience of your life. If you can accept both things, then this is the life for you. If you don't understand what I mean, continue coaching and you will.

DID YOU KNOW?

★ Leon's favorite routine was during the Denali All Star days. They added fur trim around the collar, sleeve cuffs, and bow of the uniform. The music had an Alaskan theme, featuring "Ice Ice Baby," "Let It Snow," and similar songs. The team competed at PacWest Nationals. At the end of the routine, little fur pieces floated in the air, making it look like snow was falling. Aside from the mess, it was a memorable moment.

★ His favorite part of cheer is tumbling. As a former gymnast he appreciates finding the sweet spot between progression and perfection.

★ Leon's family comes from a strong Mexican background, and his name, Leon, means "lion." And his zodiac sign is Leo, so choosing his spirit animal was simple.

- ★ He runs an auto restoration workshop and works each day with his sons building classic cars from the frame up.

- ★ Leon trained, coached, and competed in jiu-jitsu and MMA for most of his life. Although it requires a certain amount of grit and strength, Leon has a softer side too. He enjoys a good rom-com. He can't help but smile when he watches them.

- ★ Superman is Leon's favorite superhero. He has unlimited strength, is humble in his daily life, loves a woman deeply, and protects those around him. He also can shoot lasers from his eyes and fly, and both are totally cool.

- ★ Leon, of course, chose the lion because it represents family, strength, energy, courage, guardianship, protection, ferocity, and authority.

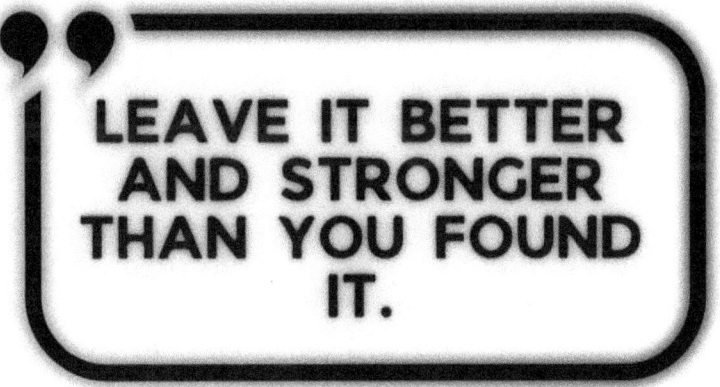

"Sport has the power to change the world. It has the power to inspire. It has the power to unite people in a way that little else does." – Nelson Mandela

NACCC

National All Star Cheerleading Coaches Congress – 2004

A WEEKEND THAT CHANGED EVERYTHING

It started with frustration—the clash of passion against pointless obstacles. "We were just frustrated that, from weekend to weekend, we were constantly changing the routines," Kristen Rosario said, "and, by definition, 'routine' means doing the same thing over and over again. And that was exactly the opposite of what we were doing."

In the early 2000s All Star cheer was booming, but rapid growth brought its share of challenges. Each event producer imposed its own rules and guidelines for what was allowed on the competition floor. For gym owners, coaches, and athletes, that meant constantly adjusting routines to meet various criteria, often requiring significant weekly changes. "Some competitions you could do a back tuck basket toss, and some competitions you couldn't," Elaine Pascale said. "Some competitions you could do a full, and some competitions you couldn't."

Such inconsistency wasn't just inconvenient, it threatened the sport's integrity and athletes' safety. After a particularly frustrating competition in the early 2000s, a group of prominent gym owners decided that something needed to change. Victor and Kristen Rosario, Elaine Pascale, Joelle Antico, and Jamie Parrish—owners of the powerhouse programs Top Gun, World Cup, and Georgia All Stars, respectively—sat down together at a picnic table in Jekyll Island, Georgia, battled the sand gnats, and made a bold decision: If the event producers wouldn't standardize their rules, the coaches would do it themselves.

"Let's sit all these companies down, and let's tell them this isn't working," Kristen said. The event producers empowered the group to carry the project forward. They understood that doing so would eliminate their competitive advantages, but they also knew it was what their customers not only wanted but needed.

This effort led to the formation of the National All Star Cheerleading Coaches Congress—NACCC (pronounced "N-A-triple-C")—an unprecedented attempt to give coaches a unified voice in shaping the sport's direction.

MIDNIGHT IN ELAINE'S DINING ROOM

The first planning meeting took place at Elaine Pascale's home with the goal of bringing order to the chaos. "Everyone ended up at my house, sitting at the dining room table," Elaine said. The group discussed how they were going to lay out the plan, what rules mattered, and which ones didn't. "I remember it was like two in the morning at one point," Kristen said. "We were delirious, exhausted, and then we started talking about colors."

An exhaustion-fueled debate over color choices—"They spent thirty minutes arguing about whether it should be pea green or sea green"—became a lighthearted moment that cemented their sense of purpose. What made the effort remarkable was its organic, grassroots spirit, a group of friends united by a shared goal of doing what was best for the kids and deeply attuned to each other's frustrations.

Later, Elaine called contacts throughout the industry, inviting coaches from across the country to attend a formal meeting in Atlanta. They needed a legal advisor to help establish the organization properly, which led them to Dennis Worley, a practicing attorney with a strong background in cheerleading.

THE FIRST NACCC ASSEMBLY

In January 2004 hundreds of coaches gathered at the Georgian Terrace Hotel in Atlanta for the first official NACCC assembly. The energy was electric. Coaches who had typically competed against each other were working together for the good of the sport. The assembly of "a couple of hundred" used a simple but effective voting system: Coaches were given colored paddles—green for "yes" and orange for "no"—to vote on proposed rules.

"We would ask, 'Do we want to vote to keep this in Intermediate?'" Kristen said. People would hold up their paddles, and we would count their votes. Survey technology didn't exist. Most people had barely started using email. The process was remarkably democratic. "Anybody who cared enough to spend the money to show up could come and vote," Kristen said.

Following the votes, a committee that included Victor, John Metz, and others stayed up until the early morning hours at Jamie's house documenting all the rules that had been approved. The next day they presented the compiled rules to the assembled coaches for a final review. "I don't think anything has ever gotten accomplished so quickly in the history of cheerleading as on that weekend," Kristen said.

The efficiency was driven by a shared purpose: to create consistency that would benefit athletes and programs across the country. By the time the weekend concluded, the NACCC had established a unified set of rules that would bring order to the formerly chaotic competition landscape. "Everybody left there so happy," Kristen recalled. "It was such a great weekend. I will definitely say it goes down as one of my favorite weekends in the history of cheerleading, because so much happened in such a short time."

BUILDING LEGITIMACY

Following that initial meeting, the NACCC established itself as a formal organization. Event producers were invited to become member companies for a $500 fee that granted permission to use the standardized rules and gave access to the coaches' "sounding board" for future decisions. That modest membership fee barely covered the organization's basic operational costs. "It paid for our stationery and the basic little things that we needed to get the information out to the companies," Victor said. "All the flights, hotels, the travel back and forth, that was all on us."

Despite limited resources, the NACCC quickly gained traction. "We had thirty of the forty event producers on board," Victor said. "Many of them were present at that meeting, and they got to see how many coaches were invested in the process." The event producers realized something profound: Their unique rules weren't drawing coaches to their events. If anything, they were driving them away. The event producers realized the NACCC could establish standard rules and allow event producers to focus on other aspects that could set them apart. For the first time, coaches had a unified voice in the sport's governance. But maintaining that unity would prove challenging.

THE TAMPA SKEWERING

While the initial assembly had been a success, translating those decisions into actionable guidelines proved difficult. At a subsequent meeting in late April 2004 in Tampa, the NACCC leadership found itself unprepared for the scrutiny of the event producers who had joined the organization. Dennis Worley recalled the tense environment: "In the meeting we were grilled, and we deserved it, because those businessmen and businesswomen were making decisions that relied on us to guide rules and divisions. We told them we were the experts. I quickly adjourned that meeting in Tampa and got us out of the room as fast as possible because we were being skewered," he said. NACC leadership promised a more organized approach within sixty days.

As the rescheduled meeting drew near, Dennis recognized the necessity for a more strategic approach. The night before the Miami meeting, he prepared an agenda and notebooks for each NACCC leader along with detailed instructions. "Victor knew about the rules," Dennis said. "Joelle knew about the money and served as the treasurer, Kristen knew about the baby steps toward creating standardized divisions, and Elaine was the cheerleader."

Dennis's instructions were clear: "When we get to your part, speak on that. For anything else, here's what you say: 'We'll be happy to discuss it.' Do not entertain their questions."

The strategy worked. This more disciplined approach helped establish the NACCC's credibility among event producers and coaches alike. For several years the organization successfully unified the sport around consistent rules and divisions.

THE VARSITY CHALLENGE

But not everyone in the industry embraced the NACCC's efforts. Notably absent from the list of member companies were those under the Varsity umbrella, primarily UCA and NCA.

To bridge that gap the NACCC leadership—including Elaine, Joelle, Kristen, Victor, and Jamie—traveled to

Memphis in June 2004 to meet directly with Jeff Webb, Varsity's founder and CEO. The NACCC group's request was simple: Join the NACCC for the same $500 fee asked of all member companies.

The meeting's awkwardness became a running joke among the NACCC leaders, who compared it to a scene from the film "Meet the Parents," wondering if they were being secretly recorded. As Elaine recounted, "No deal. No deal. And we walked out of there going, 'What the hell did we just do?'" The outcome was disappointing because they didn't really care who joined and who didn't, but they wanted one unified version of rules and divisions.

THE USASF EMERGENCE

In the spring of 2005 the NACCC Board made one final attempt to unify the industry and attended a second meeting in Memphis, this time with officers of the newly formed USASF and Varsity. Following the meeting NCA, UCA, and CHEERSPORT each agreed to join, which marked the moment when the rules and divisions were unified.

"The thirty-some companies that we had on board with the NACCC began to join the USASF because of the perk of a world championship," Victor said. To offer bids to The Cheerleading Worlds you had to be a member of the USASF. The event producers believed this was the direction the industry was going, and they jumped on board. One by one, NACCC member companies began leaving the organization.

On June 30, 2005, faced with dwindling membership, the NACCC officially merged with USASF, becoming the organization's coaches' committee. The merger brought both benefits and challenges. While it preserved some of the coaches' influence, it also diluted their independent voice within the larger organization. On August 22, 2005, the NACCC Board officially dissolved the organization, noting that their baby steps were complete. They had achieved the goal of unifying All Star.

For Elaine, the decision to sign the merger agreement was painful but necessary. "I had two companies left," she said of the NACCC's final days. After consulting with her athletes at World Cup, she made the difficult choice to join USASF.

LEGACY AND IMPACT

While the NACCC's formal existence was relatively brief—approximately twenty months from inception to merger—its impact on All Star cheer was profound and lasting. The NACCC continued as the Coaches Committee under the USASF until 2008. The organization established fundamental principles that continue to guide the sport, including standardized divisions, consistent safety rules, and the concept that coaches should have input into the sport's governance. Many of the rules first codified at that Atlanta hotel still form the backbone of today's competitive structure.

"We were the driving force pushing everybody on one scoresheet and everybody getting the same safety rules,"

Elaine said. But to this day, the goal of a single scoresheet has not been achieved.

For Dennis, the NACCC represents a pivotal moment in All Star cheer's evolution. "I was in charge of helping those people's visions come to life," he said. "And those were the people I idolized in this industry."

Victor and Kristen Rosario view the NACCC as a catalyst for uniting the industry. That seemingly trivial debate over the shades of green highlights the fact that, even while building a sport's infrastructure, these pioneering gym owners and coaches never lost their humor or humanity. Each of them was honored by the USASF in 2017 and awarded the USASF Pioneer Award for their contributions to All Star.

THE LESSON OF THE COLORFUL PADDLES

The NACCC's most enduring legacy may lie not in its specific rules or structures but in a powerful principle—that the coaches closest to the athletes should have a meaningful voice in the sport's governance. The sight of hundreds of coaches lifting green or orange paddles to vote on rules showcases a vibrant democratic spirit in All Star where passion and knowledge, rather than commercial interests, drive participation.

The NACCC's brief yet powerful existence reminds us of the remarkable achievements possible when competitors unite for a common goal. In just one weekend in Atlanta they achieved what committees and corporate boards often take years to accomplish.

For today's All Star community—some of whom never have heard of the NACCC—this history provides context for understanding how the sport's competitive structure has evolved. More important, it offers inspiration for how coaches and gym owners might continue to shape cheerleading's future, emphasizing the importance of every coach having a voice and a right to vote on what they believe is right for the sport.

The lesson of those green and orange paddles remains relevant today. When passionate people unite around a common purpose, they can transform an industry. Sometimes, the most important conversations happen around a dining room table at two in the morning when the only thing left to debate is whether the shade of green should be pea or sea.

"Making All Star a safer sport by establishing fair and consistent rules and competition standards." – USASF

USASF
United States All Star Federation – 2003

THE GREAT UNIFICATION: HOW THE USASF CHANGED ALL STAR FOREVER

(Note: If you've already read the history, skip down to "The Birth of Structure" below.)

Varsity decided to become more involved in All Star. And Jeff Webb believed that, if Varsity was going to be more invested in All Star, then All Star needed unified rules to assist in making the sport safer for the athletes. The USASF was created as a result of a brainstorming session with Jim Chadwick, Jeff Webb, Kris Shepherd, Bill Seely, Greg Webb, and a few other Varsity employees.

Jim Chadwick felt strongly that Varsity should be involved in All Star and that the world of All Star needed a standard set of divisions, guidelines, and rules.

Jim figured it would take about $500,000 to set up the organization properly. He arranged a meeting with the top twenty event producers, explained his vision, and asked each one to contribute $25,000 to help get the organization started. Everyone declined. He even asked his uncle, Lawrence "Herkie" Herkimer himself, but he also said no.

Jeff Webb agreed with Jim that a structure for All Star was necessary, so he agreed to have Varsity completely fund the new organization. Varsity was owned by a venture capitalist, and Jeff was not looking forward to explaining this new expense.

On January 29, 2004, the US All Star Federation Inc. was established with the sole mission of bringing safety and cohesion to All Star by creating a standard for the sport. CHEERSPORT was the first event company to join, followed by Athletic Championships.

The USASF's core principles still aim to make All Star a safer sport through fair and consistent rules and competition standards. The organization credentials coaches, certifies judges, sanctions events, and updates safety guidelines, all to promote the best possible environment for All Star cheer and dance athletes to train and compete.

The USASF was launched with a mission to unify the sport, but how would it persuade event producers to join? A prestigious, invitation-only event would set the standard for all, so the inaugural USASF World Cheerleading Championship was organized to showcase fourteen teams at Disney World in Orlando, Florida, in 2004. Originally launched as a season-ending celebration to promote the USASF, the event aimed to establish the most prestigious competition that every producer, gym, and athlete would aspire to join, uniting the sport and setting a standard. In 2005 the first Worlds bids were earned at events nationwide. International teams at The Cheerleading Worlds showcased the global spread of All Star cheer. Jeff Webb leveraged Varsity's longstanding relationship with ESPN to have the first Cheerleading Worlds broadcast nationwide on the network.

"The annual Cheerleading Worlds event is a dedicated tribute to the expertise, athleticism, determination, and shared passion that characterize All Star cheerleading," the USASF website says. Over 10,500 All Star athletes from twenty-five nations converge annually for The Cheerleading Worlds, the ultimate reward for the athletes' hard work, training, and dedication.

Producing the World Championships gave the USASF the ability to create the standard rules and divisions the sport so desperately needed. Event producers united to establish a standard for their competitions, leading to the birth of sanctioned events. To qualify as a sanctioned event, you had to adhere to the USASF's established guidelines. For instance, nine-panel mats, which evolved into a nine-panel spring floor, became the standard. Remarkably, before those standards were set, event producers could use any type or size of mats they chose. Events could kick off at 6 a.m. and run until midnight, so the USASF established regulations focused on athlete well-being and the sport's growth.

THE BIRTH OF STRUCTURE: CREATING THE USASF

> "The goal was to elevate the sport of All Star, get everyone on the same page, and make it a great experience for the athletes." – Amy Clark

In the early 2000s the All Star cheer industry experienced explosive growth and, with it, significant challenges. With no standardized rules or safety standards, event producers operated independently with their own scoring systems and safety and rules requirements. The need for structure had become increasingly apparent to many industry leaders. What emerged from this need was the United States All Star Federation (USASF), an organization that would fundamentally transform competitive All Star cheer and help legitimize it as a sport.

THE GENESIS OF AN IDEA

Steve Peterson joined the team, then Les Stella was added to organize the rules and credentialing standards, which included working with the NACCC to determine proper skill guidelines and progressions. Amy Clark, who would go on to become one of its most influential early leaders, was another early contributor.

It's clear from numerous accounts that Varsity Brands, under Jeff Webb's leadership, was the driving force behind the USASF's initial backing and financing. This investment would later spark both praise and criticism within the industry. The fact remains that many event producers were asked early on to contribute financially and work together to get the organization started, but most initially declined, except for Varsity and CHEERSPORT.

THE MISSION TAKES SHAPE

In 2004, when the USASF was established, its primary objective was to determine a framework for an industry that had previously functioned without centralized oversight. Amy Clark compares the initial concept to "a chamber of commerce" within the All Star cheer industry: "The goal was for all of us to elevate the sport of All Star on the same page and make it a great experience for the athletes but not have to recreate the wheel for each of the individual members."

The organization sought to unify a fragmented industry by establishing fair play, standardized rules, credentialing of coaches, and creating The Cheerleading Worlds, a prestigious championship designed to be the premier event for All Star teams. The goal of the championship was to elevate the sport and create a place for the best of the best to compete. Being invited to The Cheerleading Worlds in itself was a huge honor, and the USASF hoped the event would serve as a goal for every athlete to aspire to as a pinnacle for All Star cheer.

Meredith Walker, another prominent figure in the USASF, highlighted the significance of those efforts. She earned her master's degree in social work, yet cheerleading had a significant impact on her. "Cheerleading provided me with the first real experiences where I was proud of myself, of my athleticism, my grit, and my determination," Meredith said. "I've stayed with it and always loved it because I know the positives that kind of teamwork can build."

BRINGING ORDER TO CHAOS: RULES AND CREDENTIALING

When Amy Clark attended her first USASF Coaches Conference in 2005, she experienced firsthand the difficulties of establishing standardization in a previously unregulated industry. "We all got credentialed, and it was crazy."

Despite its tumultuous start, the credentialing program was an essential first step in establishing professional coaching standards. Coaches are now required to articulate their understanding of how to teach skills safely as well as to recognize the considerations associated with each skill at every level. Credentialing gave coaches validity and established All Star cheer as a professional career.

The creation of standardized rules was another monumental undertaking. Les Stella was instrumental in creating the first comprehensive rulebook and is recognized for assisting in the drafting of the initial set of cheer rules. This official documentation represented a crucial advancement in recognizing cheerleading as a formal sport. "Les did a really nice job with pulling the rules together and getting people on the same page," Amy said.

Along with the development of the rules came a USASF glossary that was the first step in unifying the terminology across the country. Prior to its creation, each region of the country used unique terms to describe the same set of skills. Finalizing the glossary facilitated nationwide communication in the sport.

THE EARLY TEAM

The USASF's early operations were remarkably lean. Regional directors, such as Amy Clark, were hired on a contractual basis to promote the mission and implement credentialing nationwide. Although Amy initially hesitated to accept the position because of family commitments—"I had a five-year-old, a two-year-old, and a business"—she ultimately played a crucial role in nearly every facet of the organization's development.

Steve Peterson, the first official hire after Jim Chadwick, was brought on to help produce The Cheerleading Worlds and to assist Jim in running the organization. Peterson took great pride in reaching out to and collaborating with all the event producers in the industry, encouraging them to become USASF members and to award bids for Worlds.

THE BIRTH OF CHEERLEADING WORLDS

Perhaps the most visible and influential creation of the USASF was The Cheerleading Worlds. This championship was the brainchild of Jeff Webb, and the event swiftly emerged as the ultimate goal for competitive All Star teams worldwide. Steve Peterson, who still directs The Cheerleading Worlds, reflected on the event's significance: "Standing at the 2007

Cheerleading and Dance Worlds, I remember realizing how momentous the moment really was. The event had doubled in size with the addition of Dance Worlds and featured around one hundred teams from over twenty countries."

Peterson saw the event as a physical manifestation of the industry's collaboration. "I am so honored to be able to work with the leaders in the industry," he said. "It's our collaboration that makes this event so special." The introduction of Dance Worlds further expanded the USASF's impact, creating an inclusive, ultimate competition that honors a wide range of immensely talented performers from diverse dance styles across the globe.

GROWING PAINS AND INDUSTRY DYNAMICS

As with any organization bringing structure to a previously unregulated industry, the USASF faced significant challenges and resistance. One persistent issue was the perception that Varsity had an outsized influence over the organization due to its prominent financial stake.

Another challenge was the diverse nature of the All Star gym landscape. There were large programs with multilocation facilities, small gyms in rural areas, and part-time gym owners who coached a team or two as a hobby. This range of business models made it difficult to implement standardized policies.

Beyond the political and philosophical challenges, the USASF faced significant technical hurdles in creating systems to manage its growing responsibilities. Building the USASF database was a massive but necessary undertaking. The first time around didn't go so well, so it had to be scrapped and the entire system rebuilt.

Despite those challenges, the USASF succeeded in creating essential infrastructure for the sport, including membership management, credentialing records, and event sanctioning systems.

EVOLUTION OF THE ORGANIZATION

As the USASF grew, so did its responsibilities and programs. What began primarily as a rules and credentialing body has expanded to include extensive athlete initiatives, background checks, and abuse prevention education.

Meredith Walker points to this evolution with pride: "As far as athlete safety goes, I would say that I'm really proud of the efforts and the investment that USASF has made in this area. And there is never any hesitation to invest in whatever is needed to do what we can as a national organization."

The membership structure also evolved. Initially focusing on event producers and gym owners and coaches, the organization eventually expanded to include athlete membership requirements for participation in sanctioned events and The Cheerleading Worlds.

A FOUNDATION FOR GLOBAL GROWTH

Although the USASF was established to meet domestic needs, its influence rapidly extended globally. Recruitment of international teams to the event by Varsity employees Karl Olson, Mike Cooper, Chantal Canales, and Robert Torres, along with the standardization of rules and the prestige of The Cheerleading Worlds, attracted teams from around the world, helping to universalize competitive All Star cheer standards.

One example, due to the creation and success of the International Cheer Union, girls in Africa can now participate in cheer programs because many governments sponsor those initiatives, having received funding from a federation to support its potential inclusion as an Olympic sport. This also holds true for Australia, Scandinavia, and numerous other regions around the world.

The formation of the International Cheer Union (ICU) vastly accelerated this global reach. Steve Peterson highlighted the inaugural ICU World Championship in 2009 as an event "whose date will be remembered in the cheerleading and dance history books." He predicted that "we will soon be able to look back at the ICU Championship on April 24, 2009, and see the start of something great for all cheerleaders and dancers, whether their preference be All Star or school."

Despite controversies and challenges, the USASF has revolutionized All Star cheerleading. From chaotic beginnings to a sophisticated organization backing thousands of gyms and athletes, this evolution is remarkable. The USASF injected structure and organization into the sport.

Amy Clark summarized what she believed the USASF has contributed to the sport: "I think it's things that make sense to people. I think the USASF brought structure and organization to the sport, and that's really what we wanted to do."

Meredith Walker emphasizes the historical context of this achievement: "We're still so young as a sport, but we have really high expectations. The USASF has been around for twenty years, and we are playing catch up with every sport in the world, trying to get there. And we are, we're getting there."

THE LEGACY CONTINUES

The creation of the USASF marked a pivotal moment in All Star cheer's history, a transition from fragmented growth to organized development. The story of the USASF's creation is, ultimately, about an industry taking responsibility for its own development by bringing structure where there was chaos, standards where there was inconsistency, and global opportunity where there had primarily been local competition. Through the vision and effort of figures like Jeff Webb, Bill Seely, Jim Chadwick, Amy Clark, Steve Peterson, Les Stella, and many others—along with the financial backing of Jeff Webb and Varsity—the foundation was laid for everyone in All Star cheer to benefit as it emerged as a recognized, respected, and rapidly growing international sport discipline.

WHAT USASF HAS BROUGHT TO ALL STAR

With years of experience and input from industry experts, the USASF developed and launched numerous outstanding programs and standards, including the following:

MEMBER VOTING: The creation of the USASF gave all members the opportunity to have a voice. The NACCC felt strongly that coaches and owners should have a voice in the decision-making process regarding the rules for their sport. Prior to the existence of the NACCC and USASF, you only had influence if you had the ear of the event producer whose events you were attending. Sadly, today less than 10 percent of members use their voice, but the opportunity is there, and taking advantage of it is encouraged. Many fought to give everyone the opportunity to have a voice. Use it.

CREDENTIALING: The USASF began the credentialing program, which was the first time All Star coaches could undergo training to demonstrate their understanding of the proper progressions and techniques that should be taught at each skill level. Professional credentialing provided coaches with validity and established All Star cheer as a professional career.

SANCTIONING STANDARDS: The sanctioning committee was created to implement standards for event producers to promote continuity across events and maintain safety standards. In addition, the USASF began providing official legal training. Shortly after, legal officials were required at every USASF sanctioned event to help enforce the rules and relieve event producers of that burden. This unique official legal standard is found only at USASF sanctioned events.

REGIONAL & NATIONAL MEETINGS: The USASF began offering regional meetings to provide training and discussion for gym owners and coaches to continue elevating the sport. Regional meetings also provided an opportunity for regional advisory boards to meet and discuss what was happening in their respective regions, thus giving more voice to the members. The regional meetings morphed into one large national meeting in 2021, which amplified the training and discussion available to members.

ATHLETE RESOURCES: USASF athlete membership provides athletes with exclusive resources and opportunities designed to help elevate their performance, both on and off the floor. USASF athlete opportunities include the following:

- *Leadership:* The USASF began Core Leadership Workshops that equip athletes with the skills to navigate everyday challenges, boosting their confidence to practice effective leadership styles, enhance communication, make informed decisions, manage conflict, and participate successfully in teams.

- *Exceptional Athletes:* USASF's CheerABILITIES and DanceABILITIES teams provide exceptional athletes with opportunities for exercise that enhance flexibility and strength, build independence and self-confidence, promote positive social interaction, and foster peer support among families.

- *Athlete Age Verification:* One of the cornerstones of fair play in All Star cheerleading and dance is adherence to age requirements. USASF uses age grids and a unique rostering system to verify that an athlete is placed on a team corresponding to their age. This approach helps keep competitions evenly matched, preventing any advantages that could arise from age discrepancies.

- *College Scholarships:* The USASF Scholarship Program awards college scholarships to outstanding member athletes, including exceptional high school athletes who are graduating seniors. Applications are open to member athletes pursuing higher education at accredited schools. Applicants must be active with a USASF member club but are not required to continue cheerleading or dancing in college. To date, the USASF has awarded approximately $1.5 million dollars to more than 300 athletes.

- *Athlete Protection:* The USASF is dedicated to fostering safe and positive environments for our athletes' physical, emotional, and social development, free from abuse and misconduct. We implement policies to address specific types of abuse and misconduct as well as practices aimed at reducing, monitoring, and governing areas where potential issues may arise.

MEMBER RESOURCES: USASF member clubs have the unique ability to elevate All Star in extraordinary ways by leveraging the expertise and resources of their network of regional directors, rules officials, and fellow members. Membership gives athletes access to the highest performance standards in All Star. Club Benefits include the following:

- Access to USASF sanctioned competitions

- Access to competitions offering bids to The Cheerleading Worlds and The Dance Worlds

- Inclusion in the USASF Club Finder

- Enrollment in the USASF Member Perks Program

- Membership in the nation's largest network of All Star club owners, coaches, event producers, and the companies that serve them

- Peer mentoring provided by Connection Leaders

- Growth and Business Builders, such as FUNdamentals and NoviceSELECT programs, to increase athlete membership

- Opportunity to contribute to the safety, integrity, and growth of All Star through committees, polls, and attendance at the national convention and regional assemblies

- Access to the Gym Insurance Program

- Weekly newsletter *2.30* with the latest All Star news

- Support from USASF Regional Directors for onboarding and support

THE USASF TODAY

The USASF remains the premier membership organization for gyms that prioritize standards in All Star and that seek a collective voice to enhance the sport.

Upon Jim Chadwick's retirement in 2021, his position as president was divided into two roles. He was in charge of both day-to-day operations and served as chairman of the board. Ali Stangle was appointed interim executive director before being named to the post permanently. Kathy Penree became chairman of the board.

Ali oversaw USASF day-to-day operations while Kathy handled the duties outlined in the bylaws for president and chairman of the board. Kathy's most significant contribution before her passing was restructuring the bylaws and board seats. Her work continues through Nicole Leago Devall, the current chairman of the board Ali Stangle, the executive director, and the USASF board members.

The original USASF Board structure included representatives from independently owned event producers. Many of those independent companies were purchased by Varsity, leading to a concentration in control. Every board member had lifetime seats with limited representation from gym owners and coaches. There were board seats for gym owners and coach advisory board seats, but those seats didn't include voting privileges. Kathy spent most of her time evaluating the bylaws, including how they could be restructured to improve the sport.

She began her mission in 2020 with the goal to diversify the board. By December of 2023 many changes already had been implemented and officially written into the new bylaws. At the time of this writing, the new structure offers seven seats with voting privileges to gym owners and coach members. No single brand will control more than three seats. There is an automatic seat for the Connection Leader chair, which also includes voting privileges. This change in structure gives gym owners and coaches the opportunity to vote for the first time.

In addition, there are several nonvoting advisory seats. There can be up to three unaffiliated directors, one former All Star athlete, and up to five at-large members. It is exciting to see the opportunity for an athlete to have a voice on the board for the first time.

Term limits also have been established. Most seats are limited to a two-year term with a maximum of three consecutive terms. In addition, the chairman of the board and the vice chairman cannot be from the same member category. The USASF, at Kathy Penree's direction, has gone to great lengths to ensure that everyone has a voice in leading All Star. "All discussions originate from committee input based on member feedback," Nicole Leago Devall said.

Members can email the board with concerns, and those concerns are discussed. Decisions are not made in isolation but based on membership input from across the country. Nicole had a great way of describing the decision structure: "The chairman, together with fellow board leaders, help steer the bus that is the USASF. The board serves as the steering wheel, the staff is the engine that keeps it running, and the membership provides the roadmap that guides the journey."

The USASF is committed to its current leadership initiatives: growth of the sport, fair play, and safety and guidelines. The growth of the sport across all facets is important. Every member of the USASF benefits when the sport is growing. Fair play for everyone not only ensures that athletes compete in the appropriate age groups and skill levels, but it continues to further legitimize All Star. Without fair play you don't have a legitimate sport. Last, a focus on proper progressions and protecting athletes' well-being is part of the safety and guidelines initiative.

For over two decades, many cheer and dance professionals have worked tirelessly to create the USASF from the ground up. The All Star community was hungry for unity, leadership, and direction. Many great strides have been made in those areas, and as the sport grows and evolves, we need to evolve with it. I believe we will continue to work together to do what is best for every All Star cheerleader and dancer who participates in our sport.

> "To support and enrich the lives of our All Star athletes and members." – USASF

There are many individuals who have poured their heart, soul, and passion into creating various aspects of the USASF to improve the sport and create incredible experiences for All Star. Thank you to the Connection Leaders, Regional Advisory Board, National Advisory Board, Rules Committee, Sanctioning Committee, Worlds Advisory Board, Exceptional Athlete Committee, Dance Advisory Board, Compliance Committee, DEIS Committee, and Athlete Advisory Council. Here are past and present staff and board members:

Amy Clark
Steve Peterson
Ali Stangle
Glenda Broderick
Angela Bruno
Andre Carter
Renee Dew
Gena Evans
Dana Fielding
Robin Galik
Kinshasa Garrett
Aricka Gates
Shauna Holm
Sarah Miller Bate
Cheryl Paquette

Christina Boulding
Damianne Albee
Catherine Calloway
Dori Dunster
Becky Herrera
Happy Hooper
Nicole Lauchaire
Ann Lehrmann
Anastasia Miller Burns
Jason Peetz
Tara Rall
Marti Reed
Kristen Rosario
Linsday Stephens,
Tammy Van Vleet

Tyler Phillips
Heather Toper
Meredith Walker

Robin Coe
Nicole Leago-Devall
Casey Winn Roadan

Past USASF employees and board members:

Jim Chadwick
Karen Wilson
Mary Wendt
Lynn Singer
Les Stella
Jeff Fowlkes
John Newby
Justin Carrier
Morton Bergue
Kathy Penree
Elaine Pascale
Joelle Antico
Debbie Love
Nicole Graham

Tegan Reeves
Jody Melton
Brad Habermel
Mack Hirshberg
Mike Burgess
Melanie Berry
Catherine Morris
Brian Elza
Dan Kessler
Roger Schonder
Cole Stott
Tina Galdieri
Brad Habermel
Peter Lezin
Carlos Onofre

Up next are some fun get-to-know-them facts about a few of the USASF's longest-serving team members.

"Dream big, work hard, stay focused, and surround yourself with good people." – Chrystal Evans Hurst

STEVE PETERSON

Vice President, Events and Corporate Alliance – USASF

EARNED WISDOM

* **Success:** Success is the constant striving to improve on the things you're responsible for.

* **Gratitude:** Steve is grateful to Lance and Carol Wagers, who were instrumental in his early development in the spirit industry and the founding of All Star, and to Jim Chadwick, who brought him into the USASF.

* **Steve's Wish:** Steve wishes everyone in All Star could work together again toward the same goals.

* **Mistakes:** The year at Worlds when the dew settled on the competition floor at the Wide World of Sports baseball stadium.

* **For Gym Owners:** Stay true to who you are and don't try to be like another owner or club.

- ★ **For Coaches:** Learn from the experts, your owners, and training courses.

DID YOU KNOW?

- ★ Steve loves golf, traveling, and snow skiing.

- ★ His favorite superhero is Batman.

- ★ He chose the dog as his animal because it is noble, faithful, loyal, protective, obedient and has excellent sensory perception.

> "Most folks are as happy as they make up their minds to be." – Abraham Lincoln

AMY CLARK
Vice President, Membership – USASF

EARNED WISDOM

★ **Success:** Success is the ability to spend time with your family.

★ **Amy's Wish:** That there would be one national championship, and the winners would go to the World Championships.

★ **To My Younger Self:** It's only cheerleading. It'll be here for you tomorrow and the day after that, but your kids are only two years old once.

★ **For Gym Owners:** Know what you're getting into. Understand the responsibilities that come with gym ownership and the sacrifices required to be a successful gym owner.

★ **For Coaches:** Once it comes out of your mouth, you can't take it back. Be careful with your words. They can crush the souls of children.

DID YOU KNOW?

★   Amy's favorite part of cheer is the combination of athleticism and artistry.

★   Amy used to be a pretty mean baton twirler.

★   She is a former gym owner and event producer.

★   When Amy's son was little, she took him to see WWE, and she loved it, partly because she loved watching her son experience it.

★   Amy's favorite superhero is Wonder Woman.

★   Amy chose the giraffe as her animal because it symbolizes vision and foresight. Its spiritual energy encourages us to look beyond immediate challenges and limitations, guiding us to embrace a broader view of the world.

"Well-behaved women rarely make history." – Laurel Thatcher Ulrich

MEREDITH WALKER
Director of Conduct and Compliance – USASF

EARNED WISDOM

★ **Success:** Success is having a positive impact on others. It's a rising-tide- lifts-all-ships mentality. Success is elevating everyone.

★ **Meredith's Wish:** That the sport's image could move away from so much glitz and pageantry.

★ **For Gym Owners:** Find a mentor. Befriend someone who has been there before and learn from them.

★ **For Coaches:** Educate yourself. To be a quality coach, you must be skilled in your craft. Remember why you're coaching.

DID YOU KNOW?

★ Meredith used to work in prisons. Her first job was as a researcher for the National Institutes of Health and Corrections. She would visit five prisons weekly and survey the inmates.

- ★ She traveled abroad by herself for the first time when she was fourteen.

- ★ Meredith's favorite rapper is Eazy-E.

- ★ Meredith loved Wonder Woman as a kid, but as an adult, Iron Man is her favorite superhero.

- ★ The hummingbird represents timelessness, healing, warrior energy, vitality, infinity, messenger qualities, affection, and playfulness.

"To be yourself in a world that is constantly trying to make you something else is the greatest accomplishment." – Ralph Waldo Emerson

HEIDI WEBER

American Spirit and Cheer Essentials (ASCE) – 2012
Celebrity – 2017
Open Championship Series (OCS) – 2019
Allstar World Championship – 2021

BREAKING INTO THE ECHO CHAMBER

While many All Star cheer pioneers began their journeys in the industry's early days, Heidi Weber's story offers a different perspective. She was a late arrival whose outsider status ultimately became her greatest strength. "I didn't get into All Star until 2012," Heidi said. "I had been really heavy in the scholastic side of cheer."

Her relatively late entry into All Star cheer came after Heidi had already established herself in the scholastic realm, having coached high school and middle school teams for nearly a decade. Growing up in San Marcos, California—ironically, the birthplace of California All Stars, one of the country's largest All Star programs—

Heidi cheered on a competitive high school team in the mid-1990s, but her path initially led elsewhere. "I literally stayed in what I would call a vacuum or an echo chamber in the scholastic side of things," she said, "with really no interaction on the All Star side at all for many years."

After moving to Oklahoma in 2001, Heidi started coaching scholastic cheer. Then a friend who coached a local high school team invited her to help at an All Star gym. The program was small with only about sixty athletes, and Heidi's involvement was initially limited because she was also running an apparel company. "I had already coached for a decade," she said. "I really wasn't interested in being fully immersed in All Star at that time."

Her apparel business, American Spirit and Cheer Essentials, became her key connection to the All Star world. While crafting practice wear and competition cover-ups for All Star teams, she quickly grew her industry network. The more competitions she attended, the more connections she forged, and the greater the demand for T-shirts. The USASF mandated that athletes must be covered when not competing, "So we were making crazy amounts of T-shirts," she recalled.

Her growing connection to the All Star community came with a distinct advantage: Heidi wasn't burdened by the industry's complex history of relationships and allegiances. "Entering the world of All Star later served me well for my position now because I didn't have any of that [baggage]," she explained. "There was no one I was tied to, because I didn't know who anybody was."

According to Heidi, her outsider perspective proved invaluable as she eventually stepped into a leadership role that required neutrality and fresh thinking.

FROM T-SHIRTS TO EVENT PRODUCTION

As Heidi's apparel business thrived, she began hearing a consistent request from her All Star customers: "We need more events." Responding to the demand, Heidi's company organized a school cheerleading competition. The success of her initial venture led to an expansion into All Star events, ultimately creating a separate brand called Celebrity. "My first real big season with Celebrity, we went from having one event in Tulsa to six," Heidi said. "You could imagine there were lots of learning curves and a lot of—we'll call them training failures—on the fly."

Despite the growing pains, Celebrity Competitions continued to grow. By 2017 it had evolved from a single local event into a significant presence in the competitive landscape. Heidi's true immersion into the broader All Star community came when she was invited to attend the Independent Event Producers (IEP) annual meeting in Las Vegas. Though she was organizing more events than some other attendees, she describes herself as "by far the greenest of all the EPs [Event Producers] that were there."

That meeting highlighted her outsider status in both amusing and advantageous ways. She recalls sitting at a hotel bar next to a man who introduced himself simply as "Eddie." Unaware she was speaking to Eddie Rios, renowned coach of Smoed California All Stars and a reality TV personality, Heidi's lack of recognition left him visibly confused and slightly annoyed. But for her, such moments were common. While occasionally awkward, her detachment from the industry's established social hierarchy would prove to be an asset.

LISTENING TO THE INDUSTRY'S NEEDS

As Heidi became more involved in event production, she stepped into a leadership position with the IEP, which was evolving into the Cheer and Dance Industry Professionals (CDIP). "The IEP was kind of becoming stagnant," she said, "so I pushed for the CDIP. When I joined the IEP there were very few people left. I think we were down to maybe twenty members."

Under Heidi's leadership as vice chair, the organization made a pivotal decision to become more inclusive and welcome all event producers. That change caused some longtime members to leave, but the strategy ultimately succeeded. The CDIP grew to fifty-six members. Through her growing connections, Heidi heard about the challenges facing the industry, and two issues repeatedly surfaced: affordability and predictability.

"The number one thing people were constantly talking to me about was they couldn't afford to continue the path they had chosen," she said. "We had all entered into this world where everything had become very bid-driven."

The bid-driven system—where teams battled all season for championship bids—was straining gym owners financially. The most successful programs were no exception. "Even the biggest brands in the industry were saying they couldn't charge one more cent," Heidi said, "or they were going to start losing athletes."

The second major concern was predictability. Gym owners found it difficult to plan their businesses when they couldn't guarantee which championship events they would attend at the end of the season.

"How am I supposed make a successful schedule when I don't know where my bid is going to come from? I have to, maybe, add another event? If I don't get the bid, how do I end my season?" Heidi felt those challenges were threatening the industry's sustainability.

THE OPEN: A DIFFERENT APPROACH

With those issues in mind, Heidi collaborated with three other event producers to create a different kind of end-of-season event, one that didn't require qualifying bids to attend. "We put this event in Universal Orlando," Heidi said. We called it 'The Open' specifically because you didn't need a bid."

The Open debuted in 2018 with fewer than one hundred teams participating. By 2019 it had expanded to a full series of events with ambitious plans to address the industry's pain points. "We had these great marketing pieces," Heidi said. "We had this really funny whiteboard cartoon commercial that we created. Gyms could choose where they wanted to go, plan their season, and save money. All the pain points were removed."

The series offered eight locations, each with unique attractions, as Heidi noted: "Do you want to go to Chicago and have an art and shopping experience? Do you want to go to a theme park? Do you want to go to the beach?"

Her marketing approach, inspired by the viral campaign for the infamous Fyre Festival, created buzz throughout the industry. But a curious thing happened. Despite the enthusiasm and the market research suggesting that gym owners wanted an alternative to the bid system, actual commitments fell short of expectations. "Ultimately," Heidi said, "what gym owners said they wanted and what they actually wanted were not the same thing."

Before Heidi could fully evaluate The Open's impact, the COVID-19 pandemic hit in early 2020, forcing the cancelation of all cheerleading events and putting the initiative on hold.

THE ALLSTAR WORLD CHAMPIONSHIP (ASWC)

As the cheerleading industry cautiously resumed activities in 2021, Heidi and her colleagues recognized they needed to adjust their approach. Despite the theoretical appeal of no-bid events, the market response made one thing clear: The prestige and motivation created by earning bids remained powerfully attractive to gym owners, coaches, and athletes. "Prior to the shutdown of COVID," Heidi said, "we weren't seeing the numbers come in the way we thought we would for those open events that people had so badly desired."

Event producer David Owens approached the group with a pivotal suggestion: "We are going to have to do a bid event. People want the bids." That reality led to the challenging question of whether they could create a bid event without repeating the problems they had set out to solve. They sat down and discussed how they could host a bid event without compromising the integrity of the bid.

The group knew they could only avoid most of the issues because, at the end of the day, they basically ended up starting a new bid-giving event. "But we can do better," Heidi said, "in trying to attack pain points that people have complained about."

In the summer of 2020 they announced the creation of the Allstar World Championship that would debut in 2021. The timing proved to be advantageous in unexpected ways. While the ongoing pandemic created severe limitations for established events, particularly those held at theme parks or corporate venues, Heidi's group was able to design its new championship with COVID restrictions in mind. The event was held at the Orange County Convention Center in Orlando, a venue with fewer restrictions than many other venues had.

In addition, their flexibility allowed them to accommodate more spectators than other championships could at the time. They even created a showcase opportunity for teams attending the USASF World Championship, which was limited in terms of how many supporters could watch each team compete. "We opened a showcase for USASF Worlds teams because Disney wouldn't allow more than 300 people in the entire facility," Heidi said. "With staff, judges, and teams, that's very few spectators."

While this appeared altruistic, it also served a strategic purpose. "We wanted them to see what others were capable of doing," Heidi said. The strategy worked remarkably well. In its second year, the Allstar World Championship experienced explosive growth, expanding from 425 teams in year one to 1,240 teams in year two. "It was like drinking out of a fire hose," Heidi said. "I may or may not have cried under a bleacher at some point." Today, the ASW team boasts over 1,600 members.

CREATING HEALTHY COMPETITION

Throughout her journey in All Star cheer, Heidi has maintained that competition within the industry—not just between teams on the floor but also between event producers and championship organizers—ultimately benefits everyone. "Creating this new option in the market is good for the consumer," she said. "You want there to be options. When you don't have anyone who is a viable advocate for a large stakeholder or a significant market share, you will not see continued benefits for the consumer."

Heidi believes the competition has already led to improvements in how events treat coaches and provide value to their customers. While Heidi advocates for options in the marketplace, she acknowledges the challenge her team has created for gym owners who must navigate different rules and scoring systems.

But Heidi sees promising signs in the way gyms are beginning to diversify their competitive paths with some programs now splitting teams between different championship tracks based on each team's unique strengths and goals. This move away from the long-standing one-size-fits-all approach in All Star cheer reflects Heidi's core philosophy: "Embrace evolution and change, because it's coming whether you like it or not. It doesn't have to mean anything bad."

She also challenges the industry's tendency toward groupthink: "It's very interesting that cheerleaders have the word 'leader' in their name and struggle with leadership and [avoiding] groupthink." Despite the challenges, Heidi remains optimistic about All Star cheer's future, particularly if the industry can separate the pursuit of competitive success from business success.

Perhaps most important, Heidi sees herself not as the originator of ideas but as a catalyst who helps bring the industry's collective wisdom to life. "So many of the things we've done, which I feel I've spearheaded, are not my ideas. They come from the industry's voice. I just was the catalyst to allow them to be okay," she said. "If you're not changing, you're dying. We have to reach a point as a group where we can accept that and be a part of the evolution."

In an industry often marked by fierce loyalty to traditions and established hierarchies, Heidi Weber took a stand as the voice of evolution. She tries to remind All Star cheerleaders that growth requires not just perfecting the same routines but also daring to choreograph entirely new ones. She has dubbed herself, "The Agent of Change."

> **"Success is seeing a dream and running toward it." – Heidi Weber**

EARNED WISDOM

★ **Success:** Seeing a dream and running toward it, accepting all the steps along the way, and then arriving at your destination no matter how long or what the journey looked like.

★ **Wisdom:** Embrace that being different can be the best thing to be.

★ **Mistakes:** Believing that people want solutions to the problems they communicate. Sometimes, people don't know what they want or aren't willing to change in order to seize the opportunity to get what they're asking for.

★ **For Gym Owners:** Forge your own path and choose to view your business as a legitimate enterprise. Create an environment where profit is a part of every equation.

★ **For Coaches:** Lean into your passion but remember that the human element is what makes you great, not banners or trophies. Wins last for a moment, but they don't always equate to success.

★ **Lessons Learned:** This whole thing isn't really about cheerleading, it's about giving people permission to be free to chase whatever they believe makes them great.

DID YOU KNOW?

★ Heidi's favorite part of cheer is stunting.

★ She graduated from high school at sixteen during her sophomore year.

★ Two of her four children are adopted.

★ Heidi doesn't like milk, sour cream, cottage cheese, mayonnaise, or any other white foods.

★ Her favorite superhero is Katniss Everdeen (*The Hunger Games*).

★ The hummingbird, her animal, represents a messenger, timelessness, healing, warrior spirit, energy, vitality, infinity, affection, and playfulness.

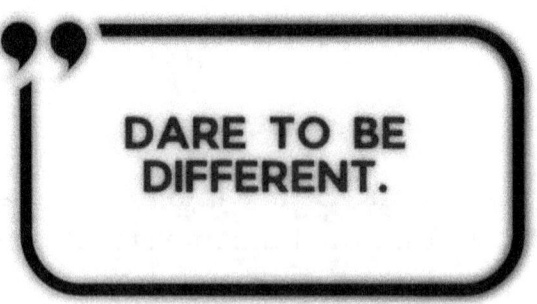

DARE TO BE DIFFERENT.

"Just another day in paradise." – Phil Collins

CATHRYN "Cat" WEEDEN

LUXE Athletics – 2014
Small Gym Association – 2018

FINDING A COLLECTIVE VOICE

In the sprawling landscape of All Star cheer, the story of the industry's evolution is often told through the lens of its largest programs, the pioneer gyms that defined All Star cheer and turned it into a global phenomenon. But in a small corner of Tulsa, Oklahoma, Cat Weeden was quietly sparking a revolution that would transform how newer, smaller cheer programs across the country operated, competed, and survived. "I didn't go into it hoping to create this leadership role for myself," Cat reflected. "I didn't go into it actually thinking we would change the landscape of All Star for small gyms."

What started as a simple effort to connect like-minded gym owners would reshape the cheerleading industry, empowering small programs that had long felt invisible in decision-making.

FINDING HER PLACE IN CHEER

Cat Weeden's rise as a small gym advocate was built on years immersed in cheer, starting far from the sport's epicenter. After moving from Oklahoma to Minnesota to North Carolina, she finally discovered cheerleading through her older sister's success on the high school team when the family moved to Michigan before Cat's eighth-grade year. Cat tried out for the school team, clueless that Michigan's cheer scene was, as she puts it, "seven or eight years behind" the rest of the country. "We didn't know that high school cheer in Michigan was completely different than any other state."

Despite that situation, she quickly excelled and felt a strong pull, not only to performing but also to the sport's creative side. Cat became obsessed with how teams were put together and how routines were designed.

Her first exposure to All Star cheer came when her high school coach received an email blast about forming an All Star team. Hundreds of kids across the state came to try out for this one team. Called Cheer! Michigan All Stars, the team practiced once a week and competed in national events, including AmeriCheer Nationals in Orlando, Florida.

It was at one such competition that Cat experienced a revelation that would shape her career. "I had never seen a double down in real life," she said. "I had never seen kids my age throwing double fulls." And Cat was captivated. She begged her parents to buy $300 worth of Mr. Video VCR tapes. (For the younger folks reading this, Mr. Video was how people watched teams back in the day. If you wanted to see another team's routine, you had to purchase the division from Mr. Video.)

Those videos became her education in elite cheer. She studied routines from Georgia All Stars, Pol County Allstars, Miami Elite, and other leading programs, and then she began incorporating elements into the eighth-grade team she was helping coach. That early experience foreshadowed what would become a hallmark of Cat's approach. Through exposure and continuous learning, anyone can develop and teach skills to anyone willing to learn.

FROM MICHIGAN TO OKLAHOMA

After high school, Cat returned to her family's roots in Oklahoma to attend the University of Oklahoma in Norman. Though she initially tried out for the OU cheer team without success, she quickly found her way into the All Star scene. As fate would have it, Cat sat next to an All Star cheerleader from the Oklahoma Twisters in her first class at OU.

What began as participation on an open All Star team quickly evolved into a coaching position. Oklahoma Twisters served as Cat's training ground for All Star coaching and directing from 2002 to 2008. She absorbed everything she could about the emerging All Star industry. This was also the start of Cat's judging career. From 2004-2014 she served as a safety, legalities, and panel judge throughout the country. "I'm a rule follower," Cat emphasized. "I do not live in the gray. I'm so black and white." This trait served her well as All Star cheerleading began to formalize its structure. "As the rules were emerging, I became obsessed with them. And I became obsessed with learning and watching videos."

With Oklahoma Twisters she gained valuable insights into program management, and the gym's philosophy of balancing cheerleading with other aspects of athletes' lives made a lasting impression. Oklahoma Twisters practiced only one day a week while most All Star programs practiced two or three days a week. The gym owners said they wanted their athletes to have time to play other sports. Such an approach to All Star cheer—viewing it as one part of a balanced childhood rather than an all-consuming commitment—would influence Cat's later philosophy as a gym owner. By the end of undergrad, Cat had cheered and competed with the University of Oklahoma All-girl, two seasons on Cheer Athletics FierceKatz, and Oklahoma Twisters Open teams. Through those experiences she learned invaluable lessons about coaching, choreography, and judging.

BUILDING LUXE

After graduating from OU with a degree in psychology after switching from international business, Cat moved to Tulsa with the man she would marry who had accepted a position with the Tulsa Police Department. After the move she completed the OU-Tulsa master's program in human relations.

In Tulsa, Cat's cheerleading career continued with coaching positions at a local gym and Tulsa Union High School where she remained the head coach for ten years. Eventually, she became the All Star director at a program called X Athletics where she spent five years developing her approach to program management.

But X Athletics faced some limitations. Located in a small town, the program struggled to advance beyond levels three or four as its more talented athletes often left for larger programs and more opportunities. Cat identified a solution. She suggested merging with a similarly sized program that had different strengths. "We had this really great coaching staff, but our kids needed more friends with stronger skills and a more competitive nature," she said. "If we put the programs together, we can probably create something really cool."

The merger was approved, and Cat was tasked with creating a new brand. Her approach to naming the program reflected her practical mindset. After watching countless hours of Mr. Video footage, she noticed one gym that appeared repeatedly, GymTyme in Louisville. "Whatever the name is," she said, "I want the L." She also knew she wanted something concise, something that would look good on uniforms and create a strong, distinctive identity.

The name "LUXE" came to her during a meal in Dallas during NCA Nationals. She sat down to eat, opened the menu, and noticed the words "Grand Lux Café." She said, "I looked at the two owners, my coach, and my tumbling director, and I said, 'Lux—that's it.'"

The choice of colors was equally pragmatic. The two merging programs had been red and blue, respectively, and neither wanted to adopt the other's color scheme. Since red and blue make purple, Cat proposed that the newly formed LUXE adopt purple as its primary color. To create a more distinctive identity, she added black to the mix, pointing out that most programs used combinations like blue and black, white and red, or black and white.

After five years as an All Star director, Cat had the opportunity to buy into ownership. But when negotiations didn't go as planned, she and her husband decided to open their own gym. In the end, the existing owners agreed to sell Cat the LUXE name, allowing for continuity for the athletes and their families. In 2016 Cat became the sole owner of LUXE, which is now operating according to her vision of what an All Star program should be. But her impact on the industry was about to expand far beyond the walls of her gym.

SMALL GYM ASSOCIATION

Around 2014 Cat noticed troubling trends in the All Star cheer industry. Policy decisions were being made that appeared to disproportionately affect smaller programs like hers. The problem wasn't necessarily malicious intent but rather a lack of diverse perspectives in the decision-making process. "The big gyms, the twelve most established gyms, they're the gyms that have been around the longest. They've earned the right to be the pinnacles of All Star because they're the strongest," Cat said. "The good thing about them was that, regardless of competitive rivalry, they communicated and worked together to move the industry forward in what they believed was in the best interests of All Star cheer."

But Cat believed that what was in the best interests of All Star cheer needed to include gyms of all sizes. At a competition Cat discussed her concerns with Angela Deacon, an owner of a small gym in Texas. Cat asked if she saw the email about a newly released change. Cat said, "I think it's really going to hurt programs our size." When Angela expressed doubt that their voices would be heard, Cat suggested gathering five or six gym owners who felt the same way and sending a group email. But first, they decided on another simple approach. They created a Facebook group called the Small Cheer Gym Association to connect small gym owners who held similar concerns. "It was such an accident," Cat admitted. "It was literally just intended to link us together. We wanted to help all the small gyms be able to connect with each other and get off our own islands."

What they discovered surprised them. The biggest issue facing small gyms wasn't external. It was their own isolation. "The biggest disenfranchisement of the small gyms we were doing to ourselves," Cat said, "because we were not participating in surveys, we were not participating in these town halls and think tanks." Often, small gym owners worked a nine-to-five career outside the gym, so it wasn't easy for them to participate in the think tanks and surveys. The association helped to catch everyone up and get them engaged.

Then their first email campaign was launched. It was modest with about twenty gym owners signing onto a thoughtfully worded message expressing concerns about a proposed policy change. Cat included a powerful metaphor that would become the association's unofficial slogan: "If the All Star cheer we see on TV is the tree, we are the roots. We are where it starts. Without us, the tree and the fruit die."

The response was immediate. "We got a conversation to happen, and by the end of that week we had a hundred owners from small gyms in the group."

When their concerns were addressed and the policy change was halted, Cat realized the power they had unlocked: The power of the small gyms lies in the collective. News spread quickly among owners of small gyms when they met at competitions. Many owners approached Cat and Angela to inquire about how they could join the group.

UNEXPECTED LEADERSHIP

As the Small Cheer Gym Association grew, eventually reaching thousands of members, it transformed from a simple communication channel into a powerful advocacy group. Cat found herself unexpectedly thrust into a leadership role. The small gyms finally felt like they had a voice, thanks to Cat and Angela's efforts and those of Tabbi McCallister, who joined them in leading the charge. But the newfound influence didn't come without challenges.

"It put us on a pedestal among small gym owners but also put us in the middle of the firing range," Cat said. "There were a couple of years that were really bad, to be honest. It was really hard. I felt like we were fighting the good fight, but large gym owners and people in power were really angry with us."

First, the association had to navigate complex definitions of what constituted a "small gym." Initially defined as programs with no more than seventy-five athletes, the threshold later expanded to 125.

Members could choose independent event producers or Varsity events. "We didn't care if you competed in Rec, D1, or D2," Cat said. "If they felt like they fit the mold, come on in." This approach sometimes created tension with midsized programs or small locations that were part of larger organizations because they didn't allow franchises to classify as small gyms even if specific locations met the small gym criteria.

The association's advocacy efforts evolved from being reactive to being proactive. When emails alone proved insufficient, they developed more sophisticated strategies. In one instance, the group asked members to contact their Varsity representatives and inform them that they would drop one competition from their schedule and not order practice wear if certain policies weren't reconsidered. "They [owners of small gyms] wanted to speak with our money and commitment," Cat said. "While one small gym making this decision wouldn't change anything, a couple hundred small gyms would send ripples. We were not asking for 'our way,' we were asking to be a part of the discussion at its root. We wanted the event producers and other companies to consider how each decision would affect small gyms. We wanted a seat at the table, and we got it."

Perhaps the most significant test of the Small Gym Association's impact came during the COVID-19 pandemic. In July 2020, as gyms were beginning to reopen, Cat posted a reflection to the group: "If this pandemic would've happened four years earlier, 50 percent of us would've closed. But we had figured out how to stabilize ourselves." The network of small gym owners that formed through the association became a lifeline during the crisis. The small gym's page blew up during the pandemic because they had no option but to work together to survive. "We fortified and strengthened each other during that time," Cat said.

What began as an effort to ensure that small gyms had a voice in policy decisions has evolved into something much more profound. The effort built a community that shared resources, strategies, and emotional support during the industry's most challenging period. And as it continues to grow, its goals grow as well. The association was on the ground floor in keeping strong parameters to qualify for DII, and it advocated for the creation of Limited Worlds divisions. It also created a network that provided owners of small gyms access to top choreographers, music producers, and industry vendors.

Looking back on her contributions to All Star, Cat was modest yet proud when she said, "I think I'm just a part of the next wave. I'm never going to be a part of the original legends in this industry. Their impact, or infamy, will go on forever. I hope that I become part of the next generation of leadership and the next generation of people that, hopefully, are not selfish, people who will pursue what keeps all gyms moving forward. The small gyms needed a voice, and I am proud to have stepped into that role for our community."

The Small Cheer Gym Association continues to provide support and a voice to small gyms. The association ensures that small gyms are part of the decision-making process. Cat still owns and operates LUXE in Tulsa, balancing her advocacy work with the daily challenges of running a successful All Star program while also being a wife to Andrew and a mom to Mayson and Brynn.

Cat Weeden has ensured that the thousands of small gyms that introduce athletes to the sport and nurture their early development remain strong and resilient. By recognizing the collective power of small gyms and creating mechanisms for them to communicate and advocate for themselves, Cat has ensured that decisions about the sport's future reflect the needs and perspectives of the entire industry, not just its largest and most visible members.

> **"Success is being better today than you were yesterday." – Cat Weeden**

EARNED WISDOM

★ **Success:** Are you a small percentage better today than you were yesterday? That's success. Whether it's your attitude, your temperament, your ability to listen, or your relationships, if you've improved, then you have been successful.

★ **Wisdom:** Acknowledge who you are. Cat said, "I can be direct and harsh, especially when I am locked in on something. People don't always like that. But I feel that the stakes are high for small gyms, so leading with passion and heart is what I've always done."

★ **Gratitude:** Cat credits her mother, Jennifer Flack, with having a significant impact on her. Jennifer is a strong, intelligent woman, and that is how Cat was raised. Cat's father, Dr. John Flack, has spent his life serving and studying underrepresented communities in health care. Cat also credits Craig Hallmark and Jeff LeForce, her bosses from Oklahoma Twisters, for their help. She also admires Ali Stangle for her ability to lead with empathy and compassion.

★ **Cat's Wish:** Cat wishes that the All Star community would continue to make lanes, create seats at the table, and make policies that help gyms of all sizes flourish. She believes creating paths for all gyms to maintain their athletes at the highest levels of our sport is the best way to fortify the future of All Star cheer.

★ **Mistakes:** Allowing people to believe that she is anti-large gym or anti-franchise. She is an advocate for small gyms; that doesn't mean she doesn't like large gyms.

★ **For Gym Owners:** Start small with what you need. Don't put yourself in debt to get started. Build a community around you and befriend other gym owners. Become an effective communicator and establish boundaries.

★ **For Coaches:** To be good at All Star cheer you have to become obsessed with it. You need to learn and adjust, because All Star is constantly changing. Be confident in what you do, but never stop learning.

DID YOU KNOW?

★ The moment the pyramid dismounts and the team has hit its routine is Cat's favorite.

★ Cat is one of five girls, and her four sisters also have names that begin with C.

★ Reading is one of her favorite activities, so she doesn't sleep much because she reads before bed. If she's ever looking down at her phone for more than two minutes, it's because she's reading.

★ She is obsessed with confetti. She keeps confetti from every event and frames it in a shadow box in her office.

★ Cat chose the fly as her animal because it symbolizes the importance of swift action and decision-making as well as the value of being nimble and responsive. She recalled a time when she was referred to as a fly. She took that and used it to empower her and hasn't looked back.

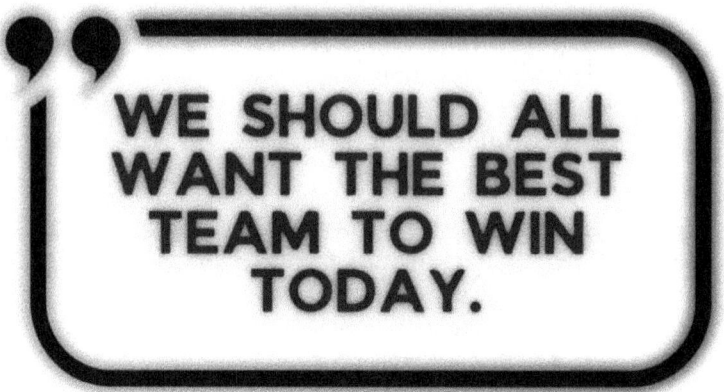

"You're always in one of three places of life: You're headed into the storm, you're in the middle of the storm, or you're coming out of the storm." – A proverb

BROOKE PLACK
Empire Cheerleading – 2014

FROM GARAGE TO EMPIRE

Many people meticulously plan for years before launching a business. Others find themselves swept along an entrepreneurial path by a series of seemingly small decisions. Brooke Plack was a public school teacher, single and broke, so her dreams of a Jamaican vacation seemed out of reach . . . until she tapped into a skill from her past: cheer. And that's when her journey to gym ownership began.

Unlike many gym owners of the previous generation who entered All Star cheer as adults, Brooke grew up in the sport during its formative years. "I cheered back when it was Intermediate, Advanced—throw what you can and don't die," she laughed, recalling the early competitive structure of the late 1990s.

As an athlete for Cheer Central, Brooke was part of a pioneering program that helped shape competitive All Star cheer. Cheer Central participated in the Junior

Olympics when cheer was first included at that level. After her time in All Star cheer, Brooke went on to cheer for the University of Arkansas Razorbacks from 2003 to 2007, gaining experience in both All Star and collegiate cheer.

Her background would prove invaluable, though she was unaware of that as she taught private cheer lessons in living rooms and front yards to fund her Jamaican vacation.

THE GARAGE

In December 2013, with $250 saved from teaching those private lessons, Brooke bought a 5-foot by 10-foot red mat from EasyFlex.com and placed it in her garage. To combat the winter chill, she borrowed an open-flame propane heater from her father, connected it to her grill's gas tank, and continued teaching after school each day. Parents would bring their camping chairs and observe while Brooke taught lessons in that garage. Before long, she was teaching Monday through Friday, 4:30 p.m. to 8:30 p.m. One day Brooke told her dad, "I'm onto something here."

The demand for her instruction grew quickly. In January 2014 she began renting space at a local fitness gym to host Saturday clinics. The response was overwhelming. Her clinics sold out with thirty kids each. By March, when she opened for regular weekly classes, 103 kids had signed up before she taught her first session. But her early success also created an immediate challenge. The fitness studio asked her to leave after just two weeks due to the crowds and parking issues. With only six weeks to find a new home for her rapidly growing business, Brooke had to act quickly.

Her resourcefulness showcased the ingenuity essential for gym owners to thrive in the early days. Between classes at the fitness studio, Brooke would toss her equipment out the back door and roll up her mats—two carpet-bonded foam strips, one cheese mat, and one octagon mat—and store them in a rented U-Haul pod.

BUILDING AN EMPIRE

When it was time to name her business, Brooke's father suggested Brooke's Cheer and Tumble, but she had other ideas. "It's not a clinic, Dad. I'm building an empire," she told him. Thus, Empire Cheerleading was born. After claiming a 2,500-square-foot spot in a small strip mall, Empire skyrocketed. In just months the gym was training 300 kids weekly in tumbling and cheer while also teaming with local rec leagues to instruct sideline cheerleaders for football and basketball.

But the conditions were far from ideal. The newly rented space included only one bathroom and a mere 1,800 square feet of mat space with tumbling practices held in front of glass windows, yet the program thrived. By 2015 Empire bought its first building and quickly doubled enrollment to 600 kids in just three months.

What makes Brooke's story remarkable is the sheer pace of her growth. While most gyms take years to build a substantial client base, Empire expanded explosively in a matter of months, bringing both exciting opportunities and significant challenges for the young business.

And Brooke was still teaching full time, attending graduate school to become a principal, and coaching two school cheer teams. Her daily routine was grueling: teach all day, arrive at the gym by 3:45 p.m., clean the facility before it opened at 4:30, coach every class until 8:30, answer parent questions until 9:10, and then do it all again the next day.

FINDING HER NICHE

Unlike the pioneers who had to educate communities about what All Star cheer was, Brooke entered the industry when All Star was already established but still evolving. That timing created a particular set of challenges. "If someone doesn't have a good experience in All Star cheer," Brooke said, "they tend to leave the sport. I'm having to teach people what All Star is *not*, because maybe they didn't have a good experience elsewhere." In an industry where many programs had already established their identities, Brooke needed to carve out a distinct position for Empire, so she focused on creating a wholesome, family-centered environment that aligned with the values of her community.

"We're in the South, we're in the Bible Belt, and it's very conservative," she said. "We've got dads going, 'My daughter's not getting out there in a crop top and two-piece at eight years old.' And I said, 'No, she's not. You're right. Not at this gym.' " Brooke's approach sometimes meant losing athletes to other programs when they reached senior age and wanted to wear crop tops, but it also attracted families who shared her values. The gym's motto became clear: "We don't care about the cartwheel. We care about the character. We're in this for our athletes to learn life skills that will benefit them for years to come."

THE ALL STAR EVOLUTION

Initially, Empire focused on competitive recreational cheerleading, an approach that Brooke noted "wasn't cool then," though it has since gained popularity. Empire would take its teams to competitions such as UCA High School Nationals and CHEERSPORT, competing with traditional cheer routines that included signs and poms. It wasn't until 2017-2018 that Empire transitioned to All Star cheer, following a pivotal Varsity University conference where Jeff Webb spoke about improving the sport's image for Olympic consideration.

"That was the first time that I truly considered doing All Star," Brooke said. Webb's speech, with its emphasis on athleticism, gave her hope to try All Star. "We still weren't doing the crop tops, and I didn't like all the hair," she said. "I'm still very traditional." As someone who participated in All Star cheer as an athlete and now owns a gym, Brooke offers a unique perspective on the sport's evolution. She describes competing at CHEERSPORT when it was "one stage in Atlanta with two curtains" where teams would perform alternately on opposite sides of the curtains.

"I try to explain to my kids that I got my first ring when I graduated from college, and now they receive rings, jackets, and all sorts of things," Brooke said. "It's much more interactive and fun so that both prep athletes and novice athletes feel like rock stars."

Brooke also witnessed the industry's growing pains firsthand, including the lack of unified scoring when she first transitioned to All Star. "We were having to change our routines every single event," she said. "Some places had a one-minute-and-a-half routine, some had a two-and-a-half-minute routine, and some had a two-minute routine."

GROWTH AND EXPANSION

Today, Empire has grown into a multivenue complex spanning three acres and featuring 11,000- and 12,000-square-foot buildings. The program offers cheer, gymnastics, ninja, tumbling, a preschool curriculum, and a full-time childcare facility that serves nearly one hundred children each day.

The gym also has launched a competitive gymnastics program that features one Level 8 athlete in its inaugural season. The addition of gymnastics represents a full-circle moment for a business that began with tumbling lessons. While growth has slowed recently, which Brooke attributes to the economy, Empire continues to expand, having opened a "brand spanking new million-and-a-half- dollar building" in the past year.

A key factor in Empire's sustained success has been staff development. Brooke takes pride in creating not just a gym but a workplace where people can build careers. "All Star cheer started out as hobbies or side projects," she said, "and now even a small gym has figured out how to turn it into careers for people."

Four years ago, four athletes graduated and remained as staff members, a development Brooke sees as "the biggest win for us ever." She emphasized the importance of recruiting and retaining staff in an industry where "people are not replaceable."

A UNIQUE PERSPECTIVE

As both a former All Star athlete and long-time gym owner, Brooke appreciates the industry's progress while acknowledging the pioneers who paved the way: "I've seen the industry grow and change so much over the years. And it's a beautiful evolution."

She expressed special appreciation for the cheer abilities program, which provides athletes with disabilities the opportunity to compete in the same environment as other teams. She said with heartfelt emotion, "When you see an entire stadium of elite athletes and parents get up to cheer on those cheer abilities athletes, that's second to none. That's not something you see in every industry."

From a lone mat in her garage to a sprawling complex serving hundreds, Brooke Plack's journey embodies the entrepreneurial spirit fueling All Star cheer's explosive growth. Her story shows that with passion, determination, and strong values, anyone can achieve greatness, even in the industry's second wave.

"When we stay focused on doing what's best for kids," Brooke said, "then I think that helps you answer all the questions and guide your business."

Empire Cheerleading, true to its ambitious name, continues to grow and evolve with ten teams and thirty-two staff members. Shaped by Brooke's experiences as both an athlete and an entrepreneur, it bridges the sport's past, present, and future.

> **"Success is not quitting." – Brooke Plack**

EARNED WISDOM

★ **Success:** As gym owners, tensions can escalate quickly because we're dealing with people's most precious resources, their children and their money. You must be willing to stick it out longer than the next guy. The ability to succeed is the ability to withstand failure and go a little further.

★ **Gratitude:** When I asked Brooke who had a significant impact on her All Star journey, she credited the USASF and Varsity University. She is grateful for the training she and her coaches received: "Those opportunities were phenomenal."

★ **Mistakes:** Delegation without adequate preparation.

★ **For Gym Owners:** Do what you say you're going to do. Stand by what you believe. You must stand for something, whatever it is.

- ★ **For Coaches:** Parents are not your friends. When working with children, you essentially have two customers. You are serving the child on the mat, but you're also serving the parent.

- ★ **Lessons Learned:** Brooke learned the hard way the importance of communication within an organization.

DID YOU KNOW?

- ★ Brooke's favorite part of cheer is the basket tosses.

- ★ She loves to hunt deer and enjoys her time in the woods. She prepares the stand and waits. After she bags a deer, she takes it to camp where she and others prepare the meat to eat.

- ★ Brooke is the host of the *Navigating Personal Growth* podcast.

- ★ Traveling is one of her favorite things. She has visited four continents and twenty countries.

- ★ Catwoman is her favorite superhero. "What's not to love?" she asks. "She wears an incredible outfit."

- ★ Brooke chose the lion as her animal because it represents family, strength, energy, courage, guardianship, protection, ferocity, and authority.

PIONEERS OF ALL STAR

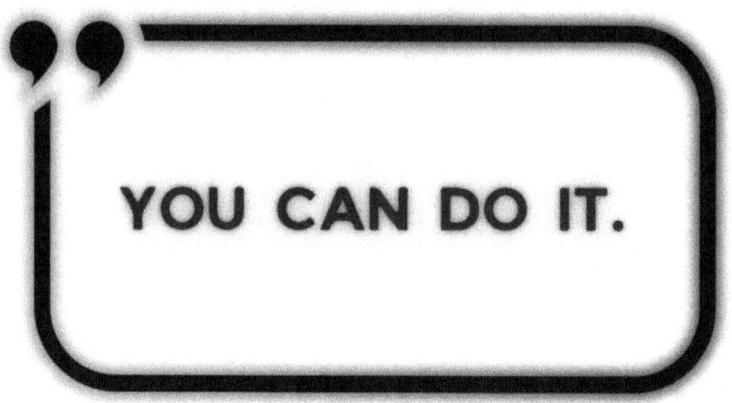

"Don't just adapt to the energy in the room. Influence the energy in the room." – @iamthandolwethu on Instagram "Define yourself by progress, not results." – Sean Guzman

KALI SEITZER & SEAN GUZMAN

Inspire Cheer Camps – 2016

TECHNICIANS AND TEACHERS

Sometimes, people find cheerleading. Other times, cheerleading finds people. Kali Seitzer and Sean Guzman's journeys into All Star cheer couldn't have been more different, yet they would ultimately lead to the same mission: elevate the sport's technical standards while transforming lives. And Kali and Sean couldn't have known how their divergent paths would eventually cross and intertwine.

KALI'S JOURNEY FROM GYMNASTICS TO ALL STAR

Growing up, Kali Seitzer was a gymnast at heart, one who insisted that gymnastics and cheerleading were not the same. "Back then," Kali said with a laugh, "gymnasts didn't have the same respect for cheer as they do now. So at the time, I didn't have respect for [cheer] either."

In her mind she was bound for the Olympics. Training under a Russian coach, Kali reached levels 8 and 9, throwing double fulls and double backs by the age of ten. But in 1996 a congenital back problem derailed her Olympic dreams. Faced with the decision between surgery or quitting, her family chose to step away from gymnastics. At just twelve, Kali felt her life collapse. She didn't want to do anything else, ever.

Enter Kevin Brubaker, the owner of Charlotte Allstar Cheerleading. Kevin had a knack for finding gymnasts who had left the sport and introducing them to cheerleading. He called Kali's mother and offered her daughter a chance to try a day at his gym. Kali was adamant that she would not participate. "I will not do cheerleading," she said. "And that's final."

But her mother insisted, and Kali showed up in full rebellion mode wearing her white velvet leotard with bare feet. She was not having it. She was determined to stay a gymnast to the core. But her resistance dissolved the moment she was placed in a stunt. The team lifted her into a prep, and Kali said, "Well, this isn't cheerleading. What is this?" That was the moment she fell in love with the sport of cheer and decided to give it a chance.

Kali quickly became one of the program's standout athletes, although her relationship with Kevin was anything but easy. "He was incredibly tough on me," Kali said. "Looking back, I needed it. I was rough around the edges. But Kevin Brubaker is a huge part of why I'm talking to you right now."

More than just a coach, Kevin became a lifeline for Kali during some difficult family challenges. By sixteen, she was already living on her own. Home wasn't stable, and she often found herself navigating adult responsibilities at far too young an age. But in the midst of all of that turmoil, Kevin Brubaker and the Charlotte Allstars gave Kali something steady to hold onto: structure, support, and purpose.

"Cheerleading became my escape, my safe space and, often, the only thing that kept me grounded," Kali said. "Kevin gave me a reason to keep pushing forward when everything was falling apart."

SEAN: BORN INTO ALL STAR

Unlike Kali's reluctant entry into cheerleading, Sean Guzman's story begins in 1999 when he was only eight years old. His sister practiced at a facility called Cheer Palace Knights where Top Gun All Stars rented space. After watching his sister practice, one of the coaches approached him and asked if he would like to cheer.

"What do I have to do?" young Sean asked.

"Show me a back handspring."

Sean tried it, landed on his head, and his All Star journey began. He joined Top Gun Bullets, the program's youth team, and never left. "About 1999 is when we all became part of the Top Gun program," Sean explained. "And that was it."

What makes Sean's story remarkable is his steadfast loyalty to a single program. "Pretty much every single day from April of 1999 all the way until now, I've spent at the university of Top Gun All Star," he said. "I have whatever is above a doctorate in All Star cheer."

That loyalty wasn't just Sean's, it became a family affair. His sister started at Top Gun, his brother also was roped in, and his mom began working there as well.

At just fourteen Sean began coaching private lessons. By his mid-teens he was participating in camps with Top Gun owner Victor Rosario. He continued coaching teams until 2017 when he took over the tumbling program and shifted his focus entirely to technical development.

FINDING THEIR PATHS

Kali's cheerleading journey continued beyond the Charlotte Allstars. After high school, Kevin handed her an application to Paris Junior College in Paris, Texas. "I'm not going there," Kali declared, and she threw the application into the trash. Kevin retrieved it and encouraged her to try, so she called the program's legendary coach, CJ Russell—then seventy years old but still coaching—who made an offer that Kali couldn't refuse. "I'll fly you out here for tryouts for free," CJ said, "and then I'll fly you back. I'll provide you with a full scholarship, and I'll fly you back and forth for Thanksgiving and Christmas."

And so Kali's remarkable collegiate cheerleading career began. She spent two years at Paris before transferring to Stephen F. Austin State University (SFA). There she earned three collegiate championship titles and proved herself in one of the most competitive cheer programs in the country. After SFA she went on to Hawaii Pacific University where she added three more collegiate national titles to her resume. "I should be a doctor for how long I was in college," she joked, "but I enjoyed every minute of it."

During her college years Kali overcame significant prejudice about her body type. Even at 115 pounds, she was considered "too big" to fly. "I didn't initially make the team at SFA," she said, "not because I lacked the skill but because they already had their formula for the mat that, at the time, included several eighty-five-pound flyers."

Rather than quitting, Kelly redirected her focus and set out to become an elite tumbler and basket toss flyer. She made it her mission to master every skill in the book. That drive led her to make history. She became the only female to complete a ball-X full on a hard floor at college nationals. Her resilience paid off. "I never got cut from a team again," she said proudly. "I made every single team and every single mat from that point forward because I decided if I couldn't contribute in one way, I'd make myself valuable another way."

After college, Kali's career took her across the country and, eventually, around the world. She worked at gyms in Texas, Hawaii, Illinois, and California. Kali has experienced nearly every role the sport has to offer. She coached at Woodward Camp and proudly represented Team USA in partner stunt as an athlete. Kali competed with Team USA and earned a gold medal. By 2014 she was traveling internationally, teaching in nineteen countries in only two years.

In 2016-2017 Kali founded Inspire, her training company that initially focused solely on tumbling but later, as her reputation grew, expanded to include stunts and baskets. Her company was built entirely on word-of-mouth referrals. It doesn't even have a website. Kali relies solely on an Instagram page and the quality of her instruction.

Sean, meanwhile, continued his development at Top Gun, becoming a respected technical authority both within the program and beyond its walls. His expertise was recognized when Shay Crawford and Debbie Love invited him to join the USASF Tumbling Education Team when Sean was only twenty-two.

THE INTERSECTION

Kelly and Sean's paths crossed in 2018 at a cheer camp in the woods of Oregon. Their connection wasn't entirely coincidental. They had been moving in the same professional orbit for some time. When they finally met at the camp, they discovered a shared philosophy regarding technical development and athlete training. After two days of working together, Sean invited Kali to Miami. She changed her flight plans and spent seven days visiting him and, the rest, as they say, is history.

Their professional partnership evolved alongside their personal relationship. They began collaborating on training sessions, camps, and coaching workshops. Together, they have developed a unique approach to technical development that combines Kali's background in gymnastics and international experience with Sean's methodical, long-term developmental perspective, honed over decades at Top Gun.

TEACHING THE TEACHERS

Over time, both Kali and Sean shifted their focus from primarily coaching athletes to training coaches and gym owners. This transition reflects their shared belief that, to truly elevate the sport, they need to focus on those who will be implementing the training on a day-to-day basis. Sean hosted nine staff training sessions in one year, a record. "I know my path in the industry is to help gym owners and coaches understand that the process takes years, decades," Sean said. Kali has drawn similar conclusions based on her travels, noting that she's conducted more coaching trainings than athlete clinics in the last two seasons.

CHEERFEST AND BEYOND

In recent years Kali and Sean have become integral to Cheerfest, an innovative camp program. Kali serves as the director, bringing her passion for athlete development to the role. "I love being able to add the little details of positivity and pumping the kids up and giving them a start to their summer," Kali said. "Maybe they're going through a tough time. Maybe things aren't great at their gym, they're not being spoken to with kindness, and they don't feel like a top athlete. But at Cheerfest, every athlete gets the chance to feel like a top athlete."

The impact extends beyond the athletes to the staff. "We're not just doing it for the kids," Kali said. "It's for everyone involved, because everyone leaves feeling inspired about the sport and coaching."

While maintaining their independent training businesses, Kali also works with Top Gun alongside Sean, creating a unique collaborative environment that allows them to balance their travels with a home base in the tumbling world.

Sean said his contribution to the sport can be summed up in one word: "Time." He said he's spent from 2 p.m. to 10 p.m. in a gym since he was approximately eight years old. And Kali sees her impact through the lives she's touched: "I feel like I positively impacted the course of people's lives for the last twenty years."

THE POWER OF CONNECTION

Throughout Kali and Sean's individual and shared journeys, what emerges most clearly is the power of human connection in shaping athletic careers and lives. Both speak of pivotal mentors who changed their trajectories—Kevin Brubaker and CJ Russell for Kali and Victor and Kristen Rosario for Sean. "They've done more for me and my family than I could have ever dreamed of," Sean said. "The second phase of my life involves trying to figure out how to repay them for everything they've done for me and to show up every single day, not for any specific outcome, but because it's the right thing to do."

Now Sean and Kali have become influential figures for a new generation of athletes and coaches. Their willingness to share knowledge, travel extensively, and invest deeply in technical development stems from a profound understanding of cheerleading's potential to transform lives.

In a sport often defined by competitive achievements and championships, Kali and Sean represent a different measure of success, one based on technical excellence, personal growth, and the long-term impact on athletes' lives. Their stories remind us that behind the flash and excitement of All Star cheer are dedicated technicians who spend decades perfecting their craft and passing their knowledge on to others.

> **"Success is *Kaizen*." – Kali Seitzer**

EARNED WISDOM

★ **Success:** Success is too often described as the result and not enough as the process. There's a term in Japanese called Kaizen. It's a term for business, and it means never-ending improvement: Success is Kaizen. Success is also the ability to withstand circumstances that you perceive as obstacles by seeing them as opportunities. Kali adds that success is also the positive impact you have on someone's life.

- ★ **Wisdom:** If you can be open-minded and willing to learn, you will be able to accept what comes and move forward. This will allow you to continually grow as a human.

- ★ **Gratitude:** Kali mentioned Kevin Brubaker and CJ Russell as having a huge impact on her life. She also credits Garrin Goznel, her coach at Hawaii Pacific University, for giving her the opportunity to stunt. She also mentioned Lisa Acoin and Kenny, who provided her with the chance to travel and teach. Sean again mentioned the significant impact that Victor and Kristen Rosario had on his life, and he also credits Shay Crawford and Debbie Love for his time with the USASF Tumbling Education Team.

- ★ **Sean's Wish:** Sean wishes the people who understand what it means to train diligently, methodically, and intelligently would be the ones to help structure the sport. He said a lot of injuries and dangerous situations occur because the resources and experiences of the specialists in their fields aren't being used.

- ★ **Mistakes:** There is no such thing as a mistake. Whatever occurred is leading you to what will happen next. Embrace it and move on. Mistakes are the building blocks of life.

- ★ **For Gym Owners:** Kali's advice is to stay open-minded, learn from others, and be patient in the process. Sean's advice is to be what you want your gym to be. If you want your gym to be good, then be a good person. If you want your gym to be successful, wake up every day and go after it.

★ **For Coaches:** Show up and try again is Sean's advice. Kali emphasizes the importance of mastering your craft. Commit to continuous growth and refinement in order to evolve into a stronger, more impactful coach every single day.

★ **Lessons Learned:** Show up every day and do the work.

DID YOU KNOW?

★ Sean's favorite part of cheer is tumbling. Kali loves it all.

★ Sean practices jujitsu. Spanish is his first language. He is an avid snowboarder. He checks the weather constantly for snow reports. Sometimes his destination will change within twelve hours of departure.

★ Kali loves nature and travel. She has visited twenty-seven countries and twenty-five states. She loves to eat crab legs.

★ Kali and Sean agreed that their favorite superhero is Eric Guzman, Sean's brother. He is a real-life superhero who has served twenty years on the Miami Police Force. He finished in the top 10 percent on his sergeant's exam and is part of the SWAT team.

★ Kali chose as her animals both the phoenix and the salmon, which symbolize rebirth, transformation, and triumph over adversity. They represent the potential for renewal and strength after facing challenges, embodying qualities such as pride, intensity, confidence, wisdom, inspiration, determination, and a spiritual desire as well as the ability to swim upstream. Sean chose the wolf, which symbolizes loyalty, perseverance, success, intuition, spirit, and an appetite for freedom, but it also can be a loner.

SUGGESTED READING FROM THE PIONEERS

- Kendall Tyler Battleson recommends *Fablehaven* by Brandon Mull.

- Justin Carrier recommends *Row the Boat* by Jon Gordon.

- Jim Chadwick recommends The Bible. He also suggests *Zen and the Art of Motorcycle Maintenance* by Robert M. Pirsig.

- Tate Chalk recommends *The Four Agreements* by Don Miguel Ruiz.

- Robin Coe recommends *Chicken Soup for the Soul* by Jack Canfield and Mark Victor Hansen and *Choose to Win* by Tom Ziglar.

- Don Collins recommends *Citizen Coke: The Making of Coca-Cola Capitalism* by Bartow J. Elmore and *From Barnum & Bailey to Feld: The Creative Evolution of the Greatest Show on Earth* by Ernest Albrecht.

- Brian Elza recommends *The Art of the Deal* by Donald Trump.

- Aaron Flaker recommends *The Energy Bus* by Jon Gordon.

- Sean Guzman recommends *Extreme Ownership* and *The Dichotomy of Leadership* by Jocko Willink.

- Brad Habermel recommends *Sapiens* by Yuval Noah Harari

- Happy Hooper recommends *The Girl with the Dragon Tattoo* series by Stieg Larsson (translated by Reg Keeland) and any book by Charlaine Harris.

- Becky Herrera recommends *Just a Minute* by Wess Stafford and Dean Merrill, and *Girl, Stop Apologizing* by Rachel Hollis.

- Ray Jasper recommends *The Diary of a CEO* by Steven Bartlett.

- Kevin Jones recommends *Failing Forward* by John C. Maxwell.

- Danny Kahn recommends *Profit First* by Mike Michalowicz and *Baby Steps Millionaires* by Dave Ramsey.

- Ladd LeBus recommends The Bible.

- Eric Little recommends *The Prince of Tides* by Pat Conroy and *Less Than Zero* by Bret Easton Ellis.

- Debbie Love recommends anything by John Maxwell on leadership; *The Power of Posture* by Naudi Aguilar and Ramon Gallegos; textbooks on biomechanics, physics, joints, and child psychology; and *The Hidden Messages in Water* by Masaru Emoto.

- Mike Martinez recommends The Bible, *Good to Great* by Jim Collins, *The Case for Christ* by Lee Strobel, and *How to Win Friends and Influence People* by Dale Carnegie.

- Jody Melton recommends *The Power Broker* by Robert Caro.

- John Newby recommends *Winning* by Jack Welch, *Good to Great* by Jim Collins, and *The Power of a Positive Team* by Jon Gordon.

- Jamie Parrish recommends *Atlas Shrugged* by Ayn Rand.

- Brad Page recommends anything by Jay Shetty.

- Courtney Pope recommends any book by Mike Krzyzewski (Coach K).

- Boog Potter recommends *Rich Dad Poor Dad* by Robert T. Kiyosaki and *Good to Great* by Jim Collins.

- Leon Reynolds recommends *Jonathan Livingston Seagull* by Richard Bach and Russell Munson.

- Angela Rogers recommends *The One Thing* by Gary Keller, *Loving What Is* by Byron Katie, and *A New Earth* by Eckhart Tolle.

- Kristen Rosario recommends anything by Dan Brown and James Patterson, describing their books as "great escapes."

- Victor Rosario recommends *Atomic Habits* by James Clear; *The Little Book of Talent*, *The Talent Code*, and *The Culture Code* by Daniel Coyle; and *Practice Perfect* by Doug Lemov and Eric Woolway.

- Stacy Rowe recommends *Leaders Eat Last* by Simon Sinek, *The Energy Bus* by Jon Gordon, and *The 7 Habits of Highly Effective People* by Stephen R. Covey.

- Bill Seely recommends *Start with Why* by Simon Sinek and The Bible.

- Kali Seitzer recommends *Relentless Optimism* by Darrin Donnelly and *The Happiness Advantage* by Shawn Achor.

- James Speed recommends *The Little Book of Talent* by Daniel Coyle and anything by John Wooden.

- Tammy Skinner recommends James Patterson, Colleen Hoover, and Freida McFadden as great ways to relax. She also recommends Dr. Seuss.

- Cole Stott recommends *Good to Great* by Jim Collins, *Make It Happen Before Lunch* by Stephan Schiffman, and *How Full Is Your Bucket?* by Tom Rath and Don Clifton.

- Orson Sykes recommends *Good to Great* by Jim Collins and *Winning with People* and *The 21 Irrefutable Laws of Leadership* by John C. Maxwell.

- Sean Timmons recommends listening to Guy Raz's podcast, *How I Built This*.

- Lance Wagers recommends *Where the Crawdads Sing* by Delia Owens.

- Meredith Walker recommends *Outliers* by Malcolm Gladwell.

- Dawn Duncan Walters recommends *Let Them* by Mel Robbins.

- Steve Wedge recommends anything by John Grisham.

- Dennis Worley recommends *Blue Ocean Strategy* by W. Chan Kim and Renée Mauborgne, *Raving Fans* by Ken Blanchard and Sheldon Bowles, and *The Innovator's Dilemma* by Clayton M. Christensen (narrated by L. J. Ganser).

"Happiness can be found, even in the darkest of times, if one only remembers to turn on the light."

– Dumbledore, from *Harry Potter and the Prisoner of Azkaban*

ABOUT THE AUTHOR

STACY ROWE

Award-winning author S.R. Fabrico (Stacy Rowe) has established herself as a compelling voice in contemporary fiction. Her debut novel, *The Secrets We Conceal*, and acclaimed Southport Series trilogy *Call Her Janie*, *Keeping Janie*, and *Janie's Hope* have earned her recognition as an emerging literary talent with a distinctive storytelling style.

Drawing from her remarkable twenty-five-year career spanning All Star cheer and dance, marketing, and sports, S.R. brings authentic depth to her narratives. Known in the cheer and dance community as Stacy Rowe, she has built an impressive legacy as a world champion dance coach, a sought-after speaker, and a long-time gym owner. Her entrepreneurial spirit extends to her roles as part owner of Premier Athletics, MotUS, The CX Brands, and The Prime Alliance where she remains dedicated to creating transformative experiences for young athletes.

Beyond fiction, S.R. has published a collection of sports journals for young athletes and a dedicated journal for women, reflecting her belief in the restorative power of personal reflection. She crafts each work with the same passion and insight that has defined her multifaceted career.

Fabrico resides in Tennessee with her husband and children where she continues to create immersive worlds that captivate readers and transport them beyond the ordinary. Her unique background and genuine storytelling prowess promise to enchant new and returning readers alike.

EARNED WISDOM

★ **Success:** Success is being brave enough to try regardless of the outcome.

★ **Wisdom:** You never know how far you can go until you go there.

★ **Gratitude:** Besides the people she mentioned in the dedication, Stacy's husband has had the greatest impact on her life. His unwavering love and support carry her forward every single day. She is grateful for her children, whom she adores and strives to set a positive example for every day. Also, her mother deserves credit for raising her to be a strong, driven woman by setting an incredible example. She also credits Tara Charlton

Smith, her coach and dear friend, for encouraging her to work hard and aspire to cheer in college.

★ **Stacy's Wish:** Stacy wishes that the industry could be unified once more.

★ **To My Younger Self:** Cherish every moment of every day. You are much stronger and more capable than you realize.

★ **Mistakes:** There are too many to list for one book. Do your best to learn from your mistakes and teach others how to avoid making them.

★ **For Gym Owners:** Take the time to get to know your staff. Continue to build your culture. That task never ends. Make sure you not only have the right people on the bus but also that the right people are in the right seats.

★ **For Coaches:** Inspire. Train your athletes to love the sport. Teach them not only to be great people but also to set high expectations for themselves so they can achieve whatever they put their minds to.

★ **Lessons Learned:** Don't put off until tomorrow what you can do today.

DID YOU KNOW?

★ Stacy's favorite part of cheer is the transitions. She loves a well-crafted transition.

- ★ Her degree is in mathematics, and she planned to be an actuarial scientist.

- ★ She also loves dance and coached it for many years.

- ★ Stacy has written four award-winning novels under the name S.R. Fabrico, which she chose to honor her mother, who passed away when Stacy was twenty-one.

- ★ Her favorite superhero is Iron Man because she loves his quick wit and brilliance. He doesn't have superhuman abilities or powers, but he does have a big brain and the courage to dream.

- ★ The whale is one of her animals because it represents wisdom, provision, intelligence, kindness, deeper awareness, nurturing, navigation, and communication. The bear is the other because it represents industriousness, instinct, healing, power, sovereignty, guardianship of the world, watchfulness, courage, willpower, self-preservation, introspection, and great strength.

ACKNOWLEDGMENTS

I am deeply grateful to my husband, who has been my biggest cheerleader. This project was no different. When I wavered or questioned myself, he reminded me to keep going. When I felt like I might never finish because the research was piling up into a mountain, he jumped in. He spent hours poring over interviews, dissecting the information, and creating a timeline for me to follow. Without his help, I may never have finished.

Thank you to my children. Your smiles brighten my world and motivate me to work harder to be the kind of mother you deserve.

I am thankful to Abel Rosa, who believed in me and encouraged Premier Athletics to open a gym with me as the manager in a small town outside of Raleigh, North Carolina. Without Abel, my life might have taken a completely different path.

Thanks to my business partners who believed in me and encouraged me along the way while I wrote this book. They offered valuable insights that helped me decide on important details. They also helped connect me with many industry professionals and pioneers who brought this book to life.

To the pioneers, thank you for your courage and vision in creating what All Star has become. To the many pioneers who are not included in this book for whatever reason—some declined, some couldn't be reached—

know that your contributions are remarkable. To those who are included here, thank you for giving me your time and for your willingness to tell your stories. It has been an honor to share them.

To my editors, Kim, Kelly, Jenn, Jody, Mike, and Story Mountain Media: I couldn't have done this without you. Thank you for your genuine care in helping me finish this project. You are rock stars who do incredible work.

I want to give a huge shout-out to Angie Ogden for helping transcribe several of the interviews as well as assisting with fact-checking, spelling of names, and a ton of other details to ensure the book is as accurate as possible. Thanks also go to Leoj Dominguez for helping design the neon signs you see at the bottom of each pioneer chapter as well as the marketing materials associated with the book.

To my OG college roommate and dear friend, Steph, who has helped me with every book. She reads them all and provides honest feedback to improve them.

Thank you, Mo Raad with The Paper House for creating an appropriate nonfiction cover that embodies All Star cheer. It was not an easy task, but you nailed it.

Thanks also go to Flaticon for providing the free animal images used at the top of each pioneer chapter.

I would be remiss if I didn't acknowledge all the gym owners and coaches who are doing the hard work every day to make a difference in the lives of children. And thanks to all the parents and athletes, especially those

I've coached over the years. Thank you for trusting me to be a part of your lives. I am eternally grateful to each of you. You taught me many lessons over the years, and coaching was one of the greatest joys of my life.

Finally, I want to acknowledge my staff and Premier Athletics. You challenge me to be a better version of myself every day. I see and acknowledge the work you do. I appreciate each of you. I am who I am because of each of you throughout the last twenty-five years.

MotUS

JOIN THE MOVEMENT

MotUS is a community of gym owners working together to help each other grow. Our vision is to imagine a gym-leading industry. Our mission is to serve gym owners and coaches; lead with courage, patience, and conviction; and empower everyone to keep athletes at the center of our actions.

We are passionate about sharing our combined experience of over 150 years. We have immense gratitude for the industry and all it has done for us, and we genuinely want to give back to help current and future generations continue to lead and grow.

As a MotUS member you receive the following benefits:

- Affiliate discounts of 10-25% off apparel, shoes, backpacks, equipment, and more
- 15% off all Prime Alliance events
- Exclusive monthly webinars
- VIP private Facebook group
- FREE Business Expo Owners Conference
- 1:1 Support
- *The MotUS Edge* podcast
- *The Monthly Scoop,* an online newsletter with updates and tips each month

Join the movement today at www.joinmotus.com or email info@joinmotus.com.

PODCAST

The MotUS Edge is a podcast cohosted by Stacy Rowe, Cole Stott, Kevin Brubaker, and Casey Jones. *The MotUS Edge* celebrates business with a focus on youth sports facility management, leadership, and motivation. Fill your cup with knowledge, laughter, affirmation, and the comfort of knowing that you're not alone. You can and will succeed with *The MotUS Edge*. Find us every Wednesday on Apple Podcasts, Spotify, and YouTube @TheMotUSEdge. Sign up to be a guest or learn more about *The MotUS Edge* podcast at www.joinmotus.com/podcast.

INDEX

A
Accidental Cheerleader, 480
Accuscore, 38, 300
ACE Cheer Company (ACE), 500, 502
ACX Jags, 425, 427
Adaptation, 177, 203, 429, 516, 552
Ahern, Diane, 166
Ahern, Shelly, 170
Alabama, 438, 500–502, 504, 534
Alamodome, 176
Alaska Athletics, 558, 561–564
Aldridge, Karen Noseff, 62
All-girl Division, 23, 283, 494, 514
All-music routines, transition to, 27, 355
All Star Battle, 74
All Star Challenge, 20, 38, 53, 98, 353, 357–361, 370, 521–527, 529
All Star Dance, 3, 12, 52, 54–55, 63, 73–74, 168, 290–291, 372, 459
All Star Dance Industry, 73
All Star Evolution, 633
All Star Facility/gym, 49, 57, 60, 67, 126, 160, 245, 297, 347, 359, 501–502, 541, 585, 605
All Star Gym Owners Association, 57
All Star Memory, 102, 507
All Star Novice Divisions, 36, 64
All Star Program, 24–25, 106, 122, 483, 492, 494, 511, 515, 533, 539, 551, 562, 604, 618, 620, 625
All Star World Championship (ASWC), 70–73, 544, 609
Alzheimer, 392
American Championships, 51, 98
American Cheer Power, 53, 131, 173–176
American Cheerleader Magazine, 31, 302
American Cheerleaders Association (ACA), 107, 236
American Spirit Championships (ASC), 75, 278–281, 283
American Spirit and Cheer Essentials (ASCE), 604–605
Anaheim, California, 168
Andrews, Serena, 66, 381
Antico, Joelle, 40, 82, 312, 317, 509, 511, 569, 597
Archie, Kendra, 170
Arnett, Kathy, 469, 476–477
Aston, Jennifer, 170
Athlete's Mind, 332
Athletes' Personal Growth, 137

Athletic Championships, 36, 44, 50, 96, 441, 449–450, 459, 539, 541–542, 579
Athleticism, xviii, 1, 23, 34, 45, 162, 338, 466, 580, 583,
601, 633
Athletics Championships, 38, 433, 444, 449, 458, 460, 495
Atlanta's Georgia World Congress Center (GWCC), 261–264
Augusta, Georgia, 287
Avery, John, 523

B
Bain Capital, 67–68, 70, 72, 543
Bantam League Cheer, 113
Bartlett, Heather, 426
Basket Toss, 29, 32, 200, 505, 568, 637, 643
Battleson, Kendall Tyler, 83, 138, 147, 651
Baylor University, 269, 336
Bergue, Morton, 83, 106, 126, 205, 213, 220, 245, 388, 391–392, 555, 597
Bid System, 69, 609
Biggest Failure, 524
Blair, Tony, 532
Bluegrass Gymnastics Training Center, 122, 434
Boggs, Bill, 160, 286, 290, 296, 356, 415
Bowles, Tanya, 358–359, 522
Bring It On movie, 214–215, 218 Brown, Derrick

"Twist", 145 Brown, Robert, 197
Brubaker, Kevin, xxiii, 35, 75, 83, 131, 265, 298, 438, 461, 640–641, 646, 648
BSN Corporation, 23
Buccat, Ronald, 224
Buckey, Cathy, 83, 112–113, 116–117, 256, 259
Building a Brand, 504
Building Gyms, 415
Burns, Anastasia Miller, 82, 596

C
California, 10, 21, 166, 168–169, 318, 354, 381, 388–389, 557, 604, 607, 643
California Specialty Camps (USA), 2, 10–11, 14–15, 313–314, 368, 384, 437, 453, 644
Camaraderie, 23, 117, 491, 515
Camp Business Models, 234, 236, 297
Campbell, Johnny (first cheerleader), 7
Carillo, George, 459
Carrier, Justin, 30, 83, 251, 396, 400–401, 597, 651
Category Scoring, 28–29, 185
Cathy Buckey Cheerleading Camps (CBCC), 113
Cathy Buckey's Influence, 116
Cathy's Wish, 118
Celebrity, 604, 606
Chadwick, Jim, 43, 82, 95–

96, 132, 239, 242, 252–253, 584, 588, 593, 597–598, 651
Chalk, Tate, 83, 412, 422, 426, 467–468, 483, 651
Champion Cheer Gym, 115, 117
Champion Cheerleading Camps, 113, 117
Champion Cup National Competitions, 117
Champion Legacy, 113
Charlesbank, 65–66, 543
Charlotte, North Carolina, 262, 288
Cheer, Aloha, 66, 381
Cheer Athletic (CA), 31, 34, 106, 221, 249, 289, 298, 301, 335–342, 397, 401, 409, 485, 562, 618
Cheer Choreography, 221
Cheer and Dance Industry Professionals (CDIP), 68–69, 72–73, 607
Cheer Extreme, 33, 144–146, 148, 192, 289, 308–309, 501, 534
Cheer Extreme Roanoke, 501
Cheer Extreme Senior Elite, 289 *Cheer Fever* film, 214
Cheer Ltd, 24, 31, 190–192
CheerABILITIES (USASF team), 590
Cheerfest, 456, 465, 645–646
CheerForce Story, 548 CheerForce's Early Growth, 551 Cheerleader Dance Team, 37, 97

Cheerleader Supply, 12, 141
Cheerleaders of America (COA), 24, 28–29, 381, 433, 436, 447–448, 513
Cheerleading, diversity in, 248–249
Cheerleading, Origins of, 3 Early Male Cheer Squads, 445
Inclusion of Women in Cheer, 9
Johnny Campbell and the First Cheer, 7
Ski-U-Mah, 7–8
World War II, 9, 11
Cheerleading Uniforms, 63, 90, 288
Cheerleading Worlds, 45–47, 54, 59–60, 289, 584, 586–587, 592
Cheerleading's Origins, 7
Cheersport, 35–36, 44, 63, 96, 98, 131, 458, 521, 574, 579, 582, 633
Cheersport Team, 35
CheerUPDATES, 56–57
Choice Events, 75, 364, 372, 527
Christian Youth Organization (CYO), 313
Churchill, Winston, 59, 539
Clark, Amy, 82, 581–584, 588, 596, 600
Clash of the Titans, 38, 358, 522–523
Clayton Valley, 21–23, 166–170, 184, 219, 388–389
Clayton Valley All Stars, 21–

23, 166–170, 184, 219, 388
Clough, Dwight, 377
Coaches, advice for, 254, 266, 275, 283, 291, 304–305, 310, 332, 343–344, 351, 402, 410, 423, 431, 442
Coe, Robin, 83, 364–365, 373, 459, 526–527, 597, 651
Coed Division, 23, 200, 494, 562
Collegiate National Championship, 114, 116, 182, 286, 354
Collins, Don, 20, 38, 83, 143–144, 360–361, 371, 522, 524, 529, 651
Concord, California, 166, 389
Concord Naval Weapons Station, 168
Connecticut Spirit, 364, 367, 369
Contemporary Era, 59
COVID-19 Pandemic, 552, 609, 624
Crabaugh, Wendy, 170
Crawford, Shay, 644, 648
Cumberland college, 433, 440, 447
Custom Music Mixing, 358
Cutthroat Competition, 523
CX Brands, 75, 255, 262, 265, 268, 456, 461–462, 465, 477

D

Dabbs, John, 481
Dallas, 18, 21–22, 56, 76, 85– 86, 104–105, 389, 405, 443, 446, 494, 549, 619
Dallas Cowboys (NFL team), 204, 352, 443, 549
The Dance Battle, 73–74
Dance Championships, 66, 381
The Dance Connection, 73, 206
Dance Majors, 56–57, 74, 383
The Dance Summit, 66, 237, 381
Dance Team, 11, 13, 37, 52, 55, 74, 97, 168, 170, 197, 200, 294, 355, 360
Dance Worlds, 51–52, 145, 585, 592
DanceABILITIES (USASF team), 590
Davis, Craig, 459
Deckard, Jessica, 560
Deep South, 192, 544
Denali Allstars, 561
Derricks, Marguerite, 206
Devall, Nicole Leago, 79, 593, 595
Dickey, Randy, 26, 57, 83, 416, 425, 429–430, 468
DII Summit, 65, 177, 237
Direction through Faith, 418
Disney World, 17, 34, 45, 61, 63, 65, 93–94, 248, 579
Division II (DII), 65
Division II Summit Competition, 177
Division I Summit, 177
Drucker, Peter, 376

E

E-Score, 152
Eastern Cheerleading Association (ECA), 20, 31, 141–142, 258, 314, 353, 511
Edmond, Oklahoma, 278–279, 282, 405, 409
1898-1981 (Early Development Era), 6
1898 (First cheerleader), 4
Einstein, Albert, 19
Elite Divisions, 62
Elza, Brian, 83, 123, 200, 459,
490, 497, 597, 651
Empire Cheerleading, 629, 631, 636
Employee stock ownership plan (ESOP), 55, 65
Encouragement, the power of, 6
Entertainment and Sports Programming Network (ESPN), 18, 91, 94, 97, 154, 238, 248, 259, 372, 526, 580
Enthusiasm, 197, 315, 367, 381, 391, 444, 501, 554, 609
ESPN Partnership, 18, 91, 94, 154, 372, 526, 580
Evans, Jerry, 206
Excel and Basix Divisions, 36

F

Fairfax, Virginia, 153
Family Cheerleading Dynasty, 146
Family Plan, 37, 50, 63, 236, 439, 524, 542
Fayetteville, North Carolina, 24, 190
Fernandez, Alex, 207
Final Destination, 59
First Cheer Camp (1945), 9–10, 198
First Televised Nationals (SeaWorld, 1980), 17
Flack, Jennifer, 626
Flack, John, 626
Flaker, Aaron, 35, 82, 304, 376, 384–385, 651
Flash Cards, 8
Florida, 17, 29, 34, 45, 52, 56, 61, 63, 65, 69–70, 72, 579, 616
Formation of USASF and NACCC, 246
The Four Agreements, 420, 651
Fowlkes, Jeff, 239, 597
Franchise, 31, 37, 94, 317, 340, 350, 369, 540, 549, 623, 626
Freehold Pop Warner Giants Team, 313
FUNdamentals Program, 292

G

Gaffney, Kathy, 83, 166, 170, 184, 219, 388
Gaffney, Lisa, 169–170
Gallup, George, 17, 92
Gamma Sigma, 8
Gandek, Kristen, 170
Gandhi, Mahatma, 509
Garner, Barry, 435
Gaynor, Bob, 169

Georgia, 116, 184, 199, 221, 231, 260–261, 438, 457, 466–467, 512, 569, 617
Georgia All Stars, 231, 285, 287–289, 471, 507, 512, 569, 617
Georgia Cheerleading Center (GCC), 288, 481
Georgia World Congress Center (GWCC), 261–264
Glielmi, Thom, 258
Glorified Private Lesson, 335
Gold Megaphone Trophy, 130
Gold Rush, 544
Golden State Spirit Association, 66, 381
Goose Creek, South Carolina, 233
Goto, Matt, 300
Gotwals, Kandy, 358
Great Competition Boom, 34
Great Lakes Cheerleading Championships, 66, 381
Great Unification, 43, 578
Greensboro, 226–228, 260, 262
Greensboro All Star Cheerleading (GAC), 226–229
Groove Experience, 55, 63, 459
The Groove Experience, 55, 63, 459
Growth of the Dance Worlds and Cheer Worlds, 584–585
Guzman, Sean, 328, 639, 641, 652
Gwinnett Convention Center, 262

Gym owners, advice for, 101, 109, 118, 126, 136, 164, 171, 180, 188, 598, 602, 613, 627, 636, 648, 658
Gymnastics Clinics for Cheerleaders, 16
GymTyme All Stars, 293, 298, 301

H

Habermel, Brad, 83, 209, 298, 301, 335–336, 342, 401, 597, 652
Hallmark, Craig, 626
Hamburg, Germany, 390
Hanbery, David, 69, 72
Hansen, Brett, 83, 346, 349–350
Harper, Ransome, 256
Harris, Jeb, 69, 72
Harvard, Angela, 66
Harvey, Dave, 490–491
Hawaii, Coastal, 66
Healthy Competition, 515, 563, 611
Henriques, Kari, 170
Herjavec, Robert, 312
Herkimer, Lawrence "Herkie", 9, 23, 42, 44, 85, 109, 167, 242, 253, 393, 579
Herrera, Becky, 83, 548, 554–555, 596, 652
Hicks, Sandye Teague, 260
Hilda' Team, 21
Hill, Ricky, 192
Hodges, Misty, 257, 298, 301
Hollywood, 38, 214, 412, 416–419, 421
Holtsclaw, Gwen, 24, 83, 190,

194
Homegrown Excellence, 561
Hooper, Happy, 83, 500, 506–507, 596, 652
Houston, 10, 76, 181, 243, 347, 396

I

Independent Event Producers (IEPs), 53–54, 63, 68–69, 75, 461, 606, 623
Indiana, 377, 379, 383, 438
Industry, COVID-19's impact on the, 543, 552, 609
Industry Evolution, 179, 186, 273
Industry Influence, 514
Innovation, 12, 19, 27, 34, 39, 288, 296, 300, 327, 329, 342, 381–383, 495–496, 516, 542, 564
Inspire Cheer Camps, 639
Intermediate Division, 39
International All Star Foundation (IASF), 51, 84, 302
International Cheer Union (ICU), 47–49, 51, 67, 82, 84, 99, 587
International Olympic Committee (IOC), 48–49

J

Jackson, Janet, 206
Jackson, Samuel L., 418
Jacksonville, Florida, 184, 313, 357–358, 436, 513
JAM Brands, 66, 98, 133, 186, 304, 376, 381–385

James Madison University (JMU), 353–354, 404
JAMfest, 35, 50, 56, 66, 376, 378–380, 383–384, 458
JAMfest Super Nationals, 35, 50, 56, 66, 376, 378–380, 383–384, 458
Jasper, Ray, 169, 205, 212, 216, 652
Jeff Webb's Enduring Vision, 99
Jones, Casey, xviii, xxiii, 75, 83, 265, 288, 416, 426, 481, 483, 487
Jones, Herff, 55, 62, 65, 239
Jones, Kevin, 23, 37, 66, 83, 129, 131, 135–136, 343, 381, 652

K

Kahn, Danny, 83, 168–169, 205, 219, 223, 388, 392, 652
Karl Olson, 48, 587
Kasemi, Marianne, 170
Kelly, Ronny, 285
Kennedy, John F., 335
Kentucky, 34, 56, 122, 197–201, 263, 378, 414–415, 433, 438, 446–447, 459, 490–497, 499
Kentucky Elite, 200, 263, 459, 490, 492–496
Kernersville, 33, 144
Kessler, Dan, 379–380, 597
King, Billie Jean, 335 Knight, Laurie, 170
Knoxville Cheer Center (KCC), 448

Knoxville Gymnastics Training Center (KGTC), 435, 447–448, 457, 539
Knoxville, Tennessee, 73, 495
Kohlberg Kravis Roberts (KKR), 75
Kramer, Roy, 154

L

Laidlow, Michelle, 170
Landry, Tom, 112, 364
Lawerence B. Herkimer Award, 321
Lawrence, 9, 23, 42, 85, 109, 170, 242, 253, 294, 393, 579
Leadership: role of women in, 416–418
LeBus, Ladd, 83, 269, 274, 652
Ledford, Jim, 468
LeForce, Jeff, 626
Legacy, 107–108, 113, 116, 124, 144, 273, 280–282, 475–476, 553, 564, 575–576, 588
Legitimacy, 97, 131, 237–238, 250–251, 409, 571
Leonard Green & Partners, 42, 543
LeTard, Tres, 83, 539, 544
Level Play, 35–36, 260
Lexington, 122, 199, 433–434
Liberty Spirit Championships, 490, 496–497
Lifelong Friendships, 79–80, 137, 316
Lifelong skill, cheer as a, 103–104

Little, Eric, 83, 204, 209, 213, 217, 652
Little Warehouse in Texas, 507
Logan, Anna Love, 82, 226, 229
Logan, Phil, 228
Longevity, 96, 123, 208, 228, 273–274, 311, 454, 475
Louisville, 34–35, 215, 257, 293–296, 382, 384, 386, 492, 494, 619
Louisville Male High School, 376
Love, Debbie, 83, 121, 124–125, 331, 597, 644, 648, 652
Lozano, Rey, 83, 169–170, 223, 290, 355–356, 361
Lyczkowsi, Mark, 358
Lyons, Randy, 397, 401

M

Macon, Georgia, 285
Madison High School, 213
Malone, Drew, 301
Mandela, Nelson, 293, 568
Marching Band, 11, 13, 29, 185, 188, 212, 218, 357
Mari, Ed, 224
Martin, Tommy, 467
Martinez, Mike, 36, 50, 83, 98, 222, 239, 433, 435, 444, 453, 457, 462, 495, 541–542, 545, 653
Mascot, 35, 112–113, 304, 377, 379, 383, 386, 396, 400, 472
Massachusetts, 300, 370

McCallister, Tabbi, 66, 622
McCary, Santwon, 300
McCullough, Leroy, 125, 192, 296, 300
McDaniel, Hilda, 19, 138, 145, 353, 361
McElreath, Kirk, 426
Medrano, Remo, 223
Meehan, Lori (Muccia), 510
Megaphones, 212
Melton, Jody, 82, 335, 342, 401, 597, 653
Memphis State University, 122
Memphis, Tennessee, 15, 148, 317, 404
Mental Game, 124
Mesquita, Windy, 170
Metz, John, 40, 571
Metzger, Jeff, 458
Miami Dade Community College, 207
Miami, Florida, 29, 261
Michael Keaton Batman Movies, 225
Michigan, 154, 438, 616–617
Mini Tramp, 16, 92
Mississippi, 89, 438
Monty, Craig, 496
Morgan, Tim, 358
MotUS, 75, 224, 255, 265, 268, 456, 461, 465, 477
Multi-location models, 506
Myrtle Beach, South Carolina, 37, 192, 267, 299, 512

N

National All Star Cheerleading Coaches Congress (NACCC), 4, 36, 40–41, 123, 246–247, 263, 289, 408, 458, 494, 568–577, 581, 589
National Championship, 21–22, 34, 114–116, 130–132, 142, 381, 404–408, 431, 491, 600
National Cheerleaders Association (NCA), 10–12, 14–15, 18, 405, 512, 514, 549, 559, 573–574, 619
Acquisition, 234
All Star National Championships, 130
High School National Championship, 21, 278, 301
Leadership, 22
Staff, 336
NC State Cheerleading, 112–115
NCA All Star National Championships, 130
NCA High School National Championship, 21, 278, 301
NCA High School Nationals, 21, 143–144, 213, 219, 286, 346, 367, 446, 453
Nevel, Bambi, 359
New Jersey, 33, 312, 315, 510
Newby, John, 60, 82, 232, 236, 238, 401, 597, 653
Nfinity, 218, 319, 412, 419–422, 509, 517
1980 (First televised cheerleading competition), 17

1985 (Term "All Star" coined), 22, 168
1982-1991 (Creation of All Star), 19
1948 (First cheerleading camp), 10
1997 (First multi-location gym business), 31, 437
1996 Summer Olympics, 416
1992-2002 (Growth Era), 25
1990s mid-decade (Golden Age of Innovation), 27
1971 (Pom-pon patent), 190
1972 (Title IX), 13
Nixon, Richard M., 13
Noffsinger, Bill, 437, 449
Norman, 85, 404, 409, 617
North Carolina, 20, 24, 33, 112, 114, 116, 354, 356, 360, 437–438, 459, 481, 521–522, 530, 534, 616
North Carolina High School Athletic Association (NCHSAA), 190–191
Notke, Tim, 335
NoviceSELECT Program, 592
Nunno, Steve, 406

O
O'Brien, Cheryl, 459
O'Brien, Julie, 36, 258
Oklahoma, Jeff, 86
Oklahoma State University, 125, 296, 437
Olmstead, Mike, 11
Olmstead, Robert, 10–11
The One, 59, 119, 155, 188, 348, 427, 460, 648, 653
The Open, 69, 543–544, 608–609
Open Championship Series (OCS), 69, 496, 543–544, 604
Orlando, Florida, 17, 34, 45, 52, 56, 61, 63, 97, 168, 314, 457, 505, 579, 616
Owens, David, 69, 72, 610

P
Paddison, Jim, 358
Page, Brad, 83, 269, 274, 653
Pan American Games, 49
Pandemic Pivot, 70, 73
Pare, Mike, 419
Parrish, Jamie, 40, 83, 285, 290, 321, 415, 494, 569, 653
Pascale, Elaine, 40, 83, 125, 144, 246, 497, 509, 511, 518, 568–569, 597
Passalacqua, Cheryl, 55, 63, 73, 459, 462
Patterson, Derick, 392 Penney, James Cash, 25 Penree, Kathy, 555, 593–594, 597
Peters, John, 207
Peterson, Steve, 83, 132, 247, 251, 581, 584, 587–588, 596, 598
Philadelphia Dinner, 246
The Pioneers of All Star Cheer, xviii, xxiii, 4, 81
Pivotal Decision, 104, 607
Plack, Brooke, 83, 629, 635–636
Plano, Texas, 106, 301, 335
Pojezny, Carol, 103–104

Pom-Pon, invention of the, 105, 173, 212
Pom-pon/pom-pom, 9, 12, 18, 105, 173, 212, 313, 500
Pop Warner Cheerleading, 509–510
Pop Warner Internationals, 510
Pop Warner Nationals, 313, 510
Pop Warner Team, 313, 357, 369
Pope, Ben, 192, 437, 449
Pope, Courtney, 57, 83, 144, 193, 308–309, 653
Postell, Joy, 456
Potter, George "Boog", 50, 83, 98, 222, 239, 433, 440–441, 447, 457, 462, 545, 653
Premier Athletics, xx, 31, 37, 50, 55, 98, 192, 444, 448–450, 456–461, 509, 515–516, 539–540
Prep Division, 62, 64, 370
Prime Alliance, 75, 456, 461, 465, 477
Private cheer gyms, growth of, 389
Pro Cheer League, 76
Professional Cheerleaders, 64
Professionalism, 53, 336, 338, 452, 460, 465, 476

Q

Q94 Rockers, 21–23, 138, 142–144, 146, 148, 150, 353

R

Raleigh, 112, 114, 262, 309, 521
Real Estate Misadventures, 427
Rebel Athletic, 62–63
Rebel Cheer Company, 21, 23, 347
Reed, Jennifer, 170
Reeves, Tegan Jemma, PhD, 83
Regional Summits, 65
Reynolds, Leon, 83, 558, 564, 653
Rhinestone Revolution, 288
Richmond, Virginia, 20, 138
Riverside Community College, 206
Robinson, Donna, 202
Roethlisberger, John, 258
Rogers, Angela, 83, 335, 342, 401, 653
Rooney, Mickey, 206
Roosevelt, Eleanor, 269
Roosevelt, Theodore, 444
Rosa, Abel, 192, 437, 449, 459
Rosario, Kristen, 83, 207, 246, 321–322, 330, 408, 568–569, 576, 596, 646, 648, 654
Rosario, Victor, 26, 39–40, 83, 119, 125, 223, 322, 326, 330, 457, 642, 654
Roswell, Georgia, 288
Rowe, Chris, 464
Rowe, Stacy, xvii, 75, 193, 265, 437, 440, 459, 461–462, 477, 654

Royal, Cenie, 205, 343
Ruiz, Don Miguel, 420, 651
Rutgers Cheerleading Program, 514
Rutgers University, 513

S

San Diego, 76, 212–213, 224, 299, 354
San Francisco, California, 313
Savannah, Georgia, 357
Schembechler, Bo, 154
Scholarship Fund, 185
Scholastic Cheerleading, 515–516
Schonder, Roger, 83, 288, 462, 472, 475, 477, 480, 486–487, 597
School Cheer, 22, 50, 106, 131, 160, 184, 347–348, 543, 559, 616, 632
Seely, Bill, 44, 83, 151, 163, 236, 578, 588, 654
Seigel, Mary Ellen, 170
Seitzer, Kali, 83, 639, 647, 654 Settlemyer, Lindsey Sitzlar, 301
Shepherd, Kris, 44, 578
Shockley, Jackie, 142
Shullaw, Danielle, 170
Simms, Tina, 193
Singer, Lynn, 83, 597 Sis Boom Rah, 7–8 Ski-U-Mah, 7–8
Skinner, Tammy, 83, 278, 281–282, 654
Small Cheer Gym Association, 66, 621–622, 625

Small Gym, 66, 177, 237, 250, 468, 561–562, 585, 615, 620–626, 635
Smith, Shannon, 37, 261, 299, 459, 535
Song Leaders and Cheerleaders of America, 24
South Carolina, 37, 151, 260, 267, 286, 296, 299, 412–415, 426, 512
Southeastern Conference (SEC), 154, 198
Southern Baptist Educational Center, 122
Southern Methodist University, 9, 85, 336
Speed Camp Innovation, 296
Speed, James, 37, 83, 257, 293–294, 297, 300–302, 322, 331, 336, 343, 385, 459, 535, 654
Spirit Cheer, 53
Spirit Express, 259
Spirit Festival, 37–38, 51, 55, 98, 298–300, 306, 364, 367, 370–371, 399, 459–460, 532, 535–536
Spirit Innovations, 66, 133, 381–382
Spirit Sports, 37–38, 51, 98, 459–460, 532, 535–536
Sports Competition, 9
Sports Supply Group, 62
Spring Floor, 26, 36, 46, 132, 199, 327, 337–338, 405, 420, 563, 580
The Stage 8 Dance Battle, 73–74

Stage 8 Dance Brands, 73–75, 456, 462
Stella, Les, 581, 583, 588, 597
Stephen F. Austin State University (SFA), 643
Steward, Damianna Albee, 60, 83, 237, 300, 532, 537
Stiller, Ben, 418
Stingray Allstars, xviii, 34, 288, 301, 465, 472–476, 480, 483–485, 487
Stingray's Remarkable Growth, 485
Stithem, Doug, 492
Stott, Cole, xxiii, 50, 54, 73, 75, 83, 462, 477, 495, 545, 597, 654
Stuart, Cris, 169
Stunt, 51, 159–161
The Summit, 59–61, 64–65, 69, 177, 236–238, 525–526, 535–536, 542, 544
Summit Events, 65, 544
Swimming, 9, 357, 513
Sykes, Orson, 83, 125, 404, 408–409, 655
Symons, Regina, 83, 131, 173, 179

T

Tampa, Florida, 65
Taylor, Edd, 169
Television Sports Network (TVS), 17–18, 92–93
Tennessee, 15, 36, 73, 90, 92, 134, 148, 161, 454, 456–457, 464, 493, 495, 515–516, 540, 546
Texas, 10, 18, 21, 56, 85, 104, 106, 443, 446, 507, 523, 525, 562, 621, 642–643
Texas Cheerleading Association, 174
Texas rises, spirit of, 347
Thalia Awards, 38, 359
Thomas, Janna, 73 Thoreau, Henry David, 269 Thorpe, Jim, 239
Tifton, Georgia, 285
Timmons, Sean, 83, 509, 517–518, 655
Tisdale, Robert, 15
Title IX, 13–14, 159–160, 162
Top Gun All Stars, 29, 39, 322–323, 325–326, 641
Tradition of Excellence, 117
Trinity Valley Community College, 215
Tuckahoe Tomahawks, 19, 139, 141, 144, 146, 148
Tull, Sabrina, 55
Tunica, 438
2018 ($2.5 billion acquisition), 66–67
2004 comedy Dodgeball, 418
2004 (ICU founded), 47–49
2004 (USASF founded), 95–98
2007 (USA Cheer formed), 159
2003-2012 (Modernization & Expansion Era), 42
2013-2024 (Contemporary Era), 59

2013 (The Summit launched), 59–61, 525
2020 (Pandemic pivot), 70–73
Tyler, Amy, 82, 226, 230, 260
Tyler, Emmitt, 35, 304, 377

U
Ulrich, Rob, 301
Under the Cherry Moon, 267
United States All Star Federation (USASF), 1, 3–4, 36, 41, 43–47, 272–273, 289, 574–598, 644, 648
United States Association of Gymnastics (USAG), 458
United Stingrays, 482–483
birth of, 482
Universal Cheerleaders Association (UCA), 15–18, 27–28, 32, 34, 457–458, 492–493, 501, 504, 514, 573–574, 633
Universal Spirit Association (USA), 2, 10–11, 14–15, 51–52, 125, 297, 299, 302, 313–314, 368, 384, 437, 453, 644
University of Alabama at Birmingham (UAB), 501
University of Kansas, 294–295
University of Kentucky, 197–198, 200, 354, 414, 446–447, 490–492
University of Louisville, 35, 215, 293–296, 298, 301–302, 336, 376–377
University of Louisville All-girl Program, 301

University of Michigan Football Coach, 154
University of North Carolina (UNC), 20, 143, 227, 257, 353–356
University of Oklahoma, 85, 192, 283, 404, 617–618
U.S. Finals, 59, 65
USA Cheer, 2, 15, 51–52, 159–160, 162, 297, 437
USA Staff, 204
USASF Emergence, 574
USASF Formation, 79, 96–98
USASF/ISASF World Championship, 302
USASF Mission, 44

V
The Vampire Diaries, 290
Vance, Serena, 193
VanVleet, Tammy, 66, 381, 555, 596
Varsity All Star, 133–134, 235, 264, 496, 524, 532, 542
Varsity Challenge, 573
Varsity Era, 495
Varsity Family Plan, 37, 50, 63, 236, 439
Varsity Spirit, 17–18, 28, 42, 51, 59, 62, 65, 67, 234, 238, 301, 396, 420, 450, 490, 539, 581
Vaughn, Vince, 418
Victory All Stars, 534
Video Replay System, 38
Virginia, 19–20, 116, 138, 142, 150, 153, 191, 228, 260, 309, 314, 353, 501

W

Waco, Texas, 269
Wagers, Carol, 22, 130–131, 205, 243, 274, 343, 350, 598
Wagers, Lance, 23, 83, 103, 109, 129, 136, 205, 287, 337, 389, 655
Walker, Meredith, 83, 582, 586, 588, 597, 602, 655
Walters, Brown, 356, 358
Walters, Dawn Duncan, 83, 122, 197, 201, 378, 655
Webb, Greg, 44, 578
Webb, Jeff, 11, 14–15, 17, 43, 48, 50, 56, 62–63, 67, 578–581, 584, 588, 633
Weber, Heidi, 68–70, 72, 83, 604, 612–613
Wedge, Steve, 24, 28, 66, 83, 171, 182–183, 187, 381, 655
Weeden, Cathryn "Cat", 66, 83, 615, 625
Weyandt's Gymnastics Program, 257–258
Who Wants to Be a Millionaire, 248
Wild wild west (era), 5–6, 19, 25, 42, 59, 67, 131, 135, 146, 206, 221, 286, 341, 466, 495, 505, 510, 522
Williams, Scott, 256
Williamsburg, Virginia, 142
Williamson, T. Lynn, 414
Witcraft, Forest, 548
Wolf Wall Pyramid, 114, 116
Worcester, 300
World Anti-Doping Agency, 49
World Championships, 46–47, 49, 51, 54, 513–514, 525, 580, 587, 600, 604, 609–611
World Cup All Stars, 33, 221, 289, 312–319, 448, 454, 509, 511–513, 515, 569, 575
World Cup Years, 511
World Spirit Federation (WSF), 38, 51, 98, 459–460
World War II, 9, 11
Worlds Bid, 45, 116, 264, 580
Worley, Dennis, 40, 60, 83, 237, 359, 370, 521, 528, 570, 572, 655

X

Xpress Brands, 53
Xtra Small Division, 67

Y

Yeager, Douglas "DJ", 56, 83
Youth Celebration, 65

Z

Zegarra, Eddie, 415
Zelinski, Dawn, 170

ALSO BY S.R. FABRICO

NONFICTION

MY JOURNAL SERIES: 52 weeks of goals, growth, and gratitude for athletes

FICTION

Sources

In addition to over one hundred interviews conducted to gather information to write this book, the author also gathered information from the following sources:

- www.study.com
- www.gophersports.com
- https://en.wikipedia.org/wiki/Cheerleading
- www.quizlet.com
- https://www.uscourts.gov/educational-resources/educational-activities/14th-amendment-and-evolution-title-ix#:~:text=Congress%20enacted%20Title%20IX%20of,It%20authorizes%20any%20federal%20agency
- https://www.billiejeanking.com/equality/title-ix/#:~:text=The%20law%20opened%20doors%20and,1057%20percent%20and%20by%20614
- https://www.merriam-webster.com/dictionary/sport#:~:text=:%20physical%20activity%20engaged%20in%20for,athletic%20game)%20so%20engaged%20in
- https://usacheer.org/history-of-cheerleading
- https://www.leonardgreen.com/
- https://www.usasf.net/about
- https://cheerunion.org/about/about/
- https://usacheer.org/about
- https://www.herffjones.com/about
- https://thecdip.com/
- https://www.varsity.com/about/mission-values/
- https://www.certifiedeo.com/blog-posts/how-many-businesses-are-there-in-america-and-what-does-it-mean-for-employee-ownership
- https://www.irs.gov/retirement-plans/employee-stock-ownership-plans-esops#:~:text=An%20employee%20stock%20ownership%20plan,stock%20bonus%2Fmoney%20purchase%20plan

- What is Rebel Athletic: The Best Cheerleading Uniforms Company
- https://www.flaticon.com/
- https://www.iasfworlds.net/
- https://mergr.com/company/bsn-sports
- https://cheerunion.org/about/what/
- https://www.baincapital.com/
- https://www.kkr.com/about/kkr-co-ceos-want-to-reach-1-trillion-in-assets-by-2030?utm_source=google&utm_medium=paidsearch&utm_campaign={campaignname}&utm_term=kohlberg%20kravis%20roberts&utm_content=Fortune-1-trillion-assets-2030&gad_source=1&gclid=CjwKCAiA7Y28BhAnEiwAAdOJUJaZ0l01YyIHfrRaVoemMmV0S9wpbKMpNHLs7iya2Thb8tEgxpi4phoCTiEQAvD_BwE
- https://www.youtube.com/watch?v=QM6bqyt6E9U

www.ingramcontent.com/pod-product-compliance
Lightning Source LLC
Chambersburg PA
CBHW050242010526
44107CB00032B/1377/J